ELEMENTARY
LANGUAGE ARTS

ELEMENTARY LANGUAGE ARTS

PHILIP DISTEFANO
UNIVERSITY OF COLORADO, BOULDER

JANICE A. DOLE
UNIVERSITY OF DENVER

ROBERT J. MARZANO
MID-CONTINENT REGIONAL EDUCATIONAL
LABORATORY, DENVER

JOHN WILEY & SONS

New York
Chichester
Brisbane
Toronto
Singapore

87-5851

Cover Design: *Phil McKenna*
Cover Photo: © *Robin Forbes/Image Bank*

Library of Congress Cataloging in Publication Data:

ISBN 0-471-86658-x

Printed in the United States of America

10 9 8 7 6 5 4 3 2 1

TO OUR CHILDREN

Gia, the twins Nicole and Jennifer
Melissa Erin
Todd and Christine

PREFACE

This book grew out of our belief that the teaching of language arts is the single most important task an elementary teacher can do. The language arts represent the communication skills of speaking, writing, listening, and reading, which form the basis for most activities that children are asked to do in their formal schooling. By presenting effective, research-based methods and content for teaching the language arts, we want elementary-school teachers to decide for themselves how best to integrate the methods and content so that their students will learn to communicate effectively.

As professors of language arts, research is very important to us. Within the past five years, an impressive amount of both quantitative and qualitative research has been conducted in language and thought development. This research, in turn, has had an impact on the way traditional language arts subjects, such as writing, reading, grammar, usage, and listening, are taught. We present the research in language and thought development, as well as research in the specific fields of speaking, writing, listening, and reading, in a meaningful way that we hope bridges the gap between research and practice. We hope that teachers who use the book will try our suggestions in their own classrooms.

As supervisors and in-service leaders in the public schools, we have asked elementary-school teachers to give us input on the practicality and usability of the suggested activities presented in the body, as well as at the end of each chapter. Most of the activities have been used successfully this past year in elementary schools. Our purpose has been to offer teachers of language arts an alternative to traditional methods of teaching that can be effective in regular classroom settings.

The text weaves an integrated approach to the language arts through each of the chapters, especially the ones on expressive and receptive communication skills. While the chapter titles may seem similar to those of other language arts textbooks, the reader will see that not only is each topic highlighted in the chapter, but that its relationship to the other language arts is explored. The text stresses the concept that the language arts are integrated with most of the school activities that children encounter.

Many people are involved in preparing a textbook of this nature. Three school districts in Colorado—Adams County #12, Northglenn; Douglas County, Castle Rock; and Boulder Valley School District—participated in this project by allowing us to visit their classrooms and work with teachers and students. Three schools in particular—Larkspur, Pine Lane, and Sedalia—shared with us samples of student writing and teaching plans, which we have included in the text.

A special thanks must be given to the John Wiley staff who worked closely with us throughout the project. We wish to thank our two editors, Mark Mochary and Carol Luitjens, for their support and encouragement. We also wish to thank Rosemary Wellner, our editing manager, and Loretta McElwee, our copy editor, for their careful work on the manuscript. In addition, we express our gratitude to Stella Kupferberg and Elyse Rieder for their excellent choice of photographs and illustrations. Finally, we offer heartfelt thanks to Miriam Navarro, our production supervisor, who kept us on schedule and worked closely with us on final page proofs.

Throughout the writing and revision process, we received many helpful comments from colleagues across the country. Among these we wish to thank Stanley I. Mour, University of Louisville; Lee Galda, University of Georgia; and Ken Kantor, University of Georgia, for their invaluable advice on the manuscript. To Johanna DeStefano of Ohio State University, who had a particular understanding of our intent, philosophy, and organization, we express our sincere and special appreciation.

Finally, we wish to thank our spouses and our children for their patience and understanding. They encouraged us while we worked nights and weekends to meet deadlines. We appreciate their support through these difficult times.

P. D.

J. A. D.

R. J. M.

CONTENTS

ELEMENTARY LANGUAGE ARTS

INTRODUCTION TO THE LANGUAGE ARTS

CHAPTER I

What Are
the Language Arts?

At the beginning of each term we make a point to ask our students what they think they will study in the class called language arts methods. Although there are a variety of answers to the question, the following seem to be more dominant than others:

"We will probably learn grammar rules."

"I hope we learn grammar rules because I don't know them."

"Language arts is creative writing."

"Language arts is correct grammar in speaking."

"Spelling is the major component of language arts."

A second question reveals more about their ideas concerning language arts. We ask our students to recall what they did in their language arts class in elementary school. Most students do not remember much about the class, or what they remember is similar to what they think they will learn in the language arts methods class, namely grammar, usage, and spelling.

Both of these questions and their answers are probably not different from the answers we would get about the components of language arts. The subject areas of language arts are many, and they integrate with each other as well as other subject areas. It is almost impossible to study any content area without using one of the language arts components of speaking, writing, reading, and listening. Yet, when our students think about the components of language arts, they think about them in narrow terms such as grammar, usage, and spelling.

Let us present to you another view of the language arts, one that you may not have thought about before, but that we feel is the backbone of the elementary school curriculum.

- writing
- reading
- listening
- speaking
- cooperating
- sharing

- translating
  print to images
- cooperating
- sharing
- listening
- speaking

In Mrs. Wright's second-grade class a group of children are busy drawing on large mural paper. The paper has been placed on tables pulled together, and several groups of two to four children are talking, planning, and drawing on different parts of the mural. The room is noisy and busy. The children move about freely to trade places, to converse with each other and the teacher, and to mix and prepare paint for the mural.

Meanwhile, several other children are busy constructing a miniature room. Using wooden sticks, toothpicks, matchboxes, miniature tiles, straw, and other sundry materials, the children are creating a model of a room that was verbally described to them but never actually seen by them.

- writing
- reading
- listening
- speaking
- getting your ideas across
- sharing
- cooperating

> In another part of the room three children are busy writing on a large piece of chart paper.
> "Okay, say, 'This is Stuart's room.'"
> "No, don't write that. Write 'Stuart lives in this room.'"
> "How about 'Stuart, *the mouse*, lives in this room?'"
> "OK, I'll write that."
> Slowly, methodically, one child writes on the chart paper, "Stuart, the mouse, lives in this room."

All of these children are working on projects related to E. B. White's classic book *Stuart Little* (Harper and Row, 1945). On the mural children are recreating Stuart's travels from the beginning to the end of the book. When they have completed their mural, they will have a visual and written representation of where Stuart went. They also will have a better understanding of the concept "to explore" as they write on the mural about where Stuart went and what motivated him to go there.

By building the miniature room children are recreating visually Stuart's bedroom described in the novel. To do this they must translate written language they have heard, and develop a mental and then physical representation of that language. Other children are required to paraphrase the same language by describing Stuart's room. The written chart will later accompany the miniature house, and the children will have experience and practice not only in paraphrasing and summarizing language but also in recreating visually what has been presented orally.

If we move from Mrs. Wright's second-grade class to Miss Pilloud's sixth-grade class, we can observe different projects with the same underlying goals and philosophies for language arts instruction. As you read this section, compare it in your mind to the definitions of language arts instruction given by our students earlier.

- reading
- writing
- listening
- speaking
- cooperating

> A group of sixth graders are completing a large chart. They have worked together in pairs to research several different climatic zones and to gather data on the types of food, shelter, and clothing needed to survive in each zone.

Climatic Zone	Average Summer Temperature	Average Winter Temperature	Food	Shelter	Clothing

- reading
- writing
- speaking
- listening
- sharing
- cooperating

- reading
- writing

Three other groups are building models of three different environments: an island off the coast of California, an island in the Caribbean, and a northern wooded forest area in upstate New York. Each has prepared a brief summary of the terrain, animal population, vegetation, and climate of each area, and a list of advantages and disadvantages of living in each.

Several other sixth graders are writing in journals. Each has assumed the role of a character in one of three books they have read. One child writes,

There was a rainstorm today. I stayed in my hut all day, and I was cold. I hope it does not keep on raining. Tomorrow I need to get more fish . . .

These sixth-grade children are busy working on projects built around the theme of "survival." They have all read three novels about children who survived on their own. The books are *The Cay* by Theodore Taylor (Doubleday and Co., Inc., 1969), *Island of the Blue Dolphin* by Scott O'Dell (Houghton Mifflin Co., 1960), and *My Side of the Mountain* by Jean George (E. P. Dutton, 1959). After children read these books, they discussed the broad theme of being able to survive alone and to "live off the land." The books and the ensuing discussion led to a detailed and lengthy study of the concept of "survival." Children *listened, discussed, read, wrote,* and participated actively in a number of other activities that increased their knowledge about science and social studies topics.

GOALS OF LANGUAGE ARTS INSTRUCTION

These vignettes present a very different view of the language arts than the one our students typically can imagine. Notice in our discussion that children were actively involved and working together in pairs and in groups, thinking, discussing, writing, drawing and creating. Notice too that children were working on social studies, math, and science concepts. To be sure, there is a time that they are instructed in spelling, usage, and reading. However, language arts instruction extends beyond instruction of specific components of the language arts, and includes activities and experiences in reading, writing, listening, and speaking that permeate the whole elementary curriculum.

What then, are the goals of language arts instruction?

1 To create in young minds a desire to learn and a love of learning through language.

2 To enable each child to communicate effectively with others.

3 To develop each child's fullest potential in listening, speaking, reading, and writing abilities.

We will discuss each goal in more detail.

1 *To create in young minds a desire to learn and a love of learning through language.* As educators we *must* see to it that we instruct children in such a way that we encourage learning through many forms and medias—discussion, drama, print, computers, and so on. If we can instill a love of learning, then we have hope for the future of these children. If we turn them *off* to learning, however, no matter how successful we are now, we have failed in the long run.

Consider adults who *can* read, but never do read. Consider adults who are so threatened and insecure about their own writing, they never attempt to write anything.

We must always, then, keep this goal as central to language arts instruction. We must teach children in such a way that they value and love language in all its forms and see a need and purpose in the various roles and functions of language.

2 *To enable each child to communicate effectively with others.* Effective communication involves many skills and abilities: (1) the ability to listen to what someone is saying to you, (2) the ability to speak to others so your ideas and opinions are accurately communicated, (3) the ability to read to obtain information and to evaluate and critique, and (4) the ability to express your ideas and opinions through writing. These abilities are learned over a long period of time, and through a variety of situations and experiences. They form the essence of what we regard as language arts instruction.

3 *To develop each child's fullest potential in listening, speaking, reading, and writing abilities.* This last goal includes much of the content most people associate with language arts instruction. In order to learn how to communicate effectively with others, children need to learn such specifics as how to spell, how to write clearly and legibly, how to pronounce multisyllabic words, and how to write a letter. These goals are important to language arts instruction, but are not the only goals of such instruction.

In sum, language arts instruction must include teaching

1 Positive attitudes.
2 Thought and language processes.
3 Specific content.

Throughout this text as we discuss each component of language arts (speaking, writing, listening, and reading), we will stress your understanding of each goal and its relationship to language arts instruction.

A COGNITIVE FRAMEWORK FOR STUDYING LANGUAGE ARTS

In order to implement these broad goals for language arts instruction, we need a framework from which to examine the components of the language arts to see how they relate to each other and to thinking and language. In Figure 1.1, we present a model of the language arts. Notice that thinking is central and permeates the model. The dashed lines enclosing the forms of language reflect the fact that thinking and language are interrelated.

One common approach to language arts is to cluster listening and speaking together as oral language skills. Reading and writing similarly can be clustered together and thought of as forms of written language. This model reflects the developmental nature of language in that we learn oral language before we learn written language.

Another way to see the interrelationships of these language skills, however, is to look at listening and reading as *receptive* language skills and speaking and writing as *expressive* language skills. We have organized our text around this model because

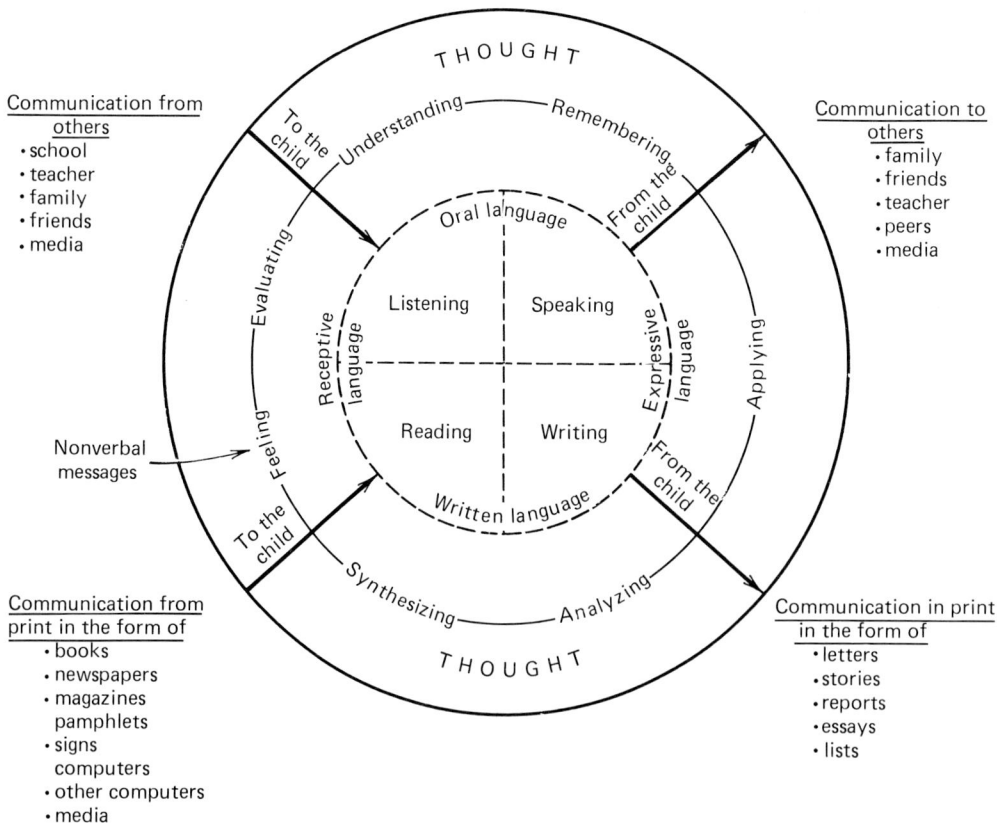

FIGURE 1.1 *A model of the language arts.*

receptive and expressive language skills are consistent with a cognitive model of thinking and language. In a cognitive model the individual is viewed as receiving input via language and expressing or generating output via language. More specifically, receptive language refers to those situations in which an individual receives information via language. Through listening and reading we receive information about the world from our environment, peers, school, media, books, and so on. This new information is added to and integrated with the old information already stored in memory. We may simply memorize the new information. We may analyze it, taking it apart and examining it in detail. We may make a judgment about that new information. Whatever we do, we add to our knowledge base through receptive language.

Conversely, expressive language refers to those situations in which we use language to express our own thoughts. We use speaking and writing to communicate language information to others. Again the thought process is prominent; we must think through, recall, analyze, and sometimes synthesize information to present it understandably to others.

In addition, the model we present displays the communicative function of the language arts. Indeed, educators sometimes use the terms "language arts" and "communication skills" synonymously. We listen and read because we want to have our needs met, we want to be entertained, we want to know something, we want to learn. We speak and write because we have something to say—that is, we wish to communicate with others. In the model, we see that the school, teacher, friends, family, and media, communicate language information to the child both orally and through print. The child also communicates language information to these same people orally and through print. The system is a *dynamic* one, changing over situations and over time to meet the communication needs of each individual.

THE ROLE OF THE TEACHER IN LANGUAGE ARTS INSTRUCTION

Educational research has shown consistently the importance of the teacher in the instructional process. Teachers can make a difference in what children learn, in how much children learn, and in children's attitudes about learning. A good teacher can create a learning environment and instruct children in such a way that they value learning, value themselves, and learn to communicate effectively with others. A poor teacher, on the other hand, can create an environment where children stagnate and develop negative attitudes about themselves and their learning.

Obviously, each potential teacher wants to be as competent as possible. Your competency as a language arts teacher depends in part on your knowledge of the content of the language arts and also on your ability to communicate that knowledge to students in a clear, exciting, and dynamic manner. Yours is not an easy task, but one that should prove to be both challenging and rewarding.

We emphasize the importance of you, the teacher, in language arts instruction for several reasons. First, we hear so much today about textbooks, computers, and other curriculum materials that it is easy to get the impression that materials do the teaching. There even are rumors that computers will soon take over the teacher's role. We have strong reason to believe that this simply will never happen. Researchers have shown that teachers are too important in the instructional process.

Second, we know that too many teachers rely too heavily on textbooks and curriculum materials. They say, "Well, the materials were written by experts and they should know." The problem with this approach is that materials are designed to be *guides*, not *masters*. For example, what may be meaningful and appropriate for average children in Detroit may not be appropriate for average children in southern Texas. Likewise, certain practices and techniques appropriate for average children may not be appropriate for gifted children. Either way, curriculum materials, and specifically language arts textbooks and materials, must be used discriminately by a knowledgeable language arts teacher. Important decisions about each individual child's needs can be made only by such a teacher.

Third, we have seen too many teachers who do not understand the nature of language learning and who, with good intentions, actually do more harm than good. For example, some teachers punish inappropriate behavior by asking their students to write, "I will not . . . ." 100 times on a sheet of paper. The next day, they may eagerly ask the same students to write a "creative writing story," forgetting that they actually are teaching children to associate writing with punishment. These teachers do not understand how children come to enjoy written language and view it as a positive experience.

As a teacher your own knowledge of how children learn language will form the backbone of your instruction. You will need to learn many things. You will need to know how we, as human beings, learn, comprehend, and remember language information (Chapter 2). You will need to know about language itself, how it is structured, what it consists of and how language differences affect instruction (Chapters 3 and 4). You will need to know how to help children express themselves effectively through speaking and writing (Chapters 5 through 9). You will need to know how to help children understand information presented to them through listening and reading (Chapters 10 through 12). Lastly, you will need to learn how to synthesize all this knowledge and develop a language arts program that enhances language learning across the whole curriculum (Chapters 13 through 15).

You may think this task is a formidable one. Our experiences with many highly competent teachers convince us otherwise. We have seen many good teachers in the language arts classroom who understand language and thought development and teach the language arts in a motivating and rewarding way.

THE RELATIONSHIP BETWEEN THOUGHT AND LANGUAGE

CHAPTER 2

Thought Development

WHAT IS THINKING?

SECOND GRADERS

...like if you saw a book and you look at it and think
   about it...

SIXTH GRADERS

...imagination
...wondering how to solve stuff
...if something's on your mind and you try and figure
   it out
...talking in your mind

OVERVIEW

In this chapter we will consider the definition of thought and how language is the representation of a specific type of thinking—a type very important to our reasoning ability. To fully understand how language operates we first must look at thinking in general. We store thoughts in three types of memory: sensory information storage, short-term memory, and long-term memory. We use the information in long-term memory to interpret the information in the other two. We interpret using our expectations about the world. This ability to interpret based on our expectations is a highly symbolic level of thinking that develops gradually in human beings.

INTRODUCTION

In the langauge arts model in Chapter 1 "thought" was central to the model and permeated it. In addition, "thought" interrelated with "language" to form the basis of language arts instruction. An important issue to discuss is what do we mean by the concept "thought." We use the term almost daily when we ask children to use their thought processes or to think about what they are doing or saying. However, we may not understand what thought is and how it is developed. In this chapter, we will look at some definitions of thought and ways it is developed in children.

Thought

Cognitive psychologists define thought as "the symbolic, mental representation of the environment—the transactional process between an individual and the environment" (Smith, 1976, p. 85). Another way of saying this is that thought is the "coding" of what we perceive with our senses. We store our representations or codifications of perceptual information in memory.

STAGES OF MEMORY

Athough we tend to use the term memory as meaning a unitary process at least three different stages of the memory process have been identified: (1) sensory information storage, (2) short-term memory, and (3) long-term memory. These three stages are in constant interaction. Sensory information storage feeds short-term memory which in turn feeds long-term memory. Long-term memory enables us to interpret information that is being processed through our sensory information storage and short-term memory. The whole process feeds back on itself in a type of mutually dependent system. Figure 2.1 depicts the interrelationship among the three types of memory.

Let us consider each memory system in more depth. Sensory information storage contains a complete picture of the world as we perceive it through our senses

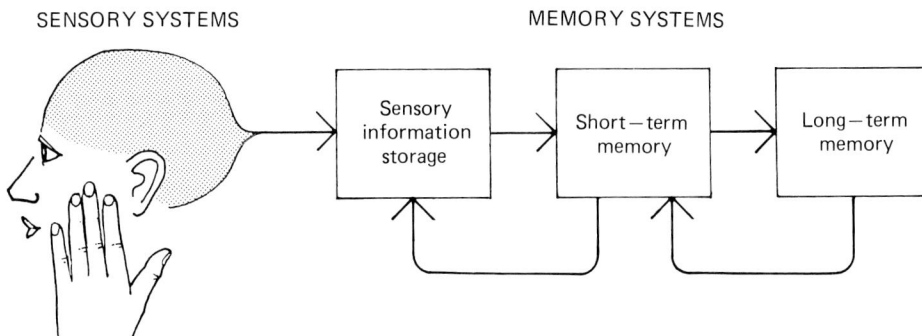

FIGURE 2.1   *The interrelationships among the three stages of memory.*

(sensory system in Figure 2.1). The duration of this picture or representation is only from .1 to about .5 second. You can observe your sensory information storage process in action by performing one or all of the activities below.

---

1   Stare at an object for awhile and then close your eyes tightly and keep them closed. Notice that the sharper images you see will linger for awhile after you have closed your eyes. This is because it takes from .1 to .5 second for your sensory information storage to clear and make itself ready for new information.

2   Clap your hands a few times very loudly. Notice that you will retain the memory of the sound for a brief period of time after the clapping has stopped.

3   Wave a pencil back and forth in front of your eyes. The shadowy image you see is, again, your sensory information storage of the image of the pencil slowly fading.

4   Press the index finger of one hand against the back of the wrist on your other hand. Notice that the sensation of being touched lingers briefly even after you remove your index finger.

Short-term memory contains far different information from that in sensory information storage. Where sensory information storage contains a fairly accurate representation of the information received from the senses, short-term memory contains our *interpretation* of the information from sensory information storage. It is at this point that we actually begin "judging" what we perceive. To illustrate, after you have passed a cow while driving on a country road, you no longer perceive the cow, you remember the image of the cow. Moreover that memory is always colored by your expectations. If you expected the cow to have one black eye and one white eye then you will remember the cow as having them regardless of whether it did or not. This explains why two people can witness the same event yet "see" totally different things. We perceive what we expect to perceive. We are constantly interpreting our sensory information.

But what do we use to "interpret" the information from sensory information storage? Our interpretation mechanism is housed in long-term memory.

Long-term memory is the "storehouse of knowledge." Without it we could do nothing. We couldn't even recognize a door as a door without long-term memory. It contains an incredible amount of information. Dr. Wayne Dyer, a popular psychologist states that

> *The brain, which is composed of ten billion, billion working parts has enough storage capacity to accept ten new facts every second. It has been conservatively estimated that the human brain can store an amount of information equivalent to one hundred trillion words, and that all of us use but a tiny fraction of this storage space (Dyer, 1976, p. 42).*

We know very little about how long-term memory operates. We are not even sure where the information is stored. But we do know that we are constantly using the information from long-term memory to interpret the outside world. That is, we use the information in long-term memory as a "template" with which we screen all information coming in through the senses. Change the template and we change the interpretation of our perception. To illustrate this, consider Figures 2.2 and 2.3.

In Figure 2.2 it is easy to see which cross bar intersects the vertical line at a right angle. But in Figure 2.3 neither cross bar appears to be perpendicular to the vertical line. In Figure 2.3 our context or template for interpreting the information has changed. We now perceive a three-dimensional rectangular object and our template in long-term memory tells us that the lines on the side of that rectangle are distorted by distance and could not possibly be perpendicular.

Using information in long-term memory we constantly try to make sense out of what we perceive; we will make our perceptions meaningful even when they are

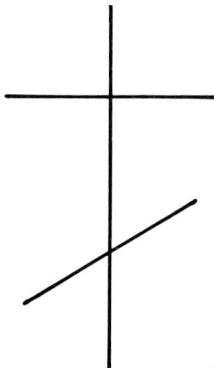

FIGURE 2.2 *Three intersecting lines.*

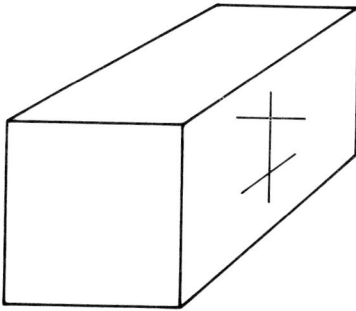

FIGURE 2.3 *Three intersecting lines: template change.*

not. To illustrate this consider Figure 2.4. The object pictured here could not possibly exist as a three-dimensional object. Yet as you look at it you will continue to interpret it as a three-dimensional one.

INTERPRETATION SYSTEM

Human beings by definition try to make sense out of what they perceive—they interpret all information as meaningful and consistent with the knowledge they already possess. Consequently they assimilate best information that is presented in a broad context. Anything presented in isolation is harder to assimilate and to recall than something presented within the context of a broad framework. Throughout this text, all drills that are recommended are usually presented in conjunction with some larger goal relative to the language arts.

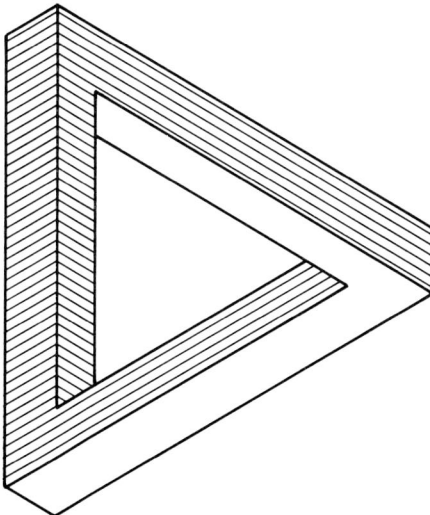

FIGURE 2.4 *Multidimensional triangle.*

How does our interpretation system work? Our prior knowledge and expectations about the information we are processing are fundamental to our ability to reason. About expectation the linguist Deborah Tannen has said:

> I have been struck lately by the recurrence of a single theme in a wide variety of contexts: the power of expectation. For example, the self-fulfilling prophecy has been proven to operate in education as well as in individual psychology. I happened to leaf through a how-to-succeed book; its thesis was that the way to succeed is to expect to do so. Two months ago at a conference for teachers of English as a second language, the keynote speaker explained that effective reading is a process of anticipating what the author is going to say and expecting it as one reads. Moreover, there are general platitudes heard every day, as for example the observation that what is wrong with marriage today is that partners expect too much of each other and of marriage.
>
> The emphasis on expectation seems to corroborate a nearly self-evident truth: in order to function in the world, people cannot treat each new person, object, or event as unique and separate. The only way we can make sense of the world is to see the connections between things, and between present things and things we have experienced before or heard about. These vital connections are learned as we grow up and live in a given culture. As soon as we measure a new perception against what we know of the world from prior experience, we are dealing with expectations (Tannen, 1979, p.137).

Tannen explains that the notion of expectation is at the root of a wave of theories and studies in a broad range of fields: linguistics, artificial intelligence, cognitive psychology, social psychology, anthropology, and psycholinguistics. To illustrate an application of the general theory of expectations consider the following passage.

> The procedure is actually quite simple. First you arrange things into different groups. Of course, one pile may be sufficient depending on how much there is to do. If you have to go somewhere else due to lack of facilities that is the next step, otherwise you are pretty well set. It is important not to overdo things. That is, it is better to do too few things at once than too many. In the short run this may not seem important but complications can easily arise. A mistake can be expensive as well. At first the whole procedure will seem complicated. Soon, however, it will become just another facet of life. It is difficult to foresee any end to the necessity for this task in the immediate future, but then one can never tell. After the procedure is completed one arranges the materials into different groups again. Then they can be put into their appropriate places. Eventually they will be used once more, and the whole cycle will then have to be repeated. However, that is part of life (Bradsford & Johnson, 1973, p. 400).

Most people find this passage difficult to understand until they find out that it is about washing clothes. You can prove this to yourself by rereading the passage now that you have that information. You will find that the words and phrases take on a new meaning. What occurred the second time you read the passage that did not occur the first time is that you consulted what psycholinguists call your *schema* about washing clothes which allowed you to immediately interpret words you could only guess at the first time. (*A schema is a type of expectation*. We will explain it in more depth shortly.) When you encountered the word *procedure* the second time you read the passage you interpreted it immediately using the information in your schema about the topic. The first time you read the passage and encountered the word *procedure* you had no way of knowing what procedure was being discussed. In fact you probably spent the rest of the time, reading the passage, going through all your schema about "procedures" trying to determine which one fit.

More precisely defined schemata (the plural of schema) are networks of information packed into units. Embedded in these packets of knowledge is, in addition to the knowledge itself, information about how the knowledge is to be used. Our schema about cars would include all the characteristics of cars (for example, what they look like, how to use them) and a representation of all the encounters we have had with cars in our lifetime. In addition to this information our schemata would include directions about how to use that information. There might also be a set of rules to tell us in which situations we should consult our schema about cars. Schemata, then, are huge information systems that govern our use of knowledge.

A schema is only one type of expectation. Abelson (1976) a well-known pioneer in artificial intelligence discusses the relationship among "scripts," attitudes, and behavior. Scripts are similar to schemata. For our purposes we can consider them the same. Basically, Abelson believes that if we can understand a person's script relative to a certain event we can predict how that individual will behave. Here we enter into the realm of motivation. In other words, we can infer a script-driven theory of motivation from Abelson's position.

A very detailed script-driven theory of human motivation is that developed by Glasser (1981) and Powers (1973). Their approach can be summarized in the following statement: We are motivated to do those things that are consistent with the way we believe the world should be.

A basic premise of this principle of motivation is that we all have scripts or mental scenarios about how the world *should be*. For example, each of us has scenarios for how we should look, how we should act in certain situations, what type of job we should have, how much money we should make, and so on. When we encounter situations that have little or nothing to do with how we think the world should be, we either ignore those situations or give them little attention. When we encounter a situation that fits our scenarios we give it a great deal of attention. That is, we attempt to manipulate the situation so that it will turn out consistently with our thoughts. To illustrate, assume you have a scenario that you should obtain a graduate degree in education. Given this, you will behave in such a way as to actualize this event—that is, make it happen. Any event in your life that might affect your going to or succeeding in graduate school will be given a great deal of attention by you. An event that does not affect your "going to graduate school" scenario will receive little attention unless that event fits into some other scenario you have.

Think back to the two classroom situations given in Chapter 1. When the children were asked to read *Stuart Little* and then to recreate his bedroom, they were using their background experiences and expectations about what the room should look like to translate print to images. The journal entry by the sixth-grader demonstrates this student's experiences and expectations about survival.

COGNITIVE DEVELOPMENT

Expectations also can be applied to the type of activities children do and how they do them. Again going back to the two examples in Chapter 1 multiple activities were being done by children rather than all children doing the same activity. Some children were speaking, some were writing, and others building. The end product of each activity was very beneficial; yet students were able to choose an activity based on their own expectations as a motivating force.

How do these expectations develop? Is there an identifiable sequence in human thought development? By looking at a few theories developed in cognitive psychology we should see a pattern to thought development.

Many psychologists have studied cognitive development in the early years. A pioneer in this field is Piaget. Stated in general terms, Piaget (1971, 1973, 1976) believes that thinking develops from the concrete to the abstract. Specifically, from birth to age two, thought is very little more than sensation, the coding of the information sent to the brain via the senses. Piaget calls this the *sensorimotor stage*. From ages two to seven, the *preoperational* stage, the child begins to produce mental images of static things and situations. From seven to eleven (concrete stage) the child begins to develop elementary classifications and relations. The child also develops the ability to understand and conceptualize processes. It is not until age 11 (*formal* stage), however, that a child is able to systematically carry out operations without relying on concrete interaction with the environment. Stated in other terms, it is not until age 11, the stage of formal operations, that the child is able to construct theories, formulate hypotheses and critically evaluate his or her own thinking. In Piaget's scheme thought gradually becomes more and more separated from present reality; as we grow older we gradually develop an abiltiy to deal with the world symbolically. It is not until we reach the level of symbolic reasoning that we can postulate a future or a reality other than the one we perceive via our senses.

At the heart of Piaget's theory is an assumption that thinking ability goes hand in hand with biological development. That is, children cannot think at a given level unless they are biologically ready for that level. Recently neurologists have added some interesting information, supportive of Piaget's contentions, to the general field of early cognitive development.

Epstein (1974 a, b) after examining the data from a number of different studies about brain and skull growth and mental development decided that enough evidence existed to support the conclusion that individuals go through brain growth spurts approximately every three years. These growth spurts, which may take as long as six months to complete, make quite a significant difference in actual brain mass. Epstein approximates the actual magnitude of the spurts at those periods to be between 35 and 85 grams, amounting to about a 3 percent to 8 percent increase in brain weight each time; four of such spurts sum to more than a 25 percent increase in brain weight by the time one becomes an adult. Epstein hypothesizes that the four major brain growth spurts occur for most children during the following periods: ages 2 to 4, 6 to 8, 10 to 12, and 14 to 16. He suggests that almost all of these age intervals could be considered turning points in Piaget's stages. In a comparison of Piaget's and Epstein's approaches, Lueers (1982) offers the graph in Figure 2.5 of the developmental stages postulated by the two theorists.

Epstein concludes that "the fact these spurts are so readily found in the data gives substantial support to the notion that the developmental processes tend to occur at certain chronological ages fairly independently of the history of the individuals" (1974 b, p. 223).

Epstein and Toepfer (1978) extrapolate the conclusion drawn about brain growth spurts to education; this rather large leap in reasoning has been heavily criticized by Lueers (1982). Epstein and Toepfer believe that because the studies on mental development show gains in student cognitive achievement at certain ages, it may follow that teaching and curriculum patterns should correspond to those patterns. They suggest that it may be relatively more difficult for teachers to initiate novel intellectual processes during the plateaus of brain growth than it is to initiate

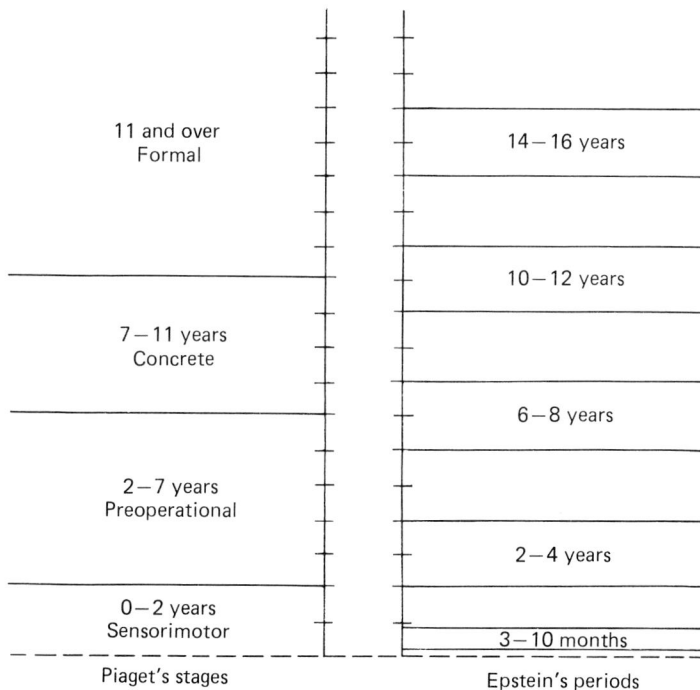

Piaget's stages	Epstein's periods
11 and over Formal	14 − 16 years
	10 − 12 years
7 − 11 years Concrete	
	6 − 8 years
2 − 7 years Preoperational	
	2 − 4 years
0 − 2 years Sensorimotor	3 − 10 months

FIGURE 2.5 *A summary of Piaget's stages of development and Epstein's period of brain growth spurts.*

these processes during the brain growth spurts. They also suggest that during plateaus in brain growth, the learning process should be characterized by the encouragement of maturation in already initiated and learned cognitive skills rather than in the acquisition of new skills.

Although they do not attach ages to their developmental levels Bruner (1960, 1964) and Klausmeier (1976) both support the notion that thinking ability develops from the concrete to the abstract. This is, individuals first learn to code and store the physical representation of their environment (how things feel, smell, taste, appear) and then gradually develop an ability to think in an abstract or symbolic fashion. Symbolic or abstract thinking does not require a sensual stimulus. That is, when we think symbolically we can picture things and situations without first perceiving them in the real world. It is at this symbolic level of thinking that we begin to develop our expectations (schemata, scripts, scenarios) about the outside world.

For example, most children at different age groups can comprehend a cause-effect relationship if the reference point for the younger children is concrete. A five-year-old knows that the reason (effect) for no dessert is that he or she did not eat any vegetable (cause). However, that same child may not fully comprehend his or her feelings of sadness (effect) after watching baby seals being slaughtered (cause). It is also at this symbolic level that language expands our thinking ability. By definition language is the symbol system for concepts that exist in the real world. The more your language grows the more symbols you have to represent the world in your mind. We might say, then, that early thought development proceeds from the concrete to the linguistic. Our ability to use language is a mirror of our ability to reason symbolically. At the risk of overdramatizing the point we might say that the language arts teacher is much more than a teacher of skills. Indeed, the language arts teacher has the responsibility of reinforcing one of the most powerful human tools—language.

SUGGESTED ACTIVITIES

1 Bring a political cartoon to class and discuss with other students what background experiences (schema) are necessary to comprehend the cartoon. Make a list of the experiences.

2 Show the political cartoon to a group of elementary children. Ask them if they can comprehend it. Did they use any background experience similar to what the college students did?

3 Observe a common object (e.g., a building). List all the properties of that object that you assume exist but do not see.

REFERENCES

Abelson, R. P. "Script Processing in Attitude Formation and Decision-making." In J. S. Carroll and J. W. Payne (eds.). *Cognition and Social Behavior*. Hillsdale, N.J.: Lawrence Erlbaum Associates, 1976.

Bradsford, J. D., and Johnson, M. K. "Considerations of Some Problems of Comprehension." In W. C. Chase, (ed.). *Visual Information Processing*. New York: Academic Press, 1973.

Bruner, J. S. *The Process of Education*. Cambridge, Mass.: Harvard University Press, 1960.

————. "The Course of Cognitive Growth." *American Psychologist* 19 (1964):1–15.

Dyer, W. W., *Your Erroneous Zones*. New York: Funk and Wagnalls, 1976.

Epstein, H. T. "Phrenoblysis: Special Brain and Mind Growth Periods." I. Human Brain and Skull Development. *Developmental Psychobiology* 7, 3 (1974):207–216. (a)

————. "Prenoblysis: Special Brain and Mind Growth Periods." II. Human Mental Development. *Developmental Psychobiology* 7, 3 (1974):217–224. (b)

Epstein, H. T., and Toepfer, C. F., Jr. A Neuroscience Basis for Reorganizing Middle Grades Education." *Educational Leadership* 35, 8 (1978):656–660.

Glasser, W. *Stations of the Mind*. New York: Harper & Row, 1981.

Klausmeier, H. J. "Instructional design and the teaching of concepts." in J. R. Levin and V. L. Allen (eds.). *Cognitive Learning in Children: Theories and Strategies*. New York: Academic Press, 1976.

Lueers, N. *An Overview of Learning Theories as an Approach to Studying Higher-Order Cognitive Thinking Processes*. Denver: Mid-continent Regional Educational Laboratory, 1982.

Piaget, J. *Biology and Knowledge: An Essay on the Relations between Organic Regulations and Cognitive Processes*. Chicago: University of Chicago Press, 1971.

————. *Problems of Genetic Psychology*. New York: Grossman Publishers, 1973.

————. *The Grasp of Consciousness: Action and Concept in the Young Child*. Cambridge, Mass.: Harvard University Press.

Powers, W. T. *Behavior: The Control of Perception*. Chicago: Aldine Publishing Company, 1973.

Smith, E. B., Goodman, K. S., and Meredith, R. *Language and Thinking in School*. New York: Holt, Rinehart and Winston, 1976.

Tannen, D. "What's in a Frame? Surface Evidence for Underlying Expectations." *Directions in Discourse Processing*. Norwood, N.J.: Ablex Publishing Corporation, 1979.

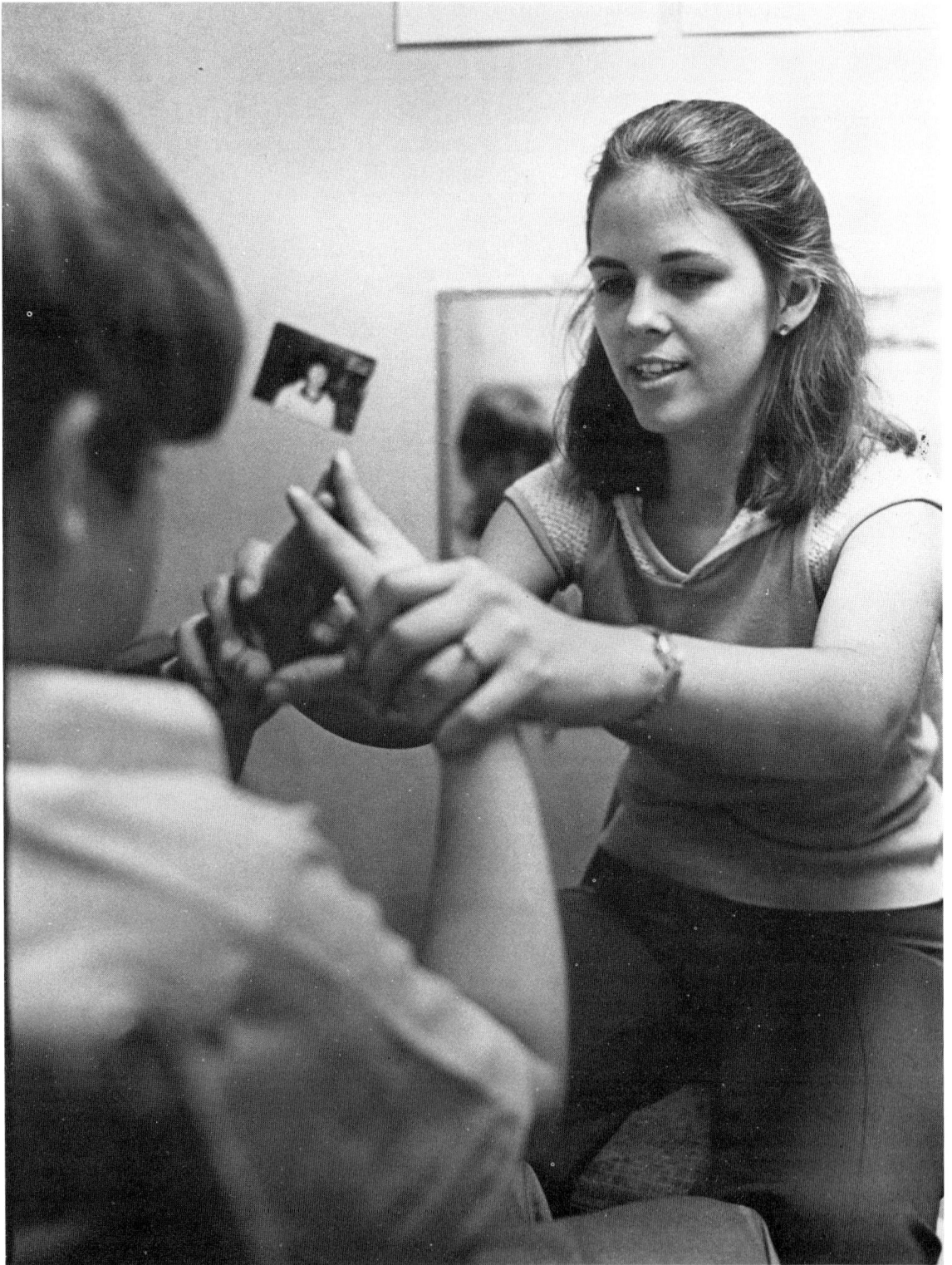

CHAPTER 3

The Nature of Language

WHAT IS LANGUAGE?
FIFTH GRADERS
...speaking, communication
...a whole bunch of phrases and sentences
...words that you put together
...Who knows how words got like they are? like
pneumonia, it could be *p...neumonia*!

OVERVIEW

This chapter begins with a brief discussion on how language and thought are related. In addition three aspects of language are dicussed: the system of language, the development of language, and the functions of language. The system of language is threefold—the sound/symbol system, the syntactic system, and the semantic system. Each system begins to develop from birth until children enter school. When children enter school, they use language in different social contexts. This ability to use language in different social contexts is called pragmatics.

INTRODUCTION

In the previous chapter, we discussed thought and thought development. It is no accident that the topic of cognition is the first area of our text and the nature of language is the second area. Vygotsky (1962) maintained that the greatest discovery of the child (language) becomes possible when a certain high level of thought and speech development has been reached. In other words, speech cannot be discovered without thinking. Speech and language have different genetic roots according to Vygotsky and follow different independent lines. At some point, the independent lines meet and thought becomes verbal and speech rational. That point occurs, according to Bloom (1970), when the three components of linguistic experience, nonlinguistic experience, and cognitive-perceptual organization interact to affect the development of linguistic competence. Bloom represents the three components schematically in the following figure.

Bloom asserts that when all three components fall in the shaded area, there is linguistic competence. However, at different times, two areas interact with each other such as linguistic experience and nonlinguistic experience, cognitive-perceptual development and nonlinguistic experience, cognitive-perceptual development and nonlinguistic experience, and cognitive-perceptual development and linguistic experience. When only two areas interact, linguistic competence does not occur.

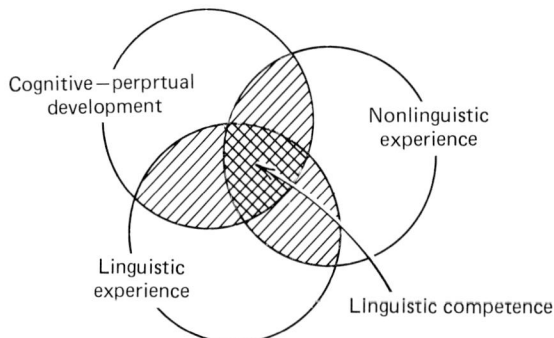

FIGURE 3.1 *Interrelationships of hypothetical components in language development. (Reprinted by permission of MIT press.)*

We already discussed two of the three areas, cognitive-perceptual development and nonlinguistic experience through thought development and expectations. Now we will look at linguistic experience.

Language at a very basic level is the labeling of thought. An example of a nonlanguage thought would be remembering an image of a tree or remembering how the tree felt, smelled, or sounded when the wind rustled through its leaves. Language enters into the picture when we use words to label those thoughts. Physiologists have postulated that different sections of the brain are responsible for storing different types of information (see Figure 3.2).

What probably happens when we remember the image of a tree is that we stimulate the visual cortex. This in turn might stimulate that part of the cortex which stores the representation of how a tree smells. Areas containing information about how a tree feels and sounds might also be stimulated. Language areas that house the labels associated with images and sensations (for example, the word "tree") are also stimulated. Of course this is a gross oversimplification of what actually happens but the gist of our discussion is fairly accurate.

The addition of these "labels" to our thoughts might at first seem like a small addition to the thinking process but it actually represents a quantum leap in reasoning power. This ability to label thought via language is the very thing that separates human thought from that of lower animal forms. Some psychologists have suggested that before language is incorporated into thought the type of thinking engaged in by humans is basically the same as that engaged in by animals. Vygotsky

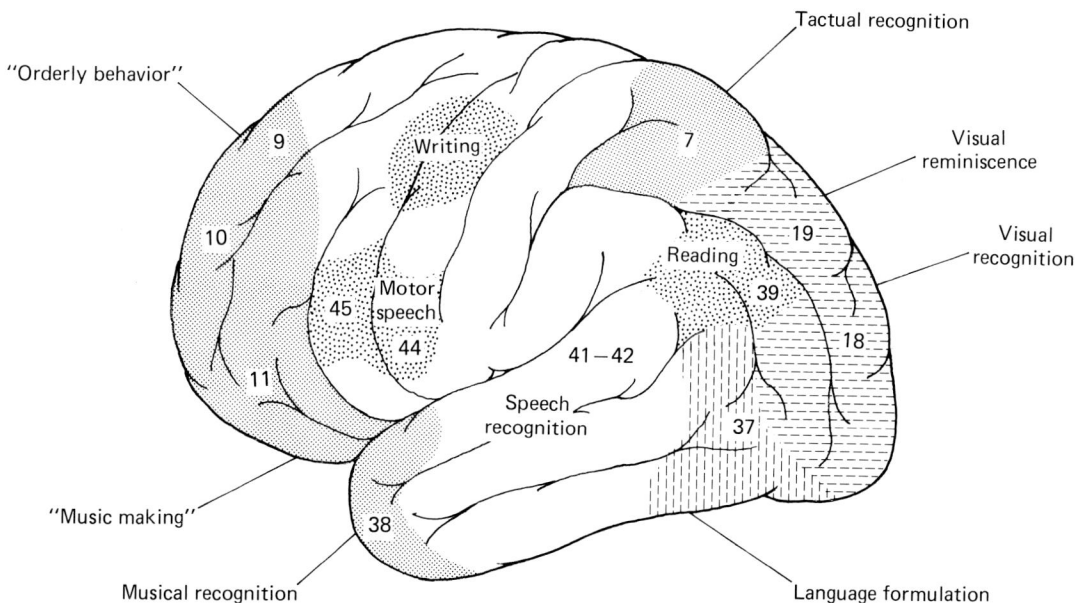

FIGURE 3.2 *Storage areas of the brain.*

(1970) felt that the prelanguage thinking of ten-month-old babies was similar and perhaps identical to the thinking of a chimpanzee.

The language system can be divided into three major areas: the sound/symbol, the syntactic, and the semantic levels.

SOUND/SYMBOL SYSTEM OF ENGLISH

When persons communicate to one another via language they usually do so by producing a stream of sounds. The number of sounds the human voice can produce is almost infinite. Yet each language uses only a small set of sounds as part of the language. The English language has approximately 36 sounds or *phonemes*. Common ones are listed in Figure 3.3.

Note that a phoneme is symbolized by a letter or some other symbol enclosed in slanted lines. The sounds made in a particular language and the rules for their organization are studied in a branch of linguistics called *phonology*. In English the sounds are grouped into two major categories—vowels and consonants. In Figure 3.3 there are 12 vowels and 20 consonants. Liquids and glides are somewhat "in-between" categories exhibiting characteristics of both vowels and consonants, although they are commonly grouped with consonants.

Vowels	Consonants	Liquids	Glides
/i/ b*eat*	/b/ *b*at	/r/ *r*ing	/w/ *w*ow
/I/ b*i*t	/p/ *p*at	/l/ *l*azy	/y/ *y*en
/e/ b*ai*t	/f/ *f*at		
/ɛ/ b*e*t	/v/ *v*an		
/δ/ b*a*t	/θ/ brea*th*		
/ə/ ros*e*s	/ð/ brea*the*		
/ʌ/ b*u*t	/t/ *t*ed		
/u/ c*oo*ed	/d/ *d*ead		
/ʊ/ c*ou*ld	/s/ *s*ame		
/o/ c*o*de	/z/ *z*est		
/ɔ/ c*aw*ed	/č/ *ch*op		
/ɑ/ c*o*d	/ǰ/ *j*am		
	/š/ *sh*ut		
	/ž/ vi*si*on		
	/k/ *c*ake		
	/g/ *g*et		
	/h/ *h*en		
	/n/ *n*eat		
	/m/ *m*ap		
	/ŋ/ ri*ng*		

FIGURE 3.3 *Common phonemes.*

The study of physical properties of sound and the manner of their articulation is called phonetics. Linguists studying phonetics would seek to determine how the various phonemes of the language are produced. They would study the similarities and differences among the sounds, the physical movements necessary for their articulation, and the vibrations that account for their accoustical effect.

Human sounds are produced by air from the lungs passing through the vocal cords in the throat and then out the body through either the mouth or the nose. In the process the sounds are intensified and shaped in different ways. The pharynx (or pharyngeal cavity), the mouth (or oral cavity), and the nose (the nasal cavity) are used to intensify sound. For this reason they are sometimes called the *resonators*. The soft palate (or velum), the hard palate, the tongue, the teeth, and the lips are used to shape sounds. They are sometimes referred to as the *articulators*. In phonetics the 36 sounds of English are described in terms of how the resonators and articulators are used to produce them. Figure 3.4 illustrates how the 36 phonemes are produced.

There is no need for a language arts teacher to know the *unfamiliar* terminology used in Figure 3.4. However, a knowledge of how sounds are produced can be a very useful tool on occasion. The terms *bilabial*, *labiodental*, and so on along the top row of the consonant chart refer to specific parts of the nasal, oral, and pharyngeal cavities. The line leading from each term identifies the specific location to which the term refers. For example, there is a line leading from the term *bilabial* to the two lips. This means that bilabial refers to the use of the two lips in the production of a phoneme. Note, that there is only one line leading from the vowel chart to the diagram. This line leads to the center of the tongue. This is because the vowels are produced solely by the position of the tongue within the oral cavity. High, mid and low refer to the position of the tongue in a vertical direction; front, central and back refer to the tongue's position in a horizontal direction. You can get a "feel" for these positions by pronouncing some of the vowels in the chart. For example, if you say the vowel sounds in the words *beat*, *bet* and *bat* (in that order) you should feel your tongue drop vertically as you say them. If you pronounce the vowel sounds in the words *bat*, *cod* and *cawed*, you should feel your tongue move backward on a horizontal plane.

In the consonant chart the words *stops*, *fricatives*, *sibilants*, *affricates*, *nasals*, and *liquids* refer to what is done to the air by the different parts of the mouth. When the air flowing from the lungs through the mouth is abruptly stopped and then let go, the resulting phoneme is called a *stop*. Note that the phonemes /b/ and /p/ are stops; more specifically, they are bilabial stops. This means that in the production of those phonemes the air flowing from the lungs is stopped by the two lips (bilabial) and then abruptly let go. The phonemes /t/, /d/, /k/ and /g/ are also *stops* but other areas of the mouth other than the two lips are used to impede the air flow. Fricatives are produced by stopping the air and letting it escape gradually rather than abruptly. The fricatives /f/ and /v/ are produced by obstructing the air using one lip and the upper teeth (labiodental).

Many speech pathologists use phonetics as the basis of their instruction. Indeed, a well-trained speech pathologist can teach a child born deaf to produce the phonemes of English by modeling the physical production of each phoneme.

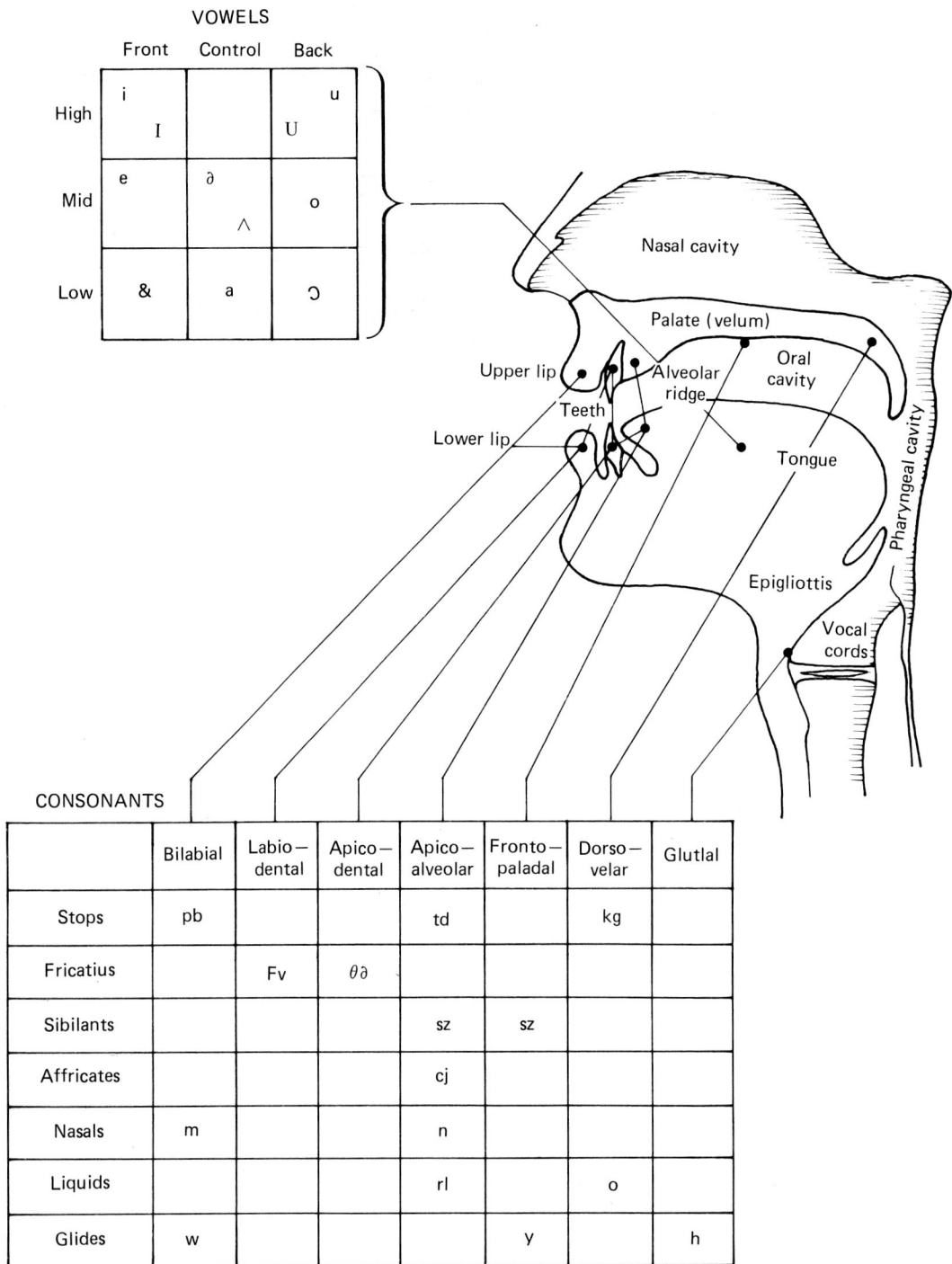

FIGURE 3.4 *Physiology of sound production.*

Because of the increasing need for communication between language arts teachers and language specialists (such as speech pathologists), it is becoming crucial that language arts teachers be aware of some basic phonetic concepts.

The final area associated with the sound/symbol system or language is *orthography*. The orthographic system of a language is relevant only to the written form of the language. Writing systems can be (1) pictographic, (2) ideographic, or (3) alphabetic. The order presented here is also their order of historic development. Pictographic writing systems are those in which the symbols relate directly to the appearance of their referents. In other words, pictures are used to represent concepts and ideas. Of course the drawback of a pictographic system is that all ideas are not capable of being pictures. Pictographic writing systems were the earliest form of writing and date back to the prehistoric times. These systems led to the development of ideographic writing. With ideographic systems each word in a language is assigned to a specific symbol which shows no relationship to the way the word is pronounced. The Chinese and Japanese have very well-developed ideographic systems of written language. English, although not ideographic in nature does employ some ideographs—mathematical signs (+, =); numerals (1, 2, 3); and abbreviations (Mr., Mrs.). With an ideographic system the reader either knows or doesn't know what the symbols mean. There are no intrinsic clues as to its meaning.

With alphabetic systems there is a correspondence between the symbols and the sounds of the language. Obviously English is an alphabetic system. But we have already seen that we don't have enough letters to go around to the 36 sounds. Consequently many letters stand for more than one sound; the letter *a* demonstrates this in the following words.

apple ate art all above

In each word the letter *a* by itself or in combination with another letter stands for a different phoneme. Of course this lack of one-to-one correspondence between the sounds of English and the orthographic symbols of English creates a great problem in reading and writing. In recent years some individuals have experimented with alternate orthographic systems to represent the sounds of English. One of the more well-known alternate orthographic systems is the initial teaching alphabet (i.t.a.) developed by Pitman & St. John (1969) in England. That orthography is presented in Figure 3.5.

The match between Pitman's orthography and the sounds of English is close to one to one. Once children have learned the initial teaching alphabet they can pronounce any word written in that orthography. Initial experimental results indicate that children can be taught to read very quickly using the i.t.a. Unfortunately when those same children try to transfer over to traditional orthography (our 26 letter system), they sometimes lose all the gain in reading ability they had acquired via the i.t.a. method.

It is safe to say that most language arts teachers have no control over the type of orthography they use to teach reading or writing. In general, the vast majority of

æ b c d cc
f<u>a</u>ce <u>b</u>ed <u>c</u>at <u>d</u>og ke<u>y</u>

f g h ie j k
<u>f</u>eet le<u>g</u> <u>h</u>at fl<u>y</u> <u>j</u>ug <u>k</u>ey

l m n œ p ɾ
<u>l</u>etter <u>m</u>an <u>n</u>est <u>o</u>ver <u>p</u>en g<u>ir</u>l

r s t ue v w
<u>r</u>ed <u>s</u>poon <u>t</u>ree <u>u</u>se <u>v</u>oice <u>w</u>indow

y z ʒ wh ʤ
<u>y</u>es <u>z</u>ebra dai<u>s</u>y <u>wh</u>en <u>ch</u>air

þ ð ʃh ʒ ŋ
<u>th</u>ree <u>th</u>e <u>sh</u>op televi<u>s</u>ion ri<u>ng</u>

ɑ au a e i o
<u>fa</u>ther ba<u>ll</u> c<u>a</u>p <u>e</u>gg m<u>i</u>lk b<u>o</u>x

u ω ω ou oi
<u>u</u>p b<u>oo</u>k sp<u>oo</u>n <u>ou</u>t <u>oi</u>l

elementary school textbooks use traditional orthography. The only orthographic issue in the teaching of elementary language arts is that of cursive versus script writing. Script writing is what we commonly call printing. Cursive writing is that system commonly used in handwriting in adults.

script   *cursive*

hello mom   *hello mom*

Elementary language arts teachers, usually provide instruction in both systems. There are many cursive systems and many methods of improving a student's "penmanship" in the use of those cursive systems. We will discuss handwriting methods in Chapter 9.

PHONOLOGICAL DEVELOPMENT

The initial stage of phonological development begins when a baby babbles. Jespersen (1925) concluded that babbling may start as early as the third week of life, but for most children it begins around the seventh or eighth week. However, this babbling has nothing to do with meaning. Many sounds produced during this babbling stage are not sounds in the English language. To refer to Figure 3.1, the linguistic experience is working but it is not interacting with the cognitive-perceptual and nonlinguistic experience during the babbling stage.

At five or six months of age, babbling is composed of consonant-vowel combinations such as "ma-ma-ma," and "goo-goo-goo." Vowel sounds exceed consonants for the first year, after which there are more consonants than vowels. According to Rebelsky et al. (1967) at about two and one-half years, almost all vowel sounds and about two-thirds of the consonants used by adults are present in children's language.

Since most school-age children have mastered the sound system of our language, we are not usually concerned about the developmental trends in phonological development. However, you may encounter a few students who have not mastered some sounds. Menyuk's data (1971) suggest that some six-year-old children may have a difficult time with the following sounds in different positions, (č, š, v, z, ð, θ, and ž). As teachers, we should look at inabilities to produce certain sounds as developmental trends. We can pinpoint the difficult sounds and see where they fit in the developmental sequence of learning sounds.

In addition to different rates of phonological development, some students are influenced by geographical location. For example, some children might say "Rat here" for "Right here," or say "pen" and "pin." These children say the words as they have heard them from persons in their immediate environment. In no way should we as teachers try to change their language system to conform to ours by saying their system is incorrect. Rather, we should let our students use their own rule system in reading and writing since they feel more comfortable with it. It may be more worthwhile to let various students compare their systems with an adult system to see, if in fact, they perceive the differences. In the next chapter on language differences, we will look at dialect.

ENGLISH SYNTAX

The second system of the English language is *syntax*, also known as grammar. DeStefano (1978) defines grammar in three ways: (1) a grammar book describing information about the patterns of a particular language, (2) grammar as it pertains to usage such as "between you and me" rather than "between you and I," and (3) grammar as "what people do when they speak their language—create sentences that are recognizable as that particular language." We will concentrate on this last definiton.

Linguists attempt to discover the particular rules that state which string of words are in fact grammatical sentences and which ones are not. The rules indicate whether the order of words is correct, the structure of words is correct, and the meaning of the sentence is clear.

In English, word order is the most fundamental aspect of syntax—that is, there are strict rules governing use of word order. To illustrate the importance of word order consider the following

The in the driveway car green belongs to Paul.

This sentence immediately sounds wrong to the native speaker of English because rules of word order have been violated. Specifically a syntax rule states (1) a modifying prepositional phrase *(in the driveway)* must come after the word it modifies and (2) a modifying adjective *(green)* must come before the word it modifies. Not all languages have the same word order restrictions. In Spanish, it is acceptable to place adjectives after the words they modify.

The structure of words has to do with morphemes. Linguists sometimes study language at the morpheme level rather than the sentence level. *Morphemes* are the smallest "meaning-bearing-units" and are either free or bound. The word "boy" is the smallest-bearing unit and is considered a free morpheme. The letters "b," "o," and "y" do not mean anything by themselves. However, together they form the word "boy." The word is free because it can stand alone in meaning. If we add an "s" to "boy" to form "boys," we now have two morphemes, the free morpheme "boy" and the bound morpheme "s." The "s" adds a plurality meaning to the word "boy" but it cannot stand by itself. This is why it is called a bound morpheme. Other bound morphemes include prefixes, suffixes, and endings showing possession such as *s* or *'s* or *s'*.

Research by Brown (1973) indicates that many of the most fundamental morphemes in the English language are acquired at a very early age and in a remarkably stable order. A listing of the fourteen morphemes that are acquired first by children learning English is presented in the order of acquisition.

---

1 Present progressive—ing (Daddy sleep*ing*)
2 & 3 *in* and *on* (*in* the car, *on* the table)
4 Noun plural—s (toy*s*)
5 Irregular past tense of verbs (*went, came*)
6 Possessive form of nouns—'s (daddy*'s* car)
7 Uncontractible copula—(*Is* Daddy here?)
8 Articles—*a, an, the*
9 Regular past tense verb forms *ed* (walk*ed*)
10 Third-person singlar verb forms -s (He play*s*)
11 Irregular third-person verb forms (*does, has*)
12 Uncontractible auxiliaries (*Is* daddy *sleeping*)
13 Contractible copulas (Mommy*'s* here)
14 Contractible auxiliaries (Mommy*'s* *sleeping*)

Not all children acquire the use of these morphemes at the same rate. Some children do not use them until age seven or eight. The vast majority of children, however, use the more common morphemes in English well before they enter school.

Our consideration of syntax has been limited to words. A major concern of syntax is the classification of groups of words. Virtually all grammars recognize the sentence as a unit of discourse.

All grammarians seem to agree that a sentence consists of two major parts. Native speakers of English have an intuitive "feel" for these two constituents. To illustrate consider the following sentence: "The old man watched the young girl playing on the swings." If you were asked to divide this sentence into two parts which of the divisions below would sound the most reasonable?

a　The old man watched ＿＿ the young girl playing on the swings.
b　The old man watched the young girl ＿＿ playing on the swings.
c　The old man ＿＿ watched the young girl playing on the swings.

Example *c* sounds more correct than the others because the basic nature of a sentence says something about someone or something. Consequently when we read or hear an English sentence we naturally break it up into "what was said" and "who or what it was said about."

In traditional grammar, which many elementary students study, these two sentence parts are called the subject and predicate. The sentence, according to traditional grammarians, would be analyzed using diagramming.

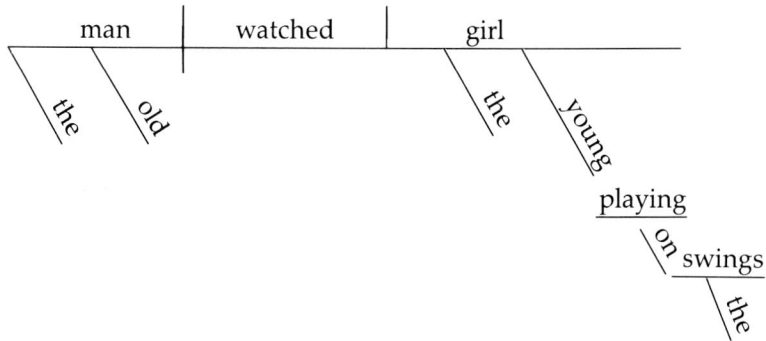

This type of diagramming separates the subject from the predicate by the vertical line cutting through the major horizontal line. Everything to the left of the line is considered to be part of the subject. Everything to the right of the line is part of the predicate.

Although traditional grammar is found in most school settings, linguists have used structural grammar for a long time to analyze sentences. The basic premise of structural grammar is that it is descriptive rather than prescriptive like traditional grammar. The structuralists collect speech from people and analyze it syntactically. Instead of using the many different parts of speech of traditional grammar and terminology for phrases and clauses (see Chapter 7), the structuralists use four basic word classes and use substitution to see if a word fits a particular class. The graphic representation of structural analysis is called *immediate constituent analysis* or IC analysis. It is used to show how parts of a sentence pattern together. Structural grammarians would analyze the above sentence in the following way.

Up to the 1950s grammars of English were useful in explaining the structure of sentences but could offer no explanation as to how two sentences with exactly the same structure could have different meanings. Consider the following example.

The shooting of the hunters was terrible.

This sentence has two possible meanings. It could mean that hunters were shooting animals and the shooting was terrible, or it could mean that some hunters were being shot and this act was terrible. In 1957 Noam Chomsky developed a syntactically oriented grammar that explained the two possible meanings of the sentence above. Chomsky stated that all sentences have two structures—one that we see or hear—the surface structure—and one that is underlying the meaning of the sentence—the deep structure. He explained the two meanings of the sentence above as generating from two different deep structures. One meaning would have the following two kernel sentences in its deep structure.

The shooting was terrible. The hunters were shooting.

The other would have these two kernel sentences in its deep structure.

The shooting was terrible. The hunters were shot.

In both meanings the second sentence was embedded in the first to produce the surface structure. To get from the deep structure to the surface structure the kernel sentences had to go through a series of "transformations," in which elements were deleted and/or changed. In Chomsky's grammar every sentence has an underlying deep structure that is changed or transformed to a surface structure. For this reason his grammar has become known as "transformational grammar." The schematical representation is given below.

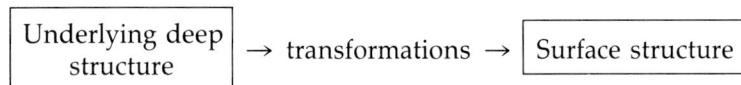

$$\boxed{\text{Underlying deep structure}} \rightarrow \text{transformations} \rightarrow \boxed{\text{Surface structure}}$$

Because of its explanatory power some cognitive psychologists have used transformational grammar as a model for language production. That is, some psychologists feel that when we speak or write our ideas are in the form of deep structure kernel sentences that we transform to surface structures.

SYNTACTIC DEVELOPMENT

At around one year of age, children speak their first words which linguists refer to *holophrases*. Holophrases can be words in adult vocabulary or they can be children's own words for things, such as "dida" for dog. When children use adult words like "milk," they do not use it as we do. "Milk" may mean "I want a glass of milk" or "I spilled the milk" or "The dog drank my milk." To understand what the child means, parents have to look for other cues, such as the child pointing to the refrigerator or to the dog hiding under the table. These first words or holophrases tend to be nouns, verbs, and interjections.

At about 18 months of age, children put together two-word sentences. Braine (1978) reports that the number of different two-word combinations increases slowly, then shows a marked increase around the age of two years. Brown (1973) conducted an extensive study of early language acquisition with three children named Adam, Eve, and Sarah. During the first two years of life, Brown labeled the children's speech telegraphic—that is, during this stage, the children's speech was made up of open and pivot words, mainly nouns, verbs, and adjectives. Other speech parts such as prepositions, articles, and pronouns were not used. Pivot-open phrases might be "allgone milk" or "pretty flowers." Again, how adults interpret telegraphic speech is through context. They have to be able to identify the context in which the child is referring when the child says a pivot-open phrase.

From the age of two and one-half to five, there is much syntax development. Nouns take on plural form. Possessive case forms, such as "my hat" for "me hat," and transformations develop. By the time children enter kindergarten, they have mastered most syntactic structures. Lee (1974) has categorized the following syntactic structures learned by five-year-old children.

---

1 Indefinite pronouns and noun modifiers (this, anybody, several).
2 Personal pronouns (I, he, who, one).
3 Main verbs (is coming, ate, was).
4 Secondary verbs.
5 Negatives.
6 Conjunctions.
7 Interrogative reversals.
8 Wh- questions.

Semantic System of English

Semantics is the study of the meaning system within a language. Before discussing the semantics of English per se we should first consider the relationship the semantic system has to the other systems. To say that English or any other language has a meaning system that is independent of the sound/symbol system or syntactic system is misrepresentation. All the systems of a language combine to produce meaning. To illustrate how syntax conveys meaning consider the following sentence.

The quarb farbled the burt.

Here the form class words have no real meaning, but from the sentence structure we do get a "sense" that something called a "quarb" did something called "farbling" to something called a "burt." Syntactically this meaning is conveyed by word order, the positions of the functor *the* and the use of the inflectional ending *-ed*. If we add known English words to this structure we obtain complete meaning.

The boy pushed the cart.

Semantics is the study of how words, word parts, and larger units of discourse convey meaning; although, as we have just seen, we can never truly discuss meaning in isolation of syntax or phonology.

Not long ago semantic studies focused on classifying the different semantic functions of a word in a sentence. Traditional grammar had attempted to categorize words into subject, verb, direct object, indirect object, subject complement, and object complement. These categories represented the semantic component of traditional grammar. However, neither traditional grammar, nor structural or transformational grammar for that matter, were able to distinguish among the meaning relationship of one word to another in a sentence.

To make a finer semantic distinction between the function of different words in a sentence, a new type of grammar was developed in the mid-1960s. This grammar, called *case grammar*, was developed by James Fillmore (1968) at Ohio State University. The first form of Fillmore's case grammar had seven different categories or semantic functions a word could perform within a sentence (see Figure 3.6).

Several other case grammars have been developed since and more case categories added for an even more specific description of the meaning relationships among words. Case grammars are used to measure language development and represent how meaning is stored in memory. To illustrate this latter use consider these sentences.

1 Bill went to the drugstore.
2 There he met his sister.
3 They bought their father a coat.

Using Fillmore's case categories, a cognitive psychologist might diagram the semantic relationships among the words in these sentences in the way shown in Figure 3.6. Such diagrams are sometimes called *cognitive maps*. Experimentation indicates that they are fairly valid representations of memory storage.

Most recently some linguists interested in semantics have turned their attention

CASE NAME	DEFINITION	EXAMPLE (italicized noun in designated case)
Agentive (A)	Typically an animate noun; instigator of action	*Mark* hit the ball.
Instrumental (I)	The inanimate object used by the agent.	Mark hit the ball with the *bat*.
Dative (D)	The animate being affected by the action of the verb.	Todd gave cookies to *Christine*.
Experiencer (E)	The animate being having the experience name by the verb.	*Gia* saw Melissa.
Factitive (F)	The object resulting from the action named by the verb.	Paul made the *cake*.
Locative (L)	The location of the event expressed by the verb.	The team played in *Chicago*.
Objective (O)	The semantically most neutral case; anything not represented by one of the other cases is assigned to the objective case.	John opened the *door*.

FIGURE 3.6 *Fillmore's Case Categories.*

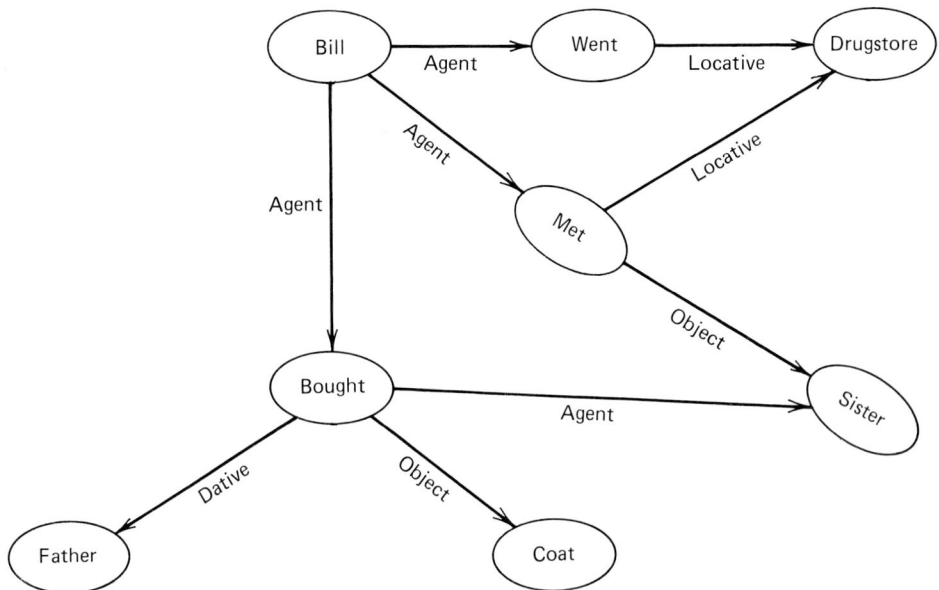

FIGURE 3.7 *Cognitive map of relationships between sentences.*

to categorizing relationships that exist between entire sentences as units rather than among the words in a sentence. Consider the following illustration.

1 The team van was broken.
2 Consequently, the team forfeited the game.

If we considered these two sentences from a case grammar approach only, we could describe the relationships the words in each sentence have with one another, but we could not describe the relationship sentence 1 as a unit has with sentence 2 as a unit. That relationship is one of causation. This is signaled by the word *consequently*.

The study of relationships among sentences as units is usually referred to as *discourse analysis*. Rather than use the sentence some discourse analysts (Marzano, 1983) use the "predication" as their basic study unit. A predication is not the same as a sentence. A sentence can be a predication but not every predication is a sentence. Basically a predication must consist of a verb form and some other words. In traditional grammar terminology a predication would include all clause forms and all verbal forms. In most cases a sentence will contain more than one predication:

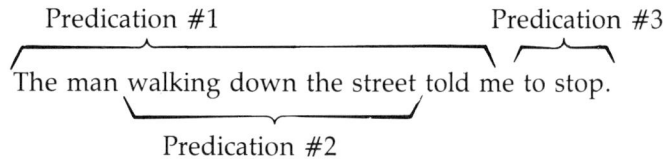

Predication #1   Predication #3

The man walking down the street told me to stop.

Predication #2

There are a number of discourse level grammars (Halliday and Hasan, 1976; Kintsch, 1974). In general the relationships they identify that can exist between predications fall into five major categories: (1) causation, (2) comparison, (3) addition, (4) time, and (5) reference. These five different types of relationships within each major category are listed here.

---

1 *Causation.*   He won the race (by) maintaining his concentration.
2 *Comparison.*   I will be there (but) I won't be happy.
3 *Addition.*   I am tired. (In fact,) I am exhausted.
4 *Time.*   They went to the game. (Afterward) they went to the dance.
5 *Reference.*   This is the book (which) should give you the most information.

It is important to note in the examples that *every relationship between propositions is signaled by a word or phrase*. The "signal words" in the examples are circled. Signal words are valuable to language arts teachers. By systematically teaching these words a teacher gives students a tool with which they can understand the general meaning of almost anything they read. In Chapter 11, we suggest strategies to teach these signal words to students.

PRAGMATICS

Besides being aware of the systems of language and their development, it is also important to understand the functions for which language is used. *Pragmatics* is the study of how and when language is used. Hanna, Hodges, and Hanna (1971) state, "Every language has the ultimate purpose of enabling man to communicate information to others; it is a means by which man's personal experience with his environment can be systematically symbolized and related to others" (p. 4). However, for communication to be meaningful and shared between a speaker and a listener, or a writer and a reader, the listener and reader must be aware not only of the actual words and expressions, but also of the social function of what is said.

Remember the message may have more than one purpose of function. Think of the many functions the term "good morning" has. It may mean the weather is nice, or another way of saying "hello," or a beginning of a sales pitch to get you to buy solar heating supplies. When children come to school, teachers need not only help them with their language from a developmental standpoint, but also to show them how language functions in many settings for different purposes.

Two systems for categorizing language have been developed by Halliday (1975) and Tough (1976). Halliday's work demonstrates that any attempt to analyze language must include consideration of form and function. That is, what the child says must be analyzed to the child's purpose for speaking, and the context or environment in which the child is speaking. Remember the earlier example of holophrases. They make sense to the listener when the listener is aware of the purpose and the context. The child says "milk" and the adult watches as the child points to the dog under the table lapping up the milk. Halliday has listed seven general uses of language.

1 *Instrumental.*   Language as a means of getting things. Examples: I want, I need.

2 *Regulatory.*   Language as a means of controlling behavior or attitudes of others Examples: Do as I tell you. Bring me this thing.

3 *Interactional.*   Language as a means of getting along with others in a social context. Examples: It is nice to see you. Pleased to meet you.

4 *Personal.*   Language as a means of expressing individuality or self. Examples: Here I come. I don't like this.

5 *Heuristic.*   Language as a means of finding out new information. Examples: Tell me why. What is this called?

6 *Imaginative.*   Language as a means of creating new worlds, making up stories, or poetry. Examples: Let's pretend.

7 *Informative.*   Language as a means of telling someone something. Examples: I've got something to tell you. I want to report on something.

You might predict that a child before entering school would use instrumental, imaginative, and informative categories. When school begins, the child is exposed to more heuristics from the teacher and begins to use this category more often. Teachers need to be aware of these categories and make sure to encourage the use of all categories in the classroom rather than spending too much time on the heuristic category. When students are asked to use all of the categories as part of their school setting, they become better language communicators.

If you are looking for a system for classifying elementary school children's language, you might want to look at the categories and strategies set up by Tough (1976). Tough's classification scheme includes seven uses of language with corresponding strategies that serve each category and reveal the child's reason for talking.

USE OF LANGUAGE

1 Self-maintaining

Strategies
1 Referring to physical and psychological needs and wants.
2 Protecting the self and self-interests.
3 Justifying behaviour or claims.
4 Criticizing others.
5 Threatening others.

2 Directing

Strategies
1 Monitoring own actions.
2 Directing the actions of the self.
3 Directing the actions of others.
4 Collaborating in action with others.

3 Reporting on present and past experiences

Strategies
1 Labeling the components of the scene.
2 Referring to detail (size, colour, and other attributes)
3 Referring to incidents.

2 Recognizing causal and dependent relationships.
3 Recognizing problems and their solutions.
4 Justifying judgments and actions.
5 Reflecting on events and drawing conclusions.
6 Recognizing principles.

5 Predicting*

Strategies
1 Anticipating and forecasting events.
2 Anticipating the detail of events.
3 Anticipating a sequence of events.
4 Anticipating problems and possible solutions.
5 Anticipating and recognizing alternative courses of action.
6 Predicting the consequences of actions or events.

6 Projecting*

Strategies
1 Projecting into the experiences of others.

4   Referring to the sequence of events.
5   Making comparisons.
6   Recognizing related aspects.
7   Making an analysis using several of the features above.
8   Extracting or recognizing the central meaning.
9   Reflecting on the meaning of experiences, including own feelings.

4   Toward logical reasoning*

Strategies
1   Explaining a process

2   Projecting into the feelings of others.
3   Projecting into the reactions of others.
4   Projecting into situations never experienced.

7   Imagining*

1   Developing an imaginary situation based on real life.
2   Developing an imaginary situation based on fantasy.
3   Developing an original story.

* Strategies which serve *directing*, *reporting*, and *reasoning* may serve these uses also.
Source: Reprinted by Permission of Schools Council Publication, 1976.

By keeping careful notes of the language functions of individual students and the class as a whole, you can promote appropriate and effective uses of language during classroom activities. In addition, you should strive to use all of the language functions yourself in the classroom to serve as a model. Sometimes, elementary teachers spend a great deal of time on task-oriented directions or questions rather than interjecting affective responses that the child may be used to from the home setting.

SUGGESTED ACTIVITIES

1   Using Fillmore's case grammar categories, diagram the following sentences.
   (a) Kate baked a souffle in the microwave.
   (b) Tom used a key to unlock the door.
   (c) Barbara bought her boyfriend a new sweater.

2   Visit an elementary classroom and observe one or two children interacting with the teacher and their peers. Classify their uses of language according to Tough's classification scheme.

3   Discuss with your peers the advantages and disadvantages of standard spelling and phonetic spelling in teaching language arts skills

REFERENCES

Bloom, L. *Language Development: Form and Function in Emerging Grammars.* Cambridge, Mass.: MIT Press, 1970.

Braine, M. "The Ontogeny of English Phrase Structure: The First Phase." In Lois Bloom (ed.). *Readings in Language Development.* New York: John Wiley & Sons, 1978.

Brown, R. *A First Language: The Early Stages.* Cambridge, Mass.: Harvard University Press, 1973.

Chomsky, N. *Syntactic Structures.* Mouton: The Hague, 1957.

DeStefano, J. *Language, the Learner, and the School.* New York: John Wiley & Sons, 1978.

Fillmore, J. "The Case for Case," In E. Bach and R. T. Harms (eds.). *Universals in Linguistic Theory.* New York: Holt, Rinehart and Winston, 1968.

Halliday, M. A. K. *Learning How to Mean—Explorations in the Development of Language.* London: Edward Arnold, 1975.

Halliday, M., and Hasan, R. *Cohesion in English.* London: Longman Ltd., 1976.

Hanna, P. R., Hodges, R. E., and Hanna, J. S. *Spelling Structures and Strategies.* Boston: Houghton Mifflin, 1971.

Jesperson. O. *Language.* New York: Holt, Rinehart and Winston, 1925.

Kintsch, W. *The Representation of Meaning in Memory.* New York: John Wiley and Sons, 1974.

Lee, L. *Developmental Sentence Analysis.* Evanston, Ill.: Northwestern University Press, 1974.

Marzano, R. *A Quantitative Grammar of Meaning and Structure: A Methodology for Language Analysis.* Denver: Mid-continent Regional Educational Laboratory, 1983.

Menyuk, P. *The Acquisition and Development of Language.* Englewood Cliffs, N.J.: Prentice-Hall, 1971.

Pitman, Sir. J., and St. John, J. *Alphabets and Reading.* New York: Pitman, 1969.

Rebelsky, F. G. et al. "Language Development—The First Four Years." In Yvonne Brackbill (ed.). *Infancy and Early Childhood.* New York Free Press, 1967.

Tough, J. *Listening to Children Talking.* London: Schools Council Publication, 1976.

Vygotsky, L. S. *Thought and Language.* New York: John Wiley & Sons, 1962.

———. *Mind in Society.* Cambridge, Mass.: Harvard University Press, 1980.

CHAPTER 4

Language Differences

HOW DO YOU ASK YOUR YOUNGER BROTHER TO GET YOU A POPSICLE?
> FIFTH GRADER
>> I don't ask. I say "Get me a popsicle."

HOW DO YOU ASK YOUR MOTHER FOR A POPSICLE?
> SAME FIFTH GRADER
>> "May I please have a popsicle, Mother."

OVERVIEW

The purpose of this chapter is to provide the background necessary to work with children who are linguistically different. Specific aspects of nonstandard language will be explored and related to cultural differences. You will learn some necessary requisites to understanding children who speak another language and the difficulties they encounter learning in an English-speaking classroom. We will explore the important topic of teacher attitudes toward language differences. We will describe some implications for language arts instruction.

INTRODUCTION

We ended our last chapter with a discussion of pragmatics and related it to the study of how and when children use language. We talked about the purposes and functions of language and how we need to examine the language of children within the social context of their environment.

As we look at children's environments, we know that some children come from a different environment, or culture, and that their culture influences their language. For example, children may come from various countries—Mexico, Cambodia, Vietnam, or Laos, speaking varying degrees of English. Other children who were born in the United States may have parents who speak another language, perhaps Spanish. Many American children speak pidgin English (in Hawaii), black English (in Detroit, New York, and other parts of the U.S.), and village English (in bush villages in Alaska). In all cases, these children do not speak the standard English or the English accepted as most appropriate for classroom use.

Children who speak nonstandard English or a different language enter the classroom with differences in language, background, and culture which will certainly affect the learning of the language arts skills. As a language arts teacher, you need to be aware of these differences, and how they affect learning, language development, and language arts instruction.

LANGUAGE AND CULTURE: IMPORTANT CONNECTIONS

It is necessary to think about how children's language reflects their environment and culture. Children are born into an existing social environment and learn to talk as their parents do. It is not surprising that children from Boston learn to pronounce car as "cah," that children from Georgia say "y'all," or that children from Mexico say "gracias." By the time children enter school, their language is deeply rooted in their home experiences (Smith, Goodman, and Meredith, 1976). This is true for all children, even those who speak "school English."

The problem arises when children who speak nonstandard English or a different language enter school and are confronted with a different and conflicting subculture (Dole, 1981a). The new subculture of the school rejects the child's language, attempts to eradicate it, and replace it with the language of the classroom, proceeding as if children had no language or cognitive abilities (Meier and Cazden, 1982). Shuy (1969) calls this the "Bonnie and Clyde" tactic of teaching English. He quotes from one observation of how English was being taught to the Pine Ridge Sioux Indians.

> *Teachers are trained to criticize (the local dialect) as "bad English," and so, no sooner does the Indian child open his mouth to speak English, than he is branded publicly as speaking incorrectly.*

No wonder these children often become "nonverbal" in the classroom!

What do we need to remember about cultural differences as we teach listening, speaking, reading, and writing to these children?

1 Children speak as their parents do; rejection of their language is a rejection of them and their parents.
2 All children are sensitive to criticisms and rejections of their language.
3 Children may have different values from their teachers and their classmates.
4 Reading materials used in our schools may not reflect the unique needs, interests, and experiences of children with language differences.

An understanding of the social context of language as well as language differences is prerequisite to designing a language arts program to meet the unique literacy needs of linguistically different children.

DIALECT DIFFERENCES

What Linguists Tell Us

We have already used the term "standard English" or "school English" to describe the language of the classroom. The term "standard English" refers to that variation of spoken English considered to carry the most prestige within the American speech community (Smith, Goodman, and Meredith, 1976). The language of national TV broadcasters most closely represents "standard English."

Wide variations exist within any language. Further, a given language will typically consist of many dialects or systematic variations in phonology, syntax, and sometimes semantics. Dialects of English differ with geographic region, ethnicity, and social status. Everyone speaks a "dialect" of English, even standard English speakers. Linguists do not assign value judgments to different dialects.

However, in our society, some dialects, like "standard English," carry the most prestige, and others, like "black English," are considered nonstandard. Nonstandard dialects typically carry negative connotations within our society, and people who speak them are considered uneducated, crude and/or illiterate. Our society, as others, has very definite value judgments about the acceptability and worth of the language we speak.

What Sociolinguists Tell Us

Language differences have been studied extensively over the last 15 to 20 years by educators, psychologists, and linguistics interested in how language works and in the effects of language differences on learning and language development. Sociolinguists study language differences and then apply their findings to education (Shuy, 1977).

Sociolinguists are largely responsible for undermining the *language-deficit hypothesis* proposed by Bereiter and Englemann (1967) and others in the 1960s. Proponents of this hypothesis argued that children who speak a nonstandard dialect are "nonverbal," and their language is "bad English," "underdeveloped," or "incorrect" (Cullinan, 1974). Our earlier example of how English was taught to Sioux Indians is a good working example of this hypothesis. Further, this hypothesis was supported by psychologists who tested nonstandard English-speaking children and found that their IQ scores were below those of standard English speakers. Thus, the nonstandard language was thought to reflect inferior cognitive development.

Several classic studies by sociolinguists such as Labov (1966) and Shuy, Wolfram, and Riley (1968) refuted the language-deficit hypothesis. They demonstrated that one dialect, black English, was a systematic, rule-governed and logical variation of English. They also found that many nonstandard English-speaking children are highly verbal with their peers, and only "nonverbal" in the more formal, standard English-speaking classroom. Additionally, they argued that nonstandard speakers could not be evaluated cognitively by tests written in and evaluated in standard English, and developed for white, middle-class children. Shuy (1977) summarizes,

> *. . . there is no problem internal to any language or dialect that affects intellectual development. The variation within a language and the way people evaluate this variation reflect the organization of the community, geographically and socially (p. 106).*

Sociolinguists have also added to our understanding of language differences through an examination of different "registers." De Stefano (1973, p. 191) defines register as "a set of linguistic forms used in given social circumstances." Shuy (1977) demonstrates the continuum of language forms in a single sentence.

1 Hey! Don't bring no more a dem crates over here!

2 Hey! Don't bring no more a dose crates over here!

3 Hey! Don't bring no more a those crates over here!

4 Hey! Don't bring any more of those crates over here!

5 *Please don't bring any more of those crates over here!*

6 *Gentlemen, will you kindly desist in your conveying those containers in this general direction? (p. 85)*

We might imagine the social setting surrounding each utterance and the person speaking it, and when it would be appropriate to use sentence 3 versus sentence 6. As we mentioned in Chapter 3, each utterance must be evaluated for its purpose within a given social context.

Sociolinguists argue emphatically that there are no rights or wrongs along this continuum, just differences. As speakers of any language and dialect, we all use different registers as we communicate with different people in different social situations. Subtle adjustments are made in vocabulary, grammar, and phonology (Shuy, 1977). De Stefano (1973), gives an excellent example of a teacher who is upset with the behavior of one of her students. "Hubert is a constant disrupter in class," she says to her principal. "Hubert has some difficulty settling down to do his work," she says to Hubert's parents. To her fellow teachers, she complains, "That kid's driving me nuts with his yackity-yacking"; and to Hubert himself, she admonishes, "Hubert, be quiet" (De Stefano, 1973, pp. 190–191). We all use registers, whether we are aware of them or not.

How does the concept of register help us understand dialect differences? We need to realize that linguists attach no value judgments to various registers or dialects; the value judgments are socially determined. In addition, we all use a range of registers for different purposes.

Nevertheless, the question of "good English" will always emerge in debates about standard and nonstandard English. Many people, argue, "Yes, what you have said is fine, but isn't it important that *everyone* learns 'good (or proper) English'?" The National Council of Teachers of English (NCTE) has responded to that statement by defining "good English."

> *Good English is that form of speech which is appropriate to the speaker, true to the language as it is, and comfortable for the speaker and listener. It is the product of custom, neither cramped by rule, nor freed from all restraint; it is never fixed, but changes with the organic life of the language (see Lightner, 1965).*

This NCTE statement helps clarify the issue: "good English" should not be equated with standard English. "Good English" involves using the appropriate register at the appropriate time.

De Stefano argues that black children do have control of registers and in fact do talk in different ways under different circumstances. She has shown that black children gradually develop more control over standard English patterns and can use them in appropriate social situations. With additional instruction, these children can learn to widen their range of registers.

Some important conclusions drawn from sociolinguistic study are summarized below.

1   *Speaking a dialect of English, any dialect, does not imply a language deficit.*
2   *Speaking a dialect of English does not imply a cognitive deficit.*
3   *We all speak in different registers, depending on the needs of a given situation.*

Effects on Learning the Language Arts

Do dialect differences affect learning the language arts skills, especially reading and writing? This question has been a topic of debate for many years. Historically, it has been demonstrated that children who speak a nonstandard dialect perform poorly in reading achievement tests. This fact poses several questions. First, does this mean that speaking a nonstandard dialect *causes* poor reading? If so, then what are the specific points of interference between the nonstandard dialect and standard English, and what do we do about such interference?

Linguists have studied extensively the dialect of black English to try to answer these questions. Several phonological and syntactic differences between black English and standard English have been identified as possible sources of interference in learning to read. For example, a black English-speaking child might say the sentence, "He passed by me" as "He pass by me," or "I tore my dress" as "I toe my dress."

Gibson and Levin (1975) argue, however, that most suggestions concerning just how phonological and syntactic differences might interfere with reading acquisition are speculative. Some educators think these differences are more problematic for teachers than for black English-speaking children. Goodman (1973) feels the problem is more one of linguistic discrimination than of linguistic interference. For example, a teacher may correct the surface structure reading of "He pass by me" and/or mistakenly conclude that the black child reading the sentence does not understand the correct tense. In fact, the child may understand perfectly well, but simply be "recoding" into his or her own dialect. Such overconcern for surface structure of superficial differences can confuse children.

In fact, many educators argue that teachers' attitudes toward the dialect may be a more important determinant of reading achievement than the dialect itself (Gibson and Levin, 1975). Some suggest that differences between the culture and values of the teacher and the child may present conflicts. These differences and teachers' not recognizing them affect the teachers' reading and language instruction for black English-speaking children. We will examine teachers' attitudes later in this chapter.

Additional sources of interferences in learning to read might be more general ones. Some educators argue that the mismatch between the child's oral language and the written language of the text could be a source of interference. Written language is more formal, structured, and organized than oral language, and does not contain the situational and nonverbal cues in oral language. Add to these already

SOME PHONOLOGICAL AND SYNTACTIC DIFFERENCES BETWEEN STANDARD ENGLISH AND BLACK ENGLISH

Phonological

Feature	*Standard English = Black English*
1 r'lessness	tore = toe
	sore = so
2 l'lessness	toll = toe
	tool = to
3 th	mother = muvver
	tooth = toof
4 ing	going = goin
	hearing = hearin
5 ed	jumped = jump
	missed = miss
6 s,es	ten cents = ten cent
	Mary's hat = Mary hat
7 sk	desk = des, desses
sp	wasp = was, wasses
st	test = tes, tesses

Syntactic

1 double negation	Tom doesn't have = Tom ain't got no
2 verb "to be"	She is always here = She be always here, or She always here
3 past tense	He walked = He walk
4 plurals and possessives	ten cents = ten cent
	Mary's hat = Mary hat
5 subject/verb agreement	John walks = John walk

existing differences the additional dialectal differences in phonology and syntax, and the task can become even more complex for linguistically different children.

Educators point to the mismatch between real life experiences and textbook experiences as a source of interference. For example, black children in New York may learn to read from readers containing stories about children on farms in the Midwest. A more striking example is when these same stories serve as basic readers for Eskimo children in bush Alaska. These children live hundreds of miles from the nearest city, and may be thousands of miles from the nearest farm. Thus, their lives and experiences are so vastly different from those in the stories they read that children have no link to the stories. Chapter 2 stressed the importance of schemata in the learning process. Applying that theory to this situation, it is easier to understand why these children have difficulty comprehending and learning from texts.

What about sources of interference in other language arts, particularly writing and spelling? Hartwell (1980) argues that while the idea of dialect interference in writing has been theorized, studies have not shown a consistent pattern of dialect-related errors in black students' writing. Instead, writing errors have been random and not necessarily related to the spoken dialect.

Hartwell argues that dialect interference in writing is related to dialect interference in reading. That is, interference in both reading and writing reflects the fact that children have not mastered the surface features of written language; they therefore turn to the phonology and syntax of their spoken language. This argument persuasively explains dialect interference in writing ("He be here" for "He is here") and in spelling ("stomack" for "stomach," "toe" for "tore").

We must keep in mind, however, that dialect interference varies among children and also for the same children between their oral and written language (De Stefano, 1972; Wolfram and Whiteman, 1971). Therefore, we cannot rely on simple answers to the question: Is there dialect interference in reading, writing, and the other language arts? Instead, we need to treat children as individuals, and determine their strengths and weaknesses on an individual basis. If we have some idea of phonological and syntactic differences between any given dialect and standard English, we should be able to pinpoint where children might have difficulty learning both oral and written standard English.

LANGUAGES DIFFERENCES: MORE INFORMATION

The International Reading Association has several excellent books for a better understanding of linguistic differences and their relationship to reading.

Cullinan, Bernice E. (ed.). *Black Dialects and Reading*. Newark Del.: International Reading Association, 1974.

Laffey, James L. and Roger Shuy (eds.). *Language Differences: Do They Interfere?* Newark, Del.: International Reading Association, 1973.

Shafer, Robert E. (ed.). *Applied Linguistics and Reading*. Newark, Del.: International Reading Association, 1979.

Shuy, Roger (ed.). *Linguistic Theory: What Can It Say About Reading*. Newark, Del.: International Reading Association, 1977.

ENGLISH AS A SECOND LANGUAGE

When we discuss language differences, we refer not only to those children who speak a nonstandard dialect, but also to those whose English proficiency may be limited due to the influence of another language. The latter children come from families and homes in which English may not be spoken at all. The children of these families, in turn, may have limited English proficiency or none at all, they may be bilingual, or they may even speak English only. Nevertheless, their home, language, and experiences are influenced by a culture and language different from that of the Anglo middle-class school.

There are an estimated four million children in this country whose native language is Spanish. These children, and an additional million other non- or limited English-speaking children do not have the advantage of learning the language arts skills in English from an English-speaking background. Many of these children, like nonstandard English-speaking children, do achieve at a slower rate than their white American peers. Thonis (1976) lists four conditions that "contribute to failure and confusion," for these children.

1 *Lack of experiences in the dominant culture from which concepts specific to the English-speaking community may be acquired* [remember the importance of schema].

2 *Inadequate oral command of the English language which is the language of the instructional program.*

3 *Lowered sense of self-esteem resulting from repeated feelings of inadequacy.*

4 *Unrealistic curriculum which imposes reading and writing English before listening comprehension and speaking fluency have been established. (p. 1)*

The question of how best to meet the needs of these children has been debated for a number of years. In 1968, Title VII of the Elementary and Secondary Education Act (ESEA) was passed in Congress. Known as the Bilingual Education Act, it appropriated funds to help non-English and limited English-speaking children especially. The funds were used to develop instructional programs to meet the needs of children from linguistically different backgrounds.

In addition, in 1974, a landmark U.S. Supreme Court decision, *Lau* v. *Nichols* strengthened the goals of the Bilingual Education Act. In this decision, the Court ruled that instruction in English to children who could not understand English was discriminatory. The Court argued that these children were excluded from participation in the educational programs because they could not speak English, the language of instruction. Schools *must*, therefore, provide children with the necessary training in the English language. The Court looked to the former Department of Health, Education and Welfare (HEW) to provide guidelines for such training.

It is important to remember that we are talking about a heterogenous group of children whose needs vary extensively, depending on the native language and language dominance of children and their parents, and the cultural differences of the family itself. HEW set up *Lau* categories to help identify and serve these children. In order to comply with the Lau guidelines, school districts had to identify non-English-speaking (NES) children and limited English-speaking (LES) children (*Lau* categories A and B, respectively) and provide suitable instruction for them.

LAU **CATEGORIES**

Degrees of Linguistic Ability to Speak English

A *Monolingual* speaker of a language other than English (no English spoken).

B *Dominant* speaker of a language other than English (speaks some English, but mostly speaks another language).

C *Bilingual* (speaks both English and another language equally well).

D *Dominant* speaker of English (speaks mostly English, but some of a language other than English).

E *Monolingual English* (speaks only English, but comes from a home where another language is spoken).

Up to this point in time, many districts did provide instruction known as ESL (English as a second language) training for non-English-speaking children for a short period of time each day. NES children spent the major part of the day in regular classrooms where English was the language of instruction. Then, for a short time daily, these children would be pulled from the regular classroom and given specific training in learning English.

Under Lau guidelines, however, in many situations ESL training was not enough. Consider, for example, situations where from 25 to 30 percent of the school population was NES or LES children whose native language is Spanish. In such cases, an ESL program would not best meet the needs of these children. A more extensive program, like bilingual education, would be appropriate.

Bilingual Education

Bilingual education may soon become an historical anachronism, as funds are presently being cut from every area of education. Nevertheless, it is an important historical development in an attempt to meet the needs of children with limited proficiency in English.

Lau guidelines forced many states to develop more extensive instructional programs for NES or LES children. Specifically, bilingual education programs were developed in areas with children in Lau categories A and B. Bilingual education is defined as an educational program in which two languages are used for instruction (La Bouve, 1977). Several types of programs were developed.

Transitional   where instruction in the first language (usually Spanish) is used as a bridge to learning English, the first language being phased out as proficiency in English increases.

Maintenance where instruction in both English and the first language continues throughout school, the goal being bilingualism and the maintenance of the culture and heritage of the first language.

Enrichment where American children develop proficiencies in a second language and learn about the cultural heritage of that language.

The most commonly accepted instructional program has been transitional in nature. Most transitional programs share at least three common elements: (1) the language of instruction is both English and the first language; (2) the cultural heritage of the first language is studied; (3) emphasis is placed on building self-esteem and self-concept. Transitional programs are developed usually for children in primary grades. In some programs, reading and writing in English are delayed until proficiency in oral English is adequate. In other programs, children learn to read and write in their native language first, then transfer to reading and writing in English when oral proficiency is obtained.

The fate of bilingual education programs lies, in part, in the hands of local school districts. Although it has been mandated by the Supreme Court that schools provide adequate instruction for these children, just how it is done is left to the schools. As schools struggle with inflation and higher costs, they have less money to invest in what some consider to be "frill" programs.

Bilingual education has always been a controversial topic. Many educators and laypeople feel bilingual education is a "frill" program. They argue that these children should be spending their time immersed in English so they can quickly and easily assimilate into the mainstream culture.

Bilingual proponents counter, however, that such "total immersion" approaches fail. Total immersion creates feelings of inadequacy, confusion, and alienation from the mainstream culture. We agree with bilingual proponents who assert that "total immersion" most often means throwing NES children into classrooms where their language and their culture are rejected, and where they are largely ignored and required to fend for themselves. "Total immersion" has been used in the past, and has a record of poor achievement, poor attendance, and low self-esteem for NES and LES children. We would concur with proponents who argue that bilingual education, where children can maintain their language and their culture, is the best alternative.

Effects on Learning the Language Arts

In Chapter 5, we emphasize the importance of oral language as a base for written language. Most children enter school with an established oral language in English to begin instruction in reading and writing in English. NES or LES children, however, begin school with an insufficient base of English oral language skills for instruction in reading and writing. These children cannot be expected to routinely proceed through the instructional program.

First and foremost, a teacher of the language arts must remember that *these children need an adequate base of oral English before they begin instruction in written English.* We cannot overemphasize this point. Teaching NES or LES children to read in English before they have an adequate understanding of English can be potentially harmful. Second language acquisition must proceed in similar sequence to first-language acquisition—from listening and speaking to reading and writing.

You or a friend may have had the experience of learning to "read" in another language before you understood the language; college courses in foreign languages sometimes are taught this way. If so, then you know the uselessness of the task, because though you can pronounce the words, you have no understanding of what you are reading.

Second, as a language arts teacher, you need to be aware of the child's self-esteem and self-concept. As NES or LES children enter school, they soon learn they are entering an environment different from their own. They may not share the value system of peers or the school. They may prefer to work in small groups rather than independently. They may prefer to be passive rather than active.

Intertwined with differences in cultural values are differences in language. NES and LES children may be very quiet and nonverbal. Their nonverbalness may be due to their values and also to their inability to understand and/or speak English. As they listen, they may be unsure of whether they understand. As they speak, they may be unsure of their vocabulary choice and their pronunciation. Thus, they say nothing rather than risk failure.

All these factors suggest that culturally and linguistically different children enter an insecure world when they enter the mainstream classroom. As a teacher, you need to be sensitive to these differences so you can make a conscious effort to build their self-esteem and make them feel more secure in their new environment. Their feelings of security will increase their willingness to take risks and to learn a new language.

BUILDING SELF-ESTEEM FOR THE LINGUISTICALLY AND CULTURALLY DIFFERENT CHILD

1 Praise what children *can* do.

2 Encourage taking a risk. Ask children to try, even if they are incorrect. Remind them that they are in school to learn and you are there to help them learn.

3 Encourage children to share with the class parts of their culture: clothes, food, toys, celebrations, music, and so on.

4 Encourage parent participation, for example, cooking their favorite home food for the class.

5 Collect and read books to children about different cultures.

6 Have LES or NES children teach the class special words in their language.

7 Create units of study for special countries in which children have a heritage.

Third, as a language arts teacher, you need to be aware that phonological and syntactic differences between NES and LES children's native language and English can interfere with learning oral and written English. The differences vary according to the child's native language. Although you do not have to speak the child's language to teach that child English, it is helpful to be aware of the major phonological and syntactic differences between the child's native language and English. Knowledge of the differences can alert you to potential problems of interference. For example, there are several sounds in English that don't occur in Spanish, "o" as in zoo, rose; "th" as in think, the; "r" as in ready, star. There is no possessive in Spanish. Thus, "Maria's house" in English becomes the "house of Maria" in Spanish. These phonological and syntactic differences can present problems for Spanish-speaking children learning English. Likewise, in any two languages, linguistic points of difference can present problems in second-language acquisition.

Below is a short quiz on myths related to working with LES and NES children. Take the test and then read the comments on each myth.

		T	**F**
1	You can't teach a child English in a regular classroom full of English-speaking students.	⎯⎯	⎯⎯
2	All limited English-speaking students learn at the same rate and can be English proficient in one year of ESL instruction.	⎯⎯	⎯⎯
3	It is best to place an NES student two or three years below age level where the English used is simpler.	⎯⎯	⎯⎯
4	A good way to help linguistically different children to assimilate is to "Americanize" their names.	⎯⎯	⎯⎯
5	All NES students are nonreaders.	⎯⎯	⎯⎯
6	If each NES student was required to attend a six-week English immersion program, the problems of working with limited English-speaking students would be solved.	⎯⎯	⎯⎯
7	The responsibility for teaching limited English-speaking students belongs to somebody else, not me!	⎯⎯	⎯⎯
8	The best teacher to assign to teach an ESL class is an English teacher.	⎯⎯	⎯⎯

Comments on Myths

1 A non- or limited English-speaking student can and should be helped to learn English in a regular classroom. As the rest of the class pursues a lesson, the NES student can be asked to repeat the name of something in the lesson, or respond to simple questions. Simple patterns (This is a _____. Point to the _____. Is this a _____?) can be used throughout the day.

2   Any group of limited English-speaking students will include slow and fast learners, students with learning disabilities, emotionally disturbed students, and so on. While the average NES student may acquire English proficiency in two or three years, a few will be fully bilingual in one year while others may require more than three years to reach that level of proficiency.

3   Placing an NES student two or three years below grade level is not generally a wise move. Any level of English is difficult to an NES student. The student is generally more comfortable surrounded by agemates. Furthermore, problems of misplacement tend to increase as the student reaches puberty.

4   Most people are emotionally attached to their names. A linguistically different student is coping with a lot and should not be asked to respond to an "Americanized" name. Learning to pronounce and using a student's name is a wonderful way of showing that the student is accepted and valued.

5   Many NES students beyond the primary grades have learned to read and write in their native languages.

6   While such an immersion program helps students become more proficient in English, they do not exit with English skills equal to their fellow native English-speaking classmates. They still require special attention and help.

7   Although teaching limited English-speaking students can be a frustrating challenge, they obviously "belong" to all of us and are everyone's responsibility.

8   That may sound logical, but the best preparation for teaching ESL is training and/or experience in teaching a second language.

Source: Reprinted with permission of Hal W. Anderson, Coordinator of English as a Second Language, Denver Public Schools, Denver, Colorado.

TEACHER ATTITUDES

Throughout this chapter, we have emphasized that educational and linguistic leaders feel teacher attitudes play an important role in language learning. If teachers and children come from a shared linguistic and cultural background, then teachers' attitudes usually are positive. If children's linguistic and cultural heritage differ, then any negative overt and covert attitudes of teachers toward these differences can affect language learning.

Unfortunately, teacher attitudes toward language reflect those of the larger society. Harvey (1975) traced the historical development of language attitudes over the last 200 years, and found that society has always regarded changes in language as negative and nonstandard dialects as inferior. He argued that "teachers must be able to accept their students as they come to school, in their language as in every other aspect of their cultural inheritance" (p. 12).

Negative attitudes of teachers toward nonstandard dialects particularly has been documented by research. Researchers have shown that teachers stereotype speakers of nonstandard dialects. Such speakers are regarded as less literate, less educated, and having less potential for learning (Blodgett and Cooper, 1973; Ford, 1974; Johnson, 1973). These negative attitudes may not be conscious; nevertheless, their message is felt by children.

The issue of negative teacher attitudes was addressed and confronted directly in a landmark court case, the *Martin Luther King Junior Elementary School Children* v. *Ann Arbor School District Board*, 1979 (Smith, 1980). After the testimony of linguists and educators, Judge C. W. Joiner of the U. S. District Court argued that one reason Ann Arbor black children were having difficulty learning to read was because of an unconscious negative attitude of teachers toward black English. Though the Court could not prescribe teaching methods, it could "require that schools help teachers understand the role of black English in the learning-to-read process" (Smith, 1980, p. 3). The school district was required to develop an extensive teacher education program to help teachers identify children who speak black English and use that knowledge in teaching them to read standard English (Civil No. 7-71861, 1979).

Our discussion has, so far, focused on teacher attitudes toward nonstandard dialects, but these arguments are also true for NES and LES children. In all cases, language and cultural differences interface with teacher attitudes. With NES and LES children, teachers often do not know about or understand the language and cultural differences between themselves and the children they teach. Dawson (1974, p. 54) summarizes the issues nicely,

> *The conflict that faces teachers in multi-cultural school settings is basically one of mis-understanding and lack of knowledge of the culture children bring to school. To work successfully, teachers need empathy, cultural understanding, and all those qualities that characterize the best in humans in any vocation.*

Then she warns:

> *Teachers have lasting effects on the children they teach. The higher the expectations teachers have for children, the greater the children will perform. Unfortunately, the opposite is also true.*

IMPLICATIONS FOR LANGUAGE ARTS INSTRUCTION

We have stressed the importance of understanding the nature of the cultural and linguistic differences of the children with whom you work. Such an understanding will help you develop a language arts program to meet the specific needs of those children. Now we will discuss some alternative instructional programs that have been used with linguistically different children.

Nonstandard English-Speaking Children

To date, no completely successful program or methodology has been found for teaching standard English to nonstandard English speakers. A variety of alternatives and programs have been tried, the success of which varies from setting to setting.

Dialect Readers   The use of dialect readers has been suggested as a possible bridge to move from nonstandard English in oral language to standard English in written language. Dialect readers are beginning reading books written in nonstandard dialect. Black English readers have been written and used with black children, but the value and usefulness of these readers is still open to debate. Cullinan (1974) and Gibson and Levin (1975) provide excellent summaries of the issues involved in the use of dialect readers. Strickland and Stewart (1974) argue against their use, in part because parents so strongly object to dialect readers for their children.

Language-Experience Materials   The use of the language-experience approach (L.E.A.) for teaching reading has been recommended (Hall, 1972; Strickland and Stewart 1974) as an alternative to dialect readers. This approach involves using words of children to develop reading materials. Children, in effect, write their own reading materials from their own experiences and in their own languages. (Refer to Chapter 11 for a detailed discussion of this approach.) In southwestern Alaska, a modification of this approach using Roach Van Allen's language experience model (Allen, 1976) has been developed and used for nonstandard English-speaking Eskimos in rural Alaska (Dole, 1981b).

Teach Standard English As a Second Dialect   Several attempts have been made to teach standard English directly to nonstandard speakers. Crowell and Kolba (1974) describe materials they helped develop (*Talkacross: Bridging Two Dialects*) to enable students "to use a second dialect if they chose to do so" (p. 69).

Debates continue, however, as to the effectiveness of these approaches.

TALKACROSS: BRIDGING TWO DIALECTS*

Content Outline: Example Copula *To Be*

1 Black English zero copula, or short form—e.g., he tired contrasted with he is tired (right now).

2 Black English uninflected be, or long form—e.g., he be tired contrasted with he is tired (all the time).

3 Forming the simple past—e.g., he tired/he be tired, you was tired contrasted with he was tired, you were tired.

4 Forming the preterit with has/have—e.g., she done been/she been contrasted with she has been.

5 Forming the preterit with had—e.g., Cora been in charge contrasted with Cora had been in charge.

6 Forming the simple future—e.g., she tired (tomorrow) contrasted with she will be tired (tomorrow).

Example of Activity Book on Copula *To Be*

You have seen that the following two kinds of sentences are used in black English: (1) He tired. (2) He be tired. The first, which we have called the "short" form, is used when you're talking about something that lasts only a short time or something that is always true about a person. The second, the "long" form, is used when you're talking about something that goes on for a long time or is repeated constantly. Compare the following sentences: Short form—She here right now. She my aunt. Long form—She be here every day. She be hanging around all the time. The equivalent for both of these kinds of sentences (He tired and He be tired) in standard English is: He's tired. That is, He's tired means the same thing in standard English as both He tired and he be tired in black English.

* By Sheila C. Crowell, Ellen K. Kolba, William A. Stewart, and Kenneth R. Johnson. Published by Instructional Dynamics, Inc., Chicago, 1974.

Non- or Limited English-Speaking Children

Elly (1981, p. 230) notes that "We have much to learn about how best to teach another language." The predominant method of instruction has been a model known as TESOL or Teaching English to Speakers of Other Languages. Donoghue (1979, pp. 414−418) identifies several important assumptions in a TESOL Program.

1 Spoken language has primacy; for example, listening and speaking skills come first.

2 Words are presented in meaningful context.

3 Basic language patterns are overlearned; for example, subject-verb agreement, noun-adjective agreement.

4 Grammar is caught, not taught; for example, children learn grammar through hearing and using language patterns, not through formal instruction.

5 There is minimal use of the pupil's native language.

6 Speech is rendered at normal speeds, not slowed speeds.

7 Culture study is an essential part of language learning.

8 Contrastive analysis is a tool for the teacher, not the pupils; for example, teachers need to know points of similarity and differences between the child's native language and English, but this information need not be presented to children.

A description of TESOL methodology would extend beyond the scope of this text. Many good books are available (see, for example, Donoghue's [1979] chapter "English for Speakers of Other Languages," or *Teaching English as a Second Language* by M. Finocchiaro, 1969). These resources should be consulted to learn more about this approach.

Once children have established an oral language base in English through approaches such as TESOL, then they can learn to read in English. Reading educators advocate a language-experience approach for bilingual children. We have therefore included a sample language-experience lesson plan appropriate for bilingual children who need continued vocabulary development in English.

LANGUAGE-EXPERIENCE LESSON FOR TEACHING READING TO BILINGUAL CHILDREN

Goals and Objectives	Children will learn new vocabulary words relating to foods found in the vegetable section of the grocery store.
Activity	Take children to the grocery store for a tour of the fruit and vegetable department.
Grouping	Total group of 20 children.
Materials	Large experience chart paper; paper, pencils, and crayons for children; fruits and vegetables purchased at the store.
Procedure	Before taking children to the store, talk about the proposed trip. Ask children to brainstorm what kinds of questions they have about their visit. Print questions on a large experience chart.

What fruits can you buy?

What vegetables can you buy?

Which foods are fruits and which are vegetables?

After the trip, return to the classroom and talk about the children's experiences at the grocery store. Begin by having them answer questions they had asked before the the trip. Record their responses on a new experience chart.

Have them compare and contrast fruits and vegetables. With real fruits and vegetables purchased at the store, have children classify the food according to food groups. Do this physically with the foods themselves and then print the classification scheme on the board.

Fruit	Vegetables
bananas	tomatoes
apples	potatoes
oranges	lettuce
grapefruit	celery

Have children draw pictures of and write about their favorite fruit and vegetable. Make these pictures and stories into a class book. Draw, color, cut out and label favorite fruits and vegetables and display them on a special bulletin board.

Additional Activities

1 Cut out favorite fruits and vegetables from magazines. Make collages. Label all fruits and vegetables.

2 Cut and grow potatoes and carrots in class. Watch and record growth.

3 Make clay models of fruits and vegetables. Label.

4 Have a feast where children bring in their favorite foods from the fruits and vegetables food groups. Ask parents to cook them in special ways.

WHEN A NEW *NES* OR *LES* CHILD ENTERS YOUR CLASSROOM . . .

Make the child feel comfortable and valued in the new environment, and give him or her time to adjust to the new situation.

Teach the child basic information about the class and the school such as where the restrooms are, where and how to order lunch, and where paper and pencils are stored.

Assign a "buddy," preferably someone who speaks the native language of the child, to help the child with the routines and organization of the class.

Determine how much English the child understands: Ask the child to point to the answer to each question.

> Where is the table?
>
> Where are the chairs?
>
> Where is the door?
>
> Where are you sitting?
>
> Where is your book?

Determine how much English the child can speak by asking questions.

> How old are you?
>
> Who is in your family?
>
> What do you like to do after school?
>
> What toys do you like?
>
> What games do you like to play?

Learn about the child's culture and develop a unit for the class to study.

Have the child teach you words in his or her native language.

Seek resource people, particularly teachers knowledgeable in TESOL, to assist you.

SUGGESTED ACTIVITIES

1 Go to the library and research the *Martin Luther King Jr. Elementary School Children* v. *Ann Arbor School Board* (1979) court case. What has happened in the school district since the court decision? Bring in your findings and discuss them with your peers.

2 Visit classrooms where there are ESL students. Observe techniques that the teachers use with these children to teach the language arts. List them and compare them to techniques that teachers use with English speaking students.

3 Interview a teacher and/or district representative. Have them identify special programs for ESL students. How do these programs differ from regular programs? What do they see as the future for these special programs?

REFERENCES

Allen, R. V. *Language Experiences in Communication.* Boston: Houghton Mifflin Company, 1976.

Allen, V. G. "Books to Lead the Non-English-Speaking Elementary Student to Literacy." *The Reading Teacher* 32, 8 (May 1979):940–946.

Bereiter, C., and Engleman, S. *Teaching Disadvantaged Children in the Preschool.* Englewood Cliffs, N.J.: Prentice-Hall, 1967.

Blodgett, E. G., and Cooper, E. B. "Attitudes of Elementary Teachers Toward Black Dialect." *Journal of Communication Disorders* 6 (June 1973):121–133.

Crowell, S., and Kolba, E. "Contrastive Analysis in the Junior High School." In Bernice E. Cullinan (ed.). *Black Dialects and Reading.* Newark, Del.: International Reading Association, 1974, 69–86.

Cullinan, B. E. "Issues in Black English and Reading." In Bernice E. Cullinan (ed.). *Black Dialects and Reading.* Newark, Del.: International Reading Association, 1974, pp. 3–13.

Dawson, M. E., ed. *Are There Unwelcome Guests in Your Classroom?* Washington, D.C.: Association for Childhood Education, International, 1974.

DeStefano, J. S. "Productive Language Differences in Fifth Grade Black Students' Syntactic Forms." *Elementary English* 49, 4 (April 1972):552–558.

———. "Register: A Concept to Combat Negative Teacher Attitudes Toward Black English." In Johanna A. DeStefano (ed.). *Language, Society and Education: A Profile of Black English.* Worthington, Oh.: Charles A. Jones Publishing Co. 1973, pp. 189–195.

Dole, J. A. "Between Language and Culture: An Alaskan Example." *Bilingual Journal* 6, 11 (Fall 1981a):10–12.

———. "A Language Development Program for Yup'ik Eskimo Children in Alaska." Paper presented to the National Association of Bilingual Education (May 1981b) ERIC Document 206 162.

Donoghue, M. R. *The Child and the English Language Arts.* Dubuque, Ia.: William C. Brown Company Publishers, 1979.

Elly, W. B. "The Role of Reading in Bilingual Contexts." In John T. Guthrie (ed.). *Comprehension and Teaching: Research Reviews.* Newark, Del.: International Reading Association, 1981.

Ford, J. F. "Language Attitude Studies: A Review of Selected Research." *The Florida FL Reporter* (Spring/Fall 1974):53–54, 100.

Gibson, E. J., and Levin, H. *The Psychology of Reading.* Cambridge, Mass.: MIT Press, 1975.

Goodman, K., and Buck, C. "Dialect Barriers to Reading Comprehension: Revisited." *The Reading Teacher* 27, 1 (October 1973) 6–12.

Hall, M. A. *The Language Experience Approach for the Culturally Disadvantaged.* Newark, Del.: International Reading Association, 1972.

Hartwell, P. "Dialect Interference in Writing: A Critical Review." *Research in the Teaching of English* 14, 2 (May 1980), 101–118.

Harvey, D. "What Teachers Believe: An Historical Investigation of Language Attitudes and Its Implications for Bidialectism in the Schools." December, 1975 ERIC Documents ED 125 288.

Johnson, K. R. "Teacher's Attitude Toward the Non-standard Negro Dialect—Let's Change It." In Johanna S. DeStefano (ed.). *Language, Society and Education: A Profile of Black English.* Worthington, Oh.: Charles A. Jones Publishing Co., 1973, pp. 177–188.

LaBouve, B. W. *Bilingual Education: A Position Paper.* National Council of State Supervisors of Foreign Languages (October 1977).

Labov, W. *The Social Stratification of English in New York City.* Washington, D.C.: Center for Applied Linguistics, 1966.

Lightner, C. "1930–1945." In Raven McDonald Jr. (ed.). *Examination of the Attitudes of the NCTE Toward Language.* Urbana, Ill.: National Council of Teachers of English, 1965.

Martin Luther King Junior Elementary School v. *Ann Arbor School District Board*, Civil No. 7-71861 (E.D., S.D., Michigan, July 12, 1979).

Meier, T. R. and Cazden, C. B. "Focus on Oral Language and Writing from a Multicultural Perspective." *Language Arts* 59, 5 (May 1982), 504–512.

Shuy, R. W. "Bonnie and Clyde Tactics in English Teaching." *The Florida FL Reporter* 7, 1 (1969), 75–82.

———. "Sociolinguistics." In Roger W. Shuy (ed.). *Linguistic Theory: What Can It Say About Reading?* Newark, Del.: International Reading Association, 1977, pp. 80–94.

Shuy, R. W.; Wolfram, W. A.; and Riley, W. R. *Field Techniques in an Urban Language Study.* Washington, D.C.: Center for Applied Linguistics, 1968.

Smith, D. E. "Dialect Dilemma: Measuring Black English." University of Michigan, School of Education. *College and School Innovator* 12, 4 (September 6, 1980):1, 4–5.

Smith, E. B.; Goodman, K.; and Meredith, R. *Language and Thinking in School.* New York: Holt, Rinehart and Winston, 1976.

Strickland, D., and Stewart, W. "The Use of Dialect Readers: A Dialogue." In Bernice E. Cullinan (ed.). *Black Dialect and Reading.* Newark, Del.: International Reading Association, 1974, pp. 146–151.

Thonis, E. *Literacy for America's Spanish-Speaking Children.* Newark, Del.: International Reading Association, 1976.

Wolfram, W., and Whiteman, M. "The Role of Dialect Interference in Composition." *The Florida FL Reporter* 9 (Spring/Fall 1971):34–38.

EXPRESSIVE LANGUAGE

CHAPTER 5

Oral Language

**HOW CAN YOU TELL IF SOMEONE
IS A GOOD SPEAKER?**
SECOND GRADERS
...if they talk baby talk, they wouldn't be ...
like if they said "pastewize" instead of "pasteurize"
...if they have a squeaky voice they wouldn't be

FIFTH GRADERS
...they don't stutter
...they don't hesitate and they pronounce the words
right

OVERVIEW

The purpose of this chapter is to provide a theoretical framework for understanding oral language development at the elementary level and to review many activities designed to improve oral language. We first discuss oral language as part of the communication act. We then show you how to use creative drama activities to foster oral language skills in children. A number of suggested activities show children how to use language to "get things done." We discuss tests designed to measure oral language and show some informal ways to evaluate children's speaking abilities.

INTRODUCTION

Using oral language is the major method of communication in the elementary schools. When children enter school, they are speaking complex sentences that have both adverbial and adjective clauses. They have a speaking vocabulary of approximately 6000 to 8000 words, and their average sentence length is around seven words. Since language is so sophisticated by the time children enter first grade, many teachers feel it is not necessary to develop oral language skills. Yet Lamb (1977), in her review of linguistic research, states that elementary teachers need to devote more time to encouraging children to engage in oral language activities such as conversations, discussions, oral reading, and dramatics.

One basis for Lamb's feelings about oral language development can be traced to research by Loban (1976). Loban examined the language development of 200 children from age five to age eighteen. A summary of his findings reiterates the importance of Lamb's statement about devoting more time to oral language development.

Loban categorized his 200 subjects as high, middle, and low in language proficiency. High-proficiency subjects excelled in the expressive language arts of speaking and writing. Their speech and writing showed exceptional ability in writing and planning. Their speaking patterns showed a sophisticated level of vocabulary as well as a careful rate of speaking that enabled listeners to comprehend what was said. The number of vocabulary words used in oral language differed among groups. For example, the high group in the first grade averaged almost eight words per sentence, while the low group averaged six words per sentence. As a matter of fact, the low group did not average eight words per sentence until they were in the sixth grade. Overall, the low ability group's oral language was characterized by very little unity and coherence as well as a meager vocabulary.

An interesting corollary to these findings is that children who were in the high-proficiency group at the first-grade level also excelled in reading and writing by the time they were in the fifth and sixth grades. Loban hypothesized that greater attention should be given to oral language instruction, especially in light of the finding that better oral language users are better readers in the latter grades. Some teachers may not see the differences in reading and writing at the primary grades and assume that the children will keep progressing at the same rate. Yet, according to Loban's findings, differences in language competence may not show up in reading and writing until the intermediate grades.

ORAL LANGUAGE AS COMMUNICATION

Our comments from second and fifth graders about what makes a good speaker are interesting. They reflect quite clearly the attitudes and thoughts that most of us have about speaking. We think of oral language and effective speaking in terms of phonology, syntax (especially grammar and usage), and semantics (particularly big words!).

Linguists, however, have a much broader view of oral language and speaking. They view oral language ability as part of the ability to communicate. A valuable tool for understanding oral language ability is gained through linguists' use of the term *communicative competence* (Hymes, 1974).

Communicative competence refers to everything the native speaker knows about language as communication. This includes the speaker's intuitive knowledge about phonology, syntax, and semantics to be sure. Communicative competence also refers to the speaker's knowledge about how to use language appropriately in a given situation. You will recall these same notions in Chapter 3's discussion about pragmatics.

The speaker, however, is not the only element in the communicative act (see Figure 5.1). In any communication two other factors converge to produce a language interaction (Tough, 1974). The *receiver* listens and comprehends through the speaker's phonological, syntactic, and semantic cues and through the receiver's own knowledge of language. Last, the *social context* determines the function and purpose of the communication.

Let us give you an example of how these notions can be applied to a language interaction. Smith (1982) provides an excellent example of a successful interaction which would be uninterpretable to us without our shared background experiences.

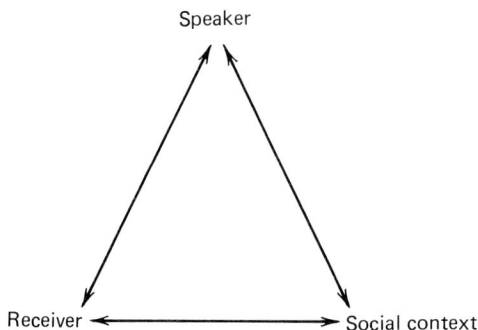

FIGURE 5.1 *A language interaction.*

More coffee*?*

Please.

In this example, the communicative competencies of the speaker and receiver interact with the social context to provide a meaningful exchange of communication. Imagine, if you will, a restaurant with a woman sitting down at a table reading a newspaper. The waiter walks over to the woman and asks her if she would like more coffee. Perhaps with the cup in her hand, she responds affirmatively and with politeness.

In this exchange, we also hope you quickly became aware of how thinking and particularly the notion of schema apply here. The speaker and receiver used their shared social context (the restaurant) and their shared knowledge base or schemata (what you do at a restaurant) to minimize talk and still communicate effectively. Little explicit language is needed.

Cook-Gumperz (1981) argues that for young children, this shared social context may play a more important role in the communicative act than it does for adults. That is, children are more "context-reliant than adults" and may rely as much on their "accumulated situational knowledge as on their linguistic knowledge" (p. 48).

Consider one of the author's five-year-old neighbors who knocked on the door and responded to the adult present with, "Is she here?" This young child assumed that the adult knew who "she" was and didn't need to communicate that information. She assumed and did not repeat the shared knowledge base they both had. In addition, she also skipped the initiating remarks common in such social contexts, namely, "Hi!"

How are these ideas important to our understanding of oral language development? First, we need to know that oral language is more than learning sounds of our language and its grammar and vocabulary. Second, we need to recognize that in developing oral language skills, we are developing communicative competence, the ability to speak and listen within the social conventions of our society.

The Nature of Conversation

To develop communicative competence in children we need to model and reinforce the social conventions of oral language. Many teachers feel children already "know" how to talk when they enter school. But consider more carefully what children need to learn, as delineated by Tough (1974).

- How to conduct a conversation.
- How to take turns.
- How to give an appropriate greeting or remark.
- How to listen.
- Ways of asking for different kinds of information.

- That other people have a point of view.
- That others' points of view may be different from our own.
- How to give a closing remark to close a conversation.
- How to speak to others and appreciate their needs.

These social conventions of language are learned only through direct experiences interacting with others and trying to make one's needs known and met. These lessons are learned with help from teachers and peers. A first grader we recently observed learned about the consequences of speaking too quietly when she read her hand-made book and was told repeatedly by several children, "We can't hear you." This young child may not have liked what her peers said, but she began to appreciate that they too have needs in the communication act.

Learning Different Registers

Learning the social conventions of language entails learning how and when to say something. An important corollary to this has already been mentioned in Chapters 3 and 4. Children need to learn different speaking styles appropriate for different situations. Earlier in this text we quoted the sentence, "Please don't move those crates over here?" and we discussed when and why you might say this sentence in different ways. Many people refer to this as "using correct grammar" (recall DeStefano's definition of grammar as it pertains to usage, such as "between you and me" instead of "between you and I.") We used the term *registers* for the different speaking styles people use depending on social context.

The effective speaker uses different registers depending on the context and the receiver of the message. It is very important to mention this again because we believe that children need to learn different registers to communicate effectively. We also believe that this concept of registers is an extremely useful one to use in working with children who speak different dialects.

For Anglo children who speak standard English, the concept of registers stresses the importance of looking at the social context. Again, remember DeStefano's example of the teacher who is complaining about her student to different people. Her remarks to the principal and to the parents are completely different from her remarks to her peers.

At the intermediate level, an excellent role-playing situation can dramatize the need for using different registers. Consider this following example.

Several boys decide to go to the video arcade after school. They invite Eddie but do not invite Eddie's best friend, Mike, because the group doesn't like Mike. Both Eddie and Mike are upset and feel angry. How can the problem be solved? Solutions can revolve around Eddie speaking to the group of boys, Mike speaking to them, or Eddie and Mike asking the teacher or another outsider to speak to the boys.

This role-playing activity has a dual purpose: (1) to solve problems and (2) to understand the relationship between register and social context. The way the boys speak to a teacher will be quite different from the way they speak to their peers. According to Duffy (1969), as elementary teachers we should show students that what is appropriate on the playground with peers, as far as register is concerned, may not be appropriate when speaking to the classroom teacher.

> In using this strategy, we are actually teaching children the use of two dialects—one which is acceptable in the home and the neighborhood and another which admits him to the company of educated society. Approaching usage instruction from such an analytical standpoint makes more sense to the linguist and is . . . a better way to teach usage than the traditional endless drill on proper usage (p. 37).

Thus, role playing activities seem to be a better method to teaching register and social context than most traditional methods.

For children who speak a nonstandard dialect of English, we believe the concept of register is especially important. As a matter of fact, we think it is the most reasonable approach to teaching standard English. Role-playing situations such as ones we have described are excellent vehicles through which linguistically different children can learn when and how to use standard English.

The role playing can and should be conducted in a supportive environment in which nonstandard English speakers can take risks, make mistakes, and learn from those mistakes. In this way we are teaching nonstandard speakers that their language is acceptable and appropriate in given situations. But, we are also teaching them the need to learn standard English as an entry into many mainstream institutions.

DEVELOPING ORAL LANGUAGE

In order to discuss the types of activities most useful for developing oral language, we will turn momentarily to the work of Britton (1970). Britton delineates the *participant* and *spectator* roles of language, both of which need to be enhanced in the elementary grades. Britton describes participant roles of language as those involving the uses of language to get things done.

- Informing people
- Instructing people
- Persuading people
- Arguing
- Explaining
- Planning

- Setting for pros and cons
- Reaching conclusions

Spectator roles of language, alternately, involve those uses of language to please ourselves first, not to please others. Experiences in the spectator role might include some of the following.

- Make-believe play
- Day-dreaming aloud
- Chatting about our experiences
- Gossip
- Traveler's tales
- Story telling
- Fiction
- Drama
- Poetry

Here we will describe activities and experiences using Britton's framework of participant and spectator roles. You can find additional activities in the spectator's role in related chapters on writing and children's literature.

EXPERIENCES IN THE SPECTATOR ROLE

Through creative drama activities such as pantomime and reader's theater, children can learn to explore real-life situations, to manipulate their bodies to express emotions and feelings, and to interpret literature. Creative dramatics can be used as an excellent starting point for developing thought processes and for moving to the participant roles of language. In addition, creative dramatics can help students enjoy and appreciate language. We agree with Moffett (1968) who states that "drama and speech are central to a language curriculum, not peripheral. They are base and essence, not specialties. I see drama as a matrix of all language activities, subsuming speech and engendering the varieties of writing and reading" (pp. 60−61).

Creative Drama

The Children's Theater Association and the National Council of Teachers of English have issued a joint statement emphasizing the importance of creative drama in the classroom. They define "creative drama" as unrehearsed drama in which "students invent and enact dramatic situations for themselves, rather than for an outside audience" ("Forum," 1983, p. 370). They further argue that drama helps participants

- Develop improved skills in reading, listening, speaking and writing.
- Develop skill in thinking analytically in acting decisively and responsibly.
- Increase and sustain the ability to concentrate and follow directions.
- Strengthen self-concept by cooperative interaction with others.
- Learn to make commitments and fulfill them.
- Learn to deal effectively with interracial, intercultural, and multiethnic situations.
- Increase motivation to learn.
- Develop individual and group creativity.

Pantomime.   A first step in teaching creative dramatics is pantomime. Even though pantomime does not involve speaking, it is an important precursor to other drama activities. Pantomime allows children the opportunity to get out of themselves and to learn to relax their bodies to express themselves more freely. Graubard (1960) divides pantomime experiences into different types, such as Mother Goose rhymes, current events, embarrassing occurrences, proverbs, advertising slogans, situations, and dramatic words. We will only discuss a few of these methods for students to use in the primary and intermediate grades.

Nursery Rhymes.   Nursery rhymes can be used with students in both the primary and intermediate levels. Select an age appropriate nursery rhyme that has strong characterization and action. Have the children sit on the floor with their eyes closed. Then read the nursery rhyme aloud and have them imagine the characters and actions taking place. Let them tell you what they visualized when they heard the story. After you have gotten their input, the children can pantomime the nursery rhymes individually, with a partner, or with a small group. For example, two students can pantomime "Little Miss Muffett" and "Jack and Jill." A group of four students can pantomime "Three Little Kittens," or "Old Mother Hubbard." Individually, students can pantomime a rhyme such as "Jack Be Nimble."

After students have completed a few pantomime activities individually or in groups, they can play a guessing game with nursery rhymes. Have groups of four select a nursery rhyme to present to the rest of the class. Give the groups time to practice the pantomime, then let each group present it to the class to guess the rhyme. If two groups choose the same rhyme, let both groups perform their pantomime. Each group may come up with a different approach to the same rhyme.

Dramatic Words.   This pantomime exercise can also be done with students in the primary and intermediate levels. On a set of cards, put the dramatic word and a possible situation involving that word. Children then choose cards and portray the word in the particular situation through a pantomime. The class tries to guess the word based on the student's particular pantomime. The following words and situations can be used in an elementary classroom.

1 *Jealousy.*   Your best friend received the bicycle that you wanted for your birthday. It has all the accessories that you wanted on a new bicycle.

2 *Sadness.*   You lost the first watch you ever had while playing on the school playground. You think it fell in a grassy area of the playground.

3 *Contentment.*   You're lying in your room listening to your favorite musical group. You have your headset on.

4 *Surprise.*   You receive a huge box from one of your relatives in another state. You open it and find the birthday present you always wanted.

Situations.   The purpose behind using situations as a stimulus to pantomime is that you can get your students to observe people, activities, and inanimate objects, and interpret them through pantomime. Through situations, students can see how actors prepare themselves for different roles by observing the movement of others. You might want to begin by having students observe some sports activities such as a basketball game or a baseball game. Students should watch how the players move up and down the court or around the field, how the players throw or catch a ball, or what they do when they are not part of the action. After they have seen the sports activity, have them discuss their observations with each other. Following the discussion, have the students pantomime the sports activity with another group of students acting as observers.

Moving toward activities, you can have students pantomime things such as doing chores around the house or participating in a hobby. This activity can be done individually rather than in groups. The students should spend some time watching others doing the activity, then they should pantomime what they have observed for the other class members. Examples of the activities could be washing a car, feeding a dog, building a fire, weaving a rug, or painting a picture. The key to pantomiming activities is to stress the importance of detail and context when the students are observing.

The third type of situation is pantomiming inanimate objects. This is the most difficult pantomime to do, and students should practice pantomiming people and activities before doing inanimate objects. Show your students various inanimate objects and discuss with them the characteristics of the objects. Let them use their senses to describe the color, size, texture, weight, smell, sound, and use of the object. After they have observed various objects, have students pantomime an object for the rest of the class. After the students have tried pantomiming classroom objects, let them observe an inanimate object on their own and pantomime it for the class. Objects to observe might be a light bulb burning out, a chair with an overweight person on it, or a machine like an electric typewriter.

Oral Reading and Reader's Theater

A different creative drama activity involves oral reading and reader's theater. Oral reading is usually done by one student, while reader's theater is done by several readers. Before sharing an oral reading, the reader must thoroughly comprehend what has been read. Using the criteria for selection of literature in Chapter 13, you can help individuals choose literature for oral reading. Tanner (1979) mentions nine points students should use to analyze a selection prior to oral reading.

1 What do unfamiliar words mean?
2 Who is speaking?
3 Who is listening?
4 Where and when does the action take place?
5 What happens?
6 When does the climax occur?
7 What is the basic mood in the selection?
8 What is the theme?
9 How does this selection keep you in touch with life right now?

For oral reading, the student chooses a poem, a short story, or an excerpt from a novel to read silently a number of times, mindful of the nine questions above. Then the student reads the selection to the audience, animating his or her face, voice, and body.

According to Tanner (1979), teachers must understand two basic principles of Reader's Theater. First, children need to explore different ways of presenting the literature for Reader's Theater. The material that the children read should shape the way they read the material. Second, the children must truly comprehend what they read and become excited about it. This way they will be able to stimulate the audience by making the literature come alive.

For Reader's Theater to work successfully in a classroom, Hennings (1982) describes the following procedures. Each child in the group reads the entire selection silently and individually. Following the first reading, the teacher assigns parts or lets the children choose a character. A second reading, this one orally, takes place with the students reading and listening to each other. The third reading is also an oral reading, but this time the play is read and acted out. The fourth reading is in front of the audience with the teacher giving the name of the reading, the cast of characters, and a short discussion of the setting or plot.

DRAMA AS A MEDIUM FOR CONTENT AREA INSTRUCTION

Some of the activities we have already mentioned can lead to another kind of informal classroom drama. This type of drama is best exemplified through the work of Dorothy Heathcote, a British dramatist who creates experience through drama, and who uses drama as a medium for instruction. It is difficult to describe the vitality and energy of the classroom drama that Heathcote creates. It is part of her genius as a leader that makes her drama successful, but it is still worthwhile here to give you some flavor for her work.

The subject of the drama is often created by curriculum: Middle Ages, King Arthur, China, Indians, early settlers (Wagner, 1976). Heathcote focuses on one part of the subject depending on age level and maturity of the students: leisure, travel, food, family, law, shelter, travel, and so on. Through questioning techniques, she then focuses on a particular moment for the classroom drama to begin. Wagner (1976) provides an example of a Heathcote drama on pirates, where she begins as the captain, "All right you lubbers, if you can show me you can get aboard my ship and hoist the sails without the usual complement of arms and legs, then you're OK as far as I'm concerned" (p. 59). And then she begins the learning experience with, "I wonder why you keep on going to sea when you know it's so dangerous" (p. 59).

Heathcote leads the drama through expert questioning and children proceed through the experience through thinking, talking, and listening. She seeks information so children themselves create the dramatic experience. She asks,

1 Information-seeking questions.
   • What time of day is it?
   • How are we dressed?
   • What did coaches look like in those days?
2 Information-giving questions.
   • How many gallons of water do we need to take on our journey?
   • Are we well supplied with blood plasma?
3 Group decision questions.
   • Shall we be in the present, past or future?
   • Are we in trouble because we are in danger or hungry?
4 Class-controlling questions.
   • How are we going to make ourselves look like soldiers?
   • Are we too tired to start the hunt today? Had we better rest first?

The children and Heathcote play out the dramatic experience. We think this type of classroom drama has enormous potential for the classroom teacher. Through this drama, subject areas can come alive. We no longer merely sit and read about the Mayflower—we can recreate the experience and "know" about it in a way that takes us beyond the printed page. We will return to Heathcote's work and creative classroom drama in Chapter 15.

EXPERIENCES IN THE PARTICIPANT ROLE

Society today places great value on oral language. Indeed, Pelligrini, DeStefano, and Thompson (1983) and others have suggested that a child's ability to use explicit oral language, that is, the ability to convey information by what is stated, is a necessary component of success in school and in learning to read and write (p. 380). For success in oral language, children need to learn to enjoy talking and listening and engaging others in these activities. The activities we described in the last section will enhance oral language enjoyment and thereby its development. We must not stop, however, with encouraging oral language in children. Many additional activities link oral language development to thinking, and can help children learn to use "explicit" oral language "to get things done" as Britton says.

When you are planning oral language activities in your classroom, you must take into account your purpose for the activities and not merely stress what Loban (1976) calls "talk and chatter." Loban also maintains that language instruction should focus on thinking and organizing one's ideas. Shane, Walden, and Green (1971), after reviewing the research pertaining to oral language instruction practices, agree with Loban that more classroom activities should increase students' fluency, effectiveness, and coherence. The activities listed below range from informal discussions to more formal activities, such as interviews or panel discussions.

Show and Tell

One method of teaching young children to speak before a group is show and tell. Show and tell stimulates oral language development as well as gives children confidence in speaking before a group. In addition, show and tell lets the students bring to the classroom experiences from home.

During show and tell, individual children talk about a game or activity or show an object that they have brought to school. As the teacher during show and tell, you need to be a role model for the other students. You should listen attentively and ask questions when you think the student doing the show and tell needs help or if you want to give more information about the activity or object. In this way you are modeling the uses of language, for explaining, persuading, and instructing. When you first try show and tell, especially with kindergarteners, you may want to tell them what to bring in, such as pictures of family members or of a special vacation. The more the child can relate to the object, activity, or game, the easier it will be to use it in show and tell. After the children have done show and tell individually for awhile, they can do it in small groups.

At the intermediate grade levels, students can do a modified version of show and tell. We've seen many classrooms where students choose a topic of interest or current event and discuss their ideas and opinions during a time period. At all grade levels, this type of experience helps children learn the importance of speaking loudly and clearly, of making their ideas understandable to others, of taking turns and other important social conventions of oral language.

Problem Solving

For upper primary and intermediate students, problem solving is an excellent device to move students from talking and listening to thinking. One way to solve problems is through a *buzz session*. During a buzz session, everyone quickly presents ideas and suggestions to a particular problem. All ideas are written down; more are judged or criticized as being better or worse than others. For the first problem-solving activity you try, you may want to do it in a whole class setting with your role being the moderator or reporting secretary. After students have done problem solving a few times, they can do it in groups with one member acting as recording secretary.

After you have decided whether to have students work in large or small groups, you then present a problem to them that will stimulate thinking. The problem should be important to the students. You may even want the students to choose their own problems to solve. As examples, you and your students might choose one of the following problems.

1 Ways to earn money for a class trip.
2 Ways to recycle newspapers and aluminum cans.
3 Ways to beautify the outside of the school.
4 Ways to get students to register their bicycles.
5 Ways to persuade the principal to have an arts and crafts show.

After you and the students have settled on a problem, you have a buzz session for approximately five to ten minutes. After their ideas have been discussed in a buzz session, tell the students to solve the problem through a problem-solving session. Students should follow these basic rules to have a successful problem-solving session.

RULES FOR PROBLEM SOLVING

1 Make sure the problem is defined.
2 Use facts from the "buzz session" and new facts to solve the problem.
3 Look for cause-and-effect relationships.
4 Everyone must participate in the discussion.
5 Listen to others and their solutions.
6 Weigh all ideas presented.
7 Choose the best solution voted on by the group.

Interviewing

A more formal type of oral language activity is interviewing. Interviewing skills not only help students to develop speaking skills, but also listening comprehension skills. An interviewer must be able to ask questions in a way the interviewer will understand and listen intently to the answers gives. Many different activities can be utilized in an elementary classroom with the interview. The activities can move from interviewing class members in a role-playing situation to interviewing family and community members for an oral history.

Before students start interviewing each other or family, they need to know the essentials of good interviewing. The first essential is good questioning strategies. We have already discussed the power of good questioning techniques as used by Heathcote. Ruddell (1978) lists four questioning strategies: focusing, extending, clarifying, and raising. Basically, focusing questions are ones that the interviewer asks to set the purpose for the interview. The focus questions provide the mental set for the way the interview will develop. The answers to focus questions can be numerous. Focus questions are general in nature and the answers should lead the interviewer to follow-up questions. If your students were interviewing one of their favorite movie stars, they might open up with the following focus question.

"What was it like growing up when you were our age?"

Ruddell's second type of question is an extending question. For an interview, a person would ask an extending question to get the interviewee to answer a question more fully. What the interviewer is looking for in an extending question is additional information of a previous answer. Let's say that the interviewee answering the above question mentions something about going to elementary school. The interviewer could come back with an extending question such as,

"Could you tell me more about your elementary school experience?"

The third type of question is clarifying. A clarifying question is directed at the interviewee when the interviewer needs further explanation about some information given. Again, going back to our hypothetical movie star, let's say that the movie star answered the above question by saying that he or she won an award for being in a school play. The interviewer could come back with a clarifying question,

"Could you give me more detail about the school play you were in?
What was the play and your role in the play?"

The clarifying question is more specific than the extending question. The extending question is then more specific than the focus question. Finally, the fourth type of question is called raising. A raising question is used in an interview when the interviewer wants the interviewee to give an opinion about something or to evaluate what was done. This level moves beyond the factual and it is here an interviewer gets feelings and opinions from the interviewee. For our fictitious movie star, the interviewer might ask,

"Why do you think your movie career has been so successful the last two years?"

We cannot stress enough the importance of asking good questions, both for your students and for you as a teacher. Stated simply, an excellent teacher asks excellent questions. We will return again to questioning techniques in Chapter 10.

The second ingredient needed for interviewing is good listening skills. What the interviewer needs to know is how to listen carefully to the answers the interviewee gives, so the interviewer knows how to react to the answer and asks the next question. When your students interview each other, they should listen very carefully to each other, and even try to trick each other to see if the other is listening.

The third ingredient to interviewing involves another language arts skill, writing. The interviewer has to listen carefully and take notes on what was said. As their teacher, you have to stress the importance of taking good notes so the youngsters do not misquote the interviewer. This might also be a good time to introduce the use of quotation marks. Since students will have to quote properly, they should know how to use commas and quotation marks in their transcription of the interview.

In addition to note-taking skills, you can discuss the use of tape recorders. Many students probably have used tape recorders, but a short lesson in how to use a tape recorder is recommended. They will be able to listen more attentively during the interview, saving the waiting to take notes until later. They can also listen to the interview many times to make sure they do not misquote the interviewee.

Depending on the time you have to use interviewing in the classroom, you should have students practicing questions, listening skills, and note-taking skills. The more students practice these skills the better they understand the interviewing process. Other language arts areas of writing through transcription and mechanics through the use of quotation marks will be improved too.

One other point needs to be stressed before students begin to interview each other. A good interviewer comes prepared to the interview. Your students should practice being good interviewers by following these six points.

1 Know the major purpose for the interview and prepare a set of questions for the purpose. Anticipate some answers so that you can be ready for the next question.

2 Ask more open-ended questions rather than close-ended questions that require a simple yes or no.

3 Be a careful listener.

4 Keep the interview within its purpose. If the interviewer wants to digress from the intended purpose, try to come back with a question that will return the topic to the purpose of the interview.

5 If you have set up a specific time period for the interview to begin and end, make sure you keep those times.

6 Be polite and friendly.

Before students interview family or community members, they should practice interviewing each other. For the initial interviewing activity, let the students find want-ads or newspaper stories about local, state, and national happenings and role play the situations. For example, with a classified ad they can role play the interview between the employer and the employee. The sports page of the newspaper is an excellent source of potential interviews between sports heroes and interviewers a la Howard Cosell.

Television also provides students with opportunities for role playing an interview. Television personalities such as Mike Wallace can serve as interview models. Students can watch different talk shows and compare interviewing techniques. Based on these comparisons, students can develop their own interview show.

Planning an interview show for the class involves work in another language arts area, use of reference skills. If there is the time, students can interview famous people, either living or dead. The interviewees—the famous people—need to research biographic data about the person. To devise questions the interviewer, as well, needs to find out information about the famous person. Such an activity could work well for an American history social studies unit. Students could role play famous Americans and have another group of students interview them. Notice here again how the language skills all come together—students read, write, talk, and listen to learn as much about their subject as possible.

Oral History

After students feel comfortable with interviewing they might want to try an oral history of their family or the community. Particular interesting books for upper elementary students are the *Foxfire* books (1972–1980) and Carol Ryrie Brink's *Caddie Woodlawn* (1975). Both books are reference books in that they describe how people lived during different historical times. The periods of time are different, but readers of these books find out about how different people at different times lived. The mechanism for writing these two books was the interview.

The students who interviewed people in the Ozarks for *Foxfire* talked to many community people to find out about growing up in the Ozark community, especially comments on how to make certain foods and supplies.

Brink's book is very different from the *Foxfire* books. The heroine in *Caddie Woodlawn* is Brink's grandmother. When Carol Ryrie Brink was eight years old, she went to live with her grandmother, and her grandmother told her many stories about growing up in Wisconsin in the 1800s. As an adult, she remembered the stories and decided to write them down in a book which became *Caddie Woodlawn*.

The children in your class can either do an oral history about their community or their family. If they choose the former, they should find older community members to interview. They can then back up their oral interviews with dated newspaper clippings. The interviews can be transcribed and written for a class project. An evolutionary report of their community can be written by the students and even presented to the community.

If the children choose the latter, they can interview older relatives. Students should ask people to retell childhood experiences or stories they heard from other relatives. During the interviews, the children can also gather information about what their relatives did for entertainment, how they traveled, where and how they got their food, how they dressed, and what toys they had. After their information is gathered, they can share their interviews with each other and write their stories to distribute to family members as presents. Or, students can recreate through drama a typical event popular in that era.

Discussion Groups

A more formal oral language activity is a discussion group. One type of discussion group is the round-table discussion. A *round-table discussion* includes a moderator or leader and four to five participants. The members deal with a problem-solving situation on a more formal basis. The leader of the group grades and assists the rest of the group and summarizes the conclusions. While the discussion group is solving a particular problem, the rest of the class can act as audience and listen to a particular group. The problem-solving activities can be similar to the ones done in a "buzz session," but the round-table discussion should be more formal. Techniques that develop effective question and answer strategies are necessary for successful inter-action in round-table discussions.

A second type of discussion group is the panel discussion. A *panel discussion* is different from a round-table discussion in that each member of the panel is responsi-ble for a particular aspect of the subject. Each member of a panel becomes as knowledgeable as possible to present information and answer questions raised by the audience. An off-shoot of the activity is to combine a panel discussion with a role-playing activity. For a social studies unit, a panel discussion can consist of students representing signers of the Declaration of Independence. For a science unit, a group of students can role play scientists speaking about nuclear energy.

EVALUATION

As described in this chapter, oral language development is a broad and varied phenomenon encompassing many language characteristics. For that reason it is difficult to speak of tests for oral language development per se. Most tests of oral language ability are articulation tests and require a trained speech pathologist for their administration and interpretation (for example, *Goldman-Fristoe Test of Articula-tion*, American Guidance Services Inc.; *Templin-Darley Test of Articulation*, Bureau of Education Research and Services, Ohio State University).

Because we have defined oral language so broadly we recommend informal methods of assessment. Specifically we suggest an adaptation of Tough's (1974) categories for oral language competence. Operationally this means you should try to

TABLE 5.1

I *Observable Behaviors*			
1 Watches when words are written down	_____ (usually)	_____ (sometimes)	_____ (seldom)
2 Paces dictation	_____ (usually)	_____ (sometimes)	_____ (seldom)
3 Pauses at end of phrase or sentence	_____ (usually)	_____ (sometimes)	_____ (seldom)
4 Appropriate title	_____ (very)	_____ (acceptable)	_____ (poor)
5 Attempts to read back	_____ (most)	_____ (some)	_____ (none)
II *Global Language Usage*			
1 Complete sentences	_____ (all)	_____ (some)	_____ (none)
2 Total words	_____ (31+)	_____ (16-30)	_____ (0-15)
3 Total different words	_____ (30+)	_____ (15-29)	0-14)
III *Refined Language Usage*			
1 Number of adjectives	_____ (9+)	_____ (4-8)	_____ (0-3)
2 Number of adverbs	_____ (3+)	_____ (1-2)	_____ (0)
3 Number of prepositional phrases	_____ (4+)	_____ (1-3)	_____ (0)
4 Number of embedded sentences	_____ (2+)	_____ (1)	_____ (0)
Total	_____3X	_____2X	_____1X
Total points	_____	_____	_____
Grand total _____			

Source: From Carol N. Dixon, "Language Experience Stories as a Diagnostic Tool" *Language Arts* 54 (May 1977) Copyright © 1977 by the National Council of Teachers of English. Reprinted by permission of the publisher and the author.

answer the following questions about each student based on your informal observation of his or her oral language use.

1 Does the child conduct conversations well with other children?

2 Does the child show an awareness of the fact that conversation involves taking turns?

3 Does the student greet you and other students appropriately in the morning?

4 Does the student appear to be a sensitive listener?

5 Is the student aware of and tolerant of other people's points of view?

6 Is the student aware of other people's needs in a conversation?

A more narrow but valuable method of oral language evaluation is Dixon's (1977). She distinguishes three types of information that can be gained about students through a language experience approach. (See Chapter 11 for a discussion of language experience.) The first type of information consists of student behaviors such as watching the teacher writing down the language experience. The second type of information consists of an analysis of students' use of complete sentences and the number of words, as well as different words, in the passage. Finally, the last type of information deals with specifics within the language experience, such as number of modifiers, phrases, and clauses.

Table 5.1 presents Dixon's language experience checklist. Dixon has quantified her categories by giving weights within each category. The total points for different individuals can then be compared with others in the same classroom. In one school, some undergraduate students who used this checklist during the beginning and end of their student teaching period were amazed at the differences in oral language ability of students in the same classroom. Others, who had pinpointed some students as probably being poor in language ability, were surprised that their total scores on the Dixon checklist were very high. What they observed were shy children in the classroom who said very little, but did have excellent oral language skills. Finally, those students, who used the checklist at the beginning and the end of student teaching, found remarkable results when they taught specific oral language skills to those students who scored low on the Dixon checklist. By giving the elementary students activities in oral language development, undergraduates saw an increase in the use of both global and refined language usage.

SUGGESTED ACTIVITIES

1 Be conscious of the different registers you use when you talk to different people in different social contexts? Can you describe some of those different registers? What groups of people dictate those different registers?

2 Interview someone other than a peer (for example, a member of a social agency, a business person) using Ruddell's four questioning strategies? Identify some characteristics of a good interview. What does it mean to be a careful listener?

3 Talk to some elementary school students about how to have a good conversation. Can you describe their level of communicative competence? What are some of their specific awarenesses about language?

4 Assume you have a student who consistently uses profanity in class. Using the buzz session technique described in this chapter, identify a possible solution or solutions to that problem.

REFERENCES

Brink, C. R. *Caddie Woodlawn*. New York: Scholastic Book Services, 1975.

Britton, J. *Language and Learning*. Harmonsworth, Middlesex, England: Penguin Books, 1970.

Cook-Gumperz, J. "Persuasive Talk—The Social Organization of Children's Talk." In Judith Green and Cynthia Wallat (eds.). *Ethnography and Language in Educational Settings*. Norwood, N.J.: Ablex Publishing Co., 1981.

Dixon, C. "Language Experience Stories as A Diagnostic Tool." *Language Arts* 54 (May 1977):501−505.

Duffy, G. *Teaching Linguistics*. Dansville, N.Y.: Instructor Publications, 1969.

Forum. "Informal Classroom Drama." *Language Arts* 60, 3 (March 1983):370−372

Graubard, P. "Pantomime: Another Language." *Elementary English* 37 (May 1960): 305−306.

Hennings, D. G. *Communication in Action: Teaching the Language Arts*. Boston: Houghton Mifflin, 1982.

Hymes, D. *Foundation of Sociolinguistics: An Ethnographic Approach*. Philadelphia: University of Pennsylvania Press, 1974.

Lamb, P. *Linguistics in Proper Perspective*. 2d ed. Columbus, Oh.: Charles E. Merrill Publishing Co., 1977.

Loban, W. *Language Development: Kindergarten Through Grade Twelve*. Urbana, Ill.: National Council of Teachers of English, 1976.

Moffett, J. *A Student-Centered Language Arts Curriculum*, K-6. Boston: Houghton Mifflin, 1968.

Pelligrini, A.; DeStefano, J.; and Thompson, D. "Saying What You Mean: Using Play to Teach 'Literate Language.'" *Language Arts* 60, 3 (March 1983):380−384.

Ruddell, R. "Developing Comprehension Abilities: Implications from Research for an Instructional Framework." In S. Jay Samuels (ed.). *What Research Has to Say About Reading Instruction*, Newark, Del.: International Reading Association, 1978.

Safer, R.; Staab, C.; and Smith, K. *Language Functions and School Success*. Glenview, Ill.: Scott Foresman & Co., 1983.

Shane, H.; Walden, J.: and Green, R. *Interpreting Language Arts Research for the Teacher.* Washington, D.C.: Association for Supervision and Curriculum Development, NEA, 1971.

Smith, F. *Writing and the Writer.* New York: Holt, Rinehart and Winston, 1982.

Tanner, F. *Creative Communication, Projects in Acting, Speaking, Oral Reading.* Pocatello, Id.: Clark Publishing Co., 1979.

Tough, J. *Talking, Thinking, and Growing.* New York: Schocken Books, 1974.

Wagner, Betty Jane. *Drama as a Learning Medium.* Washington, D.C.: National Education Association, 1976.

Wigginton, E. *Foxfire.* Garden City, N.Y.: Doubleday, 1972.

———. *Foxfire 2.* Garden City, N.Y.: Doubleday, 1973.

———. *Foxfire 3.* Garden City, N.Y.: Anchor Press/Doubleday, 1975.

———. *Foxfire 4.* Garden City, N.Y.: Anchor Press/Doubleday, 1977.

———. *Foxfire 5.* Garden City, N.Y.: Anchor Press/Doubleday, 1979.

———. *Foxfire 6.* Garden City, N.Y.: Anchor Press/Doubleday, 1980.

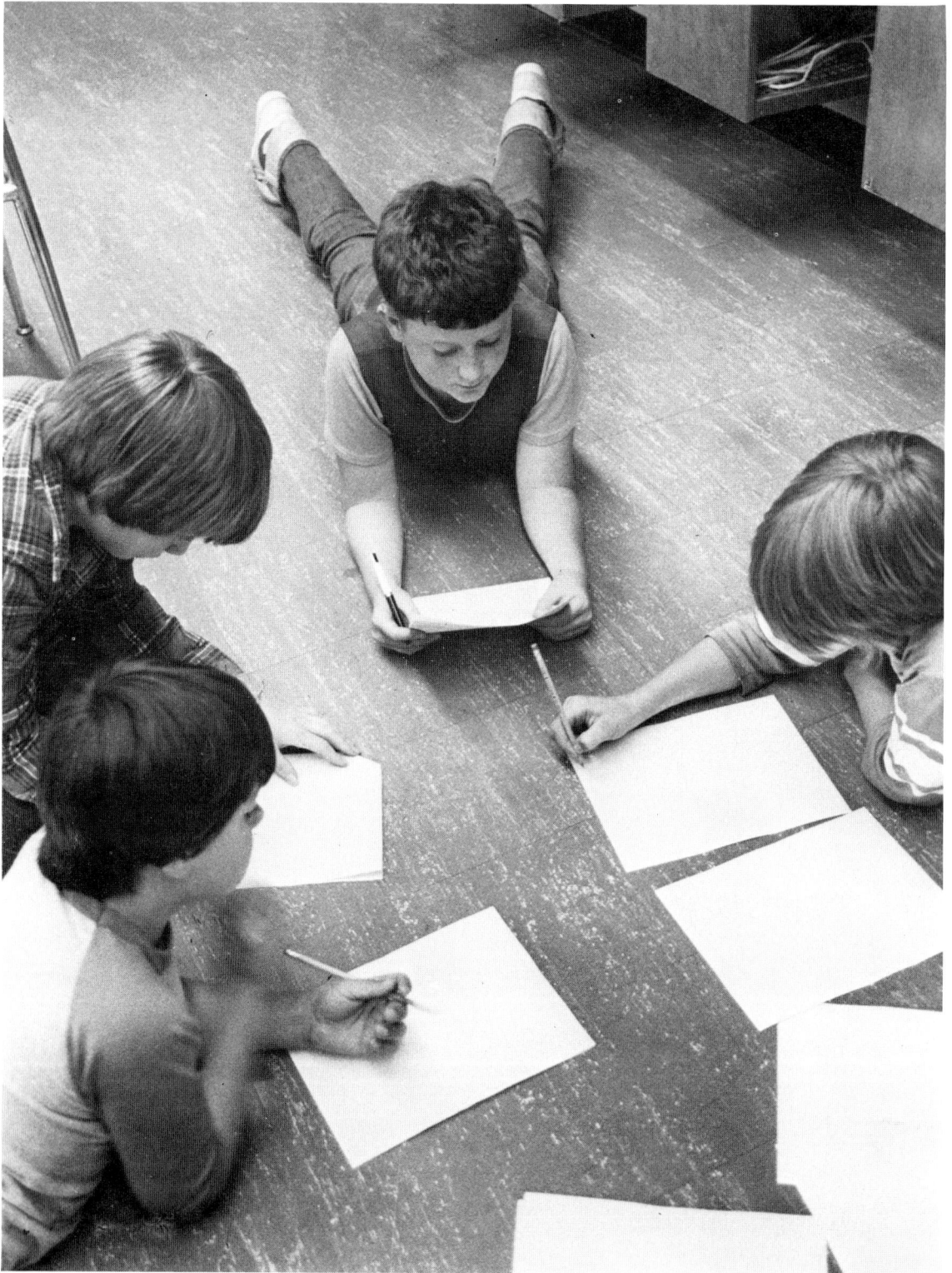

CHAPTER 6

Writing

WHAT'S THE HARDEST THING ABOUT WRITING?
SECOND GRADER
...if you don't know a word

SIXTH GRADER
...you have to think of an idea and then lots of little
ideas to go with it
...getting it all together

WHEN DO YOU ENJOY WRITING?
FIFTH GRADER
When you can choose your own subject

OVERVIEW

The purpose of this chapter is to describe both the writing process, focusing on expressive, transactional and poetic writing types, and audience characteristics. In addition, effective techniques for carrying out a teacher-student conference are presented. Methods for publishing writing and evaluation of writing are discussed at the end of the chapter.

INTRODUCTION

When children enter school, they are ready to write. They have spent quite a bit of time before school drawing with crayons, making up stories as they draw, and scribbling down stories that go with the drawings. Graves (1983) maintains that 90 percent of all children come to school thinking that they know how to write and 15 percent thinking they know how to read. What better motivation for you as a teacher than a group of first graders who are convinced they know how to write. Yet, in the average elementary classroom, writing is not a daily activity. In fact, writing takes place only one out of every 10 days. When writing does take place, students are asked to write on assigned topics instead of choosing their own. Their first drafts become filled with red ink circling every spelling and punctuation mistake. Their second drafts, if they do them, are evaluated by the teacher and returned to the children who dispose of them immediately. Maybe this brief description of how writing is sometimes taught is too harsh, but our position is that writing is too important to be taught once every 10 days. Read below what one first-grade teacher has done with writing during the first week of school.

Mary Ellen Giacobbe (1981) reports that she started to teach writing the first day of school. She gave children sheets of unlined paper and told them to write. One child after tracing her hand and adding some other things such as the sun, flowers, and lines wrote:

THE TRCE WAS TACAN A WEC.

(The turkey was taking a walk.)

The child then crossed out the "T" in "TACAN" and substituted a "W." She crossed out "A WEC" and wrote "D THE HALL." Her sentence now read:

THE TRCE WAS WACAN D THE HALL.

(The turkey was walking down the hill.)

In one writing period, this student planned her writing assignment through drawing, wrote what she wanted to say about the subject and revised her writing to say something else. Giacobbe did not circle the misspelled words or say that they were wrong. She did nothing *but* praise the child for such an informative piece, and the child kept writing.

You might feel that the child needed immediate work in spelling or that writing should be halted until the child learned spelling words that she could use in writing. But what the child was doing was inventing the spelling to get her meaning across to the reader. In Chapter 8 we talk more about invented spelling and why children choose the spelling they do for words, but for now, we want to emphasize that invented spelling is very natural and should be encouraged so students will write and not fear writing because they are not using standard orthography.

Not only can children write and want to write, but teachers can find out more about students through their writing than through most tests they may give. Armstrong (1982) in *What's Going On?* details the intellectual development of an eight-year-old girl who kept a diary in words and pictures of a growth of a seed. After reading the diary, Armstrong realized that the diary "recorded not only the physical growth of the seed which Sarah had planted but also her own intellectual development as she watched her plant grow and attempted to describe its successive stages" (p. 56).

THE WRITING PROCESS

Before looking at how we might teach writing in the elementary grades, we need to discuss the writing process. In the last 10 years, the writing process has been substantially researched. Graves (1983) discusses the writing process around the terms of choice, rehearsal, and composing. Other researchers such as Cooper and O'Dell (1977) talk about the writing process as being composed of prewriting, writing, and revision. Glatthorn (1982) speaks of exploring, planning, drafting, and revising. Whatever terms we use to describe the process does not matter. What matters is that the research in the past decade shows that the writing process can be separated into stages, and teachers need to be aware of the stages so they can provide ample time for students to work in these stages.

Another characteristic of the writing process is that the stages are recursive rather than linear and sometimes they overlap. Graves (1983) talks about rehearsing while composing. During composing, the writer may feel that there is not enough information and begins to rehearse by talking about other ideas or asking questions of others. The process is one of getting ideas down on paper, checking them out with someone else and rewriting so the message is clear and coherent to the intended reader.

Using the terms of choice, rehearsal, and composing, let's see how a second and a fifth grader began the writing process.

Choice.   Hilary, a second grader, talks to her teacher about seeing the movie, *Bambi.* Her teacher encourages Hilary to write something about the movie to share with her classmates. Hilary agrees and begins rehearsal.

Rehearsal.   Hilary goes over to the art center and picks up crayons and paper. She draws a deer in a forest with big bushes, trees, and other smaller animals. With an orange crayon, she draws fire. When the teacher asks Hilary about the picture, Hilary tells her that Bambi is looking for her mother who died in the fire. Hilary then begins to jot down words such as "fire," "deer," "Bambi," "mother." Next Hilary begins to compose.

Composing.   Hilary calls her teacher and asks for help. "I don't know where to begin," she says, "should I start from when my mom and dad said they would take me?" "What do you think?" says her teacher. "I think I'll start with the fire in the forest." Hilary then begins to write, "Once upon a time . . ." and after three sentences she stops. She asks her teacher to read what she has written. The teacher says that Hilary might want to read her partial story to her friend, Kim. Hilary reads and Kim listens. When Hilary finishes, she announces that she will take the paper home and finish it. Kim tells her not to forget to say how the campers started the fire and offers a few more suggestions.

Choice.   Christopher, a fifth grader, tells his teacher that his father bought him a telescope from a mail-order catalog and some of the parts were missing. His teacher encourages him to write a letter to the company telling them the parts were missing. Christopher agrees and begins to write.

Rehearsal.   Christopher lists the parts that were missing and then asks the teacher if he may go to the library during recess since the library has the catalog. In the library, he checks to make sure he understands the written guarantee and checks the spelling of the missing parts.

Composing.   He writes his letter and asks his teacher to help him with format. She directs him to a book with a business letter form in it, and Chris uses it as a model. When he is finished, his teacher checks the letter for information as well as paragraphing, sentence structure, and word choice. Chris rewrites the letter in pen following his teacher's suggestions and gets ready to mail it.

Both students followed the same process but their purpose for writing was very different and so was the audience. Hilary was telling a story to her friends; Christopher was writing a letter to an unknown person or persons. Both had the motivation to write based on personal experiences.

FUNCTIONS OF WRITING

Both of our writers, Hilary and Christopher, had different purposes for writing and their language represented their purpose. Even though she was not prompted by the teacher, Hilary began her story with "Once upon a time . . . ." When children come to write they draw on their pool of language experience which helps them to know what kind of language to use in certain types of situations. Hilary had listened to or read so many stories that it was natural for her to begin the story in that way.

Britton et al. (1975) categorized the functions of writing into three categories—expressive, transactional, and poetic. Expressive writing is very much like a written speech, reflecting the writer's thoughts and feelings. The writing jumps around, and the writer expects the reader to follow along because the reader has had similar experiences. Remember that Kim tells Hilary to put in the section about how the fire started, as well as other suggestions. Expressive writing is basic in that it should be a part of every grade level writing class as well as other content classes besides language arts. It is crucial for trying out and coming to terms with new ideas. It is a good way for two students or student and teacher to carry on a dialogue with each other as a learning experience.

Another term for transactional writing is school writing. When Christopher wrote to the telescope company, he was writing a transactional paper. He had to be precise about the missing telescope items and had to follow proper format and structure so the reader will take him seriously and make sure Christopher receives the missing parts. Although content is foremost in all writing, format and structure become equally important in transactional writing. A comparison can be made between expressive and transactional writing and speech registers (discussed in the last chapter on oral language).

Poetic writing can best be described as the type of writing that is either fantasy or fiction. It doesn't matter whether there is any truth in poetic writing. The writer takes for granted that the reader will experience what is written rather than using his or her own experiences. The reader does not question if the writer's schema is different from the reader's.

Writing that children do in school should be on a continuum between expressive and poetic. The writing should not be limited to just the language arts class nor should only transactional writing occur in the content areas of science, math, and social studies. Students in those classes can use expressive writing quite effectively. Although she works with students older than elementary students, Salem (1982) uses expressive writing to teach mathematics.

AUDIENCE CONSIDERATIONS

Another distinction between Hilary's and Christopher's papers is their audience. Hilary wrote for her classmates; Christopher for an unknown audience. In school, children write mostly for the teacher. However, the teacher may play different roles as the reader of children's writing. In distinguishing between the different sorts of audience found in school writing, Britton et al. (1975) suggest the following categories

1 Child to self.
2 Child to trusted adult.
3 Child to teacher as partner in dialogue.

4 Child to teacher seen as examiner or assessor.

5 Child to his/her peer.

6 Child to unknown audience.

In the classroom we should make every effort to have students write for different audiences so that they will find out that what they say is determined by the audience. Although we will discuss evaluation later, it is important to mention now that when students write for different audiences, the evaluation of the writing must take into account the audience. For example, when students are writing for themselves in a journal or diary, you probably do not want to do any type of evaluation. When you are reviewed as the trusted adult by the child, you certainly do not want to red mark the paper. What we recommend is that you evaluate very few of the students papers and when you do, let them know that the purpose of writing is evaluation. However, early on in their writing, students should be writing for themselves, their peers, and you as trusted adult.

CHOICE

Writing and Oral Language

For either expressive or transactional writing, students can use oral language as their basis for choosing a writing topic. Kantor (1980) says that "the child's skill in speaking is a key that can unlock the front door of the writing house, even though it may not unlock all doors within the house" (p. 75). Many of the activities from the last chapter on oral language can be used as prewriting activities for a writing assignment.

In the early stages of writing, children have a tendency to be cautious with words and sentences. They are concerned with spelling and other mechanical aspects of writing. While their language outside of the classroom is natural and honest, their language is sometimes tense and unnatural. By helping students tap their schemata of personal experiences through talking, you can show students that they have many ideas for writing and, more importantly, help them to take control of their own language and manipulate their language rather than have the language manipulating them. Below are some examples of using oral language in the classroom to stimulate writing activities.

Memories

Children have very vivid memories of recent and past experiences. You can tap these memories by listing categories on the board and asking students to list specific incidences under some or all of the categories. The activity can be done with the whole class, small groups, and even individually. The following categories can be used as a starting point.

1 *Childhood memories.*   Memories of family, friends, and other relatives, how you spent your holidays and vacations, happy and sad experiences.

2 *Exciting days.*   First day of school, sports days, music days, birthdays, new brothers and sisters.

3 *Future.*   School years, short-range plans, long-range plans, summertime, holidays.

4 *Interests.*   Books, movies, television, sports, music, hobbies.

Word Shaking

An activity using a brainstorming technique is word shaking. In a *Celebration of Bees*, Esbensen (1975) describes how she talks about poetry with children by "emphasizing again and again that the poet wants to use ordinary, everyday language in new ways; to make the language open new doors and windows for us; and to let us see old familiar things as though we'd never seen them before." Esbensen's method of word shaking is to get the teacher to fill the blackboard with words from the children for a poetry assignment before they start to write. With younger children, this technique gets the words already in their oral vocabulary in front of them in visibly written form. You and your students brainstorm words to describe the wind, snow, rain, or whatever they wish so they can see that they do have words to write poetry.

Word shaking can be done by individuals or small groups. Remember to accept all words and ideas that your students give. The procedure is to select a topic. Let's select "the ocean." In a large group setting ask students to call out words that describe the ocean. You may end up with a blackboard filled with words such as,

thunder	ships	fearful	dancing
roar	ocean liners	crashes	cold
blue	whales	booms	rainbows
green	calm	soft	salty
gentle	hostile	angry	white

The following poem was written by a third grader using some of the words from the brainstorming session.

The ocean roars like a circus
of lions when thunder is heard.
It's gentle and dancing under the rainbow.

Brian, Age 8

Free Writing

Kantor (1980) recommends free writing as a way for using talking as an entry to writing. The purpose of free writing is to make writing as natural as talking. Elbow (1973) insists on free writing at all levels. He says that writers should let their ideas flow freely without regard to form and structure.

Free writing can either be unstructured or structured. In unstructured free writing, you have students write for 10 or 15 minutes without stopping or thinking about what they will say next. The important thing is to keep the words flowing across the paper. They are not to worry about spelling, mechanics, or usage. If they cannot think of anything to say, tell them to write "I can't think of anything to say" over and over again until something occurs to them. Students sometimes find free writing difficult at first, but after a few times, they tend to see that they have many ideas flowing on their papers.

Structured free writing occurs when you tell students to concentrate on one of the five senses, such as listening, and record the sounds they hear around them. A short field trip outside of the building might set the mood for students to jot down sounds that they hear. Below is an excerpt from a fifth grader doing a structured free writing assignment.

> *The lawnmower roars, spurts, sputters, dies. The high grass clogs the blades. Children playing soccer in the field—laughter, cheers, screams, clapping. Animals barking, meowing as they scamper playfully around the park. Spring is here. A rain cloud appears and droplets drip on the sidewalk cooling the afternoon.*
>
> *Diane, Fifth Grade*

Other structured free writing involves music and poetry. You can have students free write to different kinds of music and with older students, you can have the music set the mood for the free writing. Begin with instrumental music so the lyrics do not distract the students, then add music with lyrics so students can free write about the music and the lyrics.

When students use anyone of the above activities or others to decide what they are going to write about, they are using their background experiences to focus on a subject. It does not matter which subjects students choose. What does matter is that children get to choose their own subjects for writing.

REHEARSAL

During the rehearsal stage of writing, the students use conversation as well as drawing, doodling, and jot listing to get ideas down on paper. It is at this stage that your role changes from the first stage. During the Choice stage you are the resource person providing many opportunities through oral language to help the students find ideas from their personal experiences for writing. During the rehearsal stage, your role changes from resource person to reinforcer.

By *reinforcer*, we mean that you have to provide support for the children. Encourage them to get their ideas down on paper and help them to decide the form of writing—a letter, a story, a poem.

During rehearsal, you may do what we call oral composing. With you or with another student, a child begins to talk through the beginning of a paper, line by line, so the details are worked out before words are actually written.

Another rehearsal technique to get children to put their ideas on paper is dictation. In the reading chapter, we discuss the importance of the language experience approach to reading. Dictating a beginning section of a story is somewhat similar to the language experience approach. For many primary youngsters, the physical act of writing may cause difficulty in getting ideas down on paper. Since you do not want the mechanical aspects to interface with the more basic skill of communicating ideas, ask the students to dictate to you, your aide, or another student the ideas they are thinking about for their compositions.

Some elementary teachers use tape recorders so students can rehearse ideas. It is similar to dictation, but the students dictate to themselves. Naturally, you have to keep in mind the problems that occur with equipment. Students record their ideas and listen to them before they start to write. Since you may not have a chance to talk to all of your students when they want you to hear their ideas, you can listen to the ideas on the tape recorder.

COMPOSING

As we mentioned earlier, rehearsal meshes with composing for many students. As they are rehearsing, students are beginning to compose. In the middle of composing, they stop and do more rehearsing. That is the recursive nature of writing. Your role during composing is one of keen observer. Let us give you an example.

Michael, an eight year old, has done some free writing and has come up with a topic about a basketball game he watched with his parents over the weekend. Michael wants to relate the enjoyable event to his classmates. He jots down some key words and draws a picture of the inside of the arena. He writes a sentence and stops. He began tapping his pencil on the desk and puts his head down. His teacher observes the behavior and walks to his desk.

TEACHER: What's wrong, Michael?

MICHAEL: I can't write my ideas about the game.

TEACHER: Have you talked your ideas through with somebody listening?

MICHAEL: No, I thought I knew what I was going to say.

TEACHER: Turn your paper over and tell me about the game.

MICHAEL: It was the first time I've seen Kareem in person. He is taller than a giant. He wore those funny goggles that made him look like he lived on another planet. Boy, could he play. Did you know he shoots a sky hook shot?

TEACHER: Okay, Michael. Now write down what you just told me. I'll be back shortly to see how your story is coming along.

This short dialogue would not have taken place if the teacher had not observed Michael having a frustrating experience with writing.

The composing stage includes many activities. It begins when ideas get down on paper and, depending on the purpose of writing, ends when the students recopy their final drafts before turning in their papers for evaluation. We are not suggesting that all papers be evaluated nor are we suggesting that all writing go through a formal revision procedure. If we look at our audience categories, we recommend that a formal revision strategy be used when children are writing to the teacher as evaluator or writing to an unknown audience. Otherwise we recommend that for the other audience categories, revision be done through the conference.

WRITING CONFERENCE

Using the work of Bruner (1978), Applebee and Langer (1983) detail the use of instructional scaffolding in reading and writing. Basically, instructional scaffolding refers to a model in which the writer learns new skills through a context where a more skilled language user provides the necessary support to aid the novice writer. The writer internalizes the tasks from the skilled language user and learns to carry out the tasks independently.

Graves (1983) describes six elements contained in scaffolding. These elements ought to be observable to someone watching you and your children in a conference setting.

1 *Predictable.* The child should be able to predict most of what will happen is a conference.

2 *Focused.* The teacher should not center attention on more than one or two features of the child's piece.

3 *Solutions demonstrated.* Teachers need to show what they mean rather than tell a child what to do.

4 *Reversible roles.* Children should be free to initiate questions and comments, to demonstrate their own solutions.

5 *Heightened semantic domain.* Both teacher and child need to have a growing language to discuss the process and content of subjects.

6 *Playful structures.* There ought to be a combination of experimentation, discovery, and humor (pp. 271, 272).

Let's look at each step briefly so you have a better feel for a conference setting.

Predictable

One purpose of the conference is for the teacher to serve as model so that other types of revision such as peer revision and self-revision can be done. Students should expect a conference at least once a week with the teacher and more than once a week in some cases. A conference should be held after a first draft and before publication. It is highly recommended that conferences be held in the same place in the classroom. During the conference, the child should do most of the talking, focusing on a set of questions that again are predictable. Below is a set of questions that can be used in a conference.

Possible Questions for Writing Conference

- Tell me about your piece of writing.
- What part do you like the best?
- Can you tell me more about it?
- Do you have enough information?
- Do you have too much information?
- How did you feel when this happened?
- Did you write your feelings?
- Why did you choose this subject to write about?
- Do you have more than one story?
- What did you learn from this piece of writing?
- What do you intend to do with the next draft?
- What surprised you in the draft?
- How does this draft sound when you read it out loud?
- Why is it important to you?
- How does this compare to other pieces you have written?
- Why?
- Underline the part that tells what the draft is about.
- Circle the part that is most exciting.
- What do you think you can do to make this piece better?
- What problems did you have or are you having?
- What is the most important thing you are trying to say?
- What works so well you'd like to try to develop it further?
- Tell them what you liked about it.
- Are you happy with your beginning and ending?

- Explain how your title fits your story.
- What are your action words?
- Can you add others?
- Can you think of a different way to say this?
- Does the beginning of your piece grab the reader's attention?

Focused

During one conference, it is impossible to cover all aspects of revision. Using the proposed sequence for the revision process (Figure 6-1), you can separate your conferences by the different steps. After the first draft, the conference would focus on the editing procedure. Following the editing procedure is proofreading which takes into account usage, mechanics, and spelling. Finally, the recopying step is saved until last when the student prepares a final copy for publication.

Since we have mentioned grammar, usage, and mechanics during this characteristic of an effective conference, we need to make a statement about their importance in the writing process. The purpose of expressive writing is for students to be

I	Writing of the first draft.	A response to an assignment which has certain guidelines
II	Editing procedure.	An examination of the first draft to determine relative strengths and weaknesses of the writing
		1 Viewing the piece of writing first as a whole, then by paragraphs, then sentences, and finally by words.
		2 Determining ways of improving and expanding on the writing
		3 Editing by the teacher, by peers, or by self.
III	Proofreading.	An examination of the rewrite for errors in the conventions of the English language
		1 Usage.
		2 Capitalization.
		3 Punctuation.
		4 Spelling.
IV	Recopying.	The preparation of the final copy in which errors in the conventions are corrected and proper manuscript form is observed

FIGURE 6.1 *A proposed sequence for the revision process.*

more concerned with expressing meaning for their own satisfaction than in conveying meaning to others. If that is its purpose, grammar, usage, and mechanics play a minor role.

As students move from expressive to transactional writing, they began to understand the desirability of adjusting surface form to meet the needs and demands of their audience. Their first drafts may be content oriented with little attention to standards of correctness, such as sentence structure, usage, and mechanics. Through the revision process, however, you can encourage students to revise and edit what they have written so they will pay attention to surface detail. Martin and Mulford (1975) offer very good advice to elementary teachers so that they avoid trying to get students to correct all mechanical faults at once.

> *The teacher should select carefully from among the child's errors when he has made more than one or two, and should then regard his selections as one, relatively unimportant element in the matter to be discussed. What is fundamental is involvement by the teacher in the substance of the child's writing. Such involvement guarantees to the child that corrections are worth taking seriously. . . .*
>
> *. . . a teacher simply has to learn to judge how much concern for the correction he can enforce without it beginning to get in the way, without it inducing in a child a false sense of priorities, or confusion. This will vary, perhaps considerably from child to child—according to his age, his ability, his interest, his flexibility, his aspirations, the effects of his past experience, of his parents' expectations, of his friends' attitudes, his attitudes to reading, to writing, to learning generally, to the teacher, to the school. . . . The list could be much extended.*

To us the important point of the quote is that young writers must understand why sentence structure, usage, and mechanics are important when they are writing for a particular audience and want to rewrite their compositions because they feel compelled to do so. When students want to learn how to improve their writing from a grammatical point of view, you can work with individuals or small groups on the particular grammar problems they are having. Our recommendation is not to teach all of the sentence structure rules, all of the usage rules, all of the punctuation and capitalization rules to the whole class. Rather, pick out particular errors in sentence structure, usage, and mechanics that either all children have used in their writing or which small groups of children have used and teach them through the context of writing rather than in isolation.

Solutions Demonstrated

This characteristic can be misinterpreted. It does not mean that teachers rewrite the papers for the children. What it means is that as you focus on a particular editing or proofreading problem, you show students through demonstration how to revise rather than to do it for them. Let's say that at one of the final conferences, you are reading over a paper with sentence structure problems. The scenario might occur as follows.

TEACHER: Alice, read over this last paragraph.

ALICE: "The train pulled to a stop. Out came the older gentleman. He was carrying a suitcase. The suitcase was big. The suitcase was heavy. The gentleman asked the conductor how to reach the mansion. The mansion was suppose to be haunted. The mansion was on 92 street."

TEACHER: Do you remember the exercise we did last week on sentence combining?

ALICE: Yes, that is where you take two sentences and write one.

TEACHER: Look at these sentences (pointing to ones that can be combined), see if you can combine them as we did in class.

ALICE: I think I can do that.

Reversible Roles

We stated earlier that we want the children to do more of the talking than the teacher. With primary students, you will find out that they will begin to ask you questions right away. They will move off the subject and ask you questions about many things or tell you about some other experience they have had. Older children, who are first encountering a conference, will sit there and wait for you to do all of the talking. After trust is established between you and the student, you will find them being more honest with you about the questions you are asking. For example, in the scenario above, Alice might have said: "I really don't know what you mean about sentence combining. Can you show me how?"

Heightened Semantic Domain

The more children confer with the teacher during the conference, the more they will understand terms used in writing. Students should use common writing terms so you can move to peer revision and self-revision. If there is a common vocabulary, students will know how to communicate with each other during peer revision. The following is an excerpt from a conference between a teacher and a fifth grader, Candi.

TEACHER: What do you think about your beginning paragraph?

CANDI: When I read it over, I can see that I am not as honest as I want to be. You know. My voice was coming out.

TEACHER: What do you plan to do with the opening?

CANDI: I think I'll change the lead so I don't sound so stuffy.

Candi used terms such as "honest," "voice," and "lead." These are writing terms that Candi has learned through previous conferences.

Playful Structures

We have all witnessed teachers who had a sense of humor. When they and their students have fun in the classroom, the work produced is a higher quality because everyone involved had a good time writing. In the first chapter of this text, we discussed the importance of developing positive attitudes. Students have too long associated writing with punishment.

Write one hundred times I will not throw spit balls at Jerry.

Writing should be fun. This means that students have to laugh about the mistakes they make and teachers laugh with the students about some of their mistakes.

After a visit from Elmer, the bunny, to one first-grade class, Matt drew this picture and added in his invented spelling the note "No one can stop the outlaw bunny." During the conference between student and teacher, Matt laughed hysterically at his picture of the bunny in "the fort." His teacher agreed that the outlaw bunny has to be stopped.

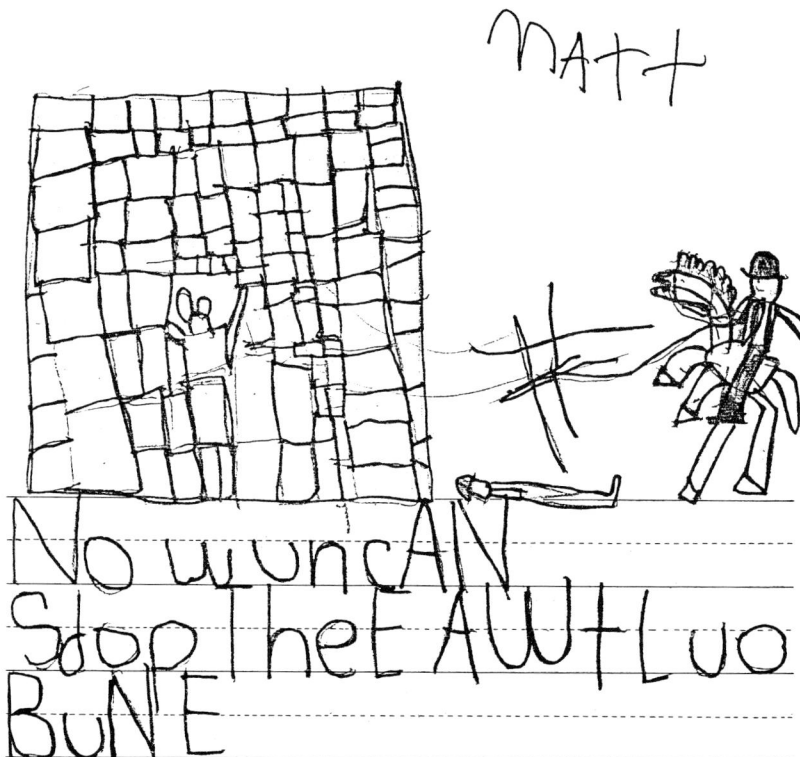

PEER EDITING

After students individually get a feel for editing by having conferences with their teacher, they are ready to do some peer editing. Using peers as editors greatly nourishes the in-class editorial process and helps the students to become self-revisionists later on. Often peers have a kind of detachment from another person's paper that allows them to make extremely helpful suggestions. Also, it seems to be that there is a transfer from learning how to help another person with a paper and the long-range goal of helping students learn to revise their own work.

The role you play in setting up peer editing is crucial. Simply pairing up students and letting them have a go at editing is seldom successful. Students must learn how to edit each other's work. You need to stress that peer editing will involve two processes. One is that the students will have to respond to each other's writing; the other, they will have to evaluate for editing each other's writing.

Responding is one of the most difficult skills to teach. It does not involve a formal evaluation or a critique of a paper. Instead, it calls for the reader to describe impressions what the paper did for him or her. Before writers receive evaluative comments and suggestions for change, they need to know how their piece affected the reader.

Questions that need to be answered by the peer editor follow along these lines,

"What do you think?"
"What went on in your mind when you read this?"
"Do you agree with what was written?"
"Did the piece of writing move you at all?"

Responses may not always be positive, and they may not give the writer the feeling that he or she has been completely successful, but they are reactions.

Besides asking students for their reactions to other students' papers, you also want them to evaluate each other's works. At first it is difficult for students to critique each other's papers, but soon they do a very good job. As students share their critiques of papers with their fellow writers, they learn not only about techniques for making their writing stronger and more interesting, but also they gain a sense of the elements of good writing as well. It is not uncommon for students to raise points about the purpose and audience of the writer, to ask for concrete details and supporting evidence, and to question the elements of logic used in the writing. To set the structure for students acting as peer editors, you might want them to follow a checklist like the one below. You might not use all of the categories for every piece of writing, but the questions should be used as guides.

Editing Checklist

Before you read through your classmate's paper, look at the following questions to help you in editing.

1 *General reactions.* What did you think? Does the writing make sense? Do you know what the author is talking about?

2 *Telling it all.* Elaboration. Are the ideas fully developed? Are there details that make people, places, and events come alive? Are there details that make the reader feel what the characters feel?

3 *Written organization.* Are events told in an interesting, logical order? Is there a beginning that creates interest? Is there action that builds interest? Is there a conclusion included that sums up the story?

4 *Paragraphs.* Do they hang together? Look at each paragraph. Does each idea or detail relate to the paragraph?

5 *Sentence sense.* Do all sentences make sense? Are they complete sentences? Do all sentences start the same way? If so, how can the writer change some of them for variety? Could some of the short sentences be combined to make them more interesting? Does the story read aloud with ease?

6 *Exactness of words.* Are the words specific? Is there a use of varied words? Are there words that relate to the senses? Is there a use of unusual expressions, word combinations and comparisons that add life to the paper?

Naturally, you would not use the checklist in its entirety, and for younger students, you may want to rewrite the questions. The idea, however, is to give the students some guidelines to begin peer editing.

When you begin peer editing with your class, you may want to begin by having the students work in pairs. The advantage of having students work in pairs is that they have the time to work in depth on one another's papers. After students feel comfortable working with each other in pairs, you can move to peer editing in small groups.

Small group work requires more advanced organizing than having students work in pairs. The students will need to know in advance when small groups will meet, and when they are to bring their first drafts to class. When students meet, they pass papers around the group so everyone has a chance to read and possibly to make notes about one another's papers before beginning a discussion.

After students feel comfortable working in small groups to edit each other's papers, you can then move to whole class editing. Working with class response as a whole is helpful in providing the writer with a variety of responses. In leading the whole class discussion, you have the opportunity to guide students' thinking to points of particular appropriateness and to model ways in which the students can respond to papers when working in pairs and small groups. As students hear other responses, they begin to sharpen their own notions about good writing.

A good technique for whole class editing is to use the opaque projector to flash a copy of the paper on a screen. Do not identify the writer of the paper. Usually after a few times, students volunteer that their papers are on the screen. Use the general criteria in the editing checklist to let the students discuss the strengths and weaknesses of the paper on the opaque projector.

Self-editing

After students have been involved in teacher editing and peer editing, they should be ready for self-editing. In self-editing, students look at their papers, not as writers, but as readers. They read their papers with a third ear. That is, they read their papers objectively, listening to what they are reading and keeping in mind their audience and purpose. Mature writers go through self-editing with the first draft of their paper. It takes a long time for writers to become a good self-editor, but when they do, writers will be writing papers that communicate their ideas to their intended audience. It should be noted here that when students do self-editing, they come back to the first step of revision—in process revision.

PUBLISHING STUDENT WRITING

''Going public'' builds student motivation to use the writing process to produce quality writing. When children share the result of choosing their own topics, revising their own papers based on their own editing decisions, they come to care more about their writing. Young writers experience great satisfaction in sharing their writing with real audiences.

A variety of ways to share students' writing exists, from simply posting it on the bulletin board to publishing it in a magazine. Marjorie Frank (1979) summarizes why sharing is important.

- Sharing is communicating.   *After all . . . one of the author's most compelling motivations for the labor or reworking and refining is the preparation of a personal statement for presentation to other human beings.*

- Sharing gets writing out into the light.   *That act of presenting it . . . of hearing it . . . of watching it live . . . of perceiving other's reactions to it . . . provides the writer with a clearer view of his work—and influences the shape of the next work.*

- Sharing increases technical accuracy.   *As kids write and publish they become spontaneously concerned about grammar and spelling and structure—and they develop as independent critics.*

- Sharing advances the craft of writing.   *If it is conscientiously used as a time for a close scrutiny of specific approaches, the sharing setting is an excellent one for elevating the techniques of writing.*

• Sharing builds self-esteem. *The fulfillment and self-respect a person feels upon bringing everything together into finished form are strengthened by the positive responses of others (p. 118).*

Ideas for Publishing Student Writing

The following ideas can be used in the elementary classroom to make sure that student writing gets published.

Classroom or School Author of Day, Week, or Month. Prominently display writing in classroom or school hallway for a featured author. Also post a biography and pictures of the authors. One theme used for these displays is "Blue Ribbon Writes."

Posting Papers. All students' first paper and more recent papers should be posted in the classroom. This allows students, parents, and others to continually monitor the students' progress.

Publishing. Many publications accept student writing for printing.

School Newspaper. Providing students an opportunity to manage a school newspaper is a wonderful way to promote the value and necessity of written communication. Writing of all ages of students can be included in a school newspaper. A feature article or column for each grade is one way to provide this.

Individual or Class Book. Students create their own books or contribute an idea or page to a class book. These can be included in a school or class library. Librarians report that student authored books are often checked out more frequently than commercial books.

Works in Progress. Seeing the importance of each component of the writing process can be enhanced by posting "Works in Progress." A "Writing" bulletin board could be prepared that displayed working drafts. Students are reinforced by seeing their drafts posted and, in allowing others to read them, authors receive editorial comments to help in revision. Brainstorming lists, interview notes, and so on, could be posted for the class to see and read.

Parent Newsletter. An excellent way to share a variety of writing is to publish them in a parent newsletter. In doing this, an attempt should be made to include writing done by student authors of all ability levels.

Third Grade News. One of our teacher friends publishes a monthly newspaper called "Third Grade News." She uses the beginning of the paper to let parents know what the children are doing in their different classes. A second section called "Star Reporters" deals with reports made by two or three children. Below is a report written about the first grade class by the reporters.

1st GRADE

They have reading groups in first grade, and they do workbook pages there and answer questions from Mrs. McNaughten and read. Around the room they have centers with different activities. They draw pictures and color, play dominoes, have games to play, and make pictures out of newspaper. They all have folders with work in them to do. They are studying Smokey the Bear.

by John, Tyler, & Brian

The next section is a poetry section. Since this was the October issue, children wrote cinquains about Halloween. A cinquain is a five-line poem with the first and last lines using either the same word or a synonym. For example,

Halloween
Spooky Ghosts
Witches Making Brew
Skeletons Singing
Halloween

The last section is a joke section and we thought you would enjoy reading one.

QUESTION: Why did Mrs. Noah ask her husband to throw a sack of cement overboard?

ANSWER: She wanted a permanent wave.

With microcomputers becoming an integral part of the elementary classroom, more publishing will come about through the use of the computer. One of the benefits of the microcomputer is that children can type in their texts, easily correct errors, and set up publishing formats in advance of their typing. In addition, multiple copies of a single piece can be published quickly for a group of children to read together. Other uses of the microcomputer are given in Chapter 15.

WRITING AND LITERATURE

Chapter 13 gives some suggestions on children becoming authors, writing about authors, and reading about authors. Here we want to stress the importance of having literature available in classroom to be used for the *choice* stage of writing. The objective of having literature in the writing classroom is not necessarily to have the children write and illustrate like a particular author. The objective is to let children enjoy the author's words, characters, and plot. If they decide to respond to the literature by trying to write a similar story, that's fine. We all try to mimic people we like whether they are writers, sports figures, or entertainers. A particular story may lead the student to read another work by the same author or write about a similar experience that one of the characters in the story had.

WRITING ACROSS THE CURRICULUM

We have already shown how writing can be incorporated into the other content areas besides language arts. Armstrong's (1982) student, Sarah was doing expressive writing through diary writing in a science class. Salem (1982) also used expressive writing in mathematics. Usually in most content area classes, however, transactional writing rather than expressive or poetic is asked of students. We recommend writing in every content area, and not just transactional writing. Any experience that a child has can be used in a writing activity. Keep in mind the sixth graders who were doing journal writing in their social studies class in the first chapter of this text. In Chapter 14, we give other examples of writing for other content areas.

WRITING CLASSROOM ENVIRONMENT

Before the writing process can be taught in your classroom, you need to provide the proper environment. In a classroom environment conducive to writing, students will learn much more about the actual process of composing than in a place where they feel uncomfortable or where writing seems unnatural. The suggestions below might help in providing a conducive classroom environment.

1 Make sure that students know that writing is expected of them as part of your class. Children write more freely than usual when they learn from the very first day that writing is a natural, useful mode of communication, and that, to participate fully in the class, they must write regularly. Elementary children should write constantly, and the teacher should make a point of showing them how writing functions as a major form of communication in the school.

Besides telling students they are going to write, you can rearrange your classroom to facilitate the writing process. If desks are movable, place them together to create worktables and conversation centers. Off to the corners of the classroom, provide some individual writing areas for students to work if they need quiet for writing and revising. The walls should be covered with cork board or some other material for displaying student writing. Going public with the students' writing should be a goal so students have the sense of accomplishment when they complete their writing assignments. Paper, pencils, crayons, pens, as well as portable typewriters, should be available for students. Finally, have a classroom library filled with books, magazines, dictionaries, and encyclopedias for students' use to generate ideas for writing and finding more information about topics.

2 Make sure that students have no fear about writing or the writing process. Since students will be involved with putting their ideas on paper, critiquing other students' writing, and having their own writing critiqued, it is imperative that they feel at ease with themselves, with you, and with other students. The first step is to make sure that students know each other's names. After students know each other, you might want to have some activities that will get students to talk about themselves. The purpose of getting students to talk about themselves is that personal experiences are the beginning writer's best resources. What the students have to say reveals information about them that you can use to motivate them further. You may find out that a student wants to play an instrument or a sport, that he or she reads widely, or has just visited a foreign country. You should use the students' information to suggest topics, draw out students as experts, or simply engage them in oral discussion. The following activities might be useful for finding out students' interests.

WRITER'S QUESTIONNAIRE

Name: _____

What do you like to be called? _____

What do you like to do on weekends? _____

What is your favorite song? _____

What shows do you like on TV? _____

Do you ever write poetry? _____

What was the last book you read? _____

What was the last movie you saw? _____

This simple questionnaire can be used at any elementary level. You can expand on it by adding questions or have the younger children answer the questions orally. The students should share their answers with you and other children so that everyone in the class knows the likes and dislikes of their peers.

A second activity involves drawing. For example, students might be given a copy of a coat of arms or one that has been cut on construction paper and asked to fill in the sections with drawings that answer the following questions.

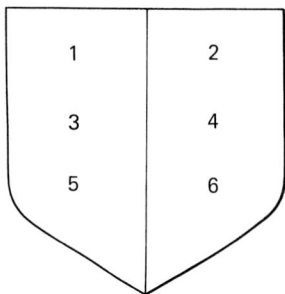

1 Draw two things you do well.

2 Draw the place where you feel most at home.

3 What would you like to be when you grow up?

4 What is your favorite saying?

5 And so on.

Students should be told that they need not be good artists to complete the exercise. The main purpose of this activity, as well as the other, is to get students to talk about themselves to their peers. They should not feel intimidated or afraid about these assignments. After students have finished a number of exercises to get to know each other, they should feel more at ease about putting their ideas down on paper.

3   Make sure that the writing classroom is a place for the development and exchange of ideas. As the teacher, you are the support factor that students need to develop their ideas. To feel successful a writer needs support. A professional writer gets support from editors and reviewers. The novice writer needs support from the teacher. A teacher's willingness to teach writing is communicated very quickly to students and the willingness strongly affects performance. Young people will write and write well in the classes of teachers whom they see as helpful and supportive. If there is no support, the students tend to write poorly.

After developing ideas, those ideas need to be exchanged. When students know their writing will be shared with others, they begin shaping and structuring their papers and learn about organization. They begin searching for the right words, the proper mixture of sentences, and the necessary information to get their point across. In other words, they begin to develop a writing style.

EVALUATION

Since the writing process is complicated, the method of evaluation needs to be reliable and effective; otherwise students will not know why they have been given a particular grade. One reason why writing has not been taught effectively in the elementary schools is that teachers, as well as students, have had a difficult time evaluating writing. Teacher variability in writing has caused problems from the standpoint that criteria for evaluation have changed as teachers are evaluating papers. As a result, students do not know what criteria were used for evaluation, and teachers have not been consistent in the way they evaluate papers.

We do not have on foolproof way to grade compositions that will eliminate teacher variability and not make students question why they received a particular grade. What we do have are suggestions for a philosophy about grading compositions and a few examples of evaluation tools that have worked for us. Let's first look at the suggestions for developing a philosophy of grading.

1 Evaluation should take place throughout the writing process. This does not mean that letter grades should be given for prewriting, writing, and revision. It does mean that the final grade should reflect how the students worked through the process of writing to get to the final product. In addition, if students are evaluated through indirect means such as feedback from their peers and you, their final grade or the finished product should reflect those indirect evaluation measures.

2 Focus your grading on methods and skills taught. Many teachers want to grade everything in all compositions. If you grade those areas that have been recently taught, you can find out whether students have understood the concepts taught. For example, if you spent time on audience and strong verbs, those would be two criteria to evaluate.

3 Give a higher value in your grading to content rather than usage and mechanics. This area is very controversial because surface errors are more easily seen and can be evaluated more easily than the use of content. Our suggestion is not to let mechanics and usage errors slip by but not to give these errors a great deal of weight in evaluation. Our position is that by having students write a great deal and helping them with all facets of content such as originality of ideas, supporting statements, and pertinent information you will get better writing with fewer usage and mechanics errors. In addition, usage and mechanics errors pop up in most writing by individuals in elementary schools as well as college. Mina Shaughnessy (1977) pointed out that subject verb agreement and pronoun reference problems persist in the writing of college students even after they have been drilled in avoiding these problems.

Writing Folders

Each student should have a writing folder to contain all the work the child has done with comments from you and peers. In addition the folder would have those papers that have been published as well as those that have not. At a glance, you should be able to see the amount of work each child has done, the number of published materials, and growth in writing based on your observation of the quality and quantity of writing.

Since you will be using conferences for revision, you can ask students at certain parts of the year to bring their writing folders to the conference. Students should be able to give you their impression about their own writing growth. By going through their folders they can pick out writing that they feel shows their competence.

Some of you will have to do more formal evaluation than the writing folders. If that is the case, you can have students choose writing from their folders for a more formal evaluation. You might have students select a sample of expressive, transactional, and poetic writing for their formal evaluation. The key point is to let them choose what they want to be evaluated. Then you can use either an analytical or a primary trait scale for evaluation.

Evaluation Scales

Holistic Evaluation.   The term "holistic evaluation" refers to looking at a composition as a whole piece rather than parts. Cooper and Odell (1977) explain holistic evaluation as

> . . . a guided procedure for sorting or ranking written pieces. The rater takes a piece of writing and either (1) matches it with another piece in a graded series of pieces or (2) scores it for the prominence of certain features important to that kind of writing or (3) assigns it a letter grade or number. The placing, scoring, or grading occurs quickly, impressionistically, after the rater has practiced the procedure with other raters. The rater does not make corrections or revisions in the paper. Holistic evaluation is usually guided by a holistic scoring guide which describes each feature and identifies high, middle, and low quality levels for each feature (p. 3).

Holistic evaluation helps you to evaluate papers more quickly, more consistently, and more pointedly. The rating is consistent because the evaluator uses the same criteria on all pieces of writing. The consistency is evident not only from piece to piece rated by the same evaluator but also between different evaluators rating the same piece.

Analytic Scales.   Two different holistic evaluation tools, analytic scales and primary trait scales, will be discussed as examples you can use in your elementary language arts classes. *Analytic scales* direct the reader's attention to specific features of the piece of writing and suggest relative point values for each feature. The grade for the piece of writing is arrived at by summing scores on the various subparts. When students receive their papers with scores from the analytic scale, they will know their strengths and weaknesses in writing. In addition, an analytic scale will contain many features, not just surface features such as usage and mechanics errors.

The most popular analytic scale was developed by Diederich (1974). The Diederich Scale was developed for the Educational Testing Service to score SAT essay examinations. Since its development, many teachers have used the scale or modified it for classroom use.

The Diederich Scale (Figure 6-2) is divided into general merit and mechanics categories. More weight is given to ideas and organization. The ratings for each item range from 1 to 5. As you would expect 1 is the lowest, 3 is the average, and 5 is the highest. The score of 2 should be used to designate below-average performance and 4 to designate above-average performance. Diederich listed guidelines for each of the criteria and these guidelines can be used by you or you can develop your own set of guidelines. Whichever guidelines you use, be sure to let your students know what they are before they turn in their papers for evaluation.

Dimensions

	Low		General Merit Middle		High
Ideas	2	4	6	8	10
Organization	2	4	6	8	10
Wording	1	2	3	4	5
Flavor	1	2	3	4	5
			Mechanics		
Usage	1	2	3	4	5
Punctuation	1	2	3	4	5
Spelling	1	2	3	4	5
Handwriting	1	2	3	4	5

FIGURE 6.2 *The Diederich scale.*

Some teachers have used the idea of the analytic scale and modified it to fit objectives they have taught. An example of a modified analytic chart (Figure 6-3) was based on the class objectives for the third grade. Notice that the guidelines are written right on the chart with the weights for each criteria. The guidelines are simple to interpret and the teacher using this scale should not have a problem grading papers. It should be pointed out that these criteria may not be the ones you use nor the weights. However, it is easy to see that this one analytic chart can be used for most writing that children do. There is an advantage to this in that students will get use to the criteria for evaluation.

Primary Trait Scale. The major difference between analytic scales and primary scales is that the analytic scales can be used for most writing, and the primary trait scale focuses on particular criteria for a specific type of writing, such as persuasion. Primary traits can be added to an analytic scale when a specific writing assignment is made or if you taught a specific trait in writing for the first time and want to evaluate it. Primary traits can focus on content in that you may want to look for logical development in a persuasive paper. The trait may focus on other devices such as voice or audience. Or the trait may focus on mechanics such as the use of direct quotes or footnotes. When students begin to write transactional papers, the primary trait scale works very well.

SUGGESTED ACTIVITIES

1 Observe a teacher and a student doing a writing conference. See if you can identify the behavior going on according to Graves' six conference characteris-

Trait	1	2	3	4	5	Weight
Capitalization	The student makes frequent errors in capitalization of sentence beginnings, story titles, initials, names, days, and months.		The student makes occasional errors in capitalization of sentence beginnings, story titles, initials, titles, names, days, and months.	The student only uses correct capitalization of sentence beginnings.	The student uses correct capitalization of sentence beginnings, story titles, initials, titles names, days, and months.	3
Punctuation	The student makes frequent errors in punctuation of dates, sentence endings, titles, and initials.		The student makes occasional error in punctuation of dates, sentence endings, titles, and initials.		The student uses correct punctuation of dates, sentence endings, titles, and initals.	3
Spelling	The student frequently misspells first-, second-, third-grade high frequency words.		The student occasionally misspells first-, second-, third-grade high frequency words.		The student correctly spells first-, second-, third-grade high frequency words.	2
Sentence Structure	The student frequently writes fragments or run-on sentences.		The student occasionally writes fragments or run-on sentences.		The student consistently uses complete sentences.	2
Format	The student uses incorrect letter or number forms, margins, spacing.		The student uses correct letter and number forms, spacing and margins, but does not indent paragraphs.		The student uses correct letter and number forms, spacing, margins and indentations.	1
Usage	The student makes frequent errors in subject-verb agreement.		The student makes occasional errors in subject-verb agreement.		The student consistently uses correct subject-verb agreement.	1
Organization	The student writes little or nothing or fragmented rambling.		The student uses some organization and development with details.		The student uses a definite sequence and organization and develops the ideas with details.	1

Reprinted by Permission of Adams County #12, Northglenn, Colorado.

FIGURE 6.3 *Third-grade writing sample criteria chart.*

tics. If you can conduct a conference, tape record it and categorize the conference questions according to the characteristics.

2 With a group of children, use Esbensen's technique of word shaking and put together a group of poems from the children.

3 Talk to primary and intermediate students about their writing habits. What kinds of writing do they do? Is one more expressive than transactional or poetic?

4 Interview two content area teachers (science, social studies or math) about their writing assignments. What generalizations can you draw about the role of writing in the content area.

5 Develop an analytic evaluation scale using the model in the text. Analyze a series of papers according to the scale. What generalizaton can be made about student performance using the scale? See if another student will evaluate the papers the same way you did using your scale.

REFERENCES

Applebee, A., and Langer, J. "Instructional Scaffolding: Reading and Writing as Natural Language Activities." *Language Arts* 60, 2 (February 1983):168–175.

Armstrong, M. "A Seed's Growth." In Mary Barr et al. (eds.). *What's Going On?* Montclair, N.J.: Boyton/Cook, Inc., 1982.

Britton, J.; Burgess, T.; Martin, N.; Mcleod, A.; and Rosen, H. *The Development of Writing Abilities*. Schools Council Research Studies, New York: Macmillan Publishing Co., 1975.

Bruner, J. "The Role of Dialogue in Language Acquisition." In A. Sinclair et al. (eds.). *The Child's Concept of Language*. New York: Springer-Verlag, 1978.

Cooper, C., and O'Dell, L., (eds.). *Evaluating Writing: Describing, Measuring, Judging*. Urbana, Ill.: National Council of Teachers of English, 1977.

Diederich, P. *Measuring Growth in English*. Urbana, Ill.: National Council of Teachers of English, 1974.

Elbow, P. *Writing Without Teachers*. New York: Oxford Press, 1973.

Esbensen, B. *A Celebration of Bees: Helping Children to Write Poetry*. Minneapolis: Winston Press, 1975.

Frank, M. *If You're Trying to Teach Kids to Write, You've Gotta Have This Book!* Nashville: Incentive Publications, 1979.

Giacobbe, M. E. "Kids Can Write the First Week of School." *Learning* 9 (September 1981):130–132.

Glatthorn, A. H. "Demystifying the Teaching of Writing." *Language Arts* 59, 7 (October 1982):722–725.

Graves, D. *Writing: Teachers and Children at Work*. Exeter, N.H.: Heinemann Educational Books, 1983.

Kantor, K. "Talking as an Entry into Writing." In Gay Su Pinnel (ed.). *Discovering Language with Children*. Urbana, Ill.: National Council of Teachers of English, 1980.

Martin, N., and Mulford, J. "Spelling, etc." In R. Larson (ed.). *Children and Writing*. New York: Oxford University Press, 1975.

Salem, J. "Using Writing in Teaching Mathematics." In Mary Barr et al. (eds.). *What's Going On?* Montclair, N.J.: Boyton/Cook, Inc., 1982.

Shaughnessy, M. *Errors and Expectations: A Guide for the Teachers of Basic Writers*. New York: Oxford University Press, 1977.

HOW TO FOOL YOUR TEACHER

(into thinking you're one of those "A" students)

1. Write neatly and clearly.
2. Keep even margins.
3. Be particular about spelling.

Before   After

Teachers are human and like most people are terribly impressed with the appearance of things. Remember "Polly Perfect"? Aren't her papers always neat as a focus of attention? Be a phony, line those numbers up and write very clearly. She'll fall for it. They always do.

CHAPTER 7

Grammar

WHY IS IT IMPORTANT TO KNOW THE EIGHT PARTS OF SPEECH IN OUR LANGUAGE?
FIFTH GRADER
So that when I speak and write I won't mess up.

REALLY?
FIFTH GRADER
Not really but that's what I learned last year.

OVERVIEW

This chapter presents a description of the three grammars found in most elementary class-rooms—traditional, structural, and transformational. Each is discussed according to its purpose along with its application to the classroom. Sentence combining, the application of transformational grammar, is discussed in its relationship to reading and writing, as well as in isolation.

INTRODUCTION

In the first chapter of this text, we pointed out that the first goal of language arts instruction is to cultivate a positive attitude about learning the different components of the language arts. A second important point was that many elementary teachers relied too much on published materials to teach the language arts as an integrated set of components representing expressive and receptive communication skills. We remind you of these two points because the topics of this chapter, *grammar*, and the next chapter, *spelling*, are ones that have been taught in isolation and, in our opinion, result in negative attitudes in children. In schools most language arts basals focus much attention on teaching grammar, and spelling is taught and graded separately from language arts. Our major purpose in this chapter and in the next is to discuss why a great deal of the language arts class time should *not* be spent directly teaching grammar and spelling, and, if you have to teach these components of the language arts, there are some methods to use to make these subjects interesting and relevant to the other language arts.

Why should grammar instruction time be minimal? Our reason is that grammar instruction will help students know something about their own language, but it will not help them to read better, write better, or understand a foreign language better. In the past, a great deal of time was spent on grammar study under the assumption that it would have a positive effect on the student's ability to use language. However, this assumption is false. In 1950, the *Encyclopedia of Educational Research* indicated that all the assumptions about teaching grammar were based on research that did not support the assumptions. The encyclopedia reported,

1 The disciplinary value that may be attributed to formal grammar is neglible.

2 No more relation exists between knowledge of grammar and the application of the knowledge in a functional language situation than exists between any two totally different and unrelated school subjects.

3 In spite of the fact that the contribution of the knowledge of English grammar to achievement in foreign language has been its chief justification in the past, the experimental evidence does not support this conclusion.

4 The study of grammar has been justified because of its possible contribution to reading skills, but the evidence does not support this conclusion.

5　The contribution of grammar to the formation of sentences in speech and in writing has doubtless been exaggerated.

6　Grammar is difficult if not impossible to teach to the point of application.

7　Formal and traditional grammar contains many items which if learned to the point of application could not have any serious effect on the learner's language usage.

8　Many grammatical rules have little or no basis in acceptable speech and writing.

9　Much of grammar based on analogy, history, logic, or an ideally perfect language may be disregarded. The only valid grammatical generalizations must be based on acceptable language practices.

These statements reinforce the notion that the time spent on grammar instruction should be minimal. Oral language development time, writing time, and reading time should not be replaced with grammar instruction with the hope that grammar will help students speak, write, and read better. Grammar instruction should have as its only purpose the analysis of the English language, and individual teachers should make a decision as to the amount of time they feel is necessary to teach children how to analyze the language. After you have decided the amount of time for teaching grammar, you then have to decide on which grammar to teach.

In Chapter 3 we described the three types of grammar found in different textbooks: traditional, structural, and transformational grammars. In *Grammar for Teachers*, Constance Weaver (1979) describes the three grammars as either grammar as product or grammar as process. Grammar as product refers to analyzing a sentence by a set of prescribed rules for identifying parts of speech or by a set of rules that determine the functions of each word in the sentence. These methods of analyzing existing sentences are ways we use traditional and structural grammar as grammar as products. Transformational grammar is grammar as process in that instead of having students analyze existing sentence, we have them produce or generate sentences based on transformational rules.

So that you will become familiar with the three types of grammar and their uses in the elementary school, we will present a description of each with some classroom applications. Personally, we advocate teaching sentence combining, an application of transformational grammar, to students so they can improve the syntactic complexity of their sentences. If you have to teach either traditional or structural grammar, we recommend that you teach them through a learning center (Chapter 15) based on individual needs rather than spending a great deal of time with the entire class.

TRADITIONAL GRAMMAR

According to Gleason (1965), the academic influence of traditional school grammar in the English language has been traced to the eighteenth century. Having its roots in the classical grammars of Latin and Greek, school grammar is modeled on these languages. To teach traditional grammar is to present the rules of grammar as prescriptions for the students to follow. The sentence is the key form in analysis of traditional grammar, and that analysis yields clausal and phrasal structures, subjects, predicates, and complements. Words within sentences are analyzed according to eight parts of speech. Each part of speech is identified by reference to a set of definitions, and the instructional approach is to apply the definitions in a deductive analysis of syntax. As we will point out in the next section on structural grammar, many definitions in traditional grammar are inaccurate when it comes to the application.

Parts of Speech

Nouns. Nouns are defined as names of persons, places, or things, and have different functions within sentences. A noun can be used as the subject of a sentence.

The *wind* blew violently.

A second function of a noun is the direct object. A direct object usually follows a transitive verb.

The pitcher threw the *ball* as fast as he could.

A third function of a noun is predicate nominative. The predicate nominative follows a linking verb and restates the subject.

My uncle was the *captain* of the team.

Another way a noun can function is as the object of a preposition. Together the preposition and the following noun constitute a prepositional phrase.

The small girl skated down the *hill*.

The fifth function of a noun is that of an indirect object. The indirect object receives the direct object.

Martha gave the *class* a treat for her birthday.

A noun also can be used as an objective complement. An objective complement follows a direct object and gives more information about the direct object.

The class elected Sara *chairperson* of the committee.

The appositive is closely related to the objective complement in that it gives more information about the subject of the sentence.

Gary, the *boy* sitting in the back of the room, is the new transfer student.

Finally, a noun can be used in direct address. The direct address calls attention to the subject of the sentence.

Bill, it is not appropriate for you to wear jeans to this meeting.

Pronouns. A pronoun is a word used in place of a noun. Because a noun is a person, place, or thing, a pronoun also refers to a person, place, or thing. The word a pronoun takes the place of is called the antecedent of the pronoun. Pronouns can be classified as being personal, relative, demonstrative, reflexive, and indefinite.

Personal pronouns refer to persons. They are classified as first person (I, we), second person (you), and third person (he, she, it, they). They are also classified as nominative (I), possessive (mine), and objective (them), depending on their grammatical function.

A relative pronoun performs a dual function in a sentence. It takes the place of a noun in the clause it introduces and it joins and relates the clause to the rest of the sentence. Relative pronouns include *who, whom, which, what,* and *that.*

She ate the candy *that* was on the television set.

I have not found the pet rock *that* Dad gave me for Christmas.

The young man, *who* played second trombone, graduated from my high school.

This and *that* and their plurals *these* and *those* are demonstrative pronouns. Demonstratives designate or point out some definite person, place, or thing. *This* and *these* point to objects near at hand; *that* and *those* point to what is more distant or remote.

The reflexive pronouns are sometimes referred to as compound personal pronouns, because they are formed by adding *self* to the singular and *selves* to the plural forms of the simple person pronouns. The reflexive pronoun first person singular and plural forms are *myself* and *ourselves.* The second person forms are *yourself* and *yourselves.* The third person forms are *himself, herself, itself,* and *themselves.*

Indefinite pronouns differ from the personal and relative pronouns in that they do not require definite antecedents. These include *none, everything, anything, something,* and *nothing.*

Verbs. A verb expresses action, being, or state of being. Verbs can be classified according to their meaning and according to their form. With respect to meaning, verbs can be categorized as transitive, intransitive, linking, and auxiliary. Verb forms are classified as either regular or irregular.

A transitive verb is one that always has an object. With a transitive verb, the action is conceived as going across or passing over from a subject to a direct object. The verbs in the following sentences are transitive verbs.

The little girl *carried* her doll in her arms.

The boy *hit* the ball over the fence.

My mother *baked* cookies for girl scouts.

An intransitive verb either shows no action at all or represents action as limited to the subject. The sentences below have an intransitive verb in them.

The artist *paints* very well.

The dog *ran* down the street.

My father *smokes* excessively.

One type of intransitive verb is the linking verb. The chief function of a linking verb is to join the subject of the sentence to some adjective or noun that identifies, defines or describes the subject. The verb *be* in all of its forms (am, is, are, was, were) is the most common linking verb. Other verbs are *appear, become, feel, grow, look, remain, stay, smell, taste,* and *sound*.

Auxiliary verbs assist the main verb in the formation of tense, voice, and mood. A main verb with its auxiliary verbs is called a *verb phrase*. *Shall* and *will* are auxiliary verbs used with verb forms to designate the future tense. *Do* and *did* are auxiliary verbs used to form the emphatic present and past tenses of verbs (do go, did go). *Have, has,* and *had* are auxiliary verbs used to form the present and past perfect tenses, such as *has talked, have talked,* and *had talked.*

The form of a verb can be classified as either regular or irregular. The classification of verbs as regular or irregular depends on the form of the past tense and past participle of the verb. A regular verb forms its past tense and past participle by adding *ed, d,* or *t* to the present tense of the verb (walk, walked, walked). An irregular verb is one that does not form its past tense and past participle by adding ed, d, or t to the present tense of the verb form, such as "swim," "swam," and "swum."

Adjectives.   An adjective is a word used to modify a noun by describing or defining it. Adjectives can be classified according to meaning as descriptive or definitive. A descriptive adjective names a quality, feature, or characteristic of the noun modified.

The *sweet* fruit added the right touch to dinner.

The children were amazed at the number of *tall* buildings.

A definitive adjective limits the application or scope of a noun by specifying quantity or number.

That house need painting.

I've hear that story *many* times.

Adverbs. Adverbs are closely related to adjectives. Adverbs differ from adjectives in that they modify verbs, adjectives, and other adverbs, rather than nouns. When classified by meaning, most adverbs can be categorized by time, place, manner, degree, and cause.

Adverbs of time may express present time, future time, past time, duration, and frequency. Examples of adverbs expressing present time are *now, immediately, today*; future time—*soon, tomorrow*; past time—*before, then, yesterday*; duration of time—*always, continuously, ever, never*; frequency of time—*again, daily, frequently, often, sometimes*.

Adverbs of place may denote position, motion toward, and motion from. Examples of adverbs expressing position are *above, below, here, there*, and *where*; motion toward—*forward*, and *onward*; motion from—*away, left*, and *right*.

Adverbs of manner usually accompany verbs of action and denote the way or manner in which the action expressed in the verb is performed. Manner adverbs are the most numerous in our language because they can be made from many other words by adding *-ly*.

Adverbs of degree denote measure or extent and usually modify adjectives and other adverbs. Examples of adverbs of degree are *just, little, rather*, and *almost*.

Finally, there are a few adverbs that express cause. They usually modify verbs, but sometimes they introduce clauses and entire sentences. Examples of adverbs of cause are *however, therefore, consequently*, and *why*.

Prepositions. Prepositions are words used with a noun or pronoun to form a phrase called a *prepositional phrase*. A prepositional phrase usually performs the function of an adjective or an adverb in a sentence.

Sally always walks home from *school*.

We like to buy ice cream *at the soda shop*.

The girls *in Room 222* won the contest.

Table 7-1 lists the common prepositions used in our language.

Conjunctions. A conjunction is a word used to join words, phrases, or clauses. In some instances, conjunctions are used to join sentences or paragraphs. Conjunctions are usually classified, according to their function in the sentence, as either coordinating or subordinating.

TABLE 7-1
Commonly Used Prepositions

about	at	but (except)	into	through
above	before	by	near	to
across	behind	down	of	toward
after	below	during	on	under
against	beneath	for	out	underneath
along	beside	from	outside	until
among	between	in	over	up
around	beyond	inside	past	with

A coordinating conjunction connects words, phrases, clauses, or sentences of equal rank. The following sentences all contain examples of coordinating conjunctions.

Gale *and* Sam have been in the same homeroom all through school.

Do you want to go to the mountains *or* to the ocean?

Mary washed the dishes *and* Tom dried them.

A subordinating conjunction joins clauses, one independent clause to a dependent clause. Examples of subordinating conjunctions are *if*, *unless*, *because*, *since*, *after*, *when*, *where*, and *while*.

Although Gale and Sam have been in the same homeroom all through school, they just met yesterday.

Interjections.   The final part of speech is called interjections. Interjections, when used, are put at or near the beginning of a sentence to express emotion or to emphasize the content of the sentence.

Wow! Did you see that touchdown.

Good heavens, I never thought the movie would end.

Hurrah! I won the election.

Teaching Traditional Grammar

As mentioned earlier, you will probably teach traditional grammar in your classroom if you are using a language arts basal. The exercises in the basals are very prescriptive, and students are asked to choose parts of speech for underlined words or choose the correct verb form or tense in a sentence.

A good technique for teaching traditional grammar to your class is to make a pretest of the different areas you want to stress. A pretest can help determine which areas the children do know. Some of your children will work in small groups or independently depending on the grammar areas they need. The following sample pretest might give you some idea as to the way you can teach traditional grammar.

SAMPLE PRETEST

Parts of Speech.   Identify the underlined words by their part of speech.

1 My sister goes to many *musical* performances. Her friends take care *of* the collection of tickets. *She* gives our *family* their *preference* of seats. She *and* two others *prepare* the refreshments. I think *that their* job is a *form* of entertainment.

Verb Tense.   Change the time in each statement from present to past.

1 They plant a garden.
2 She uses a shovel.
3 The boys water the soil.
4 The girls place the seeds in the soil.
5 We fence the yard in.
6 All of us wait for the plants to grow.

Adjectives.   Write a sentence of your own using each of the following nouns. Include at least two adjectives in your sentence modifying the noun. The first one is done for you.

1 building—The *tall, gray* building is being demolished.
2 friend
3 store
4 music
5 camera
6 food
7 book
8 river
9 skateboard
10 animal

After giving the pretest, you can score it based on a proficiency level for each grammar area. Some teachers have used 80 to 90 percent proficiency level for each area as their cut-off point. When you have graded the pretests, you will then have an idea of what areas of traditional grammar the whole class needs, small groups need, and individuals need. The next step is to set up some activities for the students based on their needs. If you find that all students need help in recognizing regular and irregular verbs, you can plan large group activities. If a small number of children need to work on identifying adjectives in sentences, you can set up some small group work. For individual students, a learning center may work the best. The learning center is described more fully in Chapter 15, but for our purposes now, you could make copies of exercises in all of the grammar areas and guide students to the appropriate exercises on an individual basis.

Suggested Grammar Activities

Most basal textbooks will give you prescriptive activities for teaching grammar, but below are some other ways of teaching traditional grammar that may be more enjoyable for students.

1 *Unscrambling sentences.*   Give students sentences from paragraphs in which the words are scrambled as well as the sentence order. With young children, you may want to scramble the word order

Swim the stream down fish the.

2 *Games.*   Many elementary teachers have developed games that students can play to learn the different parts of speech. Below is an example of the "Grammar Race."

Directions:
a Make a racing board similar to the one shown.

b On numbered index cards, print a sentence and underline one word.

c Students choose a card and identify the part of speech of the underlined word.

d If the answer is correct, the student moves his or her car one space.

e The student who finishes first wins.

3 *Grammar password.* This activity is based on the idea that one word is related to many others. Focusing on one part of speech, nouns for example, follow the TV game show of students' giving each other clues to guess the hidden word.

Hidden word: *trees*   Clues: leaves
                                 forests
                                 woods
                                 bark

STRUCTURAL GRAMMAR

Structural grammar is somewhat similar to traditional grammar although you will see some dissimilarities. The structural linguists of the 1950s sought to describe English as it was actually spoken without prior notions of its elements or structures. This basic goal of the structuralists, describing language, differs markedly from the traditional grammarians who wanted to prescribe what the language should be.

Structuralists tried to avoid attaching definitions to words such as nouns, verbs, adjectives, and adverbs because they thought definitions were not helpful when it comes to language. For example, if we define in traditional terms a noun as a name of a person, place, or thing, the following words would be classified as nouns: *door*, *toy*, and *window*. However, in the following sentences, these words are adjectives rather than nouns.

The *door* handle was broken.

The *toy* soldier stood on the shelf.

The *window* washer unhooked his safety straps.

In an effort not to attach traditional terms to structural grammar, the structuralists devised *form class words* which are basically nouns, verbs, adjectives, and adverbs. These form class words are described by the way they change forms, the position of the words in a sentence, and the kind of structure word that precedes the word in a sentence.

In addition to form class words, structuralists also described English in terms of sentence patterns. Roberts (1962) developed 10 sentence patterns that make up all possible simple sentences in the English language. Because the sentence patterns may be useful in a classroom they will be presented with a brief explanation.

Sentence Patterns

In describing sentence patterns, it is appropriate for us to use traditional grammar terms since most of you are familiar with them.

Pattern 1	Noun	Be	Adjective
	The soup	is	hot.

This first sentence pattern consists of a noun used as a subject, a *Be* verb and an adjective which is called a predicate adjective. You know that you have a Pattern 1 sentence if you can take the adjective (hot) and place it in front of the noun (soup). For example,

The hot soup is hot.

Pattern 2	Noun	Be	Adverb
	The bed	is	upstairs.

The second sentence pattern is similar to the first except that an adverb is used instead of an adjective. In some cases, the adverb is also called an uninflected word in that you cannot form the comparative and superlative. Other words that fit the third space are *yesterday, tomorrow, outside,* and *inside.*

Pattern 3	Noun	Be	Noun
	Bill	is	my brother.

In the third sentence pattern, the noun following the *Be* verb is called a predicate nominative. That is, it can be interchanged with the subject and not lose meaning. To test whether you have a Pattern 3 sentence, change the subject with the predicate nominative.

My brother is Bill.

Pattern 4	Noun	V(Int)
	Ducks	swim.

In the Pattern 4 sentence, there are two parts. One is a noun used as a subject, and the other is an intransitive verb that cannot have an object; nor can it be made into the passive voice.

Pattern 5	Noun	V(trans)	Noun^2
	The mare	won	the race.

Pattern 5 differs from Pattern 4 in that the verb is a transitive verb and there is a second noun. In traditional grammar terms, the second noun is the direct object. You can test for the Pattern 5 sentence by changing the sentence from the active voice to the passive voice.

The race was won by the mare.

Pattern 6	*Noun*	*V(Trans)*	*Noun³*	*Noun²*
	The man	gave	Sally	the pony.

The noun² in the Pattern 6 sentence is the direct object of the sentence, and the noun³ is the indirect object. You can test for the Pattern 6 sentence by adding the words *to* or *for* to the indirect object.

The man gave the pony to Sally.

Pattern 7	*Noun*	*V(Trans)*	*Noun²*	*Noun²*
	The class	elected	Marsha	secretary.

Pattern 8	*Noun*	*V(Trans)*	*Noun²*	*Adjective*
	The people	considered	the politician	honest.

Patterns 7 and 8 are infrequently used in the English language. The noun² and the adjective are called objective complements and say more about the direct object. The objective complement follows certain verbs such as *elected, considered, thought,* and *chose.*

Pattern 9	*Noun*	*LV*	*Adjective*
	The children	became	sleepy.

Pattern 9 sentence are similar to the Pattern 1 sentences in that a predicate adjective is used. The structuralists make a difference between the *be* verbs and the linking verbs (LV). If you forget the linking verbs, check the traditional grammar section. As with the Pattern 1 sentences, you check for the Pattern 9 sentences by taking the predicate adjective and putting it in front of the subject.

The sleepy children became sleepy.

Pattern 10	*Noun*	*LV*	*Noun*
	Bill and Kathy	remained	friends.

The final sentence pattern is similar to Pattern 3 in that the second noun is the predicate nominative, but it follows a linking verb instead of a *be* verb. The test for a

Pattern 10 sentence is the same as a Pattern 3. Switch the predicate nominative with the subject.

> Friends remained Bill and Kathy.

Structural Grammar in the Classroom

At the primary level in the elementary school, linguistic blocks can be used to develop and reinforce the 10 sentence patterns. A linguistic block has a word imprinted on each side and is colored for the different parts of speech. Barbara Graves (1972) used color-coded blocks for the U.S. Office of Education First Grade Study. She used blue for nouns, red for verbs, green for adjectives, white for noun determiners (a, an, the), yellow for conjunctions, orange for adverbs, gray for prepositions, purple for pronouns, and brown for punctuation. By beginning with a simple pattern such as Pattern 1, the teacher would lay out nouns, verbs, and adjectives. The students then begin to build sentences focusing on the *be* verbs, nouns, determiners, and adjectives. One sentence might be

> Tom is smart.

Another student can change any one of the words to make a new sentence. Examples might be

> The girl is smart.
>
> Tom is sad.
>
> Tom is happy.

After students have substituted words, give them a sentence where they substitute phrases and clauses as well as individual words. Give students a sentence with words, phrases, and clauses enclosed by brackets and let them substitute sets of words to change the meaning.

> The [big,] [black,] [dog] [ran] [down the street] [with a bone] [in its mouth.]
>
> The short, white cat walked up the stairs with a bell around its neck.
>
> The slender, gray horse galloped around the track with its rider on its back.

Another possibility for the primary grades is to use a modified "cloze procedure" in which the teacher prints a sentence on the board with a word missing. The children try to list as many possible words that fit the blank that makes sense. For example,

> We heard the _____ in the jungle.

Words that might fit are *monkeys, elephants, lions, tigers,* or *zebras.*

Connie ————————————— to school.

Words that might fit are *hopped, ran, skipped, walked,* or *hobbled.*

TRANSFORMATIONAL GRAMMAR

The transformationalists use phrase structure rules and transformations to describe their grammar. Phrase structure rules state ways in which the components of a sentence may be written. The following phrase structure rules will generate a large number of sentences.

1 Sentence ⟶ Noun phrase + Verb phrase (S → NP + VP)
This rule states that a sentence can be written (→) as a noun phrase plus a verb phrase.

2 NP ⟶ Determiner + noun
         Proper noun
         Pronoun
This rule states that a noun phrase may consist of a determiner (a, an, the), and a noun or a proper noun or a pronoun.

3 VP ⟶ (Auxiliary + Verb)

4 Auxiliary ⟶ Tense + (Modal)
This rule specifies that an auxiliary must include tense and may include a modal.

5 Tense ⟶ Present
            Past

6 Verb ⟶ V (Trans + NP)
         V (Intrans)
         V (Linking + Complement)
The final rule states that a verb may be either transitive with a noun phrase, an intransitive verb, or a linking verb with an predicate nominative or adjective.

Given these six rules, you can analyze surface structures by utilizing a tree diagram. For example, the deep structures of the following two sentences:

The girl might hit the boy. (and)

The winner is Bill.

would look like this.

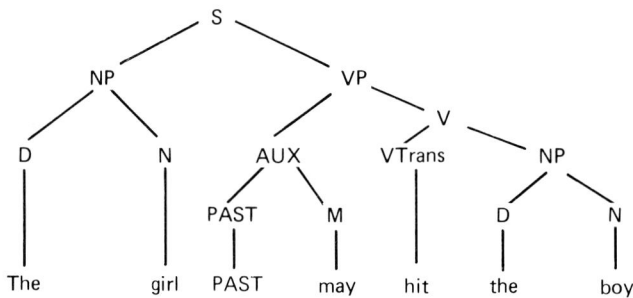

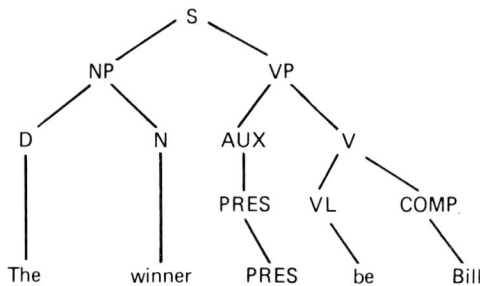

Transformations are the means by which negatives, questions, deletions, and additions appear in sentences. Some common transformations include

Negative—The boys did not go to school.

Passive—The car was driven by Bill.

Negative-Passive—The car was not driven by Bill.

Question—Did the boys go to school?

Negative-Question—Didn't the boys go to school?

Teaching Transformational Grammar

Although transformational grammar may be the way to study the language since it gets at meaning, it has been difficult for children to learn phrase structure rules and transformations. As a matter of fact, the transformationalists would not want young children to learn the rules but to understand that they are capable at a very early age to generate a large number of sentences with many transformations.

One procedure teachers can use to show students they have the ability to generate sentences is *sentence combining*. Sentence combining has been an effective tool for increasing syntactic maturity in writing (Mellon, 1969; O'Hare, 1973). Sentence combining can be cued or uncued. Cued sentence combining gives students specific direction for putting two or more sentences together. For example the following sentences

> The gentleman walked through the store.
> The gentleman stole the necktie. (who)
> The gentleman walked out the door. (and)

tell the student to add a *who* clause and a coordinating prepositional phrase by the word *and* to combine the three sentences to

The gentleman who stole the necktie walked through the store and out the door.

Other cues are crossouts, underlining, and the use of punctuation.

> The man ate the sandwich.
> The man was *old*.
> ~~The man~~ drank the soda. (,)
> ~~The man~~ then took a nap. (, and)
> The nap was *peaceful*.

Using the above cues, we would come up with the following sentence.

  The old man ate the sandwich, drank the soda, and then took a peaceful nap.

William Strong (1973) developed an uncued sentence combining technique. Strong's method is to give students a set of sentences and let them combine them anyway they wish. The rationale behind Strong's method is that students will use their intuitive language ability to generate sentences using a variety of forms such as phrases and clauses. It is not necessary to teach students terms from traditional grammar but instead to let the students create sentence naturally. Combine the sentences below.

> Two horses meet.
> They began to fight.
> They rear on their hind legs.
> Their legs are powerful.
> They circle each other in a dance.
> The dance is deadly.

You probably came up with a sentence similar to

Two horses meet and begin to fight, rearing on their powerful hind legs and circling each other in a deadly dance.

The method used to combine these sentences was the verbal, a verb ending in *ing*. It makes more sense to us to have students discover verbals by generating sentence using verbals rather than by giving students a definition of a verbal, participle for example, and have students underline the participle in a sentence.

As we stated at the beginning of this chapter, we feel that sentence combining is the best method for teaching grammar in the elementary school. Sentence combining follows the natural language development that we discussed in Chapter 3. In addition, sentence combining also follows how we view expressive language. The sentences are being generated by the student rather than being analyzed by the student. In the latter case, the student is a passive participant; in the former, the student is an active participant.

GRAMMAR AND WRITING

In the last chapter we discussed the importance of revision when your students are writing transactional papers. The importance of sentence combining becomes clearer when we look at it in relationship to the revision stage of writing. During a conference, you can point out to students which sentences could be combined to make the writing sound smoother than it does. Below is a set of sentences taken from a third grader's composition on gymnastics. This set could be rewritten using sentence combining techniques.

> *In gymnastics, we are going to have another show. I am going to do the bars. I am going to do the beam also. I am going to do the vault and I am going to do the mini-tramp. Boy are those things hard! You really have to work!*

When students revise using sentence combining, they improve the syntactic level of their writing, thus making it more enjoyable to read. The student revised the above passage as follows,

> *In gymnastics, our class is going to have another show. I am going to perform on the bars, beam, and vault. Also, I am going to do the mini-tramp. We really have to work because those things are hard!*

GRAMMAR AND READING

In Chapter 3 and Chapter 11 we discussed how certain words (because, since, in fact) signal the reader to make a connection between two or more propositions. Sentence combining exercises can be developed to focus such categories as causation or comparison to show children the importance of the signal word to comprehension at the sentence level. The following types of activities can be used.

The game ended. (Because,)

The boys went home.

The game ended.

The boys went home (because)

The directions for combining these two sentences deal with the position of the word in parentheses and whether it is capitalized and punctuated. The first set of sentence would be combined as follows

Because the game ended, the boys went home.

The second set would be combined

The game ended because the boys went home.

The position of the signal word indicates its meaning. Other sentences could be used for sentence combining based on the signal words.

GRAMMAR AND THE COMPUTER

Bradley (1982) reports using word processors with sixth graders to teach sentence combining. Chapter 15 will state other uses of the microcomputer but it seems that it should be mentioned here. Students used three different word processors to combine a series of sentences. We prefer that students use their own sentences in writing for sentence combining, if possible. When they combine their own ideas, it has more meaning for them. The microcomputer served as a motivational device for the students and when students were asked to write a composition after they combined sentences using the word processor, they did use more syntactically mature sentences in their writing.

SUGGESTED ACTIVITIES

1 Analyze at least two different language arts basals to see which of the three grammars are being used. You may find that some texts use a combination of grammars.

2 Interview a primary and intermediate language arts teacher to find out what grammar they teach, why they teach the particular grammar, and how much time they spend teaching the grammar.

3 Develop and try out a grammar game based on traditional grammar. After you have used the game, evaluate the effectiveness of it.

4 Teach sentence combining to a small group of children. Use either a cued or uncued set of sentences. When you are finished have students develop their own set of sentences for combining.

REFERENCES

Bradley, V. N. "Improving Students' Writing with Microcomputers." *Language Arts* 59, 7 (October 1982):732–743.

Gleason, H. A., Jr. *Linguistics and English Grammar*. New York: Holt, Rinehart, and Winston, 1965.

Graves, B. "A Kinesthetic Approach to Building Language Power." *Elementary English* 49 (October 1972):818–822.

Mellon, J. *Transformational Sentence Combining: A Method for Enhancing the Development of Syntactic Fluency in English Composition*. Champaign, Ill.: National Council of Teachers of English, 1969.

O'Hare, F. *Sentence Combining: Improving Student Writing Without Formal Grammatical Instruction*. Urbana, Ill.: National Council of Teachers of English, 1973.

Roberts, P. *English Sentences*. New York: Harcourt Brace Jovanovich 1962.

Strong, W. *Sentence Combining*. New York: Random House, 1973.

Weaver, C. *Grammar for Teachers*. Urbana, Ill.: National Council of Teachers of English, 1979.

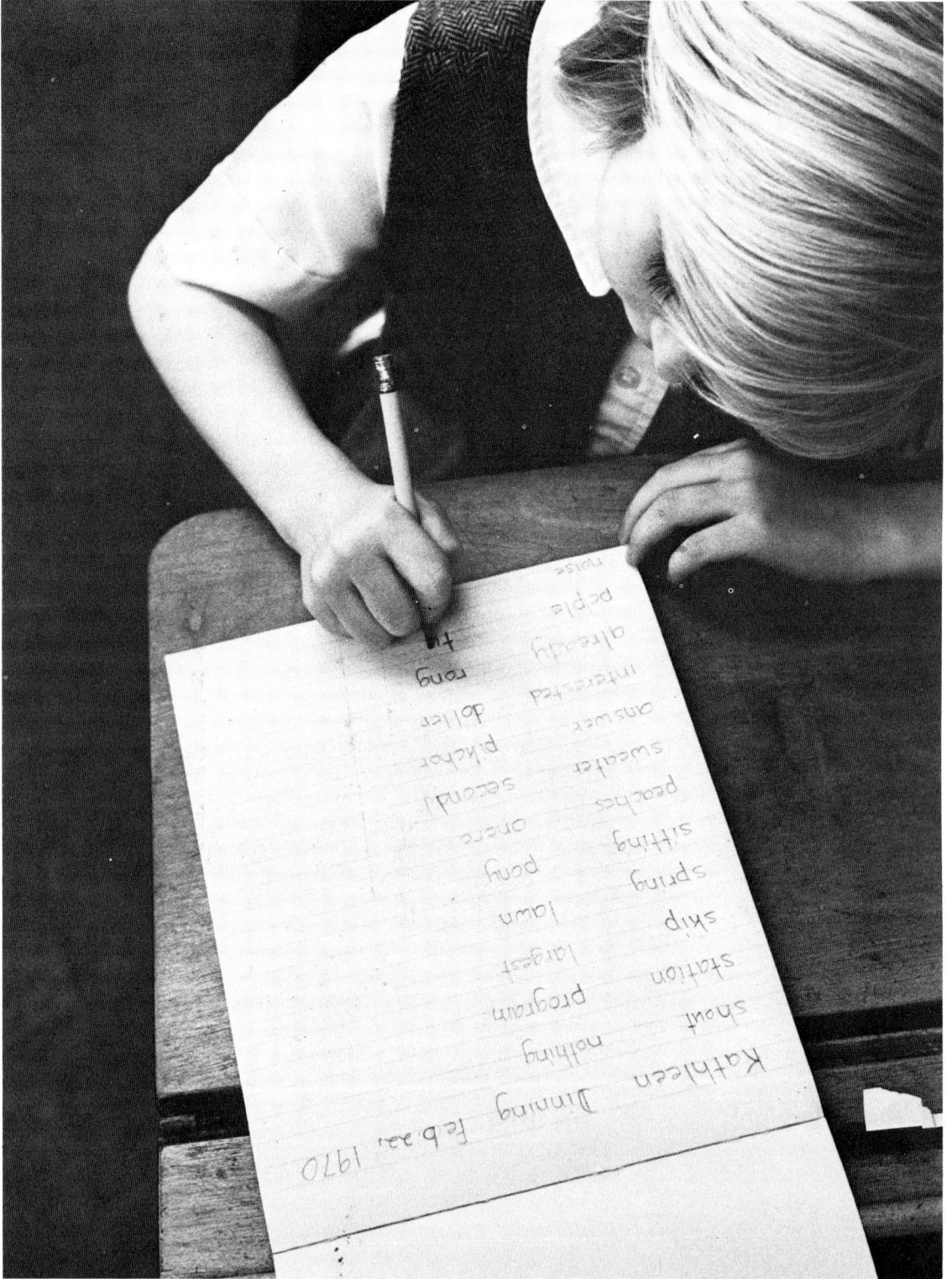

CHAPTER 8

Spelling

WHAT IS YOUR FAVORITE SUBJECT?
FOURTH GRADER
Spelling.

WHY?
FOURTH GRADER
Because I get 100s on all the tests.

WHAT IS YOUR WORST SUBJECT?
FOURTH GRADER
Writing because my teacher tells me I can't spell.

OVERVIEW

This chapter begins with a section on invented spelling. Primary teachers need to be aware that invented spelling is a natural phenomena and they should encourage children to invent spellings rather than discourage them. In addition, we discuss a spelling program at the primary level based on high frequency words and students' writing. At the intermediate level, we discuss spelling and meaning, using word families as our technique for teaching spelling.

INTRODUCTION

In probably no other area in the language arts is there such a discrepancy between what we know and what we teach than in spelling. Most elementary schools have adopted spelling series and teach and grade spelling as a separate subject from the other language arts. The spelling series dictate what words should be taught to children without any regard to what the children bring to the classroom as far as their language and background experiences, and if students will ever use the words in their writing.

In addition, the methods for teaching the spelling rules in the basals consist of going over the words on Monday followed by activities throughout the week and a test on Friday. These activities may take up anywhere from 30 to 40 minutes per day. Following the test on Friday, children seldom, if ever, use the words in their writing or, for that matter, see the words in reading.

In this chapter we will present some alternative methods of teaching spelling with emphasis on the development of spelling. For those of you whose curriculum requires teaching a formal spelling program, we will recommend one possibility for choosing words and a method that should not take you more than one hour per week. As with grammar, we recommend very little direct teaching of spelling to your students.

INVENTED SPELLING

In Chapter 6, we discussed that children come to school ready to write before they are ready to read. One way to discourage their interest in writing is to begin a formal spelling program before the second grade or to discourage their use of invented spelling when they are writing their ideas.

It is not unusual for kindergarten or first-grade teachers to be amazed or even appalled when they see "hare" for "cherry," "jragin" for "dragon," "chruk" for "truck," or "bad" or "bed." These invented spellings, according to Read (1975), show that children seem to pay special attention to the sounds of words. They are, in a way, more proficient in sounding out words than we are.

Think about the first letter in the word "hare." What is the sound the letter "h" makes? It makes the sound that begins the word "cherry" (āch).

For the next two words "dragon" and "truck" and their invented spellings "jragin" "chruk," Read also makes a case for the phonetic basis of the invented words. Before the second letter (r) in English, "d" and "t" are affricated—that is, they are released slowly with a resulting "shh" sound. The affrication is then generalized by the students to other words which begin with a "j" or "ch" rather than a "d" or "t." In addition, these children do not have any trouble with "d" or "t" beginning consonants when they are not followed by "r," ("toy" or "dog").

Although some of you may feel that the fourth example is one of carelessness, Read again gives a phonetic rationalization. Children have a difficult time with short vowels or lax vowels since they are not directly related to their sounds as the tense vowels are. As a result, children use a letter-name strategy and try to represent the lax vowel by the closest tense vowel. The closest vowel letter to the sound of the vowel in "bed" is "a," resulting in the misspelling "bad." Later on, what occurs is that students learn about the short vowels and they generalize the rule and misspell the long "a" sound in "came" with a short "e" (ceme).

These invented spellings correspond to the sophisticated phonological developments of language that we discussed in Chapter 3. Gentry (1981) using Read's research as well as his own delineates five major stages in the development of young children. These five stages presented by Wood (1982) (Figure 8-1) describe the developmental levels that children follow generally through the end of the first grade or the beginning of the second grade. Once you are aware of these stages, you can encourage children to invent words rather than to tell them that "ch" spells "chuh" in "chicken" when the child spells "truck" with a "ch." The child already knows that "ch" is the beginning of the word "chicken."

Invented Spelling in the Classroom

Our position is that invented spelling should be encouraged in the early primary grades. Both Clay (1975) and Giacobbe (1981) let their children write frequently, not worrying about or correcting the spelling but letting them write to convey meaning to themselves, their peers, or teacher. As the children move toward transactional writing that we discussed in Chapter 6, they can then work on revising their writing and the spelling can be corrected. However, we encourage invented spelling and writing so children will learn the importance of expressing their ideas to others.

FORMAL SPELLING AT THE PRIMARY LEVEL

Beginning at second grade, some schools insist that students be in a formal spelling program. If that is the case, you will have to decide where you will get the words for the program. We believe that you can gather words from two sources, children's writing and a list of high frequency words.

Stage	Characteristics	Examples	Implicit Under-standings Shown
Deviant	Random ordering of letters and other symbols known by child, sometimes interspersed with "letter-like" marks.	b + B p A = monster ≠ PAHIε = giant	Speech can be recorded by means of graphic symbols.
Pre-Phonetic	One, two and three-letter representations of discreet words. Letters used represent some speech sounds heard in word.	M S R = monster P = pie D G = dog	Speech is comprised of discreet words. Recorded speech consists of written words. Specific letters stand for specific speech sounds.
Phonetic	Spellings include all sound features of words, as child hears and articulates them.	P P L = people ChroBL = trouble	Every sound feature of a word is represented by a letter or combination of letters. The written form of a word contains every speech sound, recorded in the same sequence in which sounds are articulated when the word is spoken.
Transitional	Vowels are included in every recorded syllable; familiar spelling patterns are used, standard spelling is interspersed with "incorrect" phonetic spelling.	highcked = hiked tode = toad come = come	It is necessary to spell words in such a way that they may be read easily by oneself and others. There are various ways to spell many of the same speech sounds. Every word has a conventional spelling that is used in printed materials. Many words are not spelled entirely phonetically.

FIGURE 8.1 *Gentry's four stages preceding standard spelling.*

Children's Writing

Hagerty (1981) found that the majority of words third graders and fifth graders misspelled in writing were high frequency words that had little phoneme-grapheme representation, like "sed" for "said" and "becuz" for "because." Using the words that students misspell in writing, you can have students develop a student dictionary based on each individual's misspelled words. The students need only to list the letters of the alphabet on top of every page in their notebook. After you have evaluated student writing through one of the methods discussed in the last chapter, each student prints the correct spelling of the misspelled word in their notebook (Figure 8-2).

cafeteria	
calendar	**C**
camel	
candidate	
canyon	
carnival	
cashier	
chief	
cocoon	
color	
committee	
commence	
conceive	
congratulate	
continuous	
crowd	

FIGURE 8.2 *Sample from a student's personal dictionary.*

High Frequency Word Lists

Rather than purchasing a spelling series, you can use high frequency lists to gather words for spelling activities. Of all of the lists available, we recommend Greene's *The New Iowa Spelling Scale* (1977) which provides an extensive and carefully screened list of high frequency words found in the written communication of children and adults. In addition, the spelling scale provides teachers with reliable information on the average or typical difficulty of each of these words in each elementary school grade. The 5507 high frequency words that comprise the scale have percentages for the number of students in grade levels two through eight who correctly spelled the words (see Table 8-2).

Using the example from the table, you can see how the scale works. Let's take the word *basement*. Only 6 percent of the third graders could spell the word while 91 percent of the eighth graders spelled the word correctly. With the scale, you can devise spelling lists for your students based on ability groups. One way to accomplish an ability group spelling list is to choose words that have a high percentage (75 to 100 percent) for the low ability students; an average percentage (45 to 74 percent) for the middle ability students; and a low percentage (1 to 44 percent) for the high ability students. Using these percentages with the table, you would have the following words for fourth graders.

Low Ability Group

ball	bat	became
balls	bats	become
band	bay	bed
bank	bear	bee

Middle Ability Group

bands	bark	base	bathing	bean	beat	beds
banker	barks	baseball	bats	beans	because	bedtime
banking	barn	basket	beach	bears	becomes	
banks	bars	bath	beam	beast	bedroom	

High Ability Group

balances	banner	barrel	basis	battle	beaten	beef
balloon	banquet	barrels	basketball	battles	beating	
banana	bare	based	baskets	beads	beautiful	
bananas	barely	basement	bathe	beard	beautifully	
bankruptcy	bargain	bases	battery	bearing	beauty	

Many teachers assume that spelling series use high frequency words, and these words are placed at their proper grade levels. Horn (1969) believed that four major factors should be involved when considering the grade placement of words: (1) frequency of occurrence in children's writing, (2) permanence of value as measured

TABLE 8-2
The New Iowa Spelling Scale

Grade	2	3	4	5	6	7	8	Grade	2	3	4	5	6	7	8
balances		2	5	18	34	52	72	bathe		2	11	20	35	54	57	67
ball	62	69	86	93	94	98	99	bathing		3	21	47	69	79	89	91
balloon	3	14	16	24	28	43	52	bats	30	56	71	77	89	94	95
balls	50	64	81	82	89	94	95	battery		8	11	26	51	73	83
banana	1	15	27	49	59	75	76	battle		2	11	37	70	86	91	95
bananas	1	8	28	29	52	54	64	battles		2	8	31	64	70	87	87
band	33	49	77	81	91	94	97	bay	23	49	79	86	92	96	99
bands	18	38	54	71	81	88	93	be	61	77	90	95	97	99	99
bank	12	58	85	91	97	97	98	beach	3	25	58	81	84	91	93
banker	7	36	66	84	91	95	97	beads		17	34	52	60	66	77
banking	7	32	63	80	89	93	96	beam		3	10	46	65	72	81	87
bankruptcy		2	3	3	9	17	19	bean		4	29	65	80	86	93	95
banks	6	36	60	76	89	95	95	beans		3	18	50	79	84	89	94
banner	5	10	32	48	72	76	87	bear	14	41	75	88	93	94	94
banquet	1	2	6	14	34	56	69	beard	1	21	34	56	72	78	87
bare	2	10	26	49	69	74	83	bearing		2	15	23	30	35	40	46
barely		2	19	29	40	53	62	bears	8	32	66	70	78	93	94
bargain	1	2	9	21	35	50	50	beast		13	50	76	85	90	92
bark	4	39	66	81	84	90	95	beat		8	33	52	81	83	92	92
barks		23	55	62	79	79	92	beaten		3	7	27	46	59	72	81
barn	16	51	66	79	88	94	96	beating		2	16	44	66	75	83	89
barrel		4	13	40	53	69	70	beautiful		2	18	36	44	67	72
barrels		3	14	26	54	63	71	beautifully		2	6	12	27	37	58
bars	4	27	53	77	87	92	93	beauty		5	16	50	62	71	78
base	6	28	50	79	88	95	96	became	11	50	80	90	95	97	98
baseball	1	17	48	82	87	91	97	because	1	14	50	80	90	93	96
based		10	30	47	62	65	81	become	35	68	78	91	94	96	98
basement	1	6	26	60	78	86	91	becomes	23	47	73	77	84	88	95
bases	1	14	37	60	77	84	87	becoming	4	24	54	65	76	79	86
basis	3	5	8	11	28	29	54	bed	52	79	85	92	96	98	99
basket	4	25	49	69	79	91	93	bedroom	19	54	71	88	93	98	98
basketball	8	16	39	65	77	84	87	beds	22	65	66	80	91	93	94
baskets	1	27	40	61	75	81	91	bedtime	10	39	74	85	87	92	93
bat	34	69	77	91	93	95	97	bee	34	58	90	90	94	98	99
bath	5	47	69	85	90	96	97	beef	8	20	41	70	82	87	94

Source: The New Iowa Spelling Scale by Harry A. Greene. Revised by Bradley M. Loomer. Division of Continuing Education, The University of Iowa, Iowa City, Iowa.

by the writing of adults, (3) difficulty of the word, and (4) the extent to which words should be placed by combinations of the above three factors or should be grouped according to some problem. Studies by Ames (1965), Hillerich (1965), and Hinrichs (1975) reported that there was no consistency among spelling series as to the words used and the grade placement of words. After listing a total of 6043 different words found in seven spelling series, Ames found that only 120 words were at the same grade placement in all series. Hillerich looked at 16 series and found agreement on grade placement for only 40 words. Hinrichs concluded that the words used for a particular grade level conformed to a particular generalization that was being emphasized.

In a recent study, Hagerty (1981) compared spelling words of eleven commercial spelling programs to a standard measure of word frequency to determine whether the spelling words at grade levels 2 through 6 were high frequency words when compared to a standard measure of word frequency. Her results showed that no one series was best across grade levels as far as having the highest number of high frequency words at each grade level. Rather, all series showed variations in their number of high frequency words found at each grade level.

Using *The New Iowa Spelling Scale*, you can see how difficult some of the words are in a spelling series. Below is a list of spelling words found in one lesson of a third-grade spelling series. Next to each word is the percentage of third graders who spelled the word correctly for the Iowa scale.

coin (15%)	point (16%)
oil (30%)	enjoy (10%)
voice (6%)	toys (78%)
join (11%)	joy (53%)
noise (10%)	royal (11%)
poison (2%)	onions (2%)
boil (13%)	radio (15%)

From our cut-off points for ability groups, only one word would be appropriate for the average group (joy) and one word (toys) for the low ability group. Although there is some indication that spelling series now being published use high frequency words, you should be careful when teaching from a spelling text to make sure the words are high frequency. Since spelling series provide teachers with exercises for word lists, it sometimes is tempting to spend quite a bit of time each day teaching spelling from a text; however, a lesser amount of time with high frequency words would be more beneficial to the student.

METHODS OF INSTRUCTION

The methods teachers use to teach spelling from a basal have been researched quite extensively. For purposes of discussion, it seems appropriate to look at the corrected-test and test-study-test methods and the use of spelling rules if you are using a spelling text. Following this section, you will be given a one-week lesson plan utilizing one of the above methods.

Corrected-Test Method

The corrected-test method has been studied since the 1940s. Basically, under this method, the students correct their own spelling test under the direction of the teacher. The research done by Horn (1947), Tyson (1953) and Christine and Hollingsworth (1966)—just to name a few—has supported this method. An added variable of a multisensory approach to the correct-test method (Kuhn and Schroeder, 1971) showed to be very positive. Most teachers of spelling use an auditory approach but Kuhn and Schroeder added a visual approach in their study. Students in their experimental group corrected their own spelling tests by listening to the correct spelling of the word and seeing the correct spelling. There was a significant increase in the number of words spelled correctly by students using the oral-visual test correction procedure. From this study it seems apparent that the self-correction method would be best accomplished by the teacher pronouncing the word, spelling it orally letter by letter, and then writing the word on the chalkboard. If a child misspells a word, he or she draws a line through it and rewrites it.

Test-Study-Test Technique

Closely tied to the corrected-test method is the test-study-test technique, also called the test-study technique. Using this method, students are given a pretest before they have seen the list of words. Immediate correction by students follows the pretest so they can discover what words they need to study for the final test. This method directly contrasts the more conventional study-test-study or study-test method in which words presented on Monday are studied in preparation for a trial test on Wednesday. Students then study the word again for the final test on Friday.

Fitzgerald (1951) advocated the use of the test-study-test approach because he thought it helped to individualize a spelling program in that students only studied the words they misspelled on a pretest. If used with the corrected-test method, the test-study-test approach enabled students to pinpoint and subsequently study their own spelling errors. Follow-up studies by Hinrichs (1975) and Hillerich (1977) both supported the test-study-test technique, stating that it was important for children to locate and correct their own spelling errors.

More recently, Blumberg and Block (1975) conducted a study in which students attempted to spell words by one of three methods: viewing the word before attempting to spell it (study-test-study method); attempting to spell the word one time prior to viewing the correct spelling (test-study-test method); or attempting to spell the word several times prior to viewing the correct spelling. Results showed that students using the second and third methods learned to spell the words more quickly than did students using the first method.

What is the best method for studying a word? The following procedure, first introduced by Ernest Horn in 1919, is still widely accepted and implemented.

1 Students pronounce the word while looking at it.

2 Students close their eyes and try to visualize the word and spell it orally.

3 Students check to see if their oral spelling of the word is correct.

4 Students cover the word and write it.

5 Students check their spelling of the word against the model. If they have spelled the word incorrectly, they begin at Step 1 again.

Spelling Rules

The teaching of rules and the use of phonics in spelling has been a controversial issue for more than 50 years (Fitzsimmons & Loomer, 1978). Behind this issue is the theory that, by learning certain rules or principles, children will be able to correctly spell words they have not studied specifically for spelling (Hillerich, 1977). However, many studies generally agree that only a few rules should be taught, and that those taught should have few or no exceptions.

In an attempt to investigate the applicability of phonic generalizations to spelling programs, Davis (1972) analyzed six spelling programs to determine how applicable Clymer's 45 phonics generalizations were to the words found in those series. She found a loss of efficiency in spelling by the application of phonic generalizations to multisyllablic words, short and long vowels, vowel diagraphs, and vowel sounds affected by 1, w, u, and r. She concluded that, as a whole, phonics generalizations were only moderately useful in teaching spelling. Her conclusion was based on the results of some of the following rules.

Generalization	*Percentage of Applicability*
In the phonogram *ie*, the *i* is silent and the *e* has a long sound (hygiene).	14%
When *a* follows *w* in a word, it usually has the sound *a* as in *was* (want).	22%
When *y* is used as a vowel in words, it sometimes has the sound of long *i* (cycle).	10%
When there are two vowels side by side, the long sound of the first one is heard and the second is usually silent (yeast).	32%

Results showed that the word-list group scored higher at all grade levels on both studied and unstudied words.

From the above studies as well as studies done by Bredin (1972) and Yee (1969) which showed that there were no differences between children's spelling scores when they were taught word lists or phonic generalizations, teachers should rely on those rules that are consistent rather than following inconsistent rules. The following list identifies the few spelling rules that apply to a large number of words with only occasional exceptions.

1 When one syllable words end in a consonant preceded by a single vowel, the consonant is doubled before adding a suffix beginning with a vowel.

hit-hitting
ship-shipping
ship-shipment

2 For words ending in silent *e* (CVCe), drop the *e* before adding a suffix beginning with a vowel and keep the *e* when the suffix begins with a consonant.

bake-baking
manage-managing
manage-management

3 The letter *q* is always followed by a *u*.

quit

4 For a word ending in a consonant and *y*, change the *y* to *i* before adding *es* or *ed*.

fry-fries
fry-fried

5 For words ending in a vowel and *y* add *s* to make a plural word.

valley-valleys
monkey-monkeys

6 English words do not end in *v*.

love
have

As a final note to the study of spelling using sound/symbol relationship rather than word lists or spelling and meaning, it might be appropriate for you to read the following poem published in the *London Sunday Times*, January 3, 1965, from J. Bland.

Hints on Pronunciation for Foreigners

I take it you already know
Of tough and bough and cough and dough?
Others may stumble but not you,
on hiccough, thorough, laugh and through.
Well done! And now you wish, perhaps,
To learn of less familiar traps?

Beware of heard, a dreadful word
That looks like beard and sounds like bird,
And dead: it's said like bed, not bead—

For goodness' sake don't call it "deed"!
Watch out for the meat and great and threat
(They rhyme with suite and straight and debt.)

A moth is not a moth in mother
Nor both in bother, broth in brother,
And here is not a match for there
Nor dear and fear for bear and pear,
And then there's dose and rose and lose—
Just look them up—and goose and choose,
And cork and work and card and ward,
And font and front and word and sword,
And do and go and thwart and cart—
Come, come, I've hardly made a start!
A dreadful language? Man alive.
I mastered it when I was five.

T.S.W.
(only initials of writer known)

Planning the Spelling Lesson

Now, that you know where to find the words for spelling and methods to use for teaching the words, let's go through a one week plan for teaching spelling. Most elementary teachers spend too much time teaching spelling. It is not necessary to devote 20 minutes or more a day to teaching spelling. Horn (1976) believed that the time allotment question was relatively meaningless unless other factors, such as methods of instruction, grade placement of words, and student abilities were taken into account. If the test-study-test method was used, he believed that the time allowed for direct teaching of spelling in excess of 60 minutes a week could be spent more productively in other curriculum areas. The following plan shows how you can spend only approximately 12 minutes a day on direct teaching of spelling.

Day 1. Using high frequency words based on Greene's *The New Iowa Spelling Scale*, you can administer the pretest to the three ability groups. The sample test table (Figure 8-3) can be used to read off words to the groups. Let Group 1 know that they will have to spell the first word in the set; Group 2, the second word; and Group 3 the third word. Say "Word 1" and read across the three words (*everyone, mice,* and *repaired*). Then go to word 2 up through word 25.

Presenting words for study in columns or lists is advantageous because students can focus on each word individually. Presenting words in context seems to detract attention from the spelling of words and focuses on the meaning of words. Remember that this is not a vocabulary exercise but a spelling exercise.

After you have read the words to the students, they should correct their own pretest. You can provide students with the correct spelling of the words in a handout. Also, you could read each word and spell it correctly while the students see

Week No. _____

Group 1	Group 2	Group 3
1. everyone	mice	repaired
2. made	mailing	margin
3. put	prove	proclaim
4. dime	desk	deposits
5. seen	setting	several
6. being	besides	bishop
7. corn	cooked	convention
8. milk	mile	million
9. seed	selling	select
10. after	already	alley
11. income	indeed	infant
12. just	kindly	kitchen
13. meat	meeting	memory
14. news	nobody	northern
15. three	ticket	thousand
16. book	boil	bonus
17. room	root	ruin
18. snow	snake	snowy
19. keep	kitchen	knit
20. city	climb	claim
21. face	fame	factory
22. goods	golden	govern
23. low	longest	lodge
24. open	outlined	ornament
25. green	grandfather	grateful

FIGURE 8.3 *Sample test table for fourth graders.*

the correct words and correct their errors by writing the correct spelling next to the misspelled word. For example,

memmory memory
kindley kindly
fase face

When students have finished grading their pretests, they should turn in their papers to you so you can record their results.

Day 2. Students are given their spelling words and instructed to study the words that they missed the previous day. They can follow the procedure discussed earlier in this chapter. You might want to give them a chart with the following categories:

1 List the words to study.
2 Look at the word and say the word.
3 Spell the word orally while looking at each letter.
4 Close your eyes, visualize the word, and spell it orally.
5 Cover the model and write the word.
6 Check the spelling of the word.
7 Write the word correctly one more time.

Days 3 and 4. These two days should be devoted to practicing the words by groups. Students' activities should only take about 12 minutes. Students should practice all of the words in case they correctly guessed a word on the pretest. The following are some suggested activities. Keep in mind that your purpose is to get students to spell the words correctly.

1 Have students write each word in a sentence. Be sure they number each sentence and underline the word.
2 Scramble the letters in each word. Ask students to unscramble the letters to find the spelling words. To make it harder, add extra letters.
3 Have the students write the words in alphabetical order.
4 Have students write a story using the spelling words.
5 Make a criss-cross puzzle or word search puzzle using the spelling words.
6 Have students write a letter to someone using as many spelling words as possible.
7 Have students write the spelling words in salt.
8 Have students write the words one at a time on each other's backs. See if students can guess what each word is.
9 Write each spelling word with some letters missing. Have the students try to fill in the missing letters.
10 Draw configuration boxes to match the words. Students fill in the boxes with the spelling words. For example,

education

geography

11 You write a story using the spelling words. Have students read the story and circle the spelling words.

12 Have students compose jingles using each spelling word in a separate rhyme.

13 Have each child select four or five words from the spelling list and write a commercial or an advertisement.

14 Write a paragraph omitting the spelling words. Have students fill in the words.

15 Have each child make a spelling dictionary.

16 Have students write a poem using the spelling words.

17 Have students write a song using the spelling words.

Day 5. Give the students the posttest. If you wish, you can grade the posttest yourself or you can have the students grade their own. Scores are recorded under the pretest scores.

It should be noted that we have taught a week's spelling lesson using this format. The students spent 60 minutes on spelling for the week, and their posttest scores increased dramatically. One teacher who used to spend 25 minutes a day on spelling now spends half that time on spelling and devotes the rest of the time to composition.

FORMAL SPELLING IN THE INTERMEDIATE LEVEL

The high frequency words will be important at the primary level and to some extent at the intermediate level. We recommend that you continue to use misspelled words in writing for students at the intermediate level. The spelling dictionary would work quite well for intermediate students. You may want to try teaching spelling using word families (Chomsky, 1970). Chomsky's technique focuses on spelling and meaning.

Spelling and Meaning

The basis behind spelling and meaning is you want to help students see that the written form corresponds to an abstract or lexical (meaning) form, not directly to what they hear. Chomsky and Halle (1968) maintain that the conventional spelling of words corresponds more closely to an underlying abstract level of representation within the sound system of the language, than it does to the surface phonetic form that the words assume in spoken language. Chomsky (1970) sees conventional orthography in its essentials as a "near optimal system for representing the spoken language."

Carol Chomsky (1970) presents a rationale for English spelling to correspond with abstract, meaning forms rather than phonetic realizations. The lexical spelling could be based on how the word sounds but if we were to do this, we would be placing meaning at a lower priority. Our point of view from the beginning of this text is that meaning is paramount in whatever form of the language arts we use. For example, when we add a suffix to a noun forming an adjective such as "nation-national" or "nature-natural," a vowel alteration occurs and we pronounce the adjective differently from the noun. It would be possible to change the spelling of the adjective to correspond to its sound, but in reality, the two words are not different in the sense of "nation-notion." They are variant forms of the same word with a very similar meaning. The phonological component, how we say the word, contains rules that operate on the lexical spelling of the word keeping the meanings of words tied closely together. Other pairs of words which keep similar appearances for meaning sake but are said differently because of phonetic variation are:

> photograph-photography
> revise-revision
> medicate-medicine
> courage-courageous

At a practical level, you can teach spelling inductively by searching with the children for a systematic reason why the word should be spelled the way it is, if a reason can be found. If children spell "really" as "relly" they need to think of the word "reality" to understand the correct spelling of "really." You must help children to go back to their schemas to find words they can use to spell correctly the misspelled word. After working inductively with children, they will get into the habit of bringing to mind related words when trying to spell a troublesome word. For example, when a child tries to spell the word "industrial" and cannot figure out if the second vowel is an *i* or an *e* or a *u*, the child thinks of an associated word like "industry" and the problem is solved.

Deductively, you can set up word families for students with letters missing and ask students to fill in the missing letter by thinking of some similar words. For example,

> criti_ize (c or s)
> medi_ine (c or s)
> na_ion (t or sh)
> gra_ual (d or s)
> righ_eous (t or ch)
> ra_ial (t, c, or sh)

Students might think of the following words: "critical," "medical," "national," "grade," "right," and "race" to fill in the correct letter. The reason we recommend this technique for intermediate students is that primary children may not use the words that fit word families since they are not high frequency words. Naturally, if you have primary students misspelling words that can be associated with word families, then by all means use the spelling and meaning techniques.

SUGGESTED ACTIVITIES

1 Collect samples of student writing from children in kindergarten and first grade. Categorize their invented spelling according to Gentry's developmental levels.

2 With a small group of children, use the test-study-test method with a list of words from *The New Iowa Spelling Scale* or another series. Compare pretest and posttest results.

3 Compare a list of misspelled words found in student writing at the intermediate level to a list of high frequency words. Are students misspelling high or low frequency words?

REFERENCES

Ames, W. "A Comparison of Spelling Textbooks." *Elementary English* 42 (May 1965): 146–150.

Blumberg, P., and Block K. *The Effects of Attempting Spelling before Feedback on Spelling Acquisition and Retention.* Paper presented at the Annual Meeting of the American Educational Research Association, Washington, D.C., March 30–April 2, 1975. (ERIC Document Reproductive Service no. ED 103 885).

Bredin D. M. *Evaluation of Third-Grade Spelling.* Bulletin, School District No. 69, Skokie, Ill., June 2, 1972.

Chomsky, C. "Reading, Writing and Phonology." *Harvard Educational Review* 40 (May 1970):287–309.

Chomsky, N., and Halle, M. *The Sound Pattern of English.* New York: Harper and Row, 1968.

Chomsky, N. "Phonology and Reading." In H. Levin and J. Williams (eds.) *Basic Studies in Reading.* New York: Harper and Row, 1970.

Christine, R. O., and Hollingsworth, P. M. "An Experiment in Spelling." *Education* 86 (May 1966):575–567.

Clay, M. M. *What Did I Write?* London: Heinemann Books, 1975.

Davis, L. "The Applicability of Phonic Generalizations to Selected Spelling Programs." *Elementary English* 49 (May 1972):706–713.

Fitzgerald, J. A. *The Teaching of Spelling.* Milwaukee, Wis.: Bruce Publishing Co., 1951.

Fitzsimmons, R. J., and Loomer, B. *Spelling: Learning and Instruction.* Iowa City: University of Iowa, 1978.

Gentry, J. R. "Learning to Spell Developmentally." *Reading Teacher* 43 (January 1981): 378–381.

Giacobbe, M. E. "Kids Can Write the First Week of School." *Learning* 9 (September 1981):130–132.

Greene, H. A. *The New Iowa Spelling Scale.* (Revised by Bradley M. Loomer.) Iowa City: State University of Iowa, 1977.

Hagerty, P. *Comparative Analysis of Selected High Frequency Words Found in Commercial Spelling Series and Misspelled in Students' Writing to a Standard Measure of Word Frequency.* Unpublished thesis. Boulder: University of Colorado, 1981.

Hillerich, R. *Comparison of Word Lists in Sixteen Commercial Spelling Programs.* Unpublished study. Glenview, Ill., 1965.

———. "Let's Teach Spelling—Not Phonetic Misspelling." *Language Arts* 54 (March 1977):301–307.

Hinrichs, R. "An Old But Valid Procedure." *Elementary English* 52 (February 1975): 249–252.

Horn, E. *Principles of Method in Teaching Spelling as Derived from Scientific Investigation.* National Society for the Study of Education, 18th Yearbook, Part 11. Bloomington: Public School Publishing Co., 1919.

Horn, T. D. "Spelling." *Encyclopedia of Educational Research*, 4th ed. New York: Macmillan Co., 1969.

———."Test, Then Study in Spelling." *Instructor* 86 (December 1976):81.

———. "The Effect of the Corrected Test on Learning to Spell." *Elementary School Journal* 47 (1947):277–285.

Kuhn, J., and Schroeder H. A. "A Multi-sensory Approach for Teaching Spelling." *Elementary English* 48 (November 1971):865–869.

Read, C. *Children's Categorization of Speech Sounds in English.* Urbana, Ill.: National Council of Teachers in English, 1975.

Tyson, I. *Factors Contributing to the Effectiveness of the Corrected Test in Spelling.* Unpublished doctoral dissertation, University of Iowa, 1953.

Wood, M. "Invented Spelling." *Language Arts*, 59 (October 1982):707–717.

Yee, A. "Is the Phonetic Generalization Hypothesis in Spelling Valid?" *Journal of Experimental Education* 37 (Summer 1969):82–91.

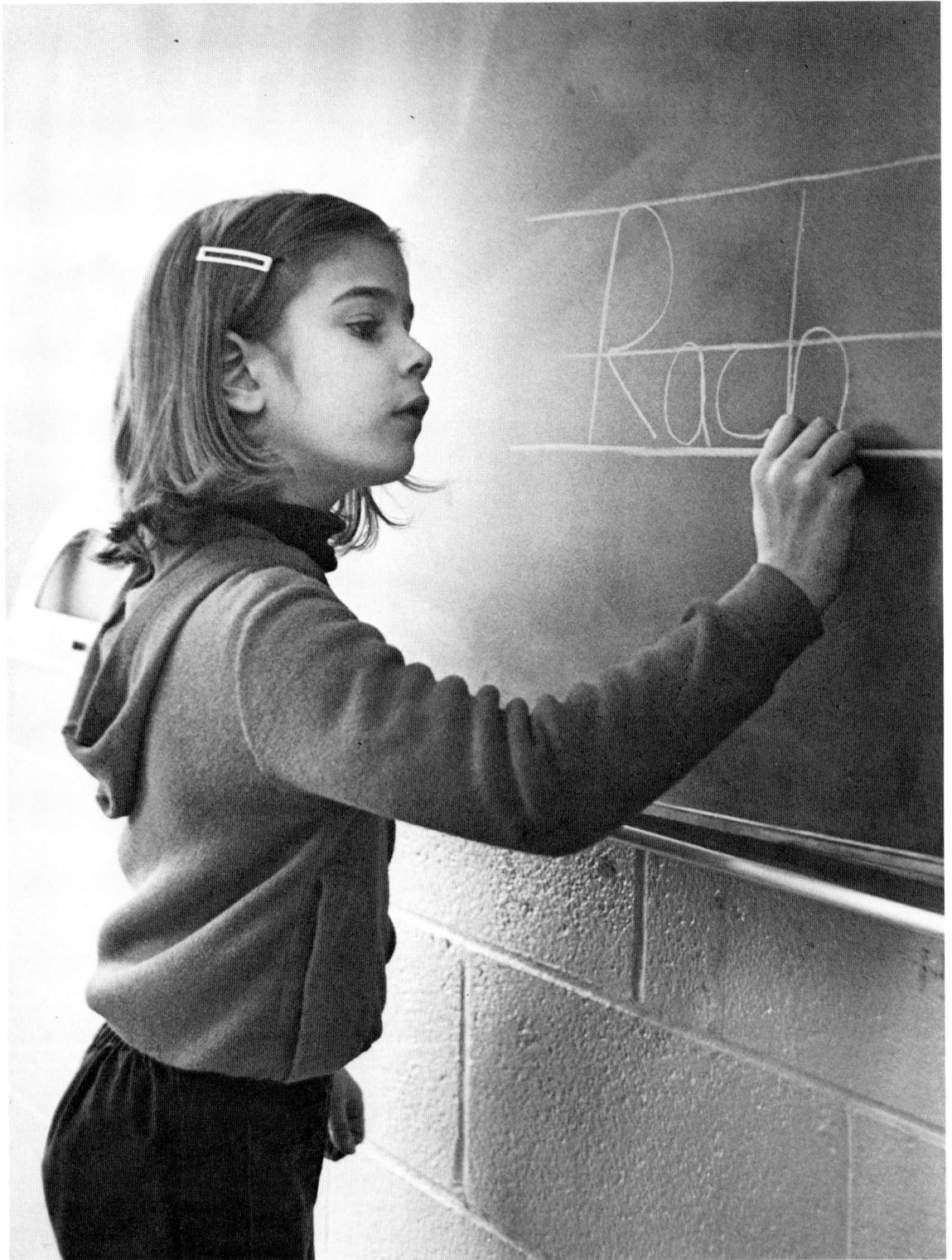

CHAPTER 9

Handwriting

WHY IS HANDWRITING IMPORTANT?

SECOND GRADERS

. . . cause then when you start cursive it will be easy.

SIXTH GRADERS

. . . so you can get good grades.

. . . if there wasn't any handwriting you wouldn't know about exploring because we wouldn't have any books to read because they had diaries in those days.

. . . my main problem in writing is that I can't even read it myself!

OVERVIEW

Handwriting is an important functional skill taught in a language arts program, a skill that is necessary for effective writing and communication. This chapter will focus on the important components of a good handwriting program. Basic goals of a program will be discussed, along with predictors of readiness for handwriting. Techniques for teaching both manuscript and cursive will be presented, based on guidelines gleaned from research on handwriting. Teaching handwriting to left-handed children will be considered next because these children require more individualized attention and direction in learning to write. Scales and checklists for the evaluation of handwriting will be presented. Lastly, the chapter will conclude with activities and ideas for maintaining interest in handwriting at the upper as well as lower grades.

INTRODUCTION

In Chapter 1, we noted that a major goal of language arts instruction was the development of writing skills. Handwriting is one of the mechanical aspects of writing. But, who is interested in the subject of handwriting? The subject certainly has not been a major topic of research over the last 50 years. Little instructional time is afforded the subject in teacher education programs. Teachers generally do not place much instructional emphasis on it and do not feel prepared to teach it. Yet the general public often is outraged by adults' inability to write clearly. Consider, for example, the sprawling, indecipherable script of doctors, or the illegible script sent through the post office daily.

Clearly, parents and educators are interested in having children learn to write legibly, and thus it is one goal of language arts instruction. Any adult who has difficulty writing, due to inadequate fine motor coordination or slow speed, appreciates the importance of good handwriting. Handwriting is a necessary component of the language arts program because it is the medium through which children first learn to express their ideas on paper. Further, even in a society dominated by typewriters and computers, handwriting remains the most convenient means of communicating on paper for the vast majority of the population.

We debated whether to include a whole chapter on handwriting or whether to include handwriting as part of the writing process. While the physical act of handwriting certainly enters into the writing process, we felt that the writing chapters should primarily focus on the thought processes only. Additionally, we felt that handwriting was a recognized component of an elementary language arts program and therefore deserved attention as a separate chapter.

We treat the skills of handwriting and spelling in a similar manner. Both are mechanical aspects of the writing process, and are necessary components of effective writing. Both are treated as functional subskills of writing. Effective writing is difficult without such skills, although effective writing goes far beyond correct spelling and legible handwriting.

BASIC PRINCIPLES OF HANDWRITING

The goals of today's handwriting program differ from those of 20 or 30 years ago. Attention to perfection and exact copying of a standard form are all but forgotten. More attention is given now to individual variation and style, with the basic goals being twofold.

- That we write *legibly*—that is, so others can read our writing.
- That we write with sufficient *speed* so we can get our thoughts down on paper.

These two goals need to be the focus of a handwriting program in the elementary grades. First, our handwriting needs to be legible enough for others to read. It does not have to be perfect. Letters do not need to be formed identically in every detail to some arbitrary standard. Clearly, letters need to be formed to approximate a standard, but individual variability is expected and accepted.

What makes legible handwriting? The following are generally accepted guidelines (Barbe, 1977).

1 *Slant.*   Consistency in slant, either diagonal right, or left, or straight.

2 *Spacing.*   Consistency in spacing.

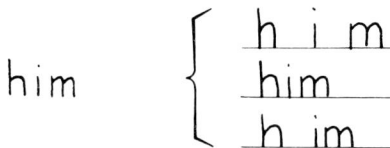

3 *Size and proportion.*   Again consistency in size—too large letters are cumbersome and take up too much space, too small letters are hard to read.

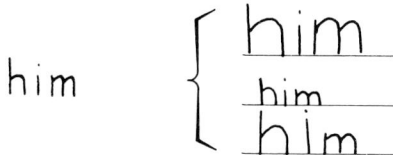

4 *Alignment.*   Again, consistency in the position of letters.

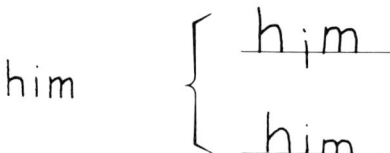

These characteristics, slant, spacing, size, proportion, and alignment, are the sub-goals of handwriting instruction. Instruction and attention given to each area will help students learn to write legibly.

Second, children need sufficient fine motor coordination and practice to become fairly adept at writing so that the act of writing does not become a tedious, tiresome task. Slow speed interrupts the thought process and makes it difficult for children to get their ideas down on paper. Common sense, though, tells us that a balance must be achieved between laborious and slow writing on the one hand and writing that is done so fast that the finished product is illegible.

These are the primary goals of a handwriting program at the elementary level. They are especially important to remember because we can easily lose sight of these goals as we proceed through detailed handwriting lessons that tend to focus on letter copy to perfection.

READINESS FOR HANDWRITING

Young children enter school with varying degrees of preparedness or readiness for learning. In the chapter on reading instruction we will mention cognitive, affective, social, and psychomotor aspects of readiness for learning. Children enter school with only partially developed large and small motor coordination. This is in part why many children cannot sit still through a kindergarten lesson, and why many children have difficulty learning to write.

The small muscles of the hands and fingers are not fully developed when children enter school. Thus, learning to write is often tedious for children; they simply can't make their hands and fingers move the way they want them to. It is informative to watch preschoolers try to color or use scissors to cut their paper. Their faces (and sometimes their protruding tongues) reflect their concentration and effort. Yet somehow the end result is always less than the expenditures of effort would indicate.

Children need practice and differentiated use of their small muscles as readiness for handwriting. At the preschool and early primary grades, the following activities and experiences are useful:

- A multitude of experiences manipulating large and small objects such as
  blocks
  puzzles
  clay
  shapes—triangles, circles, squares, colored chips
  rods
  peg boards, legos, beads
- Learning handedness (right-hand and left-hand) and feeling comfortable using one or the other

saluting the flag
throwing a ball
playing "Simon Says"

- Activities designed especially for developing fine motor coordination; practice with

cutting and pasting
coloring
dot-to-dot
tracing
using a pencil
drawing
finger painting

By presenting these activities, however, we do not mean to suggest that they are sufficient, in and of themselves, to build readiness for handwriting. Readiness for handwriting must be considered in the larger context of readiness for writing. Children need to understand the purposes for handwriting and how handwriting relates to communication through written language.

Marie Clay (1975) describes observations she made of five year olds as they learned to write. Clay emphasizes the purposefulness of children's writing and she argues that children should not be taught formal lessons in handwriting until *after* they have had considerable experiences writing. How did the children she observed learn to print? Clay describes and suggests these alternatives.

- Drawing pictures and having the teacher write dictated captions (this is the language-experience approach).
- Tracing over the teacher's script.
- Copying captions.
- Copying words around the room.
- Remembering and writing words independently.
- Inventing words (and inventing spelling as you will recall from the last chapter).
- Receiving a written copy from the teacher.

Notice in these suggestions how handwriting is *integrated into* the other forms of the language arts. Children come to see the purposes of handwriting, how handwriting functions in the context of written language, and how handwriting relates to reading, writing, spelling, and even speaking.

Clay argues that we can evaluate children's readiness for written language through their early attempts at writing. She recommends looking at (1) the highest level of language organization, from alphabetic, up through a paragraphed story; (2) the message quality, from having a concept of signs (letters, punctuation) to successful composition; and (3) the quality of the directional principle, from no evidence of direction to extensive text with appropriate arrangement and spacing.

These characteristics of awareness of written language are crucial for readiness for handwriting. Although they may seem to be useful only for writing readiness, we would agree with Clay that instruction and practice in handwriting should not proceed until there is an awareness of the *cognitive* information necessary to understand *what handwriting is for*. At the beginning stages of writing, then, handwriting should not be the focus of instruction. Once children have sufficient cognitive information about handwriting and writing and sufficient experience in writing, then formal instruction can begin.

TECHNIQUES FOR TEACHING HANDWRITING

Teaching Manuscript

The appropriate handwriting style for beginning writers is still debated (Peck, Askov, and Fairchild, 1980). Some researchers (Barbe and Lucas, 1974; Plattor and Woestehoff, 1971) argue that manuscript or print script writing should be taught and maintained throughout life. Others (Kaufman and Biren, 1979; Mullins et al., 1972; Thurber, 1975) argue that cursive or a hybrid of cursive should be taught and maintained and that manuscript or print script should be eliminated entirely. The debate continues, largely spawned by individual experiences and beliefs rather than by experimental evidence in favor of one or the other.

Despite the debate, manuscript, or print script writing, is still the style that is most commonly introduced to beginning writers in the United States today. Proponents argue that it is easiest for young writers to learn and it builds success quickly. Manuscript consists of three basic strokes. These strokes can be easily learned, after which all letters can be reproduced.

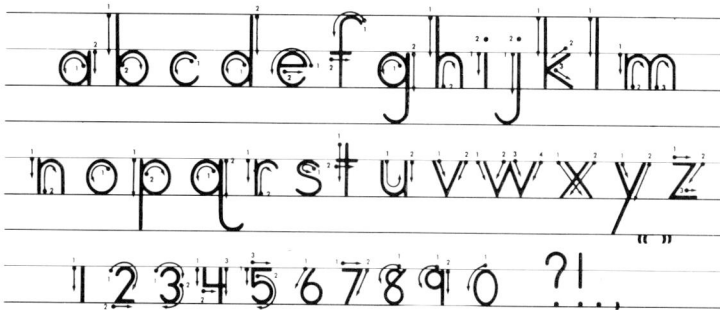

FIGURE 9.1 *Sample of manuscript writing. (Used with permission from* Creative Growth with Handwriting, *Second Edition. Copyright © 1979, Zaner-Bloser, Inc., Columbus, Ohio.)*

Formal Instruction

Formal instruction in handwriting typically begins sometime in first grade. Teachers should provide beginning writers with unlined paper and regular-sized pencils. Unlined paper is recommended at the initial stages when there is no attention to alignment, spacing or proportion. Although the large thick pencils have been recommended in the past, they are not advantageous for beginning writers. Thurber (1975, p. 17) argues

> *The average adult has a hand size two to two and a half times larger than an average first grader's hands. In order to determine what size primary pencil an adult, learning to write, would use, the primary pencil size [would need to be] enlarged two and one-half times. This [would] result in a pencil as large in diameter as a broomstick!*

Formal instruction begins with the teaching of the three basic manuscript strokes and then, the combination of those strokes into letters. Two different strategies for teaching children to combine the strokes are:

1 The "ball-and-stick" method.

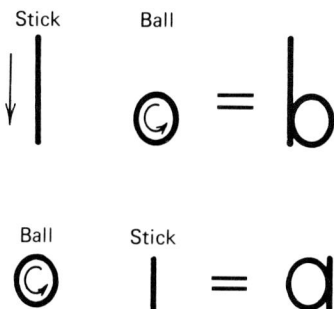

2 The "retrace" method.

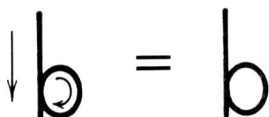

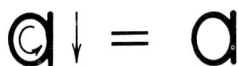

$$\downarrow \mathsf{b} = \mathsf{b}$$

$$\mathsf{a}\downarrow = \mathsf{a}$$

Both strategies are used in first grade classrooms today. There is at least some evidence, however, that the retrace method is superior because it allows children to see each letter as a whole and because it makes the transition to cursive writing easier (Barbe, 1977).

While practice and instruction in learning to print often occurs individually or in small groups, formal instruction is usually done in large groups. The teacher demonstrates on the chalkboard the appropriate letter formation and gives detailed verbal instructions to children. Children are asked to watch the teacher's demonstration so they can see the correct letter formation, and then they are asked to copy the letters on their papers. Slovik (1976) found this procedure to be the best combination of strategies to be used to teach handwriting.

To check each child's letter formations, teachers should walk around the room to make sure that children are forming their letters correctly, and also to praise and encourage success. Such positive feedback is important for children as they are learning to write, and prevents children from practicing incorrect letter formation which is awkward and can present future difficulties.

Additional principles for successfully teaching manuscript writing to young children are listed below.

1 Be aware of individual differences in handwriting readiness. Do not allow "grade level" to be the sole determinant of curriculum.

2 Allow children to sit in a comfortable position. Both feet do not have to be placed squarely on the floor, nor does a child have to sit up straight. Likewise, however, do not allow children to be slouched over in their seats or write while their heads are on the desks.

3 The pencil should be held in a comfortable grip; there is no one "correct" way of holding a pencil. Moderation is the key—not too tight, not too loose, not too high, not too low.

4 Lower-case letters should be taught first, followed by upper-case letters.

5 As the letters are introduced and practiced they should be grouped into words as soon as possible. The use of the names of children in the class is highly motivating for teaching writing.

6 Make sure each child has a clear comfortable view of the chalkboard as the letters are introduced and practiced.

Continued Practice

During the second and third grades, children need continued practice and refinement of letters and strokes. Handwriting instruction at these levels is often corrective in nature, helping children relearn letters that were learned incorrectly and strokes that are made in the wrong direction. Additionally, at this point the teacher can help children attend to proper spacing, alignment, size, and proportion—important elements of legibility that are often too complicated for beginning writers to learn. Last, children can learn to appreciate their good handwriting, and feel successful as writing becomes easier and more under their control.

TEACHING CURSIVE WRITING

Beginning Cursive

Sometime in the second or third grade most children develop an intense desire to learn "real" writing or cursive writing. They often beg their teacher to teach them, eager and highly motivated to learn. Often they have learned some cursive letters, and can recognize or, perhaps, write a cursive " *g* " or cursive " *p*." The transition between manuscript and cursive is therefore not problematic, especially when children are eager to learn.

When are children ready to make the transition? No completely reliable scales exist, and chronological age or grade level is certainly no index. Some guidelines would include

- The desire to learn cursive.
- The ability to read cursive writing.
- Sufficient fine motor coordination evidenced by ease in manuscript writing.
- A sufficient manuscript style, not perfect, but adequate.
- The ability to write all the manuscript letters by memory.
- A slanting or joining of manuscript letters.

Cursive writing differs from manuscript in several aspects. The primary difference and one that is most felt by children is the continuous stroke used in cursive. The pencil or pen is not lifted from letter to letter, but instead is lifted at the end of each word. This style allows for faster speed in writing, which is the major reason why proponents of a cursive style advocate its continued use. Second, many letters are formed differently in cursive, for example, f and *f* , s and *s* , b and *b* . In addition, cursive writing has a slight slant to the right, differing from the vertical formation of letters in manuscript. Figure 9-2 is an example of upper-case and lower-case letters in cursive writing.

Commercial handwriting series provide teachers with specific directions on the

FIGURE 9.2 *Sample of cursive writing. (Used with permission from* Creative Growth with Handwriting, *Second Edition. Copyright © 1979, Zaner-Bloser, Inc., Columbus, Ohio.)*

introduction of cursive writing to children and need not be described here. A brief outline of general guidelines appears below.

INTRODUCTION TO CURSIVE

Guidelines

- Help children become aware of the differences between manuscript and cursive, for example, differences in continuous stroke, letter formation and slant.
- Introduce the cursive letters which most resemble those in manuscript first, for example,

$$a, \; o, \; i, \; t, \; c$$

- Teach the continuous stroke first, saving the introduction of the slant until children are somewhat comfortable connecting letters.

$$it \; = \; it \; = \; it \; = \; it$$

- Special attention should be given the letter r, which, research shows is the most difficult letter to form and causes the most illegibilities.
- Be sure to teach each letter separately. Research has shown that children cannot transfer the learning of strokes in one letter to those of another.

D'Nealian Manuscript: An Alternative

We mentioned earlier in this chapter that there is considerable debate over the best handwriting style to be introduced to children. Some argue that manuscript should be eliminated completely; others argue that cursive should be eliminated completely. A third alternative has been proposed recently (Thurber, 1975) which combines some elements of manuscript and cursive. Known as the D'Nealian manuscript, this style combines the natural rhythm established by the continuous stroke of cursive and the legible letter formation of manuscript print (see Figure 9-3). It is intended to be used at the early primary level and then to help in an easy and smooth transition to cursive. Others propose that the D'Nealian style be used as the preferred style at all age levels. Thurber (1975) provides a very detailed and thorough explanation of

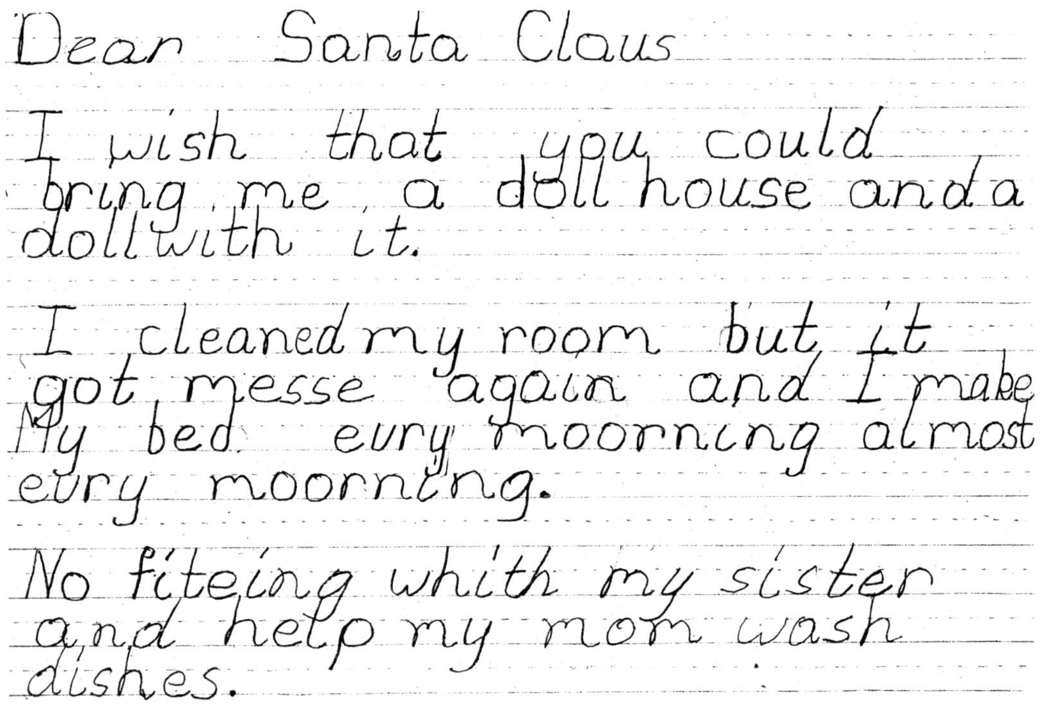

Dear Santa Claus

I wish that you could bring me, a doll house and a doll with it.

I cleaned my room but, it got messe again and I make My bed evry moorning almost evry moorning.

No fiteing whith my sister and help my mom wash dishes.

FIGURE 9.3 *Student sample of D'Nealian script.*

the rationale and methodology of D'Nealian manuscript. A commercial series is also available now, (see Figure 9-4) and many school districts have adopted this style as an alternative to teaching traditional manuscript and print writing.

THE LEFT-HANDED CHILD

The preceding discussion provided some general guidelines about teaching handwriting to average primary children. However, children who are left-handed need special attention to learn cursive handwriting. They require some different strategies from the ones already discussed.

Teachers need to make instructional adjustments for children who show a preference for using their left hands. Left-handed children are forced to conform to a right-handed society, and a written language system designed to meet the needs of a right-handed person. The difficulties encountered in writing with your left hand become apparent if you take a pencil, for a minute, and attempt to write your name with your left hand. Notice (1) you must reverse the direction of your paper, from a left tilt to a right tilt; (2) you must move your pencil toward your body instead of away from your body; (3) you automatically slant your writing to the left rather than

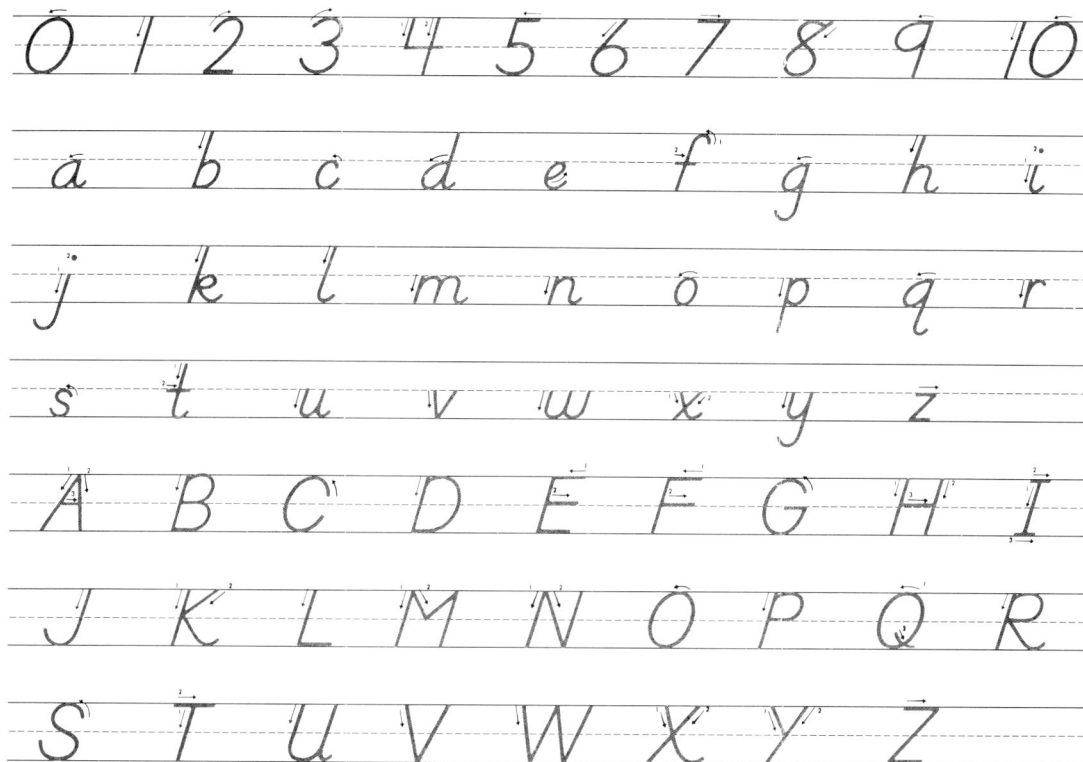

FIGURE 9.4 *D'Nealian handwriting. (Used with permission from* D'Nealian Handwriting, Book 1, *Copyright © 1978, Scott, Foresman and Company, Glenview, Ill.)*

to the right. All of these factors account for the problems in handwriting experienced by left-handers.

These problems can be overcome, however, with the help of a sensitive teacher who is aware of and provides for individual differences. Often, simple awareness of these potential problems can help a teacher adjust instruction. For example, the teacher needs to be aware that left-handers cannot simply copy the right-handed teacher's demonstration. So, after the teacher demonstrates a letter on the board, he or she can then move to the left-hander's desk to help the child make the necessary adjustments. Often times, the problems of left-handers can be nonexistent with the aid of a sensitive teacher who is willing to adjust instruction accordingly.

Based on a review of the research, Howell (1978) makes these additional recommendations for left-handers.

- Using the blackboard to help prevent or eliminate "hooking."
- Turning desks so that light will shine over the right shoulder.
- Adjusting desks to be slightly lower than for right-handed children to aid in seeing what is being written.

- Positioning the paper to the left side of the desk in front of the left arm to ease the toward-the-body movement of the arm.
- Segregating all left-handers so they may help each other and remind each other of correct approaches.
- Seating all left-handers in the front right corner of the room in order to see the teacher's writing on the chalkboard or projector screen from the same angle as they see the writing on their own turned papers.
- Individualizing the instruction.
- Teaching left-handers to use pushing strokes rather than pulling strokes.
- Teaching left-handers to make a few directional letters first, such as f, p, b or those that face right and have downward strokes.
- Using great care in teaching all letters of the alphabet emphasizing beginning points, movement directions, and sequences.

EVALUATION

Periodic evaluation of children's handwriting is necessary to ensure ongoing progress and to provide corrective feedback. A number of different evaluation techniques can be used to provide children with the necessary information they need to improve their handwriting.

Several different formal scales are available. Commercially published series provide their own scales or models which reflect high, average, and low handwriting ability for each grade level. Transparency overlays are also available. Using these, it is possible to evaluate how each letter conforms to a standard in size, spacing, proportion, and alignment.

Both of these types of evaluation instruments should be used with caution. Recall the primary goals of a handwriting program are legibility and speed. Strict conformity to a perfect standard is unnecessary and does not allow for a range of individual styles and variations that, in fact, reflect each individual's character and personality.

Thus, we recommend the use of informal methods for evaluating handwriting. A diagnostic-prescriptive model can be followed, where a teacher can prescribe practice on certain letters or subskills—such as spacing or size—based on children's handwriting during formal instruction and also daily practice.

Children can evaluate their own handwriting and make suggestions for future practice. Even in the early primary grades they can circle on their practice paper the letter or word they think is best. In addition, a simple checklist can be used.

HOW GOOD IS MY HANDWRITING?

	Yes	*Needs Improvement*
1 Slant—are all my letters straight?	_____	_____
2 Size—are all my letters the same size?	_____	_____
3 Spacing—are all my letters the same distance apart?	_____	_____
4 Alignment—do all my letters sit on the line?	_____	_____
5 Can someone else read my handwriting?	_____	_____
6 Is my handwriting neat?	_____	_____
7 Do I try my best?	_____	_____
8 What letters do I need to work on?		_____

An additional technique for showing improvement is to gather handwriting samples monthly. Create handwriting file folders for each child and place a sample of the child's handwriting from September to June. This is an excellent way to demonstrate growth in handwriting. Children love to watch their own improvement. In addition, the samples can be used as evaluation instruments themselves. In individual conferences the teacher and the child can examine strengths and also areas for improvement. Material for additional practice sessions can result from these conferences.

Additional Notes

Practice in handwriting must be made functional and meaningful to children. Excessive drill and copying turn off children's desire to write. As a language arts teacher you need to constantly remind children *why* they need to write legibly and neatly and to help them maintain an interest in handwriting. Tompkins (1980) and D'Angelo (1982) provide excellent ideas for teaching manuscript writing through "bear hunts" for younger children and calligraphy for older children.

In addition, as a model of good handwriting, you need to put forward your best effort in handwriting. The emphasis and importance you place on handwriting will be mirrored by your students.

SUGGESTED ACTIVITIES

1 Interview a primary and intermediate teacher to find out how they teach formal handwriting. How much time do they spend per week in whole group instruction and practice?

2 Collect a sample of primary students' papers and analyze them according to the criteria we discussed in this chapter.

3 Observe different first-grade students. Determine the different levels of readiness for handwriting. How does this relate to their readiness for invented spellings and for writing?

REFERENCES

Barbe, W. B.; Lucas, V.; Hackney, C. A.; and McAllister, C. *Zaner-Bloser Handwriting Workbook: Manuscript.* Columbus, Oh.: Zaner-Bloser, Inc., 1977.

Barbe, W., and Lucas, V. H. "Instruction in Handwriting: A New Look." *Childhood Education* 50, 4 (February 1974):207–209.

Clay, M. M. *What Did I Write?* London: Heinemann Books, 1975.

D'Angelo, K. "Developing Legibility and Uniqueness in Handwriting with Calligraphy." *Language Arts* 59, 1 (January 1982):23–27.

Howell, H. "Write on, You Sinistrals!" *Language Arts* 55, 7 (October 1978):852–856.

Kaufman, H. S., and Biren, P. L. "Cursive Writing: An Aid to Reading and Spelling." *Academic Therapy* 15, 2 (November 1979):209–219.

Mullins, J; Joseph, F.; Turner, C.; Zawadyski, R.; and Saltzman, L. "A Handwriting Model for Children with Learning Disabilities." *Journal of Learning Disabilities* 5, 5 (May 1972):306–311.

Peck, M.; Askov, E. N.; and Fairchild, H. "Another Decade of Research in Handwriting: Progress and Prospect in the 1970s." *Journal of Educational Research*, 73, 5 (May/June 1980):283–298.

Plattor, E., and Woestehoff, E. S. "Toward a Singular Style of Instruction in Handwriting." *Elementary English* 48 (December 1971):1009–1011.

Slovik, N. "The Effects of Different Principles of Instruction in Children's Copying Performances." *Journal of Experimental Education* 45 (Fall 1976):38–45.

Thurber, D. "D'Nealian Manuscript: A Continuous Stroke Print." ERIC Document, No. ED 169533, 1975.

Tompkins, G. E. "Let's Go on a Bear Hunt! A Fresh Approach to Penmanship Drill!" *Language Arts* 57, 7 (October 1980):782–786.

RECEPTIVE LANGUAGE

CHAPTER 10

Listening

HOW CAN YOU TELL IF SOMEONE IS A GOOD LISTENER?
SECOND GRADERS
> . . . because if you weren't listening you wouldn't know
> how to do the page.
> . . . if he's quiet, looking straight at the teacher.
> . . . if you ask him a question and he knows the answer.

SIXTH GRADERS
> . . . if someone is paying attention to the teacher.
> . . . if someone is concentrating on the subject.

© King Features Syndicate, Inc. 1973.

OVERVIEW

Children as well as adults can recognize someone who is a good listener. Good listening habits are important in the classroom, in our social encounters and in our society as a whole. In this chapter you will learn more about the art of listening and how good listening habits can be fostered in children. In the first section of the chapter we will discuss what is known about listening and how listening is part of the thinking-language model presented in this text. We will also discuss how listening relates to the other receptive language skill, reading. Developing good listening skills in children is the subject of the second section. In this section we will link up what you learned about oral language development to good listening skills. You will learn how to lead group discussions to foster good speaking and listening habits and how to develop good questioning techniques for leading children beyond talking and listening to thinking. Different purposes for listening will also be discussed and activities to develop listening for specific purposes will be presented. Next the diagnosis and evaluation of listening will be discussed. You will learn about available tests of listening assessment and also about informal observations and checklists to use for diagnosis and instruction in listening.

INTRODUCTION

Why is listening important? It is an essential component of oral language and also of the thinking-language model we presented at the beginning of this text. To learn to communicate well, we must learn to be good listeners. At an interpersonal level, we all have experienced relating a story to someone or telling someone about a problem and knowing that the person is not listening to us. How can we tell? Sometimes the person will be inattentive—his or her eyes move constantly or are distracted easily by noises. Sometimes the person will constantly bombard us with questions unrelated to what we are saying. When it is clear to us that someone is not listening, our reaction is almost always one of annoyance or distrust. Further, in this situation we realize that communication is lacking or nonexistent.

Effective communication extends beyond the interpersonal level and becomes important for us as members of society as well. Educators, business persons, politicians, and other professionals are becoming increasingly aware of the importance of good listening skills. Large private corporations now sponsor workshops on effective communication through good listening (Montgomery, 1981a). Business consultants discuss the financial costs of ineffective listening to businesspersons and frequently list recommendations to improve one's listening ability. Robert Montgomery's (1981b) *Listening Made Easy* specifically addresses the issue of good listening habits for businesspeople.

Lastly, and perhaps most importantly, good listening skills have become essential in an era of increasing mass media. Sophisticated techniques of persuasion and propaganda have become commonplace in our society, and literate citizens must be able to evaluate critically that which they hear.

LISTENING AS A LANGUAGE SKILL

Listening—Defined

Before we discuss listening in the classroom, we need to look at how listening functions as a part of the language arts. What is listening? At first glance, the answer to this question seems obvious. Many people would quickly respond that listening is hearing. Such a definition clearly falls apart, however, on inspection. We often "hear" a song on the radio, for example, although we may not "listen" to it. We may hear noises or people talking while we are working, yet we do not listen to them. Listening, then, clearly includes hearing, the physiological component, but also includes some kind of attention to what is being heard.

Sara Lundsteen, the most noted educator in the field of listening, defines listening as "the process by which spoken language is converted to meaning in the mind" (Lundsteen, 1979, p. 1). In this definition Lundsteen takes the definition of listening one step further. Listening not only involves a physiological component and an attending component, but also a comprehension component, a connection between what is heard and what is already known. Comments from our second and sixth graders at the beginning of this chapter indicate that they, even at a young age, are aware of the attending and thinking components of listening.

COMPONENTS OF LISTENING

Physiological

Includes two components:

1 Auditory acuity—the ability to hear.
2 Auditory perception—the ability to discriminate among sounds, to blend sounds together, to hold sequences of sounds in memory.

Attention

Focusing, becoming aware, selecting cues from the environment to attend.

Comprehension

Getting meaning from what is heard, associating the sounds to something already known.

Sticht et al. (1974) refer to this listening process as "auding" because of the focus on speech and on language comprehension, as opposed to simply "hearing." We are using this definition because it best reflects the position of listening taken in this chapter. Throughout the chapter we are discussing listening as language comprehension of whole units of discourse rather than as isolated segments of language. Remember that listening, unlike reading, is not a new experience for children as they enter school. They have had at least five years of experience in listening. Lundsteen reinforces this position by arguing that "the most helpful role that listening can play in reading for meaning probably lies in a broad general background of listening comprehension, more so than in specific auditory discriminations for isolated sounds" (Lundsteen, 1979, p. 9).

This chapter will therefore focus on listening as a language comprehension skill rather than on listening as auditory perception. In Chapter 11 we discuss improving auditory perceptual skills, as there is evidence to suggest that auditory training programs enhance reading readiness skills and early reading skills (Lyon, 1977). In this chapter, however, our goal will be to develop a broad understanding of listening comprehension as a language arts skill.

AN INFORMATION-PROCESSING MODEL FOR LISTENING

How does "auding" or listening occur? Sticht et al. (1974) propose an information-processing model similar in many ways to the model Goodman and others have proposed for reading. (We will present Goodman's model in more detail in Chapter 11.) For now, however, recall in Chapter 2 on thinking how information is acquired and stored. The assumptions underlying the information-processing model of listening include

1 Listening is an active information-processing activity under the control of the individual.

2 Listening occurs when language is processed from the sensory information storage, through short-term memory and into long-term memory (recall how this assumption is consistent with the process noted in Chapter 2).

3 Listening requires selective attention to certain stimuli in the environment.

4 Listening is a process whereby new information is related to prior knowledge (recall schema from Chapter 2).

5 Listening involves the generation of hypotheses or predictions about what is to be heard.

Table 10-1 provides a visual representation of the listening process. Notice we use the words "bottom-up" and "top-down." Cognitive psychologists use the term "bottom-up" to refer to processing when the emphasis is on detail first and on larger units of information second. "Top-down" refers to the emphasis on the gist or big idea first, and finer details second.

TABLE 10.1
Listening as Information Processing

Top-Down Model	*Bottom-Up Model*
Long-term memory	Long-term memory
(prior knowledge or schemata leads to generation of hypotheses about what is heard)	(relate new conceptualizations to prior knowledge, develop new schemata)
Short-term memory	Short-term memory
(existing schemata affects recoding)	(recode auditory stimuli into meaningful conceptualizatons)
Sensory information storage	Sensory information storage
(existing schemata affects selective attention to stimuli)	(selective attention to auditory stimuli)

The process of listening, like that of reading, can be viewed as an hypothesis-testing or problem-solving activity (a top-down process). Sticht et al. (1974) argue that:

> *This ability requires [the establishment of] some cognitive goal, and then [the seeking of] information which will achieve that goal. Selective attending is very much a problem-solving activity, in which external information that satisfies some cognitive requirement is sought. To selectively attend [one] has to know what type of information is needed to solve a cognitive problem (1974, p. 52).*

Listening often begins with the generation of hypotheses about what we will hear. We generate these hypotheses based on our expectations. Our expectations, in turn, are derived from our purposes for listening, and our existing schemata, our cumulative learned knowledge about the world and about language. Based on these expectations, we make predictions about what we will hear. We then selectively attend to spoken language to confirm or disconfirm our predictions. Notice we have the three components of communication as identified by Tough (1974) in Chapter 5—the speaker, the receiver, or listener, and the social context.

LISTENING AND ITS RELATIONSHIP TO READING

In Chapter 5 we discussed the important relationship between speaking and listening as oral language skills. We will return to that important relationship later in this chapter. Now, however, we want to point out some important characteristics shared by both listening and reading.

As a language arts skill, listening closely relates to reading because both skills involve the individual in receiving input via language. Recall in Chapter 1 that we identified listening and reading as *receptive* language skills. We said that it is through listening and reading that we receive information about the world from our environment, from peers, school, media, books, and so on. This new information is added to and integrated with our existing schemata. We clearly see the interdependence of language and thinking here. Language influences thought and through the expressive skills—speaking and writing—thought influences language.

In Chapter 11 you will see more clearly how the information-processing model of reading is similar to the one we present here for listening. In addition to the similarities cited here, two additional components need to be addressed.

First, both listening and reading must be processed serially, or one after another, rather than simultaneously (Sticht et al., 1974). In this regard, reading is easier than listening, because in reading one can go back to retrieve information not processed originally. Under normal circumstances, one cannot retrieve information lost serially through listening.

Second, as languaging agents, both listening and reading contain redundant information. Redundancy in the language allows for predictability. For example, spelling patterns and syntax allow for predictability in reading, and intonation and grammatical structure allow for predictability in listening. Sticht et al. argue that such predictability improves the efficiency of information processing.

What are some of the practical consequences of the similarities between listening and reading? Lundsteen lists three consequences of educational significance: analogous features, vocabulary, and common skills of thinking and understanding. We have expanded these ideas below.

1 *Analogous features.* The process of learning to read may involve finding analogies between listening and reading. For example, when children learn to read they always superimpose the symbols onto the sounds; they "read aloud." This aural/oral component of reading is crucial for beginners; they learn to associate sound and symbol together to learn that reading is language based just as listening and speaking are.

2 *Vocabulary.* Lundsteen aptly points out that reading is built on the language base of oral language, listening and speaking. "Book language" or vocabulary has to be familiar to be meaningful to the child. Thus, the vocabulary base of listening is directly related to what is understood in reading. Lundsteen suggests, "the ability to listen seems to set limits on the ability to read" (1971, p. 3).

3 *Common skills of thinking and understanding.* Researchers have found strong relationships between tests of reading and tests of listening in general (Dole, 1982; Duker, 1969; Spearritt, 1972). In addition, taxonomics of reading subskills developed by educators have generally followed the same lines as taxonomies of listening subskills. That is, listening and reading both seem to include such skills as the ability to follow a sequence, to recognize inferences, to find the main idea, and supporting details, and to evaluate what is read or heard (Devine, 1976, 1978).

There are three primary differences between the listening and reading processes.

1 When you listen to someone you do not have the luxury of "looking back" as you do when you read. What you hear is stored in sensory information storage and short-term memory and there is a limit to how long that information stays and how much information can be accommodated.

2 When listening you usually have many nonverbal cues to help you interpret what is being said. These nonverbal cues might be likened to the nonlinguistic visual cues you receive when reading (for example, pictures).

3 There is a much wider variation in sound patterns than there are in letter patterns. That is, when people speak they express words with a wide variety of pitch, tone, intensity, and so on. Hence, to identify which phoneme is being used is a much more complex task (theoretically) than identifying which grapheme (letter) is being used.

If you get the impression that listening is a much more complex task than reading you are correct. However, listening is not a more difficult task. This is because we are far more practiced at listening than we are at reading. We grow up in a aural world. From birth we are constantly presented with sounds that are to be interpreted as concepts, principles and events. By the time we reach school age we are veritable masters at "decoding" language presented in oral form. This is not the case with the printed word. Relative to the spoken word we decode printed information only a fraction of the time. In a sense, reading is a highly "unnatural" means of obtaining information in our society. It demands the learning of an entirely new symbol system (letters). Until we master this system our highly efficient "top-down" process of interpreting information is short circuited by the "bottom-up" demands of the symbols.

Regardless of the differences, it is clear that listening and reading have strong associations with each other as receptive language skills. A teacher can use these associations to improve both listening and reading in the classroom and to make the transition from listening to reading easier. Lundsteen (1979) presents some practical classroom applications based on the commonalities shared by both skills. We have expanded on these ideas below:

Teachers need to attend to

1 *Readiness for school learning.* Listening and reading form the base for general learning in the classroom.

2 *A relaxed social situation.* Listening and reading are nurtured in an environment where there is freedom to explore, take risks, experiment.

3 *Larger units of comprehension.* Listening and reading activities must be made meaningful through attention to whole stories, plays or dramatizations rather than isolated, fragmented units of language.

4 *Common analogous signals.* The relationships between listening and reading can be related to children by showing them how punctuation relates to verbal intonation; for example, a verbal pause compares to a comma, a raised voice compares to a question mark.

5 *Critical thinking and emotional aspects.* Critical thinking and analysis may occur more easily in a reading situation; appreciation or creative reaction may occur more easily in a listening situation. Children need to participate in both types of experiences.

DEVELOPING LISTENING SKILLS

Setting the Classroom Climate

In Chapter 5 we presented student activities to foster the development of oral language skills. Many of those activities involved listening as well as speaking. In this chapter we want to focus more on teacher behaviors to foster both listening and speaking skills.

Good speaking and listening skills do not occur "naturally," but are the result of training, instruction, and a desire to communicate effectively. Such training and instruction begins at the kindergarten level, and needs to be fostered at every grade level throughout elementary school and beyond. When and how does the training begin? It begins on the first day of school when you, the language arts teacher, first meet your students. It begins informally and with you acting as a role model of the ideal listener. In order for good listening skills to develop, the teacher must set an emotional and affective climate in the classroom that fosters good listening. The scenario at the primary level might occur as follows

CHILDREN: (Seated on the floor at the front of the room)

TEACHER: (In center, seated in small chair) We have already talked about some rules in our class this morning. I would like to talk about another rule which I consider to be one of the most important ones we have. (On board she

reads:) ''Be a good listener.'' Who can tell me what that means? What is a good listener?

CHILD: You listen to the teacher.

TEACHER: Yes, and how can you tell if someone is a good listener? What does a good listener do?

CHILD: Doesn't talk.

CHILD: Listens to someone when they talk.

CHILD: Pays attention.

TEACHER: Yes, a good listener does not talk while others are talking. A good listener pays attention. A good listener thinks about what someone is saying. A good listener looks at the person who is talking. Let's write these ideas on a chart and we'll hang the chart up so we can remember what to do to be a good listener.

> ## Be a Good Listener
> To be a good listener, you should:
>   1. Not talk when someone is talking.
>   2. Look at the person who is talking.
>   3. Pay attention to what the person is saying.
>   4. Think about what the person is saying
>   5. Ask good questions.

This chart would then be put up on the chalkboard. The next day and on succeeding days, you would remind children about good listening habits.

What we have just described is absolutely crucial for good listening habits to be instilled in children. A classroom climate of support and trust must be developed and nurtured by you, the language arts teacher. Such a climate does not evolve naturally, but instead is the result of careful planning and constant work with the children in your class. Formal lessons on listening are not essential. The climate can be developed informally during various periods of the day.

Children need to be encouraged to be active listeners not only during sharing time or during discussions, but also during math, social studies, and science—

whenever someone is talking. Children do not need punitive reminders to "be quiet and listen," or constant negative comments or punishments when they are not listening. Instead, children should be *encouraged to listen, shown how to listen,* and *rewarded* for demonstrating attentive behavior. We describe more specific behaviors for teachers in Chapter 15 on classroom management.

Developing the kind of classroom climate we have described is one of the most important tasks of a teacher. It should be clear that a supportive classroom climate is essential for developing good listening and speaking skills. In addition, such a climate builds self-concepts, positive attitudes, and a desire to learn. Recall from Chapter 1 that these too are essential goals for language arts instruction.

Group Discussions—Listening and Speaking Combined

Effective interchange of communication is difficult to foster in a classroom where the teacher does all of the speaking and the children do all of the listening. In such a classroom listening skills and oral language are not improved. Instead, children learn to become passive rather than active information processors and often learn to "tune out" that which is heard. Moreover, children will not learn the social conventions of language in such an environment.

The alternative classroom where active listening and oral language is fostered is one in which children interact with one another and with the teacher frequently. Children meet in small and large groups often, and participate actively in the communication process. Active listening involves thinking about, reflecting and acting on that which is spoken, and group discussions are perhaps the most effective means to this end. Below are some purposes and times for different kinds of group discussions.

GROUP DISCUSSIONS

When?	**Why?**

• Reading groups	• discussions of
	  Characters
	  Theme
	  Plot
	  Comparison to other stories
	  Appreciation of story

• Social studies	• Small group projects • Map-making strategies • Discussions of ethics

- Science
  - Experiments
  - Following directions
  - Discussions about ecology
- Math
  - Constructing graphs, charts
  - Solving word problems
- Expressive arts
  - Making a collage, mural
  - Discussions about music appreciation
  - Writing a play
  - Role plays, dramas

TRY THIS

To understand the importance of interchange in effective communication, try this with a peer or with an intermediate grade child if you are working in a classroom:

Draw the following shapes on a large piece of paper (each rectangle is 1 inch by 2 inches).

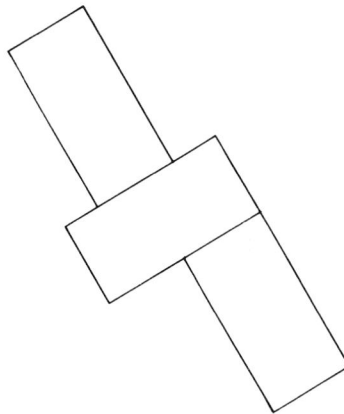

Now, taking this large piece of paper, try to describe this design to another person or persons so that they can draw an exact duplicate of the design on a piece of paper. Do not let them see your paper and do not let them ask any questions.

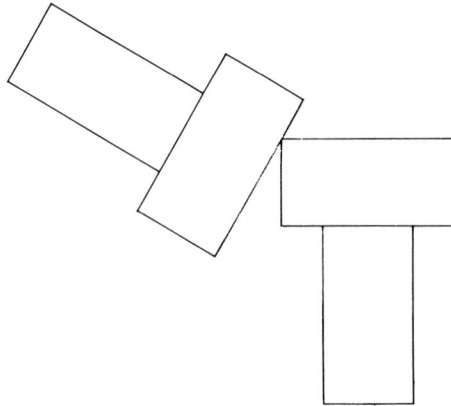

Again, have the same person or persons try to duplicate this drawing. This time although they cannot see your paper, *do* allow them to ask questions at any time.

Now compare the two drawings of your peers or children. Ask these questions.

Which drawing took longer?

Which drawing was more accurate—the one in which feedback was allowed or not allowed?

How did you feel when you were not allowed to ask questions?

Which leads to more effective communication—when questions are allowed or not allowed?

Next, examine the implications of these results for teaching and learning. Learning takes place more easily and with more positive attitudes and results when communication is two-way rather than one-way. Listening is not a language arts skill that should be taught in isolation or as a passive skill. Children need to be active listeners and will learn to do so when speaking and thinking are involved.

The Role of the Teacher in Leading Group Discussions

Group discussions in the elementary classroom should be frequent and guided by an expert leader who can teach about the *process* of communication as well as the *content* of discussion. In this section we want to discuss the role of the teacher as a leader in both *process* and *content*.

First, it is important to remember that in a group discussion children learn much more than simply the topic of the discussion. We discussed this briefly in our chapter on oral language development. Recall Tough's (1974) delineation of the social conventions of language—how to behave, how to take turns, how to ask for different kinds of information. These conventions are learned through the guidance of a teacher who does not assume these skills are known to children.

Consider, for example, a situation we observed in one classroom

TEACHER: We're going to read a story today about Rufus, the dog. Does anyone here have a dog? (Children raise hands.) Can you tell me about your dog, Marie?

MARIE: My dog ran away and we couldn't find him. So, we went to my aunt house and my cousin she has a new bike and she let me ride it.

This type of conversation is typical in content and in form of primary grade children, especially. Notice that Marie did answer part of the teacher's request for specific information. However, Marie associated her run-away dog with going to her aunt's house and then changed the subject completely to talk about the bike (probably foremost on her mind). Notice also that Marie made two usage errors—"aunt house" and "my cousin she."

How should the teacher respond to teach the *process* of communication? There are a number of alternatives similar to:

"It sounds like you enjoyed your bike ride at your *aunt's* house. Did you find your dog?"

"And what happened to your dog, Marie? Did you find him?"

But not:

"It's aunt's house, not aunt house. And it's my cousin *has*, not my cousin *she has*."

"We're *not* talking about your bike ride. Who wants to begin our story?"

In the first two alternatives, the teacher models good listening and correct usage, responds to the content of Marie's comments and still brings her back to the subject through further questioning. In the second examples, the teacher responds negatively and ignores the *content* of Marie's comment. What do you think Marie would learn from the latter exchanges? Probably, something like "keep quiet and don't volunteer again."

Thus, there are more and less effective ways to lead a group discussion. An effective teacher needs to learn to teach the process of communication and along with that the content as well. It is difficult to separate the two actually, because they go hand in hand.

We must warn you at the outset that leading a group discussion is not an easy task to learn. Barker (1982, p. 13) argues that

> *Spontaneity is a key to successful group communication, but such spontaneity makes careful analysis and organization of the message rather difficult . . . teachers involved in group communication tend often to structure their presentations tightly and to reduce possible spontaneous discussion which might arise from the presentation . . . this practice not only reduces motivation to learn but actually may inhibit the learning process.*

An undergraduate student recounted a class discussion she observed which highlights Barker's remarks and demonstrates the effects of a teacher's inability to effectively lead a group discussion.

The teacher was conducting a social studies lesson with a group of third graders. The children were reading from their texts and looking at a picture of a man standing on a barren rocky piece of land. The teacher asked, "If your land was rocky and dry, how would you get food? How would you get food if your country looked like this?" The third graders raised their hands,

"You could plow it more."

"You could work the land."

"You could fish to get fish."

"Hunt the animals."

"Try to grow your own food in the garden."

The teacher became increasingly irritated at the children's responses. "Now, how many of you grow all your food in your own garden? Now you can't tell me you grow all your food!" One child quickly raised his hand and blurted out, "I know, the supermarket!" The teacher's response was, "Now, how is the supermarket going to get food if you can't grow your food?" Next, a child remarked, "You could move!" The teacher responded, "Well, that's better." Another child then said, "Get it from other countries." "Yes," replied the teacher exasperated, *"trade!"*

The interchange of communication between this teacher and her students can be analyzed in detail to demonstrate several important points about leading group discussions and about effective communication. First, Barker's observation about teachers' overstructuring their presentation is clear in our example above. The teacher asked a question with the sole purpose of drawing out of the children the concept of "trade." It is our guess that this social studies lesson revolved around the concept of "trade," and that was the objective the teacher had in mind. This mind-set, however, narrowed the focus of the discussion and, more importantly, eliminated a problem-solving exchange of communication.

Second, it is clear that the teacher was not "listening" to her third graders. Earlier we remarked that listening must involve thinking about and reflecting on that which is heard. Obviously, the teacher was looking for the correct response, "trade," and did not think about some good responses the children gave. For example, fishing and hunting and the supermarket are three perfectly acceptable responses to the teacher's question. Although these were acknowledged, the teacher indicated through her language that she was angry at the children's responses.

The importance of developing good communication and good questioning techniques is crucial for any leader of a group discussion. This teacher could have engaged her children in an excellent problem-solving activity by asking the same question but just responding to children's answers differently. She should have responded by asking better questions. Consider these alternatives.

	TEACHER: If your land was rocky and dry, how would you get food?
	JOHN: You could plow it more.
Here you have done several things:	**TEACHER:** O.K., John, let's suppose you plowed and plowed it and it still looked like this. Then what would you do?
1 Acknowledged to John that you listened to him.	**JOHN:** You could water it more.
2 Told John his idea was worthwhile	
3 Forced John to think through his idea to solve a problem.	
Here again you are responding thoughtfully and have shown you have listened. You are also forcing children to think through different alternatives and the consequences of these alternatives.	**TEACHER:** Yes, O.K., because the dry land obviously needs water. And then you might get food to grow. But John, let's suppose you watered it, but it still wouldn't grow anything. Then what would you do?
	MARY: You could fish to get fish.
	TEACHER: Sure, that's another way of getting food. What else could you do?
	JOHN: Hunt the animals.
	TEACHER: Yes, you could certainly do that. Why don't we write all of your good ideas on the board. (Teacher does this.) Any other ideas?

The group discussion would proceed in this way until children have exhausted all their ideas about ways to get food. This type of discussion allows for spontaneity, encourages children to think, and enables children to feel they have made a positive contribution to the group. A positive interchange of communication has taken place when children feel that they can speak and listen and are valued for their ideas.

Another way to accomplish this same goal is through drama. In Chapter 5, we mentioned Dorothy Heathcote. Interestingly enough, in two superb films entitled *Building Belief* (Pts. I and II), Heathcote demonstrates how to effectively draw children into an activity similar in content to the one this teacher tried with her students. Heathcote shows how to accomplish the same goal through a problem-solving drama, and succeeds with warmth, caring, and a valuing of students and their ideas. (See Chapter 5 to help you recall how Heathcote used questioning techniques in drama to teach process and content.

We now want to summarize some guidelines for leading group discussions.

GUIDELINES FOR LEADING GROUP DISCUSSIONS

- Be sure that the physical arrangement of the children allows for exchange of ideas—make sure children can see you and each other and are not too crowded or too far apart.
- Remember to be a role model of a good listener. Pay attention, maintain eye contact and respond verbally or nonverbally in a way that lets each speaker know you are listening.
- Do not do most of the talking. Let children do the talking.
- Praise children who are being good listeners.
- Ask questions frequently (but do not bombard children with questions).
- Accept responses of children in a positive way.
- Allow children between 5 and 15 seconds to answer questions. After you ask a question give children time to reflect. Their responses will be more thoughtful, more reflective as a result.
- Try not to have a preset answer in your mind when you ask a question. Sometimes this is unavoidable, but always consider alternative responses and accept these whenever possible.
- Demonstrate good listening skills and require children to do the same in every subject area, during math, social studies, science, etc. throughout the school day. Make it a habit and require that children do the same.
- When possible teach through modeling and questioning the process of communication as well as the topic of discussion.

GUIDELINES FOR GOOD QUESTIONING TECHNIQUES

- Do not ask questions and then answer them yourself. If you ask a question, let the children answer it.
- Call on different children to answer questions. If one child is not participating, ask that child a question you know she or he can answer.
- Always allow at least five seconds "wait time" after you ask a question before you call on someone to answer it.
- Ask questions that begin in a variety of ways.
- Allow children to respond to questions divergently as well as convergently.
- Ask questions that allow children to integrate their existing schema with new information.

     What would you do if?
     What will happen if?
     How would you feel if?
     Has anything like this happened to you?
     How would you use this?

- Ask children to analyze information, synthesize information, and evaluate that which they hear about and read.

LISTENING FOR DIFFERENT PURPOSES

We have already discussed the listening process as one in which we generate hypotheses about what we will hear. The hypotheses we generate are derived from our existing schemata, the knowledge we have about the world. These hypotheses, in turn, determine our purposes for listening and the extent to which we listen. For example, if we are planning a picnic or ski trip, we may "hear" the news, but then listen attentively to the weather report, because we know that that information is of particular interest to us. If someone is giving us directions, we pay close attention to the details of the discourse because, based on our past experiences, we know that we will later have to recall the directions in exact sequence. If we listen to a campaign speech, we listen carefully to thoroughly analyze and evaluate what is said; past experiences have taught us that ideas and events are sometimes misinterpreted by politicians.

Clearly, we listen with discretion and with varying degrees of intensity depending on our purposes. We are always using our existing schemata as we listen. Our schemata help us determine our purposes for listening. Conversely, if we know what to listen for, we can better tap into our schemata and therefore listen more effectively. In this next section we will discuss listening for different purposes. We have divided this section into two areas: (1) informational listening, or listening for specific information and (2) critical listening, or listening to evaluate and judge the validity of what we hear. As each area is discussed, we will present activities to help children improve listening skills and thereby learn to communicate more effectively with others.

Informational Listening

Particularly in the elementary years, children spend a great deal of time listening for information. They listen to the teacher while directions are being given. They listen to each other during oral discussions. They listen for instructions about how to solve a math problem, how to run a computer, how to conduct a science experiment, how to pronounce a word.

The teacher can plan activities and experiences that will increase children's abilities to listen for specific information. Below we have outlined and included activities in some specific areas of informational listening in which elementary children engage daily. In these activities and whenever possible we would encourage listening to be taught in conjunction with the other language arts and content areas rather than in isolation. It is our belief that you will be more likely to teach listening in this way and that the interrelationships between listening and the other language skills will be clearer to children through this interrelated approach.

Listening to Oral Directions

At the simplest level, children need to learn to listen to oral directions. When we asked children how they could tell if someone was a good listener, we were struck by how many responded that good listeners "would know how to do the worksheet." Training children to listen carefully while you give instructions on how to complete a task takes time and patience. It also takes teacher expertise to learn to give directions so that children will understand them. Some basic rules to remember are

- Make sure you have everyone's attention before you begin giving directions—encourage children to be active listeners.
- Make sure every child can clearly see you and also any materials you are using to give directions.
- Make sure your directions are clear and concise.
- Allow children to ask questions.
- Do not reprimand children for asking a question so long as they show some signs of paying attention.
- Ask one or two children to repeat the directions in their own words.

It is important to remember that you do not teach children to listen to directions by punishing them when they don't, or by refusing to answer their questions. It is also important to remember that children's successes in following directions are as much a function of your giving them good directions as it is of their listening to your directions.

There are additional activities to use in the classroom on an informal basis to help children become better at listening to directions. For example

1 When a poem or story chart is written on the board, call on several children to go to the board and

Circle all the rhyming words.
Draw one line under words that end in *ed*.
Put an X over a word that is a synonym for courage.

Tell children to listen carefully to your directions because you will not repeat them. Children always enjoy this "game"; it is more than a game, however, because it encourages active listening and comprehension.

2 Have several children prepare lists of step-by-step instructions on how to perform a simple task like tying a shoe or drinking from a cup. Let them decide on the tasks and then choose other class members as listeners to perform the tasks. Pair a listener and a speaker; the listener must do exactly what he or she is told and cannot ask questions. Discuss the results in terms of what it takes to "listen" effectively and also to "communicate" effectively.

"How did you do?"
"Did you follow all the directions?"
"If not, where did you go wrong?"
"Why were you not able to follow directions?"
"How will this help you next time in following directions better?"

THE LISTENING CENTER

An effective way of reinforcing listening skills is through the use of a listening center. Headphones, tapes, and storybooks make the listening center a quiet area of the room where children can work individually on listen skills inter-related with other subject area material such as reading, writing, science, or math.

Listening centers might include several activities such as,

- Reading along in a new storybook.
- Reading newly created books into a tape recorder and having others listen to their stories.
- Following directions on making an art project or a game.

- Drawing pictures of a scene that children hear about through a tape recording.
- Listening to directions for a math worksheet.

Listening centers can be an additional tool for the teacher in improving listening skills. These centers must be used carefully, however, or they can produce wasted energy. Durkin (1978) warns that children should not be placed at listening centers doing the same activity day after day. If the listening center is always used to have children simply read along in a book, children can learn to "tune out" the book, thereby not listening at all. Remember to have an established *purpose* for listening at the center and to *vary* the types of activities you present.

Listening for Sequence

Listening to detect sequence is another type of informational listening skill needed by elementary children. This skill requires us to listen to and store in memory a particular sequence of ideas, actions, or events, often for later recall or for drawing inferences and conclusions. The skill is a foundational one for critical listening and also for critical reading. For example, children need to learn to recall a particular order in which an event occurred to fully evaluate the impact of that event or the consequences of the event. Some activities to help children listen for sequence include

1 Read (or have children listen to) a story with a set sequence as part of the plot, for example, *Drummer Hoff* by Edward Emberley (Prentice-Hall, Inc., 1967). Cut out flannelboard characters of the story. Have children verbally recall the story and place each event on the flannelboard in appropriate order.

2 Read *Stuart Little* by E. B. White to children. First, have them agree on a list of major events in the story; then have them decide on the order of those events. In groups children can draw pictures and number each major event. This activity can be done with any story.

3 Have children sit in a circle. Begin with one child who says, "I'm going to Argentina and I'm taking. . . ." Children then repeat what they heard in exact sequence before adding their own onto the list.

4 Take several pictures or slides of a pet or a child doing something in a particular sequence—for example, a cat jumping from a chair, a child getting ready for bed. Place the pictures in random order on the chalkboard. Tape record children as they create a sentence for each picture. Then play back the tape, and have children place the pictures and their sentences in the correct sequence. This is an excellent activity for interrelating listening and speaking. Children could also write their sentences and read them.

5 Read a series of sentences to children in random order. Add an irrelevant sentence or one that does not make sense in the series and have children identify that sentence. Then have them place the sentences in the correct order. For example, read the following sentences:

The children came back to school after the trip.
The children received a tour of the museum.
The children rode on the bus.
The children went on a field trip.
The children played kickball in P.E.

First, have children identify the irrelevant sentence. Then have them place sentences in the correct order.

Listening for the Main Idea and Details

Another important foundational skill in listening involves the ability to identify the main idea and details. When listening to small units of discourse or larger units, children must learn to note the specific details of the message and also the most important idea. These skills are often best taught as prerequisites to the same skills in reading.

Direct instruction in teaching main idea and details is needed if we want children to become proficient. This does not mean that we can delegate the worksheet to teaching main ideas and details. Teachers can directly teach these skills in several ways.

- Begin by reading aloud or listening to tapes of short paragraphs with clearly identifiable main ideas and accompanying details.
- Work through the tapes or reading to ensure that children understand why a particular idea was chosen.
- Ask questions like
  1. What is the main idea?
  2. How do you know? Tell me what sentences gave the clues.
  3. Name some details.
  4. How do you know these are details? Where in the paragraph or story did you get a hint?
- Draw visuals or models to demonstrate relationships between the main idea and details.
- See if children can spot irrelevant information or information that does not address the main idea or the details.

Chapter 11 discusses teaching for main idea and details. You might want to read the short section on main idea in that chapter, because instruction in listening and in reading often reinforce each other. In addition, the activities used in reading are interchangeable with activities used in listening. We would encourage you to use activities in both modes when teaching main ideas and details as well as other skills mutual to both listening and reading.

Critical Listening

The ability to listen critically requires moving beyond processing the information heard. Critical listening requires thinking about and evaluating incoming oral information in the light of existing schemata. In our era of mass media, the importance of critical listening becomes obvious. We often gaze in wonder and amazement at people who invest their entire savings of $10,000 to receive a "genuine $25,000 diamond," or the people who invest their hard-earned savings in some get-rich-quick scheme they hear about or read. As educators we have an obligation to train children to be literate and critical consumers in our society. Teaching them to think critically through listening and reading is an important means to this end.

Teaching critical thinking skills through listening should begin in the early primary grades and continue throughout elementary school and beyond. Many teachers think that primary grade children are too young to learn to think critically. We believe, however, that even kindergartners can benefit from lessons and questions requiring critical listening skills.

At the lower grade levels, critical listening instruction can begin with a simple book by Patricia Ruben entitled *True or False* (J. B. Lippincott, 1978). In this book simple pictures are presented with true-false questions requiring children to examine the picture and evaluate the veracity of a statement read with the picture. For example, one picture shows two girls smiling at each other holding hands and the teacher reads, "These girls are friends. True or false?" The pictures and statements require children to go beyond the statement given and, using existing schemata, draw inferences about a given situation.

Primary grade children can also work on critical listening skills by being asked appropriate questions that require them to think through an event or a situation. For example, children can listen to the story *Goldilocks and the Three Bears* and then discuss if Goldilocks should have entered the bears' house. Children can also listen to stories like *Six Chinese Brothers* by Cheng Hou-tien (Holt, Rinehart and Winston, 1979) and decide which parts of the story could really happen and which parts could not. They can also simply listen to stories read aloud by the teacher on a daily basis (see Chapter 13 on children's literature) and decide if they like the story or not and why. All of these activities are important ones for building critical listening skills at an early age.

As children reach the intermediate grades, a variety of activities can be developed to teach the components of critical listening that children need to learn.

- Sorting out relevant from irrelevant details.
- Judging the worthiness of a speaker as an authority on his or her subject.

- Evaluating the content of a presentation for emotional overtones.
- Differentiating real from make-believe.
- Differentiating fact from opinion.

One intermediate teacher we know uses critical listening to help develop an understanding of different periods in American history for her fifth graders. When children study the Mayflower, for example, the teacher has children listen to a recording entitled *"The New World"* from *Our Nation's Heritage Series* by the Chevron School Broadcast Company (1970). This particular recording is a dramatic presentation of common people as they make the 3000-mile journey across the Atlantic Ocean. Children listen to peasants as they talk about their difficulties on the voyage. They hear the captain shouting orders to his mates. After listening to these recordings, children take the point of view of the voyagers and write about how it would feel to travel during those times. They also listen to one person on the Mayflower and, based on dialect and speech, they must decide what part of the ship these voyagers would be on. Recall that Heathcote uses similar techniques in classroom drama. For now we need to emphasize that these activities build a critical thinking attitude on the part of children because they help children view the world from different perspectives and under different conditions.

Three wonderful children's books about listening are worthy of your attention. All deal with using your senses to "listen" and we recommend them for all students.

The Other Way to Listen by Byrd Baylor.

If You Listen by Charlotte Zolotow.

The Song by Charlotte Zolotow.

Another effective technique for teaching critical thinking skills through listening involves propaganda analysis. The Institute of Propaganda Analysis has assisted educators in identifying specific propaganda techniques used in the mass media. Intermediate grade children can study about these techniques and identify specific propaganda techniques they hear on TV and radio. These techniques can also be identified in magazine advertisements, thereby strengthening critical reading skills as well.

An extensive unit could be written on propaganda techniques since these techniques daily have real-life application to children. Specific types of propaganda techniques are given below.

1 *Bandwagon.* This technique tries to persuade the consumer that everybody is doing or buying something; therefore the consumer should too.

2 *Card stacking.* In this technique persuaders present only opinions, facts, and information that favor their position or product—and ignore information that disfavors their ideas or products.

3 *Glittering generality.* This technique utilizes words with connotative meanings (old-fashioned, motherhood, freedom) to influence or persuade without evaluation of the facts.

4 *Name calling.* Persuaders use derogatory labels or remarks to persuade, again without evaluation of the facts.

5 *Plain folks.* Persuaders identify with the common person on the street, the plain folks, in order to convince or persuade.

6 *Testimonial.* In this technique, a famous person gives a testimonial about the value of an idea or product—the product or idea becomes associated with that person.

Children can be taught these propaganda techniques and then asked to identify them in TV and radio commercials. They can keep log books recording the TV commercials they watch at home, the types of propaganda that are used, and an evaluation of the real message being sent.

TV LOG BOOK				
Date	Time	Commercial	Type of Propaganda	What Are They Really Saying
2/9	7:05 P.M.	Rolaids Spells Relief	Testimonial (Roger Staubach)	Famous person uses Rolaids
			Plain folks	So do common people; everybody uses Rolaids; you
			Bandwagon	should too
2/10				

In addition, have children cut out magazine ads that use propaganda techniques and identify various types of persuasion. This activity involves critical thinking about what is read as opposed to what is heard, and should be used as an integral part of a unit on propaganda analysis.

Additional activities for a unit on propaganda analysis might include

1 Constructing a bulletin board with examples of the different kinds of propaganda identified in commercials.

2 An in-depth study of words used in ads and commercials to evaluate their denotative and connotative meanings (see also Chapter 13).

3 Having children rewrite ads or commercials changing the type of propaganda used *or* without any form of propaganda.

4 Evaluating the effectiveness of various commercials and then evaluating their effectiveness on a five-point scale.

5 Having children write scripts advertising their own products using different types of propaganda techniques.

6 Role playing the selling of their products.

In sum, we can say that critical listening and critical reading both involve a critical evaluation of encoded information. The activities developed for critical listening and critical reading (see Chapter 11) can be used interchangeably. We further encourage you to try to think of ways in which you can alter activities so that they can be used with both of the receptive communication skills.

PUTTING IT ALL TOGETHER: STRATEGIES FOR LISTENING/READING CONNECTIONS

Earlier we discussed and presented some classroom applications of the similarities between listening and reading as receptive communication skills. Two additional teaching strategies can be used to enhance both listening and reading comprehension. Both strategies focus on thinking and analyzing what is heard and read, thereby helping children apply and transfer existing schemata to new language processing.

The first strategy is the listening-reading transfer lesson developed by Cunningham (1975, 1982). In this lesson children learn and practice a particular comprehension skill through listening before they learn the same skill in reading. First, children listen to a selection and respond to the purpose set by the teacher. Then, children read a similar selection and respond to the same purpose. For example, a teacher might wish children to learn to differentiate relevant from irrelevant information. The teacher might first read a paragraph telling children to think carefully about each sentence and identify the sentence that does not make sense in the selection. Several paragraphs could be presented and analyzed until children are capable of identifying irrelevant sentences. As a follow up the teacher would present several similar paragraphs to children in written form. Children would then be asked to draw circles around the irrelevant sentences.

The listening-reading transfer lesson can be used for different purposes and with a variety of comprehension skills. We recommend this type of lesson especially for helping children to understand the need to bring existing schemata to both the listening process and the reading process.

The second technique was developed as a reading activity by Russell Stauffer (1975) but can also be used as a listening activity. Called the Directed Listening/ Thinking Activity (or DLTA), this strategy requires children to generate hypotheses or make predictions about what they will hear and then listen to confirm or disconfirm their predictions. This strategy is an application of the information-processing model of listening that we presented earlier in this chapter. It requires children to integrate new information with existing schemata, selectively attend to auditory stimuli for a set purpose, and become active rather than passive listeners.

The DLTA can be used with a read-aloud book read by the teacher at any grade level. The teacher would proceed thus

PREDICTIONS: "Based on the title of the story and the pictures on the cover, what do you think this story might be about? What makes you think so?"

The teacher might write children's responses on the chalkboard or simply repeat them. Several ideas should be solicited from children. Next, the teacher would read the story to the children, and stop to check on predictions midway through the story.

CONFIRMATIONS: "Now, based on what you have already heard, who wants to change their predictions. Why? What new evidence do you have?"

"How do you think the story will end? Why do you think so? What evidence do you have?"

The teacher would then read the rest of the story, having children listen to find out if their predictions are accurate. At the end children would discuss the conclusion of the story and whether or not their hypotheses had been confirmed.

This activity teaches children to take risks and to make predictions based on information that they already have. Again, existing schemata can be called up to be integrated with new information.

EVALUATING LISTENING COMPREHENSION

Lundsteen (1979, p. 81) defines the best listener as one "who most consistently, in the least time and in the greatest variety of circumstances, most closely approximates the speaker's meaning in the widest variety of spoken material." Thus, a complete profile of a listener would incorporate listening for different purposes in a wide variety of circumstances and situations. Such a profile is obviously difficult to compile, particularly in formal testing. In this section we will discuss some available formal instruments to measure listening. Most of the section, however, will focus on informal assessment techniques you can use in your class to begin to develop a profile of your children as listeners.

Formal Instruments to Measure Listening

In our opinion, the education profession is still without a first-rate instrument for the measurement of listening. However, there are a number of commonly used tests to test listening related skills.

The Illinois Test of Psycholinguistic Ability (published by the University of Illinois at Urbana) contains 12 subtests and can be used with children ages two to ten. Of the 12 subtests the ones most pertinent to listening are Auditory Reception, Auditory Association, Auditory Sequential Memory, and Auditory Closure.

The Wepman Auditory Discrimination Test (published by Language Research Associates) can be administered to children between the ages of four and nine. To administrate the test, children are presented with word pairs and asked to discriminate changes in frequency, intensity, and pattern of auditory stimuli. The Illinois Test of Psycholinguistic Ability and the Wepman Auditory Discrimination Test measure a student's ability in the mechanics of listening.

There are also a number of standardized tests that focus on a child's listening comprehension. The Sequential Test of Educational Progress Listening Test (published by the Educational Testing Service in Princeton, New Jersey) is available in two alternate forms for each of four levels which go up through grade six. The general format of the test is that the teacher presents information orally and then asks the students questions about that information. Students respond by selecting options from multiple-choice items. The test purports to measure plain-sense comprehension, interpretation, and evaluation-application.

The Cooperative Primary Tests (published by the Educational Testing Service) also contains a listening comprehension subtest useful for children in grades 1.5 to 3.0. Again information is presented to children orally; they then respond to multiple-choice items about that information. The test measures a student's ability to identify associated or illustrative examples, recall specific elements, interpret the ideas presented and draw inferences.

The Durrell Listening-Reading Series (published by Harcourt Brace Jovanovich) compares a child's listening ability with reading ability. It has forms that assess vocabulary and sentence comprehension for grades one through six.

Informal Methods for Assessing Listening

Most classroom teachers do not have the time or the need for a formal assessment of listening comprehension. Informal techniques can give an accurate picture of children's overall listening abilities.

Criteria for evaluating listening effectiveness can be set up with children and then used by teachers in their own informal observations or by the children themselves. One advantage of teacher observations is its flexibility—you can evaluate listening under a variety of circumstances. To have children evaluate themselves requires them to become more aware of their own listening skills. A listening list could be developed as a group and may include the following items.

Does the student

1 Have a purpose for listening?
2 Look at the speaker?
3 Appear interested?
4 Maintain attention?
5 React thoughtfully?
6 Ask pertinent questions?

Teachers can use these simple criteria to evaluate children under a variety of conditions, for example, during discussions, when oral instructions are given by the teacher and by other children, during a film or filmstrip, when the teacher is reading aloud. This information also can be effective feedback for children; they can learn under what conditions they listen best.

Wolvin and Coakley (1979) recommend that children make listening log books. Intermediate grade children can use these logs to evaluate their listening by recording how much time they spend listening. Waking hours can be divided into 15-minute intervals and children can record how much time they spend listening, speaking, reading, writing, and in nonverbal communication. The importance of listening becomes evident through this type of activity. Children can write detailed descriptions of their listening experiences and their reactions to these experiences to help them evaluate their behavior and how well they listened.

Example

Listening Log: 12/2—late afternoon
1 Type of listening:
mother scolding
Reaction:
I did not pay attention because I've heard it all before. She yelled at me for not cleaning my room, but I was too busy trying to leave the room to get to my softball practice.

Checklists, log books, informal discussions, and the role model you as a teacher create can help children develop good listening skills. These skills do not necessarily require direct instruction in the isolated skill of listening, but instead can result from careful attention and consideration to listening as one of the four language arts skills.

SUGGESTED ACTIVITIES

1 As you listen to someone be aware of all the assumptions you are making about what they say. How is this an example of "top-down" processing?

2 Be aware of how you know someone is listening to you when you speak. What verbal and nonverbal cues do they give you that they are paying attention to what you say?

3 For one night keep a log book of the different commercials you see on television and the various propaganda techniques employed in those commercials.

4 Observe a language arts teacher leading a discussion. List the techniques he or she uses that are described in this chapter (for example, convergent and divergent questions, accepting students' responses, listening to students).

REFERENCES

Barker, L. L. (ed.). *Communication in the Classroom.* Englewood Cliffs, N.J.: Prentice-Hall, 1982.

Cunningham, P. "Transferring Comprehension from Listening to Reading." *Reading Teacher* 29 (November 1975):169–172.

———. "The Chip Sheet: Improving Listening and Reading Comprehension." *Reading Teacher* 35, 4 (January 1982):486–488.

Devine, T. "Listening and Reading." ERIC Document ED 132523, 1976.

———. "Listening: What Do We Know after Fifty Years of Research And Theorizing?" *Journal of Reading* 21, 4 (December 1978):269–304.

Dole, J. A.; Harvey, S. A.; and Feldman, V. "The Development and Validation of a Listening Comprehension Test as a Predictor of Reading Comprehension." Paper presented at the American Educational Research Association Conference, April 1982.

Duker, S. "Listening." In R. L. Ebel (ed.), *Encyclopedia of Educational Research*, 4th ed. New York: Macmillan, 1969, pp. 747–752.

Durkin, D. *Teaching Them to Read.* 3rd ed. Boston, Mass.: Allyn and Bacon, 1978.

Lundsteen, S. W. *Listening: Its Impact on Reading and the Other Language Arts.* Urbana, Ill.: National Council of Teachers of English, 1971.

———. *Listening.* Urbana, Ill.: National Council of Teachers of English, 1979.

Lyon, R. "Auditory-Perceptual Training: The State of the Art." *Journal of Learning Disabilities* 10, 9 (November 1977):564–572.

Montgomery, R. L. "Are You a Good Listener?" *Nation's Business* (October 1981): 65–66, 68.(a)

—————. *Listening Made Easy.* New York: AMACOM, 1981. (b)

Spearritt, D. "Identification of Subskills of Reading Comprehension by Maximum Likelihood Factor Analysis." *Reading Research Quality* 8 (Fall 1972):92–111.

Stauffer, R. *Directing the Reading Thinking Process.* New York: Harper and Row, 1975.

Sticht, T.; Beck, L.; Hauke, R.; Kleiman, G.; and James, J. *Auding and Reading: A Developmental Model.* Arlington, Va: Human Resources Research Organization, 1974.

Tough, J. *Talking, Thinking, Growing.* New York: Schocken Books, 1974.

Wolvin, A. D., and Coakley, C. G. *Listening Instruction.* Urbana, Ill.: Eric Clearinghouse on Reading and Communication Skills, 1979.

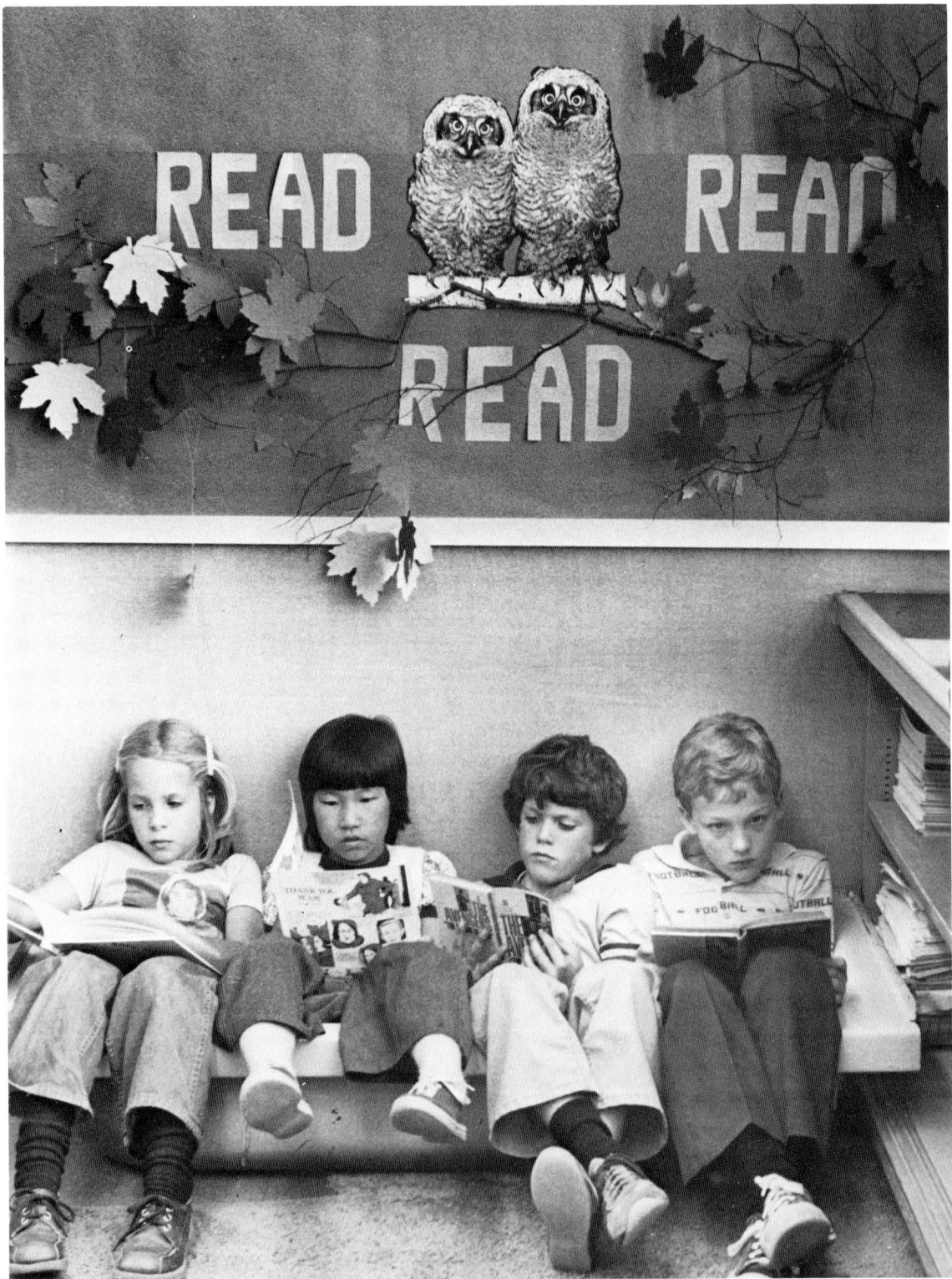

CHAPTER 11

Reading Instruction

WHAT IS READING?
SECOND GRADERS
   . . . learning how to read words.
   . . . learning compound words like
       ketchup, like "catch" and "up."

SIXTH GRADERS
   . . . learning.
   . . . thinking.
   . . . understanding.
   . . . something the people can enjoy.

WHO IS A GOOD READER?
FIFTH GRADER
   . . . my mom . . . she reads every night and she enjoys
       it too.

OVERVIEW

The purpose of this chapter is to give you a general overview of reading as part of receptive communication. We will discuss reading readiness, and help you set up criteria to tell you when children are ready to learn to read. You will learn about the major components of reading instruction, focusing on comprehension at the word, sentence, and schema levels. Then you will learn about the three major approaches to the teaching of reading, the language experience approach (L.E.A.), the individualized reading approach (I.R.) and the basal reader approach. Lastly, we will discuss the evaluation of progress in the reading program, and give you guidelines for both the formal and informal evaluation of your students.

INTRODUCTION

In earlier chapters we stressed thought and language because knowledge gleaned from cognitive psychologists and from linguists has been so instrumental to understanding language arts skills. The oral language chapter demonstrated the importance of schema for speakers and listeners, in their understanding of the social context of the message. The writing chapter emphasized the importance of the oral language base and of thought again. In the listening chapter we presented a listening model in which we make predictions about what we will hear based on existing schemata and knowledge of language. Here we will again see the importance of the thinking-language model in understanding the reading process. You will notice, too that the model we present will be similar to the listening model since the receptive skills of listening and reading are related.

THE READING PROCESS

In Chapter 10 we presented an information processing model of listening which we said was also applicable to the reading process. We will now explain that model in more detail to show you how it applies to both receptive language skills.

Prior to 1967 the common-sense belief about the reading process was something like the following: "Reading is a precise process. It involves exact, detailed, sequential perception and identification of letters, words, spelling patterns and large language units" (Goodman, 1976, p. 497). We have already referred to this approach as a bottom-up approach. Bottom-up refers to any process in which the emphasis is on detail first and larger units of information second. Relative to reading a bottom-up model suggests that reader's primary goal is to decode the words that he or she is reading rather than comprehend the overall message. Second graders have a bottom-up model of reading when they respond that reading is "learning how to use words" and "learning compound words." A bottom-up model does not take into account the use of schema. Prior to the late 1960s most models of reading were basically bottom-up.

In the late 1960s Kenneth Goodman attacked the common-sense bottom-up model of reading in his now famous article entitled, "Reading: A Psycholinguistic Guessing Game" (1976). Based on a top-down schema oriented model of reading, Goodman offered this alternative view of the reading process.

> *Reading is a psycholinguistic guessing game. It involves an interaction between thought and language. Efficient reading does not result from precise perception and identification of all elements, but from skill in selecting the fewest, most productive cues necessary to produce guesses which are right the first time. The ability to anticipate that which has not been seen, of course, is vital in reading, just as the ability to anticipate what has not yet been heard is vital in listening (1976, p. 468).*

Goodman developed his theory of reading by studying the mistakes or "miscues" of children as they read aloud. He found that when reading children did not seem to rely most heavily on the sound/symbol system as much as they did on what seemed "logical." In other words, they anticipated and read what seemed to fit best into their schema about what they were reading. Often they make substitutions like "there" for "here," "home" for "house" and "Dan" for "Don."

In the model, Goodman argues that the reading process is initially a top-down one in which you, the reader, try to identify the appropriate schema with which to interpret what is being read. From your schema you generate hypotheses about what you expect to read. You then use those hypotheses to guide what you look at and how you initially interpret what you see. Of course you also use your knowledge of language to guide and interpret what you see (for example, in the sentence: John threw the _____, your knowledge of syntax and semantics tells you the missing word can't be "jumping" or "house"). You then test that interpretation to see how logical it is in light of your hypotheses. If your choice fails this test of logic you go back and try to gather more information to make another tentative choice about meaning. If you can't make an initial guess about the meaning of what you see, you look for more information until you can. If your choice is acceptable you assimilate the information and continue reading.

This, then, is our model of the reading process. The importance of schema and language are obvious. We read based on our existing knowledge base of the world and our knowledge of language. The two come together and influence the message we receive from the written text. As we discuss particular components of the reading process we want you to keep these facts in mind.

READINESS FOR PRINT

The model of reading we have presented makes clear the prominence of cognitive and linguistic abilities in the reading process. These abilities are developed gradually over children's preschool and school years. In this section we want to focus on these abilities necessary for learning to deal with print.

The whole area of reading readiness is controversial and has remained that way for decades. Because our society places a high value on reading, we tend to look for simple answers to the reading dilemma. Some writers, not necessarily educators, have argued that children can learn to read at an early age and that they would benefit from early instruction in reading. This idea has a great deal of popular appeal to parents, especially parents who distrust our educational system and want to teach their children themselves. Thus, numerous popular books have been marketed that encourage and instruct parents how to teach reading to their babies. This popular belief, however, is neither supported nor endorsed by leading experts in reading, and there remains a large gap between what parents believe about reading readiness and what reading authorities "know" about reading readiness.

Current thinking among educators today emphasizes an individualized and broadened interpretation of reading readiness. In years past a blank endorsement of a particular chronological age (a child must be six) or mental age (a child must have an I.Q. equal to that of a six year old) determined beginning reading instruction. Now, educators urge teachers to look at children as individuals, assess where they are on the "readiness" scales, and teach them what they need to know.

Additionally, educators have begun to think of reading readiness in the broader context of readiness to deal with print. Current research and thought emphasizes helping children learn the purposes and functions of written language through early experiences with writing as well as reading. Some experts even argue that children should learn to write before they learn to read and that these experiences in writing teach them what reading is all about. We will return to this argument in more detail later.

Components of Reading Readiness

When we refer to readiness for reading, we refer to a myriad of experiences and abilities which children need so that they can deal with print. At the simplest level, children need to be able to see and hear adequately. Beyond that they need to be able to distinguish likenesses and differences visually—that is, differentiate an *n* from an *r* or a *p* from a *q*. They need to be able to distinguish likenesses and differences auditorily—that is, hear the difference between "pin" and "pen" and "pan." Additionally, they need a certain amount of visual-motor coordination—the ability to turn a page, hold a book, color, write, and cut and paste. All these skills are typically associated with reading readiness. We will not discuss them in detail here, but instead will focus on the thinking and language components so necessary for reading.

LANGUAGE AND CONCEPT DEVELOPMENT

The ability to read is a cognitive and language-based ability. Children who have expanded vocabularies, use complex sentence structures and have sophisticated concepts about the world have a head start in their readiness for print. When they encounter language in their readers, they are more likely to be able to connect that language to their existing schemata. For example, compare the responses of two six-year-old girls' encounter with a story about the ocean. Jennifer lives in Denver and Tina lives in Rhode Island. Because Tina has had numerous sensory experiences with the ocean (the sound of the waves, the smell and taste of salt, the feel of the sand), she probably will have an enriched vocabulary about the ocean and therefore a better understanding of the story she reads. Jennifer, on the other hand, may have seen pictures of the ocean, but she is unlikely to have the background and vocabulary to comprehend the story as well as Tina.

In addition to knowledge and language awareness of general concepts, children have to know some very important common concepts as prerequisites to reading. To give you a better example of this, consider this sentence.

The dog is sitting under the table.

To understand that sentence children need to have more than just an idea or concept of "dog" and "table"; they also must have a concept of "under." Having knowledge of that concept, they then can imagine in their minds the table with the dog sitting squarely underneath. Thus, young children must learn the important concepts of "under," "on," "over," "near," "far," and so forth. Many kindergarteners have not developed these concepts.

Do you see why knowlege of these simple concepts is so important to reading readiness and how this knowledge relates to language development? In even the most simple reading material these concepts are used constantly. In the sentence presented earlier, imagine what happens when a child thinks that "under" means "on," or "beside?"

The dog is sitting under the table.

The dog is sitting on the table.

The dog is sitting beside the table.

Clearly, an understanding of these concepts is a prerequisite to comprehension of these sentences.

DEVELOPING A SCHEMA FOR BOOKS

All of the components of readiness that have been mentioned—visual and auditory skills, visual-motor coordination and language/conceptual development—are not, in and of themselves, complete and entirely adequate barometers for determining when a child is ready to read. You may encounter a child whom you feel is competent in all these areas, but still is not ready for books.

Take a minute to review what we know about books and print. In order to read, we need to know certain things, like

1 Where the front of the book is.
2 Where the title of the book is.
3 Where the words are versus where the pictures are.
4 On what page the story begins.
5 How to turn the page.
6 Which page to turn and in which direction.
7 Which page to begin reading.
8 Where to begin reading:
   left to right and top to bottom.

Children vary in their knowledge about these concepts when they enter school. The variation is due in large part to the kinds of experiences the home provides in establishing a literate environment for the child. Children have a head start in homes where there is an abundance of books, in homes where parents and siblings read often and value reading, or in homes where they themselves are read to. Recall the fifth grader who said his Mom reads a lot and enjoys it too. This child probably knew at the age of three or four what a book is for and how to hold a book. In contrast, those children who grow up in a home environment where literacy is not valued have a harder time comprehending what written language is all about. They have to learn in the classroom the purpose for written language and how written language relates to oral language. We discuss this in further detail in Chapter 13 on children's literature, but we feel it is important to mention now because the home environment shapes children's readiness for print.

We must also mention the importance of attitudes in readiness for books. Children's attitudes will already be developed in the home, although it is also true that children can have positive attitudes toward reading, but still not be ready to read. How does the child feel about learning to read? Does she or he want to sit down and listen to a story? Does she or he express or show an interest in the pictures, or more importantly, in the words? Does she or he ask you what a word "says?" Does the child understand the relationship between the words and what you are speaking? Does the child act interested and ask questions, or wiggle around or look up and away at other visual or auditory stimulation? All of these behavioral characteristics are reflective of children's readiness for reading. This readiness can be discerned by you, an observant teacher. Very clearly, the most important point we can leave with you is that you should never force children to read before they are "ready" for it.

THE CHILD WHO IS READY TO READ IS A CHILD WHO*

Listens

to directions without interrupting.

to stories and poems for five or ten minutes without restlessness.

Hears

words that rhyme.

words that begin with the same sound or different sounds.

Sees

likenesses and differences in pictures and designs.

letters and words that match.

Speaks and Can

stay on the topic in class discussions.

retell a story or poem in correct sequence.

tell a story or relate an experience.

Thinks and Can

give the main ideas of a story.

give unique ideas and important details.

give reasons for opinions.

Understands

the relationship inherent in such words as up and down, top and bottom, little and big.

the classifications of words that represent people, places and things.

Experiences

everyday activities and events commonplace for the peer group.

loving concern from adults.

Adjusts

to change in routine and to new situations without becoming fearful.

to opposition or defeat without crying or sulking.

to the necessity of asking for help when needed.

Plays

cooperatively with other children.

and shares, takes turns, and assumes a share of group responsibilities.

and can run, jump, skip, and bounce a ball with comparative dexterity.

and has adequate eye-hand coordination.

Works

without being easily distracted.

and follows directions.

and completes each task.

and takes pride in his work.

Feels good about him or herself and her or his contributions to the group.

Source: From The Parents and Reading Committee, International Reading Association.

READING AND WRITING: EARLY CONNECTIONS

Earlier we mentioned that some educators argue that children can and should learn to write before they learn to read. This idea runs counter to traditional thinking about the sequence of learning the language arts.

$$\text{listening} \rightarrow \text{speaking} \rightarrow \text{reading} \rightarrow \text{writing}$$

Graves and his associates in the University of New Hampshire Writing Project (refer to Chapter 6) provide good evidence, however, that children *can* and *do* benefit from early experiences in writing. We already mentioned the work on Marie Clay (1975) in our chapter on handwriting. She too stresses the importance of a creative writing program as a necessary part of every beginning reading program.

To understand why these and other educators make these early connections between reading and writing, you need to understand some theoretical links between oral and written language. Remember that children enter school with a wealth of knowledge about language through their four to five years of experience in the oral mode-listening and speaking. As they enter school they need to learn written language. Writing is an excellent medium through which those connections can be made.

Clay (1975) convincingly explains how and why children can learn about reading through writing. She argues that creative writing makes children pay attention to the details of written language and to the hierarchy of sequential units in print—sentences to phrases to words to letters. Recall from the handwriting chapter that

Clay evaluates readiness for *writing* in terms of knowledge of language organization, understanding of a message, and sense of directionality. These same characteristics are equally important as components of reading readiness. Does the child understand what a word is, what a sentence is? Does the child understand the concept of sign, that a sign represents a message? Does the child know that reading occurs from left to right?

Marie M. Clay (1972) has developed a test that evaluates children's understanding of and readiness for books and for written language. The test is individually administered to children, and asks such questions as: How do you hold the book? Where is the front of the book? The test is designed to evaluate children's knowledge about written language and is an excellent resource for teachers to help determine children's readiness for print.

In Chapter 9 on handwriting we stressed the importance of children's early experiences with writing for handwriting readiness. Here we again stress the importance of early experiences with writing for reading readiness. The two are tied together theoretically because they both are aspects of written language. Thus, reading and writing need to be tied together in the classroom so children can understand the important connection. Early writing experiences generate early reading experiences and help children become comfortable with written language. Late in this chapter we will describe a more specific technique for linking reading and writing via the language-experience approach. For now we will just reiterate that some kind of writing program is essential for reading readiness as well as for writing readiness.

READING INSTRUCTION

Current thinking (Goodman, 1967; Kohlers, 1969; Pearson and Johnson, 1978; Smith, 1978) as well as longstanding reading pedagogy (Huey, 1908) emphasizes the crucial role that comprehension plays in reading. Reading, like each of the language arts skills, is thinking process, and the ultimate goal of all reading instruction is toward the improvement of comprehension. When children first learn to read, an inordinate amount of energy and time is spent on bottom-up processing and the graphophonic relationship because children cannot translate the symbols into sounds. Even at this time, however, the purpose of reading instruction must be to help children learn to associate what they read with what they think and what they know. We are delineating two areas here—reading as "decoding," as translating symbols into sounds—and reading as "comprehending," that is, understanding what an author is saying. This dichotomy is not often understood by many people who think reading *is* decoding.

To illustrate this point we will recount an extraordinary visit to one classroom. One of the authors visited a class and heard the oral reading of a bright, precocious eight-year-old Laotian child who had been in this country less than a year. This little boy read flawlessly from a fourth-grade reading text. He could pronounce every unfamiliar word he encountered, breaking each word into syllables and carefully sounding out each syllable. It required little time to realize, however, that he had absolutely no idea of what he was reading; he was simply "barking at the words." On the other hand, why *should* he be able to comprehend the story? It was about the 1968 landing on the moon. There was nothing in his experience or background to lay the foundation for understanding any of the words or concepts—astronaut, moon, space, orbit, rocket—or the sequence of events in the story. This child could "decode" the words; he could translate the symbols into sounds. He could not, however, comprehend the story; he did not understand what the author was saying.

We have already discussed receptive language processing as being top-down or bottom-up. The decoding process itself forces on children a certain amount of bottom-up processing. When children first learn to read, they are forced to pay close attention to the morphemes and even graphemes on a page. Thus you have children who "word-read": "Sam . . . went . . . to . . . school . . . late . . . today." Even for these children, however, reading must also be a top-down process for comprehension to occur. Children must be able to relate the story to something they know; it must be meaningful to them. If it is not, then beginning readers will not come to understand that important connection between written language and ideas. Further, later on, even after they can decode, they will not connect their reading with their past existing schemata, their experiences and their ideas.

In this section we will present the comprehension of written language at three levels: the word level, the sentence level and the schema level. We will suggest some skills and abilities necessary for comprehension at each level and provide you with specific teaching strategies for improving comprehension of progressively larger units of discourse.

COMPREHENSION AT THE WORD LEVEL

At the beginning and most basic level, reading requires an accurate decoding and comprehending of individual words. Decoding refers to the act of translating a written symbol, "cat" for example, to its oral counterpart /cat/. In order to decode, children need: (1) to know the graphemes and their corresponding phonemes; and/or (2) to understand the essential nature of the graphophonological relationship—that is, that written symbols correspond to oral sounds, "cat" and /cat/. Beyond this, however, comprehending at the word level requires an understanding of what the words mean. Thus, children who can decode "cat" may not comprehend at the word level until they can connect the grapheme symbol "cat" with an image or concept of a cat in their heads. As we discuss different methods for teaching beginning reading, or reading at the word level, it is important to understand this distinction. What we are saying is that all decoding must be accompanied by comprehending for reading to occur even at this most basic level.

Methods of Teaching Decoding

Beginning reading focuses on the decoding process, the process whereby children learn to translate written symbols to their oral counterparts. The two opposing methods of teaching decoding, *phonics* versus *whole-word*, have received a great deal of attention in American society and the popular press. We will discuss each in detail.

The phonics method is one of several types of synthetic methods (Durkin, 1978). These bottom-up methods are called "synthetic" because they always proceed from part to whole. In other words, learning to read begins with learning isolated letters and sounds and then proceeds by blending those sounds together to decode words. The primary focus of study is on the graphophonic relationship. It is believed that once children can "crack the code" then they will have learned to read.

A typical sequence of instruction using a synthetic method would proceed in the following way.

1 You would teach children to discriminate and then identify all the letters of the alphabet.

2 You would then teach them to associate the correct sound to the symbol—"1" says /1/, "b" says /b/, and so on.

3 You would then teach them to blend or synthesize the sounds together to make words.

"bat" would be taught
"a" says /a/   "b" says /b/   "bbbaaa"
"t" says /t/—"ba . . . ttt"   "bat"

Synthetic methods of teaching beginning reading rely on the notion that our language is basically phonemically regular. Earlier in this book however, we mentioned that our alphabet consists of 26 graphemes and 36 or more phonemes. Thus, we have, at best, an imperfect match between letters and their corresponding sounds. In the phonics method, children are taught rules that they can apply when they come to an unknown word. These rules enable children to decide which phoneme to use with a given grapheme. Some rules you may remember learning yourself:

1 *CVC pattern.* When a vowel occurs between two consonants, then the vowel has a short sound.

bat
can
top

2 *CVVC pattern.* When two vowels are together between two consonants, then the first vowel has a long sound, and the second vowel is silent.

leap
float

3 *CVCE pattern.* When a vowel occurs between two consonants followed by an "e," the vowel has a long sound.

hope
ride
cane

In addition to teaching rules for vowel sounds, a set of rules for syllabication is taught so that multisyllabic words may be decoded.

You also may remember learning these rules:

1 When two vowels occur between two consonants, divide between the consonants.

gar/den
pil/low
win/dow

2 When two vowels occur between one consonant, divide before or after the consonant.

a/lone
be/hind
to/gether

Programs vary in the extent and intensity of teaching these phonics rules to children. Aukerman (1971) describes numerous programs on the market and the degree to which they emphasize teaching the rules. Some programs such as *Breaking the Sound Barrier* (Aukerman, 1971, pp. 94–95) consist of a handbook of detailed pronunciation rules to be taught directly to children. Programs like this lie on the extreme end of the continuum of synthetic methods. Many good basal reader series use a synthetic method for teaching beginning reading, but also rely on other methods as well.

Before discussing these other methods in detail, we want to mention one other synthetic method which you may hear about. This method is often referred to as the *linguistic approach* to teaching reading. This method is often confused with a phonics method, and we think this confusion should be clarified.

The linguistic approach originated in the late 1950s and early 1960s with the work of Fries (1955) and Bloomfield and Barnhardt (1961). They were among the first linguists to take an active interest in reading and to try to apply knowledge gleaned from linguistics to the field of education. They argued that our language is basically phonemically regular, and that children could learn to read easily once they discerned this regularity.

A number of similarities exists between the linguistic method and the phonics method, so much so, in fact, that teachers often do not understand the differences between the two. Both methods are based on the assumption that our language is phonemically regular. Both methods begin by teaching the graphemes and then

TAT, TAM, AND SAM

I see Tat, Tam, and Sam

at the mat.

Tat, Tam, and Sam sat

at the mat.

The rams and Sam sat

at the mat.

From *The Palo Alto Reading Program*, Book One, Second Edition by Theodore & Glim et al., © 1975 by Harcourt Brace Jovanovich, Inc. Reprinted and reproduced by permission of the publisher.

their corresponding phonemes. Both methods thus emphasize the sound-symbol relationship, and the synthetic method of learning words.

Careful examination of linguistic readers, however, reveals differences between the two methods. In the linguistic method, children are *not* taught the rules. Instead, they are exposed to the regular patterns of the English language in their reading materials. Therefore, in linguistic readers, vocabulary is carefully controlled so that word families such as MAT and SAT are introduced and reinforced repeatedly throughout each story (see example). In this way children learn the rules indirectly without being taught them. Thus, the linguistic method emphasizes the learning of word families as opposed to the learning of pronunciation rules. The phonics method does not control the exposure to new words and new word patterns, and children are required to sound out each new word as it occurs in context in the reading material.

Before completing this discussion of synthetic methods, an additional comment is in order. Many proponents of synthetic methods focus on the decoding process only. Oftentimes they fail to recognize the importance of comprehension even at this most beginning level. Some assume that children already make the connection between the letters, the word, and its referent. Others assume that comprehension will automatically come later, or can be taught later. Observations of first-grade classrooms will quickly reveal children who spend hours on hours learning how to decode using a bottom-up synthetic method, but who do not understand the connection between the word they decode and its referent. Some children figure this out on their own; others do not.

Analytic Method

An alternative procedure for teaching beginning reading is known as the analytic method, also commonly referred to as the "look-say" or "whole-word" method. Using this method teachers teach children to read whole words *before* teaching them the particular letters and sounds. Sylvia Ashton-Warner (1963) used this method in teaching "key words" to her Maori children. She simply asked them what words they wanted to learn each day and then she wrote them down on small cards. Each word was learned as a whole word—that is, c-a-t was learned as "cat." Of course, children must be repeatedly exposed to these words. Simply telling a child one time is no assurance that the word will be remembered. In basal reader series the words are repeated frequently (remember encountering "*See* Dick, *see*. *See* Jane run.") Sylvia Ashton-Warner put the words on small cards and filed them in a word bank. Children took the words out of their word banks daily and made sentences with them, copied them, and repeated them.

Later, the "sight words" that the children have learned are used to teach them about the graphophonic relationship. Beginning consonants, blends, vowels, and other phonic skills are learned based on generalizations the children derive from their word cards or chart stories.

TEACHER: ''Mary, you have the words 'come,' 'can,' and 'cap.' Look at the words carefully. What sound does the 'c' make in each of these words?''

Analytic methods of teaching beginning reading rely on the notion that language must be meaningful for it to be learned. Proponents of this method emphasize that children need to learn to decode whole words from the very beginning, thereby enabling them to see the connection between spoken and written language immediately. They argue that by using the synthetic method, teachers fragment language into meaningless pieces, and children fail to learn the connection between print and language.

The controversy continues. Which method is the best method to teach beginning reading? Proponents of each side cite extensive research to support their positions. Both methods have been used successfully *and* unsuccessfully with different children. Perhaps the more pertinent question to ask is: Which method best leads to comprehension at the word level and beyond *for which children*? An excellent teacher can certainly use either method and still help children make the connection between print and language. Many children will not make this connection on their own. It is our viewpoint that for beginning readers especially, the analytic method enables that connection to be discerned more easily.

COMPREHENSION AT THE SENTENCE LEVEL

Despite the controversy surrounding beginning reading instruction, traditionally it has been easier to teach beginning reading than to teach reading at the more advanced levels. It is easier to teach children to comprehend words than it is to comprehend sentences, paragraphs, and whole stories. These larger units of discourse are syntactically and semantically more complex, and make more linguistic and cognitive demands on the reader.

In the past, teachers have had little assistance or guidance in how to teach reading beyond the word level. Wolf, et al. (1967) listed several factors that have contributed to this: (1) inadequate definition of specific skills involved, (2) inadequate instructional materials, and (3) lack of instruments to evaluate performance and growth. Recent research in propositional analysis, however, (Kintsch, 1974; Schank, 1973; Thorndyke, 1977) has assisted educators in understanding some of the complexities in these larger units of discourse. This understanding has enabled educators to develop instructional strategies to help children comprehend at the sentence level and beyond.

Comprehension at the sentence level refers to understanding the relationships that exist between words within a sentence and also between sentences themselves. In Chapter 3, we listed five major categories that describe relationships within and between sentences. We also mentioned that these relationships are always signaled by a key word or phrase.

Below is a discussion of four major categories of propositions included in Chapter 3—causation, comparison, addition, and time—along with instructional strategies for teaching comprehension at the sentence level. We also refer you to an excellent resource book, *Teaching Reading Comprehension* (Pearson and Johnson 1978), which includes additional categories and instructional strategies.

Relationships Between Propositions

Causation.   Young children often read sentences without a clear understanding of how the sentences fit together. Understanding cause-and-effect relationships seems to be a particularly difficult task for children. When cause and effect is explicitly stated by certain signal words, the task becomes somewhat easier. For example, in the sentence

He needed food *so* he went to the store.

the word *so* signals the reader that one event caused the other event. In this sentence the cause comes first, the effect second, and the signal word "so" provides the connective link from one event to the other. By teaching children to look for the signal words and to know what these words mean, we can help children understand cause and effect.

The task becomes somewhat more difficult, however, with certain signal words. Some signal words suggest a reverse order of cause and effect. For example in the sentence

The party ended *because* Bill went home.

we need to teach children that the event coming *before* "because" is the *cause* of the event coming after "because." In this particular case it is essential that children understand which event was the cause and which was the effect.

Unfortunately, some causal relationships are not signaled by key words at all and therefore must be inferred. For example, in the sentence

Bill went home and the party ended.

a cause-and-effect relationship is implied but not signaled by a key word. Here the reader needs to use his or her prior knowledge and experience to connect the two propositions together and to understand which event caused the other.

Comparison.   Understanding comparative relationships between propositions requires children to see the differences between propositions. At the proposition level, signal words are often used to assist the reader in drawing these contrasts. In the sentence

I will be there, *but* I won't be happy.

the word "but" signals a contrast between an event and the feeling about the event. In the sentences

> Bill is tall. *In comparison*, his brother is short.

the words "in comparison" signal that one attribute is in direct contrast to another.

Again, teaching children to understand comparative relationships begins by teaching the signal words and what they mean. Based on these signal words, children then identify the two attributes and note how they are dissimilar, or how one relates or contrasts to the other.

Addition. Addition is used here as a general category of propositons which restate, rephrase, embellish, or order attributes, ideas or events. Children need to understand when and in what ways:

1 One proposition restates another.

> I am tired; in fact, I am exhausted.

2 One proposition is an example of another.

> He does many things well. For example, he is excellent at cards.

3 One proposition simply adds more information to another.

> He is tall and he is handsome.

4 One proposition is a paraphrase of another.

> He does many things well. He cooks. He sews.
> In all, he is an excellent homemaker.

Time. This last category refers to understanding time relationships between propositions. This task is a particularly difficult one for children, as concepts about time and the sequence of events develop slowly during the elementary years. Many young children do not understand the meaning of simple signal words like "before" and "after." Clark (1971) found that children use the order of oral presentation of a proposition to determine the sequence of time. Thus in the sentence

> They went to the dance *after* they went to the game.

many young children will list going to the dance as the first event and going to the game as the second event. Thus, with time relationships it is especially important that children understand the meanings of the signal words, and have extensive practice reordering events in the correct sequence.

Instructional Strategies

Below we have listed several instructional strategies to be used to teach comprehension at the sentence level. Many suggested strategies can be used to teach one or more of the four general categories described. In addition, we try to show you how to modify the strategies for different age and ability levels.

- Teach children to look for signal words. You might post charts in which the signal words are listed.

- Teach children the meanings of the signal words. Primary grade children need to learn even simple signal words like "before" "after," "while." Intermediate grade children need to learn the meanings of signal words used in their content area texts, "first," "second," "third," "last."

- As you are reading stories to children, occasionally pick out a paragraph with signal words and discuss it with them. For example, read the paragraph

  She was so *busy thinking* that *she was unaware of thick muddy clouds that blocked out the sun.* Nor *did she hear the menacing rumble of thunder. She was almost knocked off the doorstep* when *a sudden gust of wind drove torrents of rain against her face.**

- Talk about the meanings of *so . . . that, nor,* and *when.* Change the sentences around and say them in a different way. Try different signal words.

- Discuss with children the effects of reversing the sentences and the word order.

  Bill went home. Therefore, the party ended.

  The party ended. Therefore, Bill went home.

  How does the meaning of the sentences change when the sentences are reversed?

- Have children make up sentences with the signal words and write them on 3 × 5 cards. Place cards in a box. Have children pull out one card at a time and: (1) name the signal word, and (2) decide if the propositions can be reversed without changing the meaning of the sentence(s).

  I will be there,
  but I won't be happy.

  Bill went home; so
  the party ended.

- Read two sentences to the children. As they listen, they should think of the correct signal words to establish a relationship between the ideas in each:

  He went to the store.
  He needed food.

  Mary is going on a trip.
  She should plan well.

* From *Sam, Bangs & Moonshine* by Evaline Ness (Holt, Rinehart and Winston, 1966).

The tire was flat.
The driver pulled over to the side of the road.

- Make large charts to display the signal words and sentences. Provide a space large enough for children to write in the signal words and the sentences, and to identify the cause-and-effect, contrast, time or addition category.

Signal Word	Sentence	Cause	Effect
because	He went to the store because he needed food.	he needed food	he went to the store

- Have young children fold a sheet of paper in half. Make up a series of sentences like

  She ate an ice cream cone after she cleaned her room.

  Have children draw a picture of each event in the order in which it occurred. Older children can make up their own sentences using the signal words in the time category and they can draw pictures to illustrate the sentences.

- Provide children with sentences from a favorite book in which they must choose the appropriate signal word.

  _____ the old lady said, "This soup looks good."

  "It looks good _____," said the hungry young man.
  "_____ it would look better
  _____ you threw in a chicken or two."*

COMPREHENSION AT THE SCHEMA LEVEL

Thus far we have examined reading comprehension at the word level and discussed how to teach children to associate a written word with its oral counterpart. We also discussed comprehension at the sentence level by presenting different relationships between propositions and listing instructional strategies for teaching comprehension of these relationships. We now want to examine comprehension of larger units of discourse, units such as a paragraph, a chapter, or a whole story or units that require the reader to use existing schema to comprehend. We will discuss four categories of comprehension at the schema level. We will then describe one particular instructional strategy for teaching comprehension at this level.

* From *Stone Soup* by Ann McGovern (Scholastic Book Services, 1968).

Main Idea-Details

We believe that children often need direct instruction in understanding the main idea and details of a paragraph. This task is not an easy one for teachers, however, particularly since paragraphs differ in their composition and in how explicitly or implicitly the main idea and details are stated.

Pearson and Johnson (1978) define the task of finding the main idea as that of being able to understand that some ideas expressed in a paragraph are examples of a more general idea also expressed within that same paragraph. Consider the paragraph:

> *Bob likes sports. He likes to play volleyball. In the winter he likes to ski. He belongs on a hockey team. In the summer he swims and plays baseball.*

We can see clearly the main idea and the supporting details. You can have your children outline the paragraph as follows:

Bob-sports
    volleyball
    ski
    hockey
    swim
    baseball

Pearson and Johnson also suggest presenting a visual model to help illustrate the relationships among these ideas.

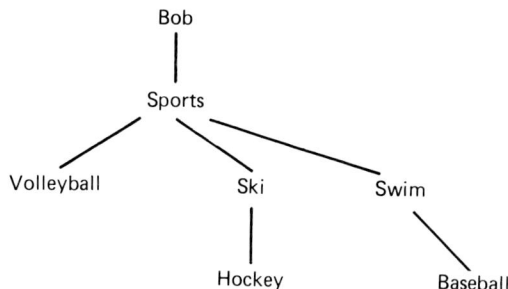

A problem you will encounter when you teach main ideas is that oftentimes paragraphs are not organized so that the main idea is explicitly stated. Similarly, details are often embedded in the sentences and are not clear to the reader. We believe that the best teaching procedure is to begin with clear paragraphs such as the one we have presented above, moving on to progressively more difficult paragraphs as children become more proficient in this skill.

In addition, this is a particularly good skill to relate to writing and to teach as a reading-writing unit. Children can read paragraphs which differentiate the main idea from details and then write paragraphs based on their experiences. For example, they can begin with a general statement and then fill in the details—for example, Last week I went to a pajama party, or When I was sick, I had to go to the doctor.

Paraphrase

Just as we expand and build concepts through synonyms, we also expand and build on comprehension through paraphrasing (Pearson and Johnson, 1978). At the schema level, paraphrasing can refer to a summarization of a story, or an expression of the gist of a paragraph or story. Children often have difficulty paraphrasing a story. This problem relates back to a more general problem mentioned earlier, that children often fail to see how sentences fit together and relate to one another and to ideas. Again, the sequence of instruction must proceed from the simple to the more complex, and from the explicit to the more implicit.

Begin by reading a simple story and having children "tell in their own words" what the story was about. In addition to this retelling procedure (Goodman and Burke, 1972), you can also ask children to tell what the story is about in one or two sentences. This is a more difficult task and will require more practice for children to learn to be concise.

Figurative Language

We are not often aware of how we use figurative language on a day-to-day basis. One of the authors became acutely aware when he impatiently said to his three year-old daughter, "Hold your horses!" to which his daughter replied, "I don't *have* any horses!"

Children must learn that not all language is to be interpreted literally. They are exposed to figurative language early in life, yet they often do not understand the real meaning behind many of our common expressions. As they progress from the primary to the intermediate grades, they need to study expressions that can be literally or figuratively interpreted. We include these expressions under schema level comprehension because comprehension of figurative language requires the reader to use existing schema in his or her head.

One of the best ways to teach figurative language is through the use of children's books. The following are most illustrative

- *Come Back, Amelia Bedelia*, by Peggy Parish (Harper & Row, 1971).
- *Play Ball, Amelia Bedelia*, by Peggy Parish (Harper & Row, 1972).
- *The King Who Rained*, by Fred Gwynne (Windmill Books and E. P. Dutton, 1970).
- *A Chocolate Moose for Dinner*, by Fred Gwynne (Windmill Books and Simon & Schuster, 1976).

In *A Chocolate Moose for Dinner* and *The King Who Rained*, pictures literally interpret the figures of speech, allowing children to see their images. Thus, the expression "Mommy has a frog in her throat" is illustrated literally. In the Amelia Bedelia books children read about Amelia who literally interprets everything she hears, that is, her matron's instructions, "Dust the furniture," "Draw the draperies," and so on.

The following activities can be used to provide children with practice in figurative language.

After reading the Fred Gwynne books

- Have children draw pictures illustrating many different figures of speech.
- Have children write or explain the figurative interpretation, the "real meaning."
- Have children role-play different figures of speech and have the class guess what the figure of speech is.
- Find headlines from newspaper stories or magazine articles that include vague terms—for example,

> "Thousands Left Homeless" or
> "Heavy Casualties Reported."

Discuss how individual students interpret "thousands," "homeless," and "heavy."

- Examine textbooks and look at statements like, "the country is large and has many people." Analyze how different people in different places—for example, New York City versus Kalamazoo, Michigan—would interpret "large" and "many."

Children need to discover that such vague terms produce indefinite and individual interpretations of what they are reading. Discuss with students when, where, and why vague terms might be useful and under what circumstances specific terms would be more appropriate.

Evaluating What You Have Read

In Chapter 5 we discussed the role of problem solving in oral language development. In Chapter 10 we discussed critical listening. Everything that we said in those chapters relates directly to teaching critical reading. What we are asking is the question posed by Wells (1981) "most important of all, and a question which applies to *all* pupils. . . . Are they encouraged to adopt an independent, inquiring and critical attitude to the information that is presented to them and the problems they are given to solve?" (p. 266)

This question is a crucial one for any language arts program. In terms of reading, children need to learn very early that not everything that is written is true. This statement seems so obvious as to be innocuous. Nevertheless, it needs to be pointed out because some children proceed through all their schooling without understanding this basic fact. Interestingly, the NAEP (National Assessment of Educational Progress) reported that 17 year-old's critical reading abilities were below what they were several years ago (NAEP Report, 1982). Some educators have speculated that we have been so busy teaching the "basic skills" in reading that we have neglected this important area of the reading curriculum.

As we mentioned in the listening chapter, we must begin to teach children at a very early age to be critical and evaluative about what they read and hear. Such training begins by asking kindergarteners "Do you think this could really happen?" and "What part of the story do you like best? *Why?*" and proceed on a continuous basis throughout the elementary grades. We are suggesting here that evaluative activities be built into the reading program on a day-to-day basis, rather than being pushed aside for a separate month of the year or a particular grade. Such a reorientation of the reading curriculum means that as a language arts teacher, you *always*

1 Ask at least some questions at the higher levels of analysis, synthesis, and especially evaluation.

2 Ask children to choose at least some of their own books and topics for study.

3 Build into your program time for oral sharing and discussion of individual opinions.

4 Ask that children provide evidence or proof of their assertions and/or opinions.

5 Ask children to be critical of what they hear and read.

Teachers are often most insecure about their abilities in teaching children to evaluate what they have read. Basal manuals do not always provide ideas for teachers. We have already mentioned the Wolf et al. study (1967) which argued that inadequate instructional materials was a major factor in teachers' failure to teach critical reading. Below we have included several instructional activities for teaching children to critically evaluate what they have read.

- Young children can learn that words have connotative as well as denotated meanings. Some words have pleasant connotations or feelings surrounding the word: *candy, vacation, Christmas;* while other words have unpleasant connotations: *homework, ugly, spinach.* Explain that the connotations of words are highly individualized; e.g., *sly* might mean tricky to one person and clever to another. Have children examine their own pleasant and unpleasant feelings surrounding many words. You can make a chart listing words and the associations children have with those words.

- Read the story *The Emperor's New Clothes* by Hans Christian Anderson. Discuss the techniques used by the swindlers to convince the Emperor to wear his new clothes. Discuss how the swindlers are like salespersons trying to sell things. Retell the story using ordinary people and a salesperson selling cars, TVs, clothes, and so on. Encourage children to include the salesperson's appeal to people's emotions and feelings instead of facts.

- Have intermediate grade children watch a sports event on TV. As they watch, record the facts of the game, that is, points scored and by whom, names of players, numbers of errors, and so on. Then have children find the newspaper articles of the same event. Read the articles and note how they compare to the facts already recorded. Then reread each article, underlining words and phrases that reflect the author's opinion or interpretation.

- Have children bring in advertising slogans from magazines and newspapers. Instruct them to rewrite each slogan in a different style. For example, if the slogan is biased, rewrite it in a factual way. If the slogan is based on facts, rewrite it in a biased way.

- Obtain several editions of a science, health, or social studies textbook. Have intermediate grade children discover how the treatment of the same topic varies from one edition to another and from one publisher to another. Notice how much space is devoted to the topic, whether or not the accounts of the events differ, how the facts are presented, and if there are apparent opinions included. Children could then make a chart comparing editions and listing possible reasons for the discrepancies.

- Read two stories to children; one that is a tall tale and one that is true. Ask children to tell you which story is true and which is make-believe. Read paragraphs from both stories and have children classify the paragraphs as true, pretend, or make-believe. Make sure they provide evidence for their classifications.

- Have children evaluate TV commercials and magazine advertisements of their favorite foods. Discuss emotional or loaded words or phrases used to appeal to the audience. List the facts stated and the opinions or beliefs stated. Are the facts distorted to present themselves in a favorable light? Is evidence given to support the facts?

Strategies for Teaching Comprehension at the Schema Level

We have already stressed the importance of schemata for comprehension. As a teacher, how do you ensure that children have the appropriate schema as they are reading? How can you help them process written language from the top, *as well as*, from the bottom? One effective technique is the Directed Reading-Thinking Activity (Stauffer, 1980). This technique is similar to the DLTA presented in the listening chapter. It requires children to identify what they already know about a story topic before they begin reading. They make predictions about the story and then read the story selection to verify their predictions. Last, children are asked to provide evidence in the story to confirm or disconfirm each of their predictions. This procedure, like the DLTA, is excellent for providing practice in processing written language from the top down.

Here is an example of a DRTA used with intermediate children who are reading Theodore Taylor's book *The Cay*.

I. Predict

Identify a purpose for reading.

> *Strategy:* Have children read the title of the book, *The Cay*. Teacher asks: What do you think this book is about? What is a "Cay?" What do you already know about this subject? What do you think you will find out? Have children look at the pictures. Revise predictions based on this additional information.
>
> *Then:* How fast or slow do we need to read this story to get the information we want?
>
> *And:* What predictions can we make about this book? Who do you think might be the main characters? What do you think they might do in this book?

II. Read

> *Strategy:* Children now silently read the first chapter to answer some of their questions. They are reading at a predetermined rate to test their predictions to see if they are right or wrong. Children can read the whole book this way or read chapter by chapter. (If they read a chapter at a time you can proceed to step III and then return to step I before reading the next chapter. Proceed through the book thus, predict-read-prove; predict-read-prove).

III. Prove

> *Strategy:* After children finish reading, conduct an oral discussion where children look at their earlier predictions to find out which were accurate and which were inaccurate. Require children to provide evidence in the text to prove their answers.
> A. What do you think?
> B. Why do you think so?
> C. *Prove* it!

An additional instructional strategy for teaching comprehension of stories is the semantic web (Freedman and Reynolds, 1980). The semantic web provides children with a visual representation of a story, and helps children see the relationships between ideas in a story. Instructions for using the semantic web are provided below.

THE SEMANTIC WEB

1 Teacher chooses one question, *the core question* as the focal point of the web. Examples of core questions include

What happened in the story?
Who were the main characters?
What did the characters do in this story?
What were the main events in the story?

The core question is written on the board as follows

What happened
in the story?

You can ask the question *before* children begin reading; this helps set a purpose to their reading. Alternatively, you can ask them after they have finished reading and continue through the week.

2 The web strands are the answers to the questions. They are visualized as follows

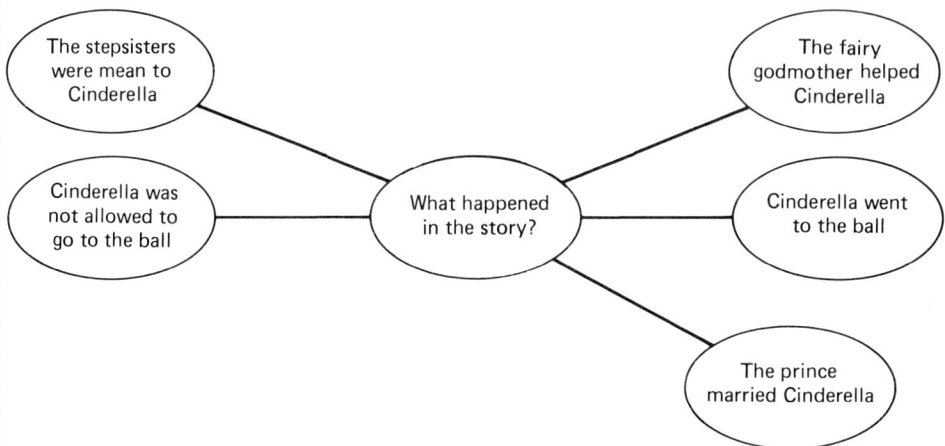

The stepsisters
were mean to
Cinderella

The fairy
godmother helped
Cinderella

Cinderella was
not allowed to
go to the ball

What happened
in the story?

Cinderella went
to the ball

The prince
married Cinderella

Children contribute each of the answers as the teacher writes them on the board. Freedman and Reynolds suggest writing the answers on a separate list and then having children decide together which answers will go on the web.

3 Once the answers have been written on the board, children then are asked to find evidence in the story to support their answers. For example, in the response "The fairy godmother helped Cinderella," children would be asked to find some sentences in the story to support that statement. The semantic web would then be expanded as such:

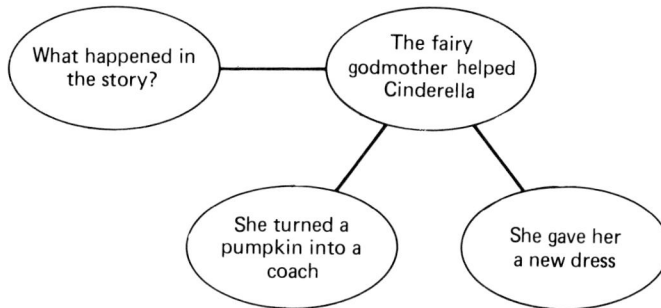

These additional circles are called *strand supports* as they provide support or evidence for the responses in the web strands.

4 Last, children are asked to look for relationships between the web strands. "How do these go together? How are they alike? For example, with the responses "The stepsisters were mean to Cinderella" and "Cinderella was not allowed to go to the ball," children might see a relationship between the two web strands, "bad things that happened to Cinderella." Similarly, they may see the remaining web strands as "good things that happened to Cinderella." These relationships would then be connected with dotted lines and identified:

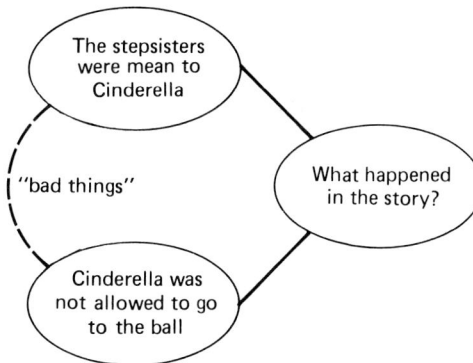

Semantic webbing provides children with a visual organization of written discourse. It can be used with a paragraph, a chapter, a story or a whole book. It assists children in visualizing and understanding the whole, and helps them see how the parts relate to the whole. It can be used before children begin reading a story, as a guide during their reading or upon completion of their reading.

MAJOR APPROACHES TO TEACHING READING

We turn now to the three major approaches to the teaching of reading, the language-experience approach, the individualized reading approach, and the basal reader approach. In this section we will describe each approach and discuss how each utilizes the other language arts skills of speaking, writing, and listening.

The Language-Experience Approach (L.E.A.)

Earlier in this chapter we emphasized the important connections between writing and reading. We also stated that many educators are now stressing the theoretical and practical links between the two forms of written language. Long before educators espoused these views, Sylvia Ashton-Warner in her book *Teacher* (1963) described a program she developed which used the reading-writing connection. Her program became the prototype of the language-experience approach (L.E.A.) to the teaching of reading. Working with poor Maori children in New Zealand, Ashton-Warner found an effective procedure for teaching children how to read. She gave each child cards with *key words* on them. The key words were words that had a very special meaning to that child, words like "love," "fear," "scared," "house," and "monster." Every day each child would tell Ashton-Warner what words she or he wanted to be recorded and then Ashton-Warner would write the words on the cards. In this way a bank of vocabulary or sight words was learned by the children. They learned the words because the words came directly from their experiences and emotions. With enough word cards, children could put the words together to form sentences and stories. Ashton-Warner then recorded the sentences and stories on paper, until the children were able to write themselves. They drew pictures to accompany their stories, and put the stories into books. The books were then shared with other students, read, and reread by all.

During the early 1960s, Doris Lee and Roach Van Allen (1963) extended the work of Ashton-Warner in their book *Learning to Read Through Experience*. Allen (1976) later described the philosophy of the language-experience approach as such.

- I can *think* about what I have experienced and imagined.
- I can *talk about* what I think about.
- What I talk about I can express in some other form.
- Anything I *record* I can recall through speaking or reading.
- I can *read* what I can write by myself or what other people write for me to read.

Explicit in this philosophy is the idea that reading is an integral part of the other communication skills of listening, speaking and writing. In teaching children to read, we begin with the experiences of children. Drawing from their experiences, we record the oral language that they use to describe what they experience. We can summarize the language-experience approach in this way:

> Begin with experiences—then children
>   *listen* to themselves and to others as they
>   *speak* about their experiences. Then they
>   *write* what they have said, and lastly they
>   *read* what they have written.

Steps in the L.E.A.

We now want to describe in detail the steps in a typical language-experience lesson to demonstrate how this approach can be implemented in a primary grade classroom.

Step 1: Begin with an Experience.   Children need some kind of motivational activity to stimulate their thinking and language production. Typically, teachers who use the L.E.A. provide their children with frequent field trips and a stimulating, activity oriented classroom. Some different kinds of experiences which stimulate thinking and language production might be

- Short walks around school.
- Field trips to a zoo, factory, post office, or TV or radio stations.
- Cooking.
- A good film.
- A good book.
- A visitor or guest speaker.
- A new animal to care for.
- Plants to care for.
- A science experiment or adventure.

Step 2: Add Oral Language, Listening, and Speaking.   We have already said that just having a variety of experiences is not enough to develop language. Experiences must be accompanied by an oral sharing of ideas, emotions, personal reactions, and so on. After a group experience, children need to talk about what they see, feel, or hear. They need to interact with each other in a discussion of their experiences and what the experiences mean to them. Refer back to our discussions on question techniques to refresh yourself on how to lead group discussions to ask good questions. As you read this interchange of ideas, notice what the teacher said to facilitate group discussion and interest.

Step 3: Add Writing.   After a period of discussion (and the time will vary depending on the grade level, the class, and the type of experience), the language-experience teacher will then record what children have said. This can be done in a number of ways.

1   *Whole class.*   You may have your whole class seated around a chart board or chalkboard while they are discussing their experiences. Then you might say

"John, tell me the part that you liked best."

and John would reply

I liked when the elephant
tried to spray me.

And you, the teacher, would write on the board *exactly* what John had said. In this way you can write several children's sentences.
If you used this procedure, you would then send children back to their seats where they would copy one or more sentences from the board.

2   *Individual.*   You also could have each child give you a simple sentence about his or her experiences and then you would write that sentence directly onto the child's paper. Language-experience chart paper is often used for this purpose. Each child draws a picture to accompany the sentence. Often, especially at the very early stages of reading, children will say what part of an experience they liked best.

Step 4: Reading.   After children complete their illustration and their sentences, they then read their sentences back to the teacher and to each other. Again, several procedures can be used here.

1   You can say
"Steve come to the board and point to the sentence that is yours. Can you read it back to us?"

or

"Who can read Steve's sentence?"

or

"Let's all read Steve's sentence."

2   You can have children break into small groups of two or three and have them read their sentences to each other, then to the total group.

Skill Building Using the L.E.A.

What we have presented are the very basic components of a language-experience approach. We have tried to show you particularly how the approach integrates the language arts and requires children to participate in a full spectrum of language experiences.

You may be wondering, however, how comprehension at the word, sentence, and schema levels are taught in this approach. Mary Ann Hall's book *Teaching Reading as a Language Experience* (1981) is an excellent reference for a detailed explanation of how to build reading skills using the L.E.A. We will give you some suggestions based on Hall's books and on other materials.

1 Use the group experience stories to build reading readiness and early reading skills. Ask children:

"Who can show me . . .
  where I begin reading?
  in which direction I read?
  where the letter "h" is?
  where the word "elephant" is?
  a word that rhymes with "ball"?
  a word that begins like "fat"?
  a word that ends in "ing"?

2 Make individual word cards with "key words" that are remembered by each child. On a 3 × 5 card, for example

elephant		zoo

Have children bring in children's shoe boxes to store their word cards. This is an excellent way to build sight words, words that children must know immediately to be able to read.

3 Have children create sentences by manipulating their word cards around. They then can copy and illustrate their sentences onto language-experience chart paper.

The	elephant	was	at	the	zoo

4 Have children categorize their word cards according to

- colors
- animals
- people
- objects
- action words
- math words

- describing words
- rhyming words
- compound words
- feeling words
- science words

They then can make word books of colors, animals, and people.

My Book of People I Know	My book of Favorite Animals

In addition, we need to mention oral language develpment in the L.E.A. Often, beginning teachers assume that they need to correct children's oral language before they record it in written form. This is especially true for teachers of children who are dialectically different. Beginning readers may dictate sentences like:

"I *goed* home after school."

Dialectically different children dictate sentences like:

"He be here."

"My sister she like music."

Teachers often are appalled when reading experts tell them to record exactly what the child says, "errors" and all. Remember however that the goal in the L.E.A. is to help children see the connection between oral and written language and to create a perfect match between what is said and what is read. Another goal is to make children feel like masters of their language. To help accomplish these goals, do not correct their language at this stage. Accept and record what each child says. When children can read and understand the nature of written language, we can teach them about "registers" and help them learn the "register" of written language. For our present purposes however, we need to accept children's language as it is.

What we have described for you are the basic components of a language-experience approach to teaching reading. We now want to reiterate these components for you.

1 The reading materials read by the children are booklets that they themselves made.
2 The booklets contain stories that are of *immediate interest* to the children.
3 The stories contain *language* that is *familiar* to the children because they themselves spoke and wrote the words.
4 Children learn reading skills.
5 Children learn to make the *important connection* between spoken and written language.

Language-Experience in the Intermediate Grades

A common criticism of the language-experience approach is that it is a method for teaching beginning reading only. Many intermediate grade teachers think that once children can read, then teachers have no reason to use the L.E.A.

If we define L.E.A. more broadly, however, we can then see that this approach is an excellent one for teaching language (including reading) skills at any grade level. The basic components of the approach can be used even after children can read. Note that the L.E.A. can be used at *any* grade level.

- The lesson begins with an *experience*.
- Students *orally share* their ideas, *brainstorm* new approaches, ideas.
- They then *write* about their ideas and create stories.
- They *illustrate* their stories and make books.
- They *read* their books to other students in their class and in the school.

The important points for any language-experience lesson are: (1) that reading is tied into the other language arts skills rather than isolated as a separate skill; (2) that the stories have intense interest to the students because they write about things that interest them; (3) that because the students write the stories themselves, the language of the stories matches the language of the students.

We would, therefore, highly encourage the use of the L.E.A. with children at all grade levels, modified depending on age and ability levels. In addition, you would want to use the L.E.A. as a supplement to your reading/writing program at the intermediate grade levels rather than as the primary approach to teaching reading. The next section shows how to expand children's reading beyond the language-experience materials that they make and read.

Individualized Reading Approach

A primary component of the language-experience approach is to have children learn to read with books they themselves have written and constructed. Thus, their first exposure to written language is one in which they see in print what they have said. We have already explained how seeing this match helps children learn the connection between oral language and written language. One problem with this methodology, however, is that children are not exposed to new language—new words, phrases, sentence structures, ideas, concepts, and so forth. Thus, the language-experience approach needs to be extended and supplemented, particularly as children move through the primary and intermediate grade levels.

The individualized reading approach (I.R.) helps extend the L.E.A. In this approach children read extensively and intensively about topics that interest them. The materials they read are called "trade books," that is, books that are not meant to be used as texts. Most often we think of library books as "trade books," although the term refers to any book other than a text—books you purchase at bookstores, paperback books, and so on. Recall from Chapter 1 the trade books that were used as a base for intergrating the language arts, such as *Stuart Little*, and *The Cay*.

Many underlying principles of the individualized reading approach are similar to those of the L.E.A. As in the L.E.A., the individualized reading approach adheres to the philosophy that children learn best when they have an intense interest in what they are learning and when learning is meaningful to them. Thus, children's attitudes toward their learning are crucial, and a primary goal becomes that of helping children develop positive attitudes toward reading.

Additionally, in both approaches reading instruction is individualized; in the L.E.A. children *write* their own reading materials, in the I.R. children *choose* their own reading materials. Both approaches encourage the use of a wide variety of reading materials for children, and the integration of the other language arts skills of listening, speaking, and most importantly, writing.

Basic Components of Individualized Reading

In her excellent book, *Reading in the Elementary School*, Jeannette Veatch (1978) describes in detail the methods and procedures used in the individualized reading approach. Veatch is considered to be one of the founders of the individualized reading approach, and has been instrumental in disseminating the philosophy of individualized reading and in providing teachers with detailed guidelines on using this approach. She, as well as other advocates of the approach (for example, see Barbe and Abbott, 1975; Duker, 1968), describes the basic components of individualized reading as follows:

1 *Self-selection of books.*   In this approach, children choose their own trade books to read. Veatch (1978) lists two criteria for selection: (a) the child must want to read the book and (b) the child must be able to read the book.

For the successful implementation of this approach, a large quantity of books of different ability levels must be available in the classroom. A good rule of thumb is to have at least five books available for every child in the class—about 125 books for a class of 25.

2 *Self-pacing.*   Another hallmark of this approach is that children proceed through the books and through instruction *at their own pace*, rather than at a predetermined pace set by the teacher, the curriculum guide, or the instructional manual.

3 *Pupil-teacher conferencing.*   In individualized reading, each child has a conference with the teacher at least two or more times per week. These intensive one-on-one sessions: (1) allow you as the teacher to diagnose and evaluate children's needs and progress; (2) serve the purpose of establishing close rapport between the child and you; and (3) assist in developing positive attitudes toward reading. Veatch points out that it is important for children to prepare for the conference—by studying one particular part of the story intensely, by preparing an oral report, or listing difficult vocabulary words. Similarly, it is important for you to keep accurate records of each conference.

4 *Record-keeping procedures.*   Both you and your children can record reading progress through the use of charts (see the sample chart). As the teacher, you should have a file on each child, keeping track of books that have been read, dates, vocabulary, comments on oral reading, word attack skills, comprehension, and so on. We also recommend that children have their own individual files in which they record their reading progress. Children as early as the second grade can keep accurate, though simple, records of their progress.

Example of Student Chart

Title of Story or Book	Date Started/Finished	Conference

Student Record-Keeping

Name: _____ *Starting:* _____ *Ending:* _____ *Book:* _____	
Silent Reading	**Reading Activity**
Composition	**Self-Reading**
Oral Reading: Make an Appointment with your Teacher to Do Some Oral Reading Each Week *Day* _____ *Time* _____ *Book* _____ *Pages* _____	**Comments**
Teacher's Check _____	

5 *Small group task instruction.* Individualized reading does not mean that children work on a completely individualized basis at all times. Teacher diagnosis of children's needs will warrant, at times, small group instruction and work periods. After several conferences you may decide to pull a small group together for instruction on understanding the main idea of a paragraph, or on prefixes and suffixes. You may want to gather a group to work together on a project or an independent study of a particular science or social studies concept.

Class Management in the Individualized Reading Approach

Of the three approaches to the teaching of reading that we are discussing, the individualized reading approach is the one that requires the most *careful* classroom management to implement. Veatch's (1978) diagram demonstrates how a typical morning would proceed using this approach (see Figure 11-1).

```
┌─────────────────────────────────────────────┐
│         1.  Planning the reading period       │
└─────────────────────────────────────────────┘

┌─────────────────────────────────────────────┐
│            2.  Self selection of books        │
└─────────────────────────────────────────────┘

┌─────────────────────────────────────────────┐
│           3.  Independent work period         │
└─────────────────────────────────────────────┘

┌─────────────────────────────────────────────┐
│             4.  Individual conference         │
└─────────────────────────────────────────────┘

┌─────────────────────────────────────────────┐
│            5.  Organization of groups         │
└─────────────────────────────────────────────┘

        ┌──────────────┐   ┌──────────────┐
        │ Instructional │   │ Independent  │
        │  purposes     │   │   work       │
        └──────────────┘   └──────────────┘

┌─────────────────────────────────────────────┐
│    6.  Sharing, follow—up, and evaluation     │
└─────────────────────────────────────────────┘

   ┌──────────────┐ ┌──────────────┐ ┌──────────────┐
   │ Instructional │ │ Independent  │ │ Independent  │
   │  group work   │ │ group work   │ │ individual   │
   │               │ │              │ │    work      │
   └──────────────┘ └──────────────┘ └──────────────┘

┌─────────────────────────────────────────────┐
│ 7.  Start over again—planning the now reading period │
└─────────────────────────────────────────────┘
```

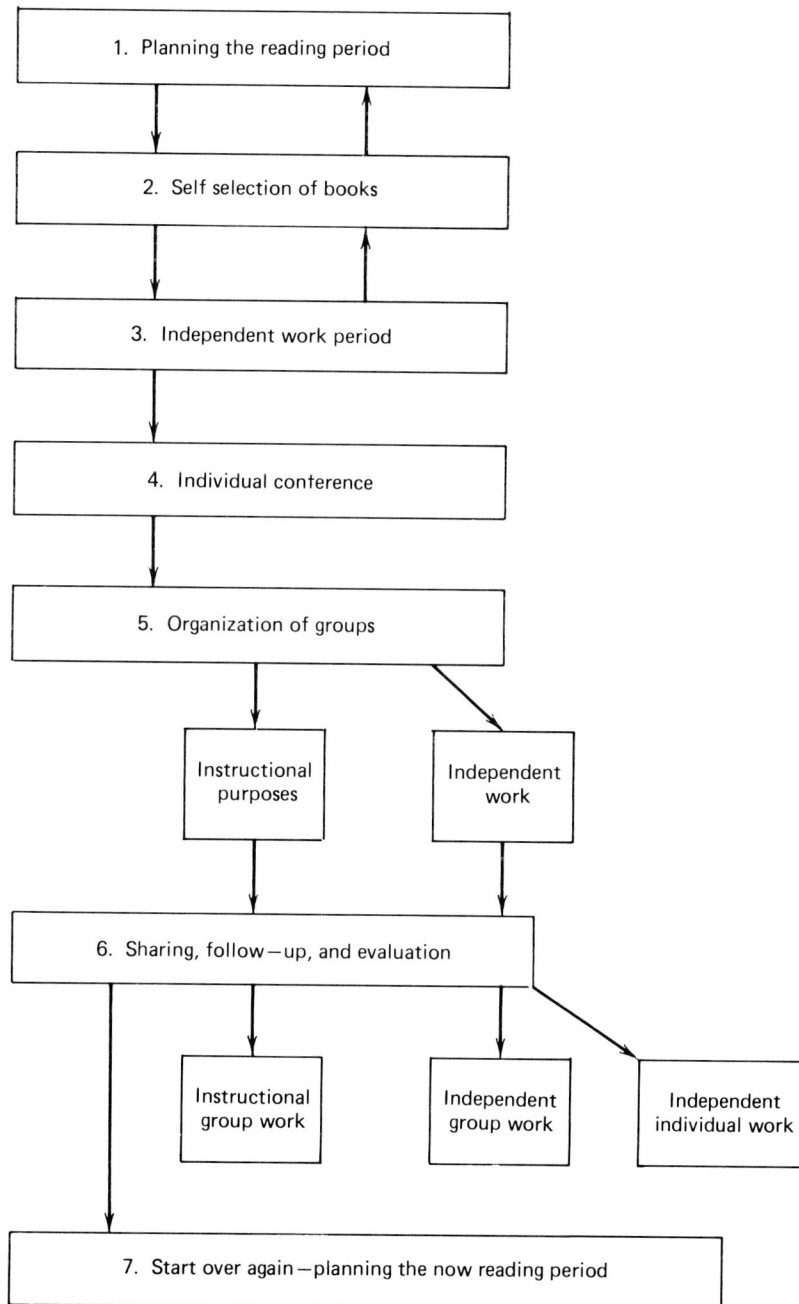

FIGURE 11.1 *Classroom management chart for individualized reading. (Used with permission from* Reading in the Elementary School, *1978, John Wiley & Sons, New York, N.Y.)*

A question you might have about this approach is, What do the children do besides read their books? The following list, along with Veatch's diagram, will help you see what children do during the reading period.

- Children spend part of *every* reading period quietly reading.
- Children individually or in groups work on projects related to a book they are reading.
  Constructing a diorama
  Making a map
  Writing a book report/summary
  Creating a script
  Writing a report
  Illustrating a book or story
  Making a book jacket
  Writing a new story or book of their own
- Children spend some time evaluating what they have done and planning the next day's activities.

Certainly, these types of activities require a certain amount of independence on the part of children. Some children, more than others, adapt themselves extremely well to the less structured environment to which this approach lends itself. All children need guidance and assistance in this approach, however, especially in the beginning. Further, you as a teacher need to be very well-organized and able to keep accurate, up-to-date, and detailed records of the children's progress. With these factors in mind, it is possible to see how such an approach can benefit children's reading.

Integrating the language arts is another added spinoff of this approach to teaching reading. The types of activities in which children engage during the reading period go beyond simply "reading." Children write often as a natural extension of their reading, and they work in groups where they share what they have read and written. Thus, all the language arts skills are in use on a daily basis.

Basal Reader Approach

We turn now to the most commonly used approach to the teaching of reading, the basal reader approach. Basal readers consist of a whole series of commercially prepared books and supplementary materials (Aukerman, 1981). This approach is a highly structured one, and one that differs extensively from both the language-experience and the individualized reading approaches. We can see the latter two approaches as extensions of each other and of the thinking-language model espoused early in the book. The basal reader approach, however, differs markedly in its orientation, philosophy, and procedures for teaching reading.

Components of the Basal Readers. Basal readers comprise the basic reading instructional material for the vast majority of American school children. Auckerman (1981) describes the essential components of basal materials as follows:

1 A series of 15 or 16 books, several for each grade level, preprimer, primer, and grades one through six.

2 Teacher's editions for each book. Each edition contains detailed lesson plans and instructions for teaching reading skills.

3 Pupil workbooks. These are soft cover expendable books that contain exercises to reinforce the reading skills taught during the reading instructional period.

4 Pupil tests. These are often group administered tests used to place students in the proper reading text and/or to evaluate progress in reading.

5 Additional supplementary materials. Many series offer a number of optional assessory materials such as boxes of word cards, tapes and filmstrips, and enrichment books.

Basal readers differ from publisher to publisher, but most series have a common core of features that distinguish them as an approach to teaching reading. The two most important features are

1 Vocabulary control. New vocabulary words are introduced in each story not randomly but rather systematically. Only a few new words are introduced in any one story, and these words are reinforced or repeated throughout the story, and then reintroduced in later stories.

2 Skill development and reinforcement skills are taught and reinforced in every lesson of the basal.

Using the Basal Reader Approach. The teacher's manual is the core of the basal reader program, and each manual includes detailed descriptions on how to teach reading. Outlined in the manual is what is called a "scope and sequence" of reading skills to be covered by the teacher during the course of reading instruction in the basals. "Scope" refers to what reading skills are covered at a particular level—initial consonant sounds, "b," "c," "f," and "m"; root words, rhyming words, compound words, "ing" endings, and so on. "Sequence" simply refers to the order of presentation of these reading skills.

A series of lesson plans are also included in the teacher's manual. Each lesson plan corresponds to a story in the basal reader. Lesson plans included in different publishers' manuals vary in details. Some tell teachers exactly what to say at every step while others provide guidelines.

In general, though, the lesson plan typically includes several parts.

1 Objectives for the lesson—this usually includes cognitive objectives such as skill development.

2 Vocabulary introduction—how to present new vocabulary words introduced in the story.

3 Motivation—questions and comments to say to children to motivate them to read the story.

4 Comprehension questions—questions to ask children during and after they read the story.

5 Skill development—specific teaching suggestions to introduce a new reading skill.

6 Pages in the workbook to assign to children as follow up after they have read the story.

These lessons are typically taught in small groups of from five to ten children in a small reading circle with the teacher. Teachers who use this approach often divide the class into three reading groups according to reading ability. The teacher's time might be divided in the following way.

	Group 1	*Group 2*	*Group 3*
Period 1 9:00–9:20	Seatwork	With teacher	Follow-up work
Period 2 9:20–9:40	With teacher	Follow-up work	Seatwork
Period 3 9:40–10:00	Follow-up Work	Seatwork	With teacher

Children can do a variety of activities in their seats. Some activities are merely "busy work," that is, work that has no instructional value to children, but is given for the purpose of keeping them busy. Other seatwork activities can include valuable worksheets or projects that involve the other communication skills of listening, speaking, and writing. These activities include listening to stories at listening centers, writing books, reading books, and illustrative stories. Some basal series provide teachers with suggestions of supplemental activities that can be used as seatwork, but most often teachers are required to create these activities themselves. We will discuss in more detail the use and value of worksheets in the last chapter of this book.

Criticisms of Basals and Some Suggestions

Prior to 1970 a great deal of criticism was leveled at basal reader series. Publishers of basals responded to those criticisms and because of the changes made in the series, the quality of basals has improved dramatically over the last 15 years. In fact, the changes have been so significant that Durkin (1978) divides her discussion of basals into the pre- and post-1970 era.

Before 1970, some common criticisms were

1 Failure to include children of ethnically diverse backgrounds in stories or pictures.

2 Almost exclusive emphasis on white, middle-class children and lifestyles.

3 Sexist roles, models and language.

4 Rigid grade level designations of books.

5 Too much emphasis on narrative fiction to the exclusion of the more expository style needed in subject area textbook reading.

During the late 1960s and 1970s major changes were made in basals. Publishers began to include stories and pictures of children from different backgrounds and lifestyles. Women and men were included in roles traditionally reserved for the opposite sex, that is, a woman carpenter, a man cleaning a house. Multilevel designations of books were substituted for specific grade levels—books now progress from levels 1–14, instead of from first grade to sixth grade. In addition, publishers have introduced more variety into the reading material included in the basals.

Even with these changes, however, criticisms about basal readers and the basal approach still abound. It is clear to us that the criticisms do not relate to the basal materials themselves, but rather to *the way basal materials are used in the class*. Thus, the criticisms are really directed against many aspects of the *basal reader approach* to teaching reading rather than the basal materials themselves. Here is a typical scenario.

Teacher calls Group 3 to the front of the class. Children sit in assigned seats in a small group with teacher in the middle. Teacher says, "Okay, open your books to page 25. Johnny, begin reading." Johnny reads out loud and teacher interrupts frequently to make corrections in Johnny's oral reading . . .

Teacher then reads comprehension question from the teacher's manual. Teacher calls on Mary who is not paying attention . . .

Teacher then asks child beside Johnny to read . . .

After all children have finished reading, Teacher begins phonics lesson, read from the manual . . .

On completion of that task, teacher says, "OK, go back to your seats and do pages 32–34 in your workbooks."

"Next. . . ."

Those of us who have observed in classrooms see this scenario frequently. Many teachers

1 Depend too much on the teacher's manual.

2 Do not provide enough motivation for reading.

3 Do not set a purpose for reading.

4 Do not tie the reading into the child's existing schemata.

5 Have children read aloud for no apparent reason.

6 Do not encourage children's appreciation for the story.

7 Ask too many factual questions.

8 Emphasize too much word-perfect reading.

9 Do not use their own imagination and creativity in the lesson.

10 Tend to make the lesson too routine and monotonous.

11 Emphasize phonics skills and deemphasize comprehension.

Some Suggestions.   Basal readers can be a rich and valuable resource for teachers. As Aukerman (1981) remarked, "Most basals provide a beautiful, varied, and interesting collection of reading materials, unequaled anywhere else in the world" (p. 12). If you wish to take advantage of these materials, a few guidelines should help you develop varied, interesting lessons using the basal reader approach.

1 Remember that the teacher's manual provides *guidelines* for you to follow; it is not to be followed word by word, page by page.

2 Remember to vary the lessons.

3 Remember to introduce the story by
   a. Tying the story into some experience with which children are already familiar.
   b. Getting children excited about reading the story.
   c. Encouraging children to make predictions about the story's plot or conclusion.

4 Remember to encourage children to become actively involved in the story—by reading, sharing aloud, guessing, discussing, asking questions.

5 Remember to give children options for reading ahead, or choosing their own stories to read.

6 Provide children with some interesting follow-up activities—writing scripts, making games, extending reading, drawing pictures, writing stories, making book jackets.

7 Remember to integrate reading with other language arts skills, particularly writing. Combine reading basal stories with writing.

READING EVALUATION METHODS

As we seek to improve children's reading abilities, we need to be able to account for how far they have progressed over a given period. There are both formal and informal measures for evaluating reading progress. Evaluations need to be based on knowledge of both the strengths and weaknesses of children's reading. Determining these strengths and weaknesses is known as *diagnosis*. Diagnosis and evaluation of reading ability should be one important focus of reading. No matter what reading approach we use, our instruction must rest on finding out what children know and don't know, and then building on those skills to improve reading ability. We will discuss formal and informal evaluation procedures.

Formal Measures of Assessment

A standardized reading test is one type of formal test that is administered to large numbers of children across the country. The test is constructed so that children can be compared to their peers.

Scores on a standardized reading tests are reported in grade equivalent scores, percentile ranks, stanine scores, or standard scores. A grade equivalent score supposedly indicates the grade level at which the student taking the test can be expected to read. For example a grade equivalent score of 6.5 would indicate that a student had a reading ability equivalent to a sixth grader in midyear. Although this is a common interpretation, it has been criticized by reading specialists.

> *Contrary to prevalent opinion, a student usually cannot be expected to read a basal reader or other material on the grade level which is indicated by a survey reading test score because this score often represents the student's frustration reading level rather than the instructional reading level. . . . In addition, the typical student who earns a grade equivalent score on a survey reading test which is considerably higher than his or her actual grade level may not possess the background of experiences or interests to be able to read up to that level. (Miller, 1978, p. 82.)*

A *percentile rank* indicates how well a student has performed relative to the students in the norming group. For example, if a student obtains a percentile rank of 40, it indicates that the student has performed as well as or better than 40 percent of students of the same age, grade, and sex who were used in the norming of the test. *Stanine scores* are similar to percentiles except that there are nine possible ranks rather than 100 as is the case with percentiles. Figure 11-2 compares stanine scores and percentile ranks to a normal distribution.

Generally speaking there are two types of standardized reading tests. A standardized *survey* test usually contains subtests that measure word attack skills, vocabulary, and comprehension. Survey tests are considered to be global measures of reading ability—that is, they provide the teacher with the general reading ability of

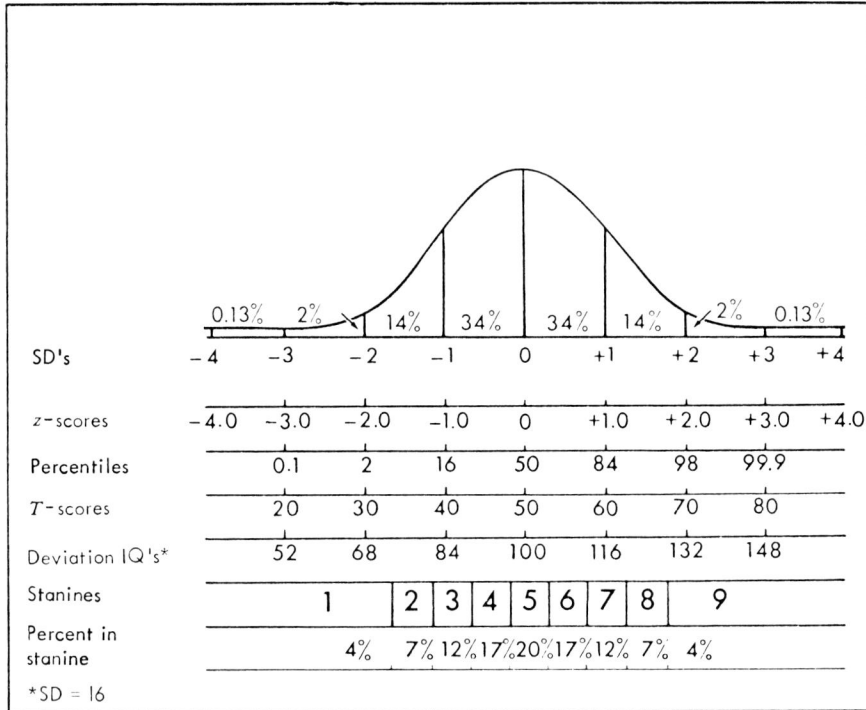

		0.13%	2%	14%	34%	34%	14%	2%	0.13%
SD's	−4	−3	−2	−1	0	+1	+2	+3	+4
z-scores	−4.0	−3.0	−2.0	−1.0	0	+1.0	+2.0	+3.0	+4.0
Percentiles		0.1	2	16	50	84	98	99.9	
T-scores		20	30	40	50	60	70	80	
Deviation IQ's*		52	68	84	100	116	132	148	

Stanines: 1 | 2 | 3 | 4 | 5 | 6 | 7 | 8 | 9

Percent in stanine: 4% 7% 12% 17% 20% 17% 12% 7% 4%

*SD = 16

FIGURE 11.2 *Corresponding standard scores, stanines, and percentiles in a normal distribution.*

the child. They are not informative about particular areas of strengths and weaknesses of a child's reading ability, and thus are not considered to be good for the *diagnosis* of reading ability. Most school districts use standardized survey tests to evaluate reading progress on a yearly basis. Some of the more commonly used survey tests are listed below.

Metropolitan Achievement Tests
(Harcourt Brace Jovanovich, Inc.).

Nelson-Denny Reading Test
(Houghton Mifflin Co.)

SRA Assessment Survey
(Science Research Associates)

Stanford Achievement Tests
(Harcourt Brace Jovanovich, Inc.)

Unlike survey tests in which a child's overall performance is measured against the performance of a norming group, criterion referenced tests measure performance against sets of specific objectives. For example, an objective might read

Given a word, the student will be able to identify the beginning sound when the word is pronounced. Criterion for passing = 10 out of 15 items.

Instead of an overall score, criterion referenced tests report scores in a dichotomous fashion (pass versus no pass) for a variety of skill areas. Below are listed some of the more commonly used criterion referenced reading tests.

Criterion Reading
(Random House)

Fountain Valley Teacher Support System in Reading
(Richard L. Zweig Associates, Inc.)

Individual Reading Skills Program
(Houghton Mifflin Company)

Patterns, Sounds, and Meaning
(Allyn and Bacon, Inc.)

Diagnostic tests are so named because they subdivide the reading process into a number of separate skill areas and then report norms or criterion scores for each skill area. Actually most criterion referenced tests can be used as diagnostic tests, while survey tests usually cannot because they do not report enough "subscores." To illustrate the types of skills tested by diagnostic tests consider the different subtests of the Stanford Diagnostic Reading Test:

Test 1: Auditory vocabulary. This evaluates a student's ability to recognize words when presented auditorily. The words used are frequently found in elementary school textbooks.

Test 2: Auditory discrimination. This evaluates a student's ability to discriminate among various consonants, vowels and their combinations.

Test 3: Phonetic analysis. This evaluates a student's ability to recognize selected letter/sound relationships.

Test 4: Structural analysis. This evaluates a student's ability to recognize syllables in words.

Test 5: Reading comprehension. This evelutes a student's ability to comprehend material read silently.

Student scores from diagnostic reading tests are commonly reported in profile charts. Figure 11-3 presents a profile chart from the Durrell Analysis of Reading Difficulty.

Some of the more commonly used diagnostic reading tests are listed below.

Diagnostic Reading Scales, Revised Edition CCTB/McGraw-Hill

Durrell Analysis of Reading Difficulty
(Harcourt Brace Jovanovich, Inc.)

Gates-McKillop Reading Diagnostic Test,
(Teachers College Press, Columbia University)

Stanford Diagnostic Reading Tests
(Harcourt Brace Jovanovich, Inc.)

Another category of reading test is the oral reading test. These tests are administered individually to students who are asked to read progressively harder passages aloud. As the student reads the passages, the teacher identifies and

Profile Chart

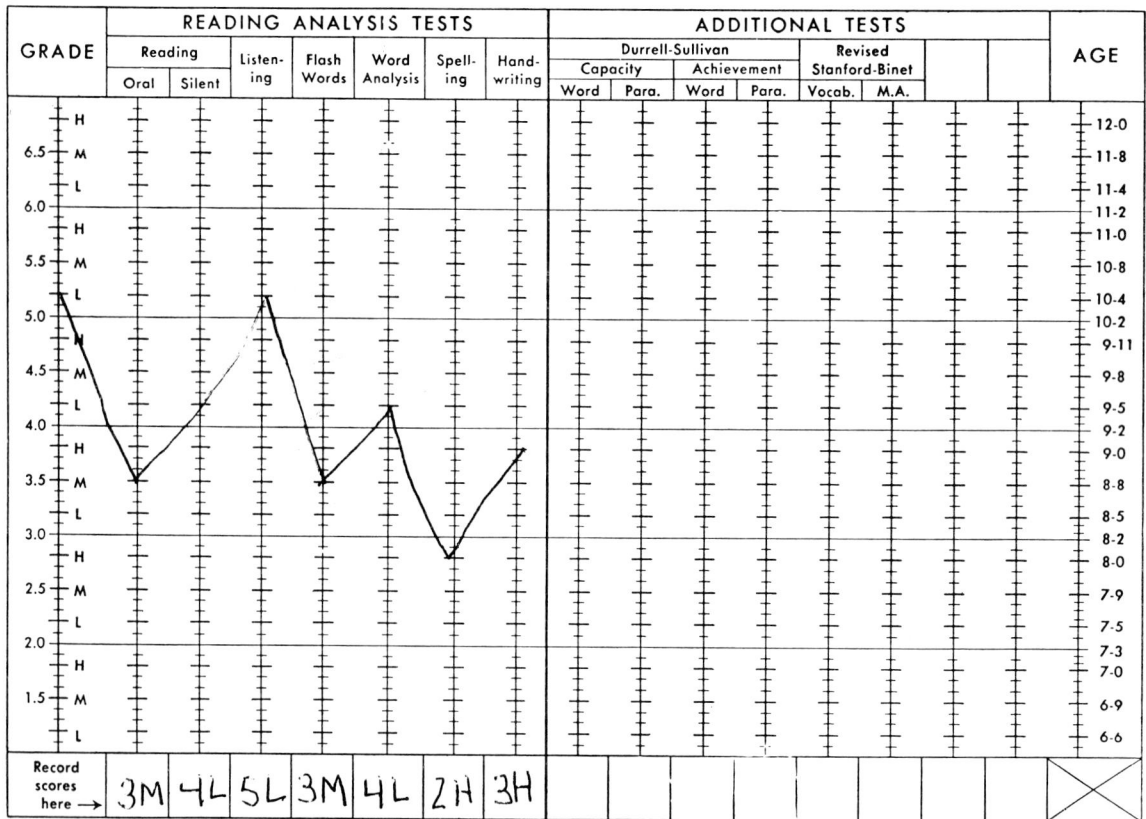

GRADE	READING ANALYSIS TESTS							ADDITIONAL TESTS								AGE
	Reading		Listen-ing	Flash Words	Word Analysis	Spell-ing	Hand-writing	Durrell-Sullivan				Revised Stanford-Binet				
	Oral	Silent						Capacity		Achievement						
								Word	Para.	Word	Para.	Vocab.	M.A.			
Record scores here →	3M	4L	5L	3M	4L	2H	3H									

FIGURE 11.3 *A profile chart from the Durrell Analysis of Reading Difficulty. (Reproduced by permission. Durrell Analysis of Reading Difficulty. Copyright © 1980, 1955, 1937 by Harcourt Brace Jovanovich, Inc. All rights reserved.)*

categorizes any errors the student makes. Some of the more commonly identified errors in oral reading tests are

Omissions.   The student leaves out a word or phrase.

Additions.   The student inserts a word.

Reversals.   The student switches the order of words ("was there" for "there was") or of letters ("was" for "saw").

Repetitions.   The student repeats a word or phrase.

One of the most commonly used oral reading tests is called the Individual Reading Inventory. Students usually begin by reading words from a set of word lists. The student's performance on this task is considered an indication of his/her sight word ability. The student then reads a series of passages. The extent to which the student avoids or makes oral reading errors is then used to calculate the student's independent, instructional, and frustration reading levels. The student's independent reading level is the highest level at which the student can read without assistance. The student's instructional level is the highest level at which the student can read with help from the teacher. The frustration level is that level at which the student makes so many errors that he or she becomes frustrated. Commonly used Individualized Reading Inventories include

Botel Reading Inventory
(Follett Educational Corporation)

Analytical Reading Inventory
(Charles E. Merrill Publishing Company)

Classroom Reading Inventory
(William C. Brown Publishers)

Informal Reading Diagnosis
(Prentice-Hall, Inc.)

Reading Placement Inventory
(Economy Company)

One of the most sophisticated methods for analyzing a student's oral reading is the Reading Miscue Inventory (Goodman and Burke, 1972). With the Reading Miscue Inventory (RMI) a teacher can measure a student's ability to use the graphophonic, syntactic, and semantic language systems when reading. To do this the teacher must ask a series of questions about each oral reading error or "miscue" the students make. Below is a list of those questions.

Question 1:   Dialect.   Is a dialect variation involved in the miscue?

Question 2:   Intonation.   Is a shift in intonation involved in the miscue?

Question 3: *Graphic similarity.*   How much does the miscue look like what was expected?

Question 4: *Sound similarity.*   How much does the miscue sound like what was expected?

Question 5: *Grammatical function.*   Is the grammatical function of the miscue the same as the grammatical function of the word in the text?

Question 6: *Correction.*   Is the miscue corrected?

Question 7: *Grammatical acceptability.*   Does the miscue occur in a structure which is grammatically acceptable?

Question 8: *Semantic acceptability.*   Does the miscue occur in a structure which is semantically acceptable?

Question 9: *Meaning change.*   Does the miscue result in a change of meaning?

When these questions are answered about each miscue, the teacher then translates the information into a set of graphs and scores which can be interpreted in terms of the student's ability to use the graphophonic, syntactic, and semantic language systems.

The scoring procedures for the RMI are very complex and considered by some to be too time consuming for most classroom teachers (Hood, 1978; Pikulski, 1974). For this reason Tortelli (1976) and others have devised modified RMIs which provide diagnostic information similar to that of the RMI, but which are less time consuming to administer and grade. Below we have included a modified RMI that can be used quickly and easily by classroom teachers to provide the important kind of diagnostic information that the RMI yields. Note that the three components of language—graphophonic, syntactic and semantic—are evaluated for each miscue.

Modified RMI

Reading	Text	Graphophonic	Syntax	Semantics
What did the child say?	What did the text say?	Was the miscue similar in spelling and in sound?	Was the miscue similar in grammar?	Did the miscue maintain meaning?
		high medium low	noun for noun, verb for verb, yes no	yes no
		Total Percentage = _____	= _____	= _____

Informal Measures of Assessment

There are a number of informal ways to assess reading progress. Not only are informal measures easier for the classroom teacher to administer and grade, but they also often provide more useful diagnostic information.

As tests become more comprehensive, the difference between formal and informal tests is becoming less distinct. For example, some reading specialists consider oral reading tests informal because they rely to a great extent on the teacher. We choose to classify them as formal because they are commercially prepared and commonly used to quantify and label students relative to their reading ability. We consider informal assessment to be that which is predominantly teacher made and less structured in coding procedures. That is, with informal assessment technique the emphasis is not so much on "measuring" a student's reading ability as it is on getting an overall impression of a student's abilities.

Probably the most valid way to informally assess a student's reading is to listen to the student read orally about information *the student has some background knowledge of*. This implies an individual assessment for each student or, at least, a grouping of students by interests. That is, after you have identified student interests organize them into small groups (three to five) based on those interests. For each group, select a piece of grade-level material. For example, a sixth-grade teacher should select material that is written for sixth graders. Each student should have his or her own copy of the reading passage. Tell students that the group will be reading the passage aloud and that they can take a few minutes to look it over. At this time, you should observe the students' prereading behaviors. In general, good readers skim over material before they read it. If it is a book they look at the table of contents or look at the pictures. If it is a short passage they might read the introductory paragraph and thumb through the entire passage reading selected sentences and phrases. If a child makes no attempt to preview the material before reading, it might be an indication that he or she does not realize the importance of prereading activities.

After prereading, have each child read a portion of the passage orally. Allow each student to read at least 100 words. As a student reads, mark on your passage any word or phrase the student mispronounces, omits, or substitutes another word for. This can be done by drawing a line through any word or phrase on which the student makes a "miscue." For example, after a student has read a 100-word section, the teacher's copy might look like the copy in Figure 11-4.

It is the number and type of oral miscues that tell you how well the student knows the words and concepts necessary to read at his or her grade level. Basically, about each miscue you should ask the question: "Is this a word or phrase the student should be able to recognize at his or her grade level?" For example, Figure 11-4 indicates that the student had miscues on the following words:

voyages

journeys

deserts

explorations

Arctic

experiences

> Sailors have often in their vogages reported seeing land even though their ship was in the middle of the ocean. When they sailed in the direction of this land they saw it would disappear.
>
> On journeys across the deserts travelers have sometimes seen a lake ahead of them. Being very thirsty, they would rush toward it only to find it gone.
>
> On their explorations of Arctic regions explorers have seen high mountains just ahead. When they tried to get closer, the mountains were not there.
>
> For a long time no one tried to explain these strange experiences. Most people probably. . . .

FIGURE 11.4 *Student's oral reading errors. (From* The Golden Book Encyclopedia, *Vol. 10, by B. M. Parker: New York: Golden Press, 1959, p. 898.)*

The teacher would have to decide which words were grade level words. These would be considered "errors"; the others would not. This is most efficiently done by consulting graded word lists. One of the best lists available for grades up through the sixth grade is that by Harris and Jacobson (1972). If the student makes five or more errors per 100 words it might be an indication that the student's sight vocabulary or knowledge of concepts is lacking. We will discuss concept development and sight vocabulary in Chapter 12.

After the students have completed reading the passage, they should be asked to "retell" what they have read. This should be done individually for each student without the others hearing the retelling. In the retelling, students should be able to recall and report all important pieces of information contained in the passage. During the retelling, it is appropriate for the teacher to ask probing questions to make sure the student remembers important facts. A child's ability to recall important information provides information about their ability to integrate what they have read into their existing schema about the topic.

The entire procedure provides informal, diagnostic information about three important aspects of the reading process.

1 The extent to which students engage in previewing or overview activities.

2 The extent to which students have the necessary sight vocabulary and store of concepts for their grade level.

3 The extent to which students integrate what they read into their existing cognitive structure about the topic.

Here we must emphasize the fact that this procedure is informal and that the conclusions you come to might have some inaccuracies. However, if done with care and common sense, the procedure can provide valuable data about a student's ability to read efficiently.

Other Informal Measures

In assessing children's progress we need to look to a multitude of sources in order to diagnose and evaluate fully. Additional sources would certainly include

1 *School records.* Oftentimes we can learn important information about children through their past school records—information such as how often children have been transferred from school to school, health problems, past reading difficulties.

2 *Interviews.* Informal interviews with children often reveal important information that can be used to diagnose reading attitudes, reading interests, and self-concept.

3 *Attitude surveys.* Specific questions can be devised and administered in oral or written form to determine how interested children are in reading, what they like to read best. For example, "My favorite book is . . .," "When I have to read, I . . .," and "To me books are. . . ."

4 *Observation.* An important source for evaluating reading progress is informal observation. Checklists can be devised for observations or you can simply jot notes on 3 × 5 cards and keep them in a file or card box.

Reading Skill	*Brenda*	*Bob*	*Gia*	*Melissa*	*Heather*	*Jeremy*	*Stephen*
Fact and opinion							
Main idea							
Figurative language							
Cause and effect							
Relevant versus irrelevant information							
Analytical reasoning							

Name of Child	**Date of Observation**

Conference:
General comments:
 	
Reading:
  Attitude
  Interest
  Risk taking
  Oral reading
  Comprehension
  Appreciation	

We want to emphasize that diagnosis and evaluation of progress are ongoing processes in teaching reading. Diagnosis is not an instantaneous process, it does not begin when you first meet the child and then stop there. Informal observation and constant contact with children necessitate a constant cycle of diagnosis and evaluation.

Diagnosis

Evaluation

As a teacher you assess and then reassess, modifying your instruction to meet the needs of the children in your class on a continuous basis. Sometimes you may want to use more formal measures of assessment, but more often you will learn to rely on your own informal measures and observations to improve the reading skills of your children.

SUGGESTED ACTIVITIES

1 Interview some preschool children about reading. Ask them some basic characteristics of reading: How do you hold the book? Where do you start? Why do people read? Describe their level of awareness about the reading process.

2 Visit a reading class being conducted in an elementary school. In observing the class, list the types of activities the teacher asks the students to do. Using the information in this chapter, categorize these activities as to their focus (for example, comprehension at word level, sentence level, schema level).

3 Analyze two or three basal readers. How are their approaches to beginning reading instruction similar? How are they different?

4 Use the modified miscue analysis described in this chapter and evaluate the reading ability of two students. What are the strengths and weaknesses of each student? Compare these results with the performance of those students on standardized reading tests.

5 Develop and implement a DRTA (Directed Reading/Thinking Activity) with a small group of students. Evaluate the success of that activity.

REFERENCES

Allen, R.V. *Language Experiences in Communication*. Boston: Houghton-Mifflin, 1976.

Ashton-Warner, S. *Teacher*. New York: Simon and Schuster, 1963.

Aukerman, R. *Approaches to Beginning Reading*. New York: John Wiley and Sons, 1971.

————. *The Basal Reader Approach to Reading*. New York: John Wiley and Sons, Inc., 1981.

Barbe, W., and Abbott, J. *Personalized Reading Instruction.* West Nyack, N.Y.: Parker Publishing Co., 1975.

Bloomfield, L., and Barnhart, C. *Let's Read, A Linguistic Approach.* Detroit: Wayne State University Press, 1961.

Clark, E. V. "On the Acquisition of the Meaning of 'before' and 'after.'" *Journal of Verbal Learning and Verbal Behavior,* 10 (April 1971):266–275.

Clay, M. M. *Concepts About Print Tests.* London: Heinemann Books, 1972.

———. *What Did I Write?* London: Heinemann Books, 1975.

Duker, S. *Individualized Reading: Readings.* Metuchen, N.J.: Scarecrow Press, 1968.

Durkin, D. *Teaching Your Children to Read.* Boston: Allyn and Bacon, Inc., 1978.

Freedman, G., and Reynolds, E. "Enriching Basal Reader Lessons with Semantic Webbing." *The Reading Teacher* 33, 6 (March 1980):677–684.

Fries, C. *Linguistics and Reading.* New York: Holt, Rinehart and Winston, 1955.

Goodman, K. "Reading: A Psycholinguistic Guessing Game." *Journal of the Reading Specialist* 4 (May 1967):126–135.

———. "Behind the Eye: What Happens in Reading." In Kenneth Goodman and Olive Niles (eds.). *Reading Process and Program.* Urbana, Ill.: National Council of Teachers of English, 1970.

Goodman, Y., and Burke, C. *Reading Miscue Inventory.* New York: Macmillan Publishing Co., 1972.

Hall, M. A. *Teaching Reading as a Language Experience.* Columbus: Charles E. Merrill Publishing Co., 1981.

Harris, A. J., and Jacobson, M. D. *Basic Elementary Reading Vocabularies.* New York: Macmillan, 1972.

Huey, E. *The Psychology and Pedagogy of Reading.* New York: Macmillan Publishing Co., 1908.

Hood, J. "Is Miscue Analysis Practical for Teachers?" *Reading Teacher* 32, 3 (December 1978):260–266.

Kintsch, W. *The Representation of Meaning in Memory.* Hillsdale, N.J.: Erlbaum Associates, 1974.

Kohlers, P. "Reading Is Only Incidentally Visual." In Kenneth Goodman and James Fleming (eds.). *Psycholinguistics and Reading.* Newark, Del.: International Reading Association, 1969.

Lee, D., and Allen, R. V. *Learning to Read Through Experience.* New York: Appleton Century Crofts, 1963.

McCracken, G. "The Newcastle Reading Experiment." *Elementary English* 30 (January 1953):13–21.

Miller, W. H. *Reading Diagnosis Kit.* New York: The Center for Applied Research in Education, 1978.

National Assessment of Educational Progress. *Reading Comprehension of American Youth: Do They Understand What They Read?* Denver, Colo.: Education Commission of the States, 1982.

Pearson, P. D., and Johnson, D. *Teaching Reading Comprehension*. New York: Holt, Rinehart and Winston, 1978.

Pikulski, J. "A Critical Review: Informal Reading Inventories." *The Reading Teacher* 28, 2 (November 1974):141–151.

Schank, R. C. "Identification of Conceptualization Underlying Natural Language." In P. C. Schank and R. M. Colby (eds.). *Computer Models of Thought and Language*. San Francisco: Freeman, 1973.

Smith, F. *Understanding Reading*. New York: Holt, Rinehart and Winston, 1978.

Stauffer, R. *The Language-Experience Approach to the Teaching of Reading*. New York: Harper and Row, 1980.

Thorndike, E. L. "Reading as Reasoning. A Study of Mistakes in Paragraph Reading." *The Journal of Education Psychology* 8, 6 (1917):323–332.

Thorndyke, P. "Cognitive Structure in Comprehension and Meaning of Narrative Discourse." *Cognitive Psychology* 9, 1 (January 1977):77–110.

Tortelli, J. "Simplified Psycholinguistic Diagnosis." *Reading Teacher* 29, 8 (April 1976): 637–639.

Veatch, J. *Reading in the Elementary School*. New York: John Wiley and Sons, 1978.

Wells, G. *Learning Through Interaction*. Cambridge: Cambridge University Press, 1981.

Wolf, W.; Huck, C.; King, M.; and Ellinger, B. D. *Critical Reading Ability of Elementary School Children* (Report of Project No. 5-1040). Washington, D.C.: Office of Education, 1967.

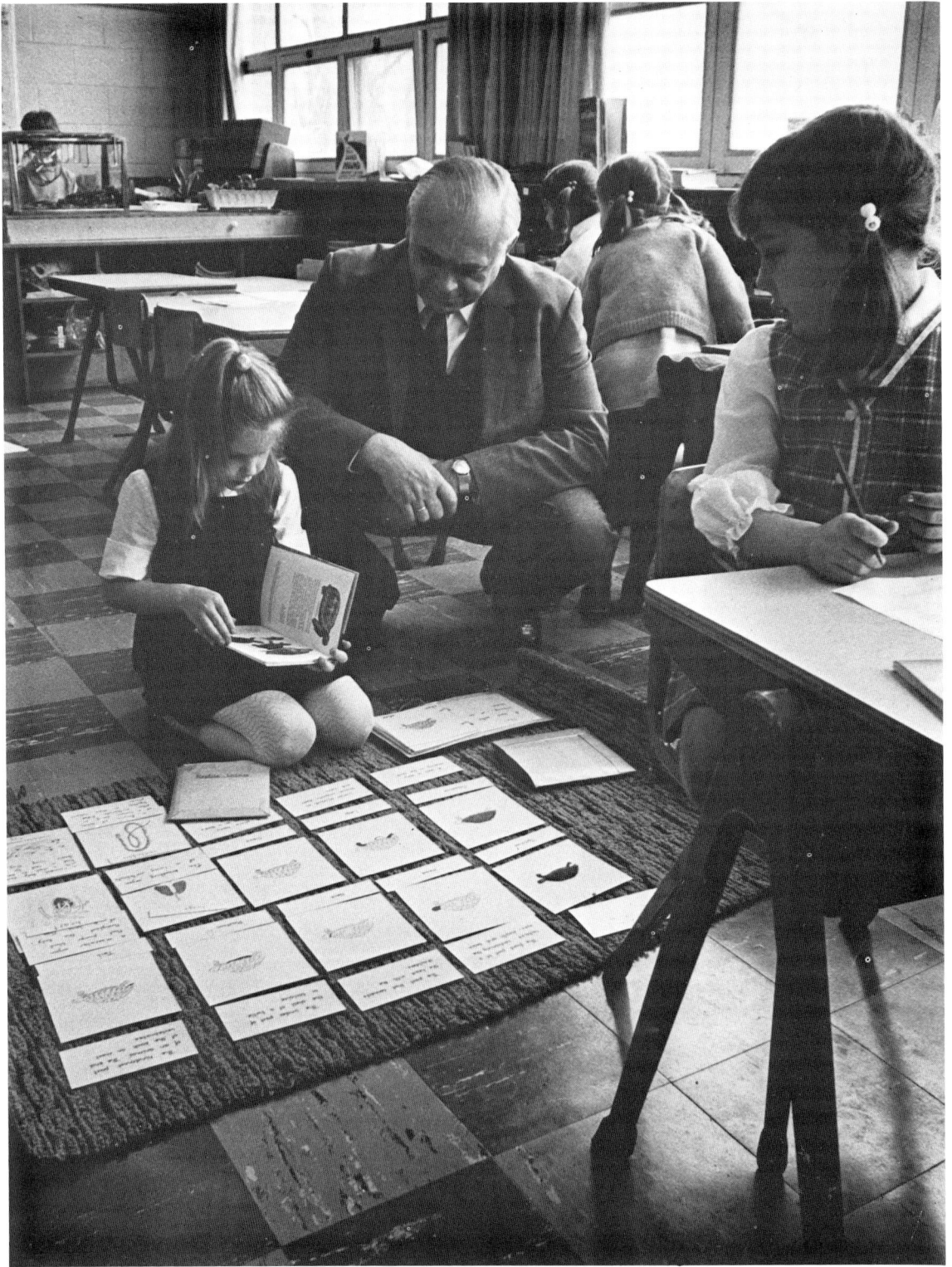

CHAPTER 12

Vocabulary
Development

WHY IS IT IMPORTANT TO HAVE A GOOD VOCABULARY?

SECOND GRADERS

...cause otherwise when you grow up you'd be really dumb.

CAN YOU THINK OF SOMEONE WHO HAS A GOOD VOCABULARY?

FIFTH GRADERS

...doctors—cause they say all these diseases, they pronounce all these sicknesses and you say, "like what?"

OVERVIEW

In this chapter we discuss four different types of vocabulary development activities: (1) structural analysis, (2) use of concept groups, (3) use of the dictionary and thesaurus, and (4) sight words. Structural analysis involves breaking an unknown word down into component parts. Concept groups are sets of related concepts that can be used to understand and learn new concepts. The dictionary and thesaurus can be used to introduce and reinforce new vocabulary. Sight words are a small set of words that form the "glue" of language and should be immediately recognizable by students.

INTRODUCTION

The importance of vocabulary development is evident from many perspectives. Anderson and Freebody (1981) report the strong relationship between vocabulary and general intelligence. An equally consistent finding has been that word knowledge is strongly related to reading comprehension. Given the importance of vocabulary development it seems self-evident that increasing a student's vocabulary might also increase the student's performance in reading and other related language arts areas.

What is vocabulary development? Within education and specifically language arts instruction it can mean many things. In general, when language arts teachers talk about vocabulary, they can mean one of four types of vocabulary. They are: (1) listening, (2) speaking, (3) reading, and (4) writing vocabulary. Each type has a very specific meaning.

- *Listening vocabulary*—those words that children can understand when they hear them spoken in context.
- *Speaking vocabulary*—those words that students correctly and consistently use in conversation.
- *Reading vocabulary*—those words that students recognize immediately when reading.
- *Writing vocabulary*—those words that students correctly and consistently use in writing.

In general, if you are trying to teach or reinforce any of these specific vocabularies you should do so in the context of the other three types. For example, when trying to improve a child's listening vocabulary you should also include activities that reinforce the other three vocabulary types. In this chapter we discuss a number of different vocabulary development techniques. Note, that as much as possible we include activities that incorporate all four vocabulary types. The specific techniques we will cover are (1) structural analysis, (2) teaching using concept groups, (3) teaching sight words, and (4) using the dictionary and the thesaurus.

STRUCTURAL ANALYSIS

The act of decoding a word by identifying the meaning of the affixes (prefixes and suffixes) and root words is called *structural analysis*. For example, if students encountered the word "bimonthly" and did not know what it means, they might be able to figure it out from a knowledge of the prefix "bi" and the root word "month." Below is a list of commonly used Latin, Greek, and Anglo-Saxon prefixes.

Latin Prefixes

ab-, abs-, a-	from, away	abstain
ad-	to, toward	adjoin
ante-	before	antecedent
bene-	well, good	benefactor
bi-	two	bimodal
circum-	around, about	circumnavigate
con-	with	concurrent
contra-	against	contradistinction
de-	down	depress
dis-	apart, opposite of	dislike
ex-	out, from	excavate
extra-	beyond	extracurricular
in-, il-, im-, ir-	not	inept, illicit, immature, irrational
in-, im-	in	infringe, impede
inter-	between	intercede
intra-	within	intramural
intro-	within	introspection
juxta-	near	juxtapose
non-	not, opposite from	nonviolent
per-	through	perforate
post-	after	postmortem
pre-	before	predetermine
re-	again, back	reclaim, recoil
retro-	backward	retroflex
semi-	half, partly	semiskilled
sub-	under	submarine
super-	over	supersonic
trans-	across	transcontinental
ultra-	beyond, extremely	ultraconservative

Greek Prefixes

a-, an-	not	amorphous, anhydrous
ambi-, amphi-	around, both	ambidextrous, amphibious
ana-	back, opposite	anaphase

anti-	against	antiwar
cata-	down	cataclysm
dia-	through	diatribe
dys-	bad	dysfunction
epi-	upon	epigram
eu-	good	euphemism
hyper-	beyond, excess	hyperactive
hypo-	under	hypotension
meta-	beyond	metaphysics
	denoting change	metamorphosis
para-	side by side, near	paraphrase
peri-	around	perimeter
prot-	first	prototype
syn-, sym-	together	synchronize, symphony

Anglo-Saxon Prefixes

a-	in, on, of	ashore, akin
be-	near, about	beside
for-	off, to the uttermost	forswear, forbear
mis-	wrong, bad	misunderstand
out-	beyond, more than	outlaw
over-	too much	overcompensate
un-	not	unbeaten
with-	against	withstand

Prefixes commonly change the meaning of the word they are added to. For example if we add the prefix *un* to the word *natural* we completely reverse its meaning. Suffixes generally do not change the meaning of words. Instead they change the word's part of speech. Below are some common suffixes marking nouns, verbs, adjectives, and adverbs.

Suffixes marking nouns: -acy, -age, -an, -ance, -ancy, -ant, -ar, -ard, -ary, -ate, -cy, -dom, -ee, -eer, -ence, -ent, -er, -ery, -ess, -ette, -hood, -ice, -ie, -ier, -ite, -ism, -ist, -ity, -ive, -kin, -let, -ment, -mony, -ness, -or, -ory, -ship, -ster, -teen, -tion, -tude, -ty, -ure, -y, -yer.

Suffixes marking verbs: -ate, -en, -fy, -ify, -ise, -ize.

Suffixes marking adjectives: -able, -ac, -aceous, -al, -am, -ar, -ary, -ate, -ble, -ent, -er, -ern, -escent, -ful, -ible, -ic, -ical, -id, -ile, -ine, -ish, -less, -like, -ly, -ory, -ose, -ous, -some, -ty, -ulent, -wise, -y.

Suffixes marking adverbs: -ally, -fold, -like, -ly, -ward, -ways, -wise.

In addition to the these prefixes and suffixes Johnson and Pearson (1978) recommend direct instruction of the following inflectional endings:

Inflected Endings

Plural
s—girls
es—watches

Comparison
er—taller
est—tallest

Tense
ed—jumped
ing—jumping
s—jumps

Possessive
's—Ann's
s'—boys'

Durkin (1976) has developed a two-step methodology for teaching students to use the information available with prefixes and suffixes.

1 With derived and inflected words, prefixes and suffixes should be mentally separated from the root so that if the root is not familiar, its pronunciation can be worked out with the help of letter-sound relationships.

2 Once a root is identified, the suffix immediately attached to it should be added. If there is a second suffix that should be added next. The prefix is added last (pp. 54, 55).

Durkin offers the following illustration of the analysis-synthesis process for derived and inflected words.

foretell	*carelessness*	*unwanted*	*unenviable*
tell	careless	wanted	enviable
foretell	care	want	envy
	careless	wanted	enviable
	carelessness	unwanted	unenviable

In addition to Durkin's generalized strategy, below are some other activities that can be used to reinforce the use of prefixes and suffixes.

• Select a root word to which many prefixes and suffixes can be added (for example, *courage*). Using a list of prefixes and suffixes and the dictionary have students generate as many words as possible.

discourage
encourage
courageous

Note that this activity helps reinforce spelling by meaning as we presented in Chapter 8.

• Have students create "new words" using common roots and affixes. For example, Johnson and Pearson (p. 102) suggest the following four sets of roots and affixes:

	A	*B*	*C*	*D*
1	trans	luno	graph	ological
2	tele	helio	vis	ic (or al)
3	proto	stella	phon	ology
4	neo	terre	trop	phobia

Students can select randomly from each column to create such new words as "telelunophonology," the study of sending sound across the moon.

• Identify a number of words from the newspaper that have roots and affixes. Have students break down the meaning of those words into their component parts.

Included under the general technique of structural analysis is the analysis of compound words. Compound words are usually defined as two separate words joined together to create a new word that has the combined meaning of the two root words. In many cases this is an inaccurate definition. For example, consider the compound word *blackboard*. It carries more meaning than those contained separately in the roots *black,* and *board*.

There are many activities that can be developed using a list of compound words,

1 *Separating compound words into their roots.* Have students discuss the independent meanings of the roots and then the combined meaning in the compound word.

Root	*Root*	*Compound*
after	noon	_____
mail	box	_____
street	light	_____

2 *Making word puzzles.* Supply students with the definitions of the root words for selected compound words. See if students can identify the compound words using these definitions.

> Animal with wings + Container used for bathing = _____
> (Answer: birdbath)

3 *Separating compounds.* Have students separate compound words into their roots and discuss the meaning of those roots. This activity helps demonstrate that some compounds are truly composites of the meaning of both root words while others are not.

4 *Finding which roots fit.* Have students draw a line from those words which can be used with the root word on the right.

foot

car

base   ball
snow
out

A final area generally considered part of structural analysis is contractions. A useful instructional technique is to present students with the uncontracted component words for contractions and have them recombine these words:

had   not   _____
was   not   _____
it   is   _____
he   will   _____
I   would   _____

An alternate exercise is to have students rewrite a passage changing all uncontracted forms to contracted, and vice versa. This usually helps demonstrate the stylistic impact of contractions.

TEACHING WORDS IN CONCEPT GROUPS

What does it mean to know the meaning of a word? Labov (1973, p. 341) has stated that "words have often been called slippery customers and many scholars have been distressed by their tending to shift their meaning and slide out from under any simple definition." Labov's position suggests that knowing the meaning of a word is not synonymous with word knowledge. It has been suggested that most articulate adults can accurately define only a small portion of the words they know and use quite effectively. In fact, it has been shown that adults have difficulty defining such seemingly simple words as *cup* (Labov, 1973); *eat* (Anderson and Ortony, 1975); *red* (Halff, Ortony, and Anderson, 1976); and *held* (Anderson, et al., 1976). How, then, can we explain the word knowledge?

To understand the word knowledge we must deal with the issue of concept development. A word is probably most accurately defined as the "label" society places on a concept. A concept is defined in a complementary fashion—"the socially accepted meaning of one or more words which express the concept" (Klausmeier and Sipple, 1980, p. 22). For example, the word *dog* is a label society uses to represent the conceptual representation of a set of four-legged animals with certain characteristics. Vocabulary knowledge, then could be operationally defined as the relationship between an individual's store of concepts and the labels society uses to represent those concepts. If this perspective is at all true, we can say that vocabulary development is akin to concept development. Let us consider how an individual might learn a new concept.

Assume that a student is introduced to the concept *domicle*. At first the student might learn that such concepts as *house* and *home* are similar to or examples of the concept *domicle*. The student might then learn that such concepts as *building* and *structure* have some similarities with *domicle* but are different in some respects. When the student establishes enough "points of reference" with which to define (not in a literal sense) *domicle* we say the student understands the concept. It is the comparing and contrasting of new concepts with previously stored concepts that culminates in what we call concept knowledge. Perhaps this is one reason why two literate individuals have trouble defining a common word in the same way. Both individuals might have different defining concepts which they use for comparative purposes. In general they have the same working knowledge of the concept but use different points of reference.

Given the validity of this model of concept development it makes sense that student vocabulary development could be facilitated if new vocabulary was presented in association with known vocabulary.

To facilitate this process Klausmeier and Sipple (1980) have outlined seven steps teachers might follow when trying to develop new concepts. Klausmeier's model was developed primarily as a theoretical framework around which to plan instructional techniques. That is, in its present form it does not lend itself to classroom use. For a language arts teacher, the following adaptation might be useful.

1 Identify the larger conceptual group that the target concept is a part of. To illustrate this first step assume that a language arts teacher wants to introduce the concept "domicile." The teacher would first try to place that concept in some larger framework. Is domicile the example of some larger conceptual group? A possible answer to this question might be the more general concept of "buildings." All buildings are not domiciles but, for the most part, domiciles are buildings.

2 Define the target concept. Some definitions of our target concept *domicile* are

   a permanent residence
   principal home
   a place where people live

3 Help students understand the meaning of the concept by pointing out examples of the concept and nonexamples of the concept which are within the framework of the larger conceptual group. For example, *houses, apartments, condominiums* are all examples of the concept domicile. *Restaurants, factories, stores* are examples of the general concept, *buildings*, but they are not examples of *domiciles*. These examples can be used in either an inductive or deductive fashion to demonstrate the meaning of the target concept.

4 Identify the vocabulary words relevant to the examples of the concept and the vocabulary words relevant to the nonexamples. Here the teacher must decide which words are important given the students' grade levels. Vocabulary pertinent to the concept *domicile* might be the words *house, home, dwelling, apartment* along with the word *domicile*.

5 Make sure the students can recognize these words by sight and can spell them correctly.

Another application of the principal of relating new vocabulary words to known words is to present vocabulary in groups or "clusters." To facilitate this a study was conducted (Marzano, 1983) in which the 7000 words (concepts) most commonly found in elementary school textbooks were categorized into 430 basic concept clusters. To illustrate the information contained in a cluster consider the following:

Grabbing/Holding Actions

	Concept	Grade Level	Syntactic Form
1	hold	1	Noun−verb
	catch	1	Noun−verb
	squeeze	3	Noun−verb
	grab	3	Verb
	grip	4	Noun−verb
	clutch	4	Verb
	clasp	5	Noun−verb
	wring	5	Verb
	clench	6	Verb
2	pick	2	Verb
	pinch	4	Noun−verb
	pluck	6	Verb
	nip	6	Noun−verb
3	hug	3	Noun−verb
	wrap	3	Verb
	cling	4	Verb
	nuzzle	4	Verb
	embrace	6	Noun−verb
	snuggle	6	Verb

This cluster's name is "Grabbing/Holding Actions." Within the cluster there are three unnamed sets of related concepts. These represent concepts with closer semantic ties than those represented by the more general cluster name. Concepts within the subcluster and the main cluster are meant to be introduced to students as sets. That is, when introducing one concept to students, the other concepts within the cluster or subcluster may also be introduced.

Teaching the 430 concept clusters in their entirety represents a major commitment in terms of time, energy, and materials. For a description of how to accomplish this see Marzano (1983). The benefits of the cluster method, however, can be gleaned without actually teaching every word in a cluster.

The clusters themselves can be grouped into larger clusters. We'll call these "super-clusters." There are only 61 of these. The names of the super-clusters listed in rank order relative to their size (how many concepts are contained in the super-cluster) are found in Appendix A. To illustrate, below is a sample of information found in Appendix A for super-cluster, "Types of People," followed by an explanation of the cluster.

Types of People:
  Number of concepts = 237
  Number of clusters   = 15

a People (General)
  RC: human, people, mankind
  GLR: 2-people; 5-self
  NC: 10

b Names for Women
  RC: woman, widow, lass,
        female, girl
  GLR: 1-girl; 6-housewife
  NC: 17

c Names for men
  RC: boy, male, sir, guy, gentle-
        man
  GLR: k-guy; 6-host
  NC: 12

d Names Indicating Youth/Age
  RC: infant, youth, child, elder,
        baby
  GLR: 1-baby; 6-infant
  NC: 20

e Names Indicating Friendship
  RC: neighbor, ally, pal, lover,
        friend
  GLR: 1-friend; 6-comrade
  NC: 17

f Names for Spiritual/Mythical People
  RC: fairy, spirit, saint, goblin,
        wizard
  GLR: 2-fairy; 6-wizard
  NC: 17

g Names Indicating Negative
  Characteristics of People
  RC: liar, gossip, enemy, grouch,
        outlaw, thief
  GLR: 3-thief; 6-pest
  NC: 28

h Names Indicating Lack of Perma-
  nence for People
  RC: guest, rover, runaway, visitor
  GLR: 3-visitor; 6-wanderer
  NC: 15

i Names Indicating Permanence for
  People
  RC: settler, dweller, resident
  GLR: 4-settler; 6-immigrant
  NC: 17

j Names Indicating Size of People
  RC: giant, midgit, pygmy
  GLR: 2-giant; 6-pygmy
  NC: 5

k Names Indicating Fame
  RC: celebrity, hero, idol
  GLR: 2-star, 6-idol
  NC: 7

l Names Indicating Knowledge of a
  Topic
  RC: expert, genius, novice
  GLR: 4-expert; 6-amateur
  NC: 7

m Names Indicating Financial Status of
  People
  RC: millionaire, miser
  GLR: 6-pauper
  NC: 4

n Family Relations
  RC: dad, mother, parent, sister,
        brother
  GLR: k-daddy; 6-niece
  NC: 45

o Names of People Indicating Political
  Disposition
  RC: democrat, patriot, socialist
  GLR: 5-confederate; 6-patriot
  SS: republican
  NC: 16

This super-cluster contains 237 concepts in all and 15 clusters. Representative words are given for each of the clusters contained within this super-cluster. Specifically, the information presented for each cluster includes

1   Representative concepts from the cluster *(RC)*. These words are representative of the characteristics of all words (concepts) within the cluster. Basically if you identify synonyms and related words for each representative word listed you will have covered the majority of concepts within a cluster.

2   Grade level range *(GLR)*. The word representing the lowest grade level at which the concept cluster appears and the word representing the highest grade level at which the concept group appears. Also identified are concepts that are found primarily in selected content areas. The following code is used for that identification

SS = social studies
SC = science
EN = English
MA = math

3   Number of concepts *(NC)*. The total number of concepts in a cluster.

How can these super-clusters be used to improve vocabulary development? Their primary utility is as a framework around which to classify and introduce the vocabulary words specific to the grade level you teach. The basic plan is for you to categorize the words you will be teaching within a unit or entire year prior to presenting those words to students. Once the vocabulary words have been categorized you present the categories to the students and establish *anchor concepts* (concepts familiar to the students) for each category. Once the anchor concepts are firmly established, new vocabulary words are introduced. For example, assume that you have identified a cluster named "Heat" as a useful grouping for a number of concepts you will introduce throughout a unit. You might identify the following anchor concepts for that cluster: *hot, cold, warm.*

Once anchor concepts have been established you can then present the cluster and the anchor concepts to the students. You might present these to students with the following introduction.

Throughout the next unit we are going to encounter some new words. These words will be similar to some words we already know.

You would then introduce the cluster names and anchor words and have students record those clusters in a personal vocabulary notebook.

As each new vocabulary word is introduced, you help the student associate the new concept with the anchor concept. The following procedures generally help form these associations.

Have the student describe the new vocabulary word as it relates to the anchor concepts. For example, assume that you want to teach the concepts *temperature* and *parch*. You might first have students describe those words in the following way.

"*parch* is making something very hot until there is no water left."

"*temperature* is how we measure how hot or cold something is."

A variation on this approach is to have students develop semantic maps or cognitive maps as described in Chapter 11. That is, for each new vocabulary word students can brainstorm to identify related concepts. The related concepts can then be displayed in an interconnected map showing the relationships among the concepts. Figure 12-1 contains a semantic map for the concept newspapers.

The next step is to have students visualize the concept being learned. Visualizing takes the form of students' picturing some concrete object or event they can associate with the concept being learned. For example the following visualizations might be made with the concepts *parch*.

"parch": The student visualizes a man walking through the desert in search of water. There is a visual closeup of the man's mouth. The word *parch* is superimposed on the picture.

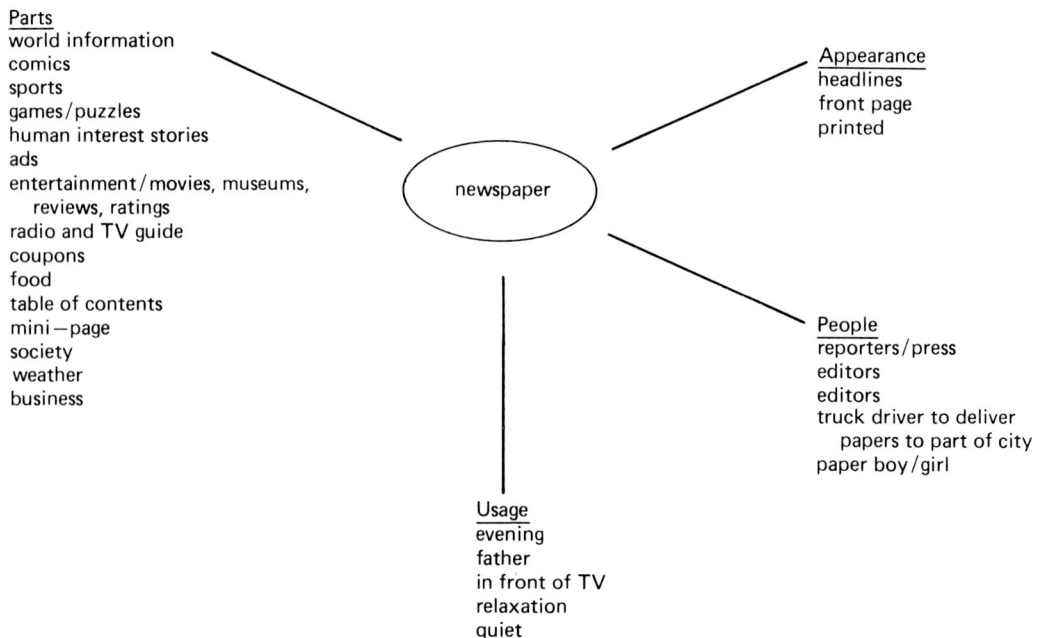

Parts
world information
comics
sports
games/puzzles
human interest stories
ads
entertainment/movies, museums,
    reviews, ratings
radio and TV guide
coupons
food
table of contents
mini—page
society
weather
business

Appearance
headlines
front page
printed

newspaper

People
reporters/press
editors
editors
truck driver to deliver
    papers to part of city
paper boy/girl

Usage
evening
father
in front of TV
relaxation
quiet

FIGURE 12.1 *Primary grade level semantic map.*

Note that within the visualization the word itself is superimposed over the scene. This helps students obtain a strong visual representation of the orthographic (letter) symbols for the spoken word. This strong visual representation will help the student recognize the word when reading and spelling it correctly when writing.

The final step is to have students use the new words in different syntactic forms. That is, nouns should be used in their singular and plural forms: temperature and temperatures.

Verbs should be used in their infinitive, third-person singular, and participial forms: parch, parches, and parched.

Also the suffixes listed in the previous section of this chapter can be used with the new concepts to produce derivational forms of the new vocabulary words.

THE DICTIONARY AND THESAURUS

Of the more than 5000 different reference books available to students the dictionary and thesaurus are two of the most powerful. Over four decades ago Thorndike (1935, 1942) said,

> *The ideal dictionary for a young learner is a book which will help him learn the meaning of any word that he needs to understand, the spelling of any word that he needs to write, and the pronunciation of any word that he needs to speak. It will give him the help that he needs when he needs it, with a minimum of eyestrain and fatigue. It will give him a maximum of knowledge and skill and power for reading, writing, and speaking for every minute that he spends. It will fit him in due time to make proper use of a dictionary for adults (p. vi).*

Johnson and Pearson (1978) identify five types of information contained in dictionaries that would be helpful to building vocabulary.

1 *Guides to locating words.* The principle guide to locating words is the alphabetical arrangement of the entry words. Most students have little trouble with the alphabet but some might have difficulty alphabetizing sets of words such as the following: *fulcrum, fulfill, full, fulsome.* Consequently, to ensure that students can efficiently use the dictionary teachers should provide practice in alphabetizing sets of words with similar alphabetical arrangements. As an aid to understanding the alphabetical arrangement all dictionaries contain guide words on each page which are the first and last words that appear on the page.

2 *Entry words.* Entry words contain information about word pronunciation, grammatical class and meaning. Of course, the entry words are the heart of a dictionary. Large dictionaries often include derived forms of the entry words with affixes, word etimologies and idiomatic expressions.

glow (glō) verb 1. to shine brightly and steadily esp. without a flame. 2. to have a bright or ruddy color. 3. to be exuberant or radiant, as with pride. noun 1. a light produced by or as by a body heated to luminosity. 2. brilliance or warmth of color, esp. redness. 3. a sensation of physical warmth. 4. a warm feeling of emotion.   OE glō   (*American Heritage Dictionary*, p. 306).

3 *Pronunciation keys.*   The pronunciation of each entry word is indicated via the use of phonetic symbols, syllabication divisions, and stress markers. The phonetic symbols most commonly used are the International Phonetic Alphabet and diacritical marking systems. The specific system used by a dictionary is usually presented at the beginning or end of the book.

4 *Abbreviations and symbols.*   To save on space many dictionaries use abbreviations and symbols. Most dictionaries include a listing of these symbols and abbreviations at the beginning of the text.

ff.	following
e.g.	for example
‡	foreign word
<	derived form

5 *Special sections.*   In addition to the information listed above many dictionaries contain special sections. Some of those special sections are

- States and cities in the United States
- Flags
- Full page maps
- Foreign monetary units
- Precious stones

Knowledge of these areas is a prerequisite to a student's effective use of the dictionary.

The thesaurus is one of the most powerful yet often underused tools for increasing vocabulary. Johnson and Pearson (1978) state that the thesaurus is "a fantastic aid to classroom vocabulary instruction" (p. 141). They also state it is not commonly used in language arts classrooms. As a result, many students are unfamiliar with its contents and its possibilities. In many respects, the thesaurus is less complicated and more useful than the dictionary. It emphasizes only one aspect of words—their meanings using synonyms and antonyms.

In essence, a thesaurus is a list of words classified according to meaning and carefully indexed and cross-referenced. To a great extent a thesaurus can be a useful companion to the concept clusters described previously in this chapter. That is, for each representative concept presented in the Appendix the thesaurus can be used to generate related concepts. Below we've listed some other instructional activities that might be used with dictionary and/or thesaurus.

1 *Using guide words.*   Using the dictionary locate the guide words found on the pages where the following words appear.

reprimand
entrust
college
animal

Next, reverse the process. List some selected guide words and have students identify one word from each page represented by the guide words. Students can report on interesting words found on those pages.

2 *Words borrowed from other languages.* Ask students to identify the origin of the following words

coyote
caribou
sauerkraut
frankfurter
lariat

3 *Using big words.* Have students identify more common words for some technical or "big" words

phenomenon
terminus
parsimonious
rostrum
syllabus

TEACHING SIGHT VOCABULARY

Many teachers use the term sight vocabulary to refer to all those words a reader can recognize immediately while reading. This definition of sight vocabulary is almost synonymous with our definition of reading vocabulary presented at the beginning of this chapter. In the discussion here we define sight vocabulary a bit differently as do Johnson and Pearson (1978):

> *. . . a relatively small corpus of words which occur in such high frequency in printed matter that they are deemed essential to fluent reading, especially in the beginning stages. Many basic sight words are neither particularly meaningful in and of themselves (but, to, far) nor picturable; thus they are often not very interesting to children. Yet they are the glue words of language which cement meaningful communication (p. 12).*

There are over 3000 word frequency lists constructed from such sources as the speech of young children, school essays, language of bilingual adults, comic books, award-winning children's literature. One of the most frequently used lists is Johnson's (1974). Johnson's first- and second-grade lists are presented below.

TABLE 1
Johnson's First-Grade Words

a	day	I	off	table
above	days	if	old	than
across	did	I'm	one	that
after	didn't	in	open	the
again	do	into	or	then
air	don't	is	out	there
all	door	it	over	these
am	down	its		they
American	end	it's	past	think
and			play	this
are	feet	just	point	those
art	find		put	three
as	first	keep		time
ask	five	kind	really	to
at	for		red	today
	four	let	right	too
back		like	room	took
be	gave	little	run	top
before	get	look		two
behind	girl	love	said	
big	give		saw	under
black	go	make	school	up
book	God	making	see	
boy	going	man	seen	very
but	gone	may	she	
	good	me	short	want
came	got	men	six	wanted
can		miss	so	was
car	had	money	some	way
children	hand	more	something	we
come	hard	most	soon	well
could	has	mother	still	went
	have	Mr.		what
	he	must		when
	help	my		where
	her			which
	here	name		who
	high	never		why
	him	new		will
	his	night		with
	home	no		work
	house	not		
	how	now		year
				years
				yet
				you
				your

TABLE 2
Johnson's Second-Grade Words

able	different	last	real	water
about	does	leave	road	were
almost	done	left	same	west
alone	each	light	say	while
already	early	long	says	whole
always	enough	made	set	whose
America	even	many	should	wife
an	ever	mean	show	women
another	every	might	small	world
any	eyes	morning	sometimes	would
around	face	Mrs.	sound	
away	far	much	started	
because	feel	music	street	
been	found	need	sure	
believe	from	next	take	
best	front	nothing	tell	
better	full	number	their	
between	great	of	them	
board	group	office	thing	
both	hands	on	things	
brought	having	only	thought	
by	head	other	through	
called	heard	our	together	
change	idea	outside	told	
church	knew	own	town	
city	know	part	turn	
close		party	until	
company		people	us	
cut		place	use	
		plan	used	
		present		

Johnson and Pearson (1978) recommend the following five-step procedure when teaching basic sight words.

1 Seeing.   *The word is written on the chalkboard, a flashcard, or a piece of paper and* spoken in an oral context. *With appropriate words* (book, table, chair) *we recommend labeling the objects themselves in the classroom. With other words* (children, party, house) *we recommend labeling a picture that exemplifies the word. However, many basic sight words are not picturable, and with them the following steps become very important.*

2 Discussing.   *After the word has been written, it should be read aloud by the teacher and by the children. Some words lend themselves to short discussions related to the* *children's environment, experiences, and interests. But, again, many basic sight words do not lend themselves to interesting discussions, and the next step is highly useful.*

3 Using. *Children are next asked to use the word in a sentence or two or to suggest synonymous words or phrases. Remember, most basic sight words are already in the speaking/listening vocabularies of young children, even though they cannot yet read them. Since many basic sight words* (the, of, which) *cannot really be discussed, it is important that they be used and reused in sentences by the children so that they clearly see the function and purpose of the words. As much as possible the sentences they generate ought to be written on the board and compared to help them see the roles played by such words as* and, then, *and* with.

4 Defining. *Providing a definition of a word is often much harder for a child (or an adult for that matter) than providing a synonym or using the word in a sentence. Again, many basic sight words are not easily definable* (have, it, let). *But whenever possible, children should be led from using to defining—in their own words, not those of a dictionary. "What does this word mean to you?"*

5 Writing. *Finally, the children should be encouraged to practice writing the words, both alone and in various contexts; for writing a word reinforces learning the word. Many teachers have their pupils keep word books or personal dictionaries in which they write new words, their meanings of synonyms, and sample sentences containing the new words (pp. 19–20).*

In addition to these techniques sight word games are available from commercial publishers and/or may be constructed quickly and inexpensively by teachers. "Feed through" games are some of those most commonly used for sight word instruction. Such games require a cardboard cutout of some object that has a window and strips of paper and cardboard with sight words listed.

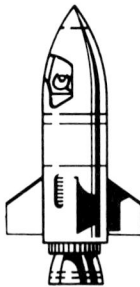

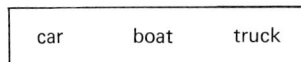

As the strip with the sight words is pulled through the window students can see only one word. Typically games are devised in which students are somehow rewarded for each correctly identified word.

SUGGESTED ACTIVITIES

1 Learn some new words using the visualizing process and related activities described in this chapter. What do you notice about your ability to remember those words?

2 Identify some important concepts for a unit you will be teaching or a unit you have taught. What are some ways you could group or cluster those concepts?

3 Become familiar with the dictionary available to your students. What are some of its more important features?

4 In a small group develop a semantic map for a few selected concepts. Use Figure 12-1 in this chapter as a guide.

REFERENCES

Anderson, R., and Freebody, P. "Vocabulary Knowledge." in J. T. Guthrie (ed.). *Comprehension and Teaching: Research Reviews*. Newark, Del.: International Reading Association, 1981, pp. 71–117.

Anderson, R., and Ortony, A. "On Putting Apples into Bottles: A Problem of Polysemy." *Cognitive Psychology* 7 (June 1975):167–180.

Anderson, R. C.; Pichert, J. W.; Goetz, E. T.; Schallert, D. L.; Stevens, K. W.; and Trollip, S. R. "Instantiation of General Terms." *Journal of Verbal Learning and Verbal Behavior* 15 (October 1976):667–679.

Durkin, D. *Teaching Word Identification*. Boston, Mass.: Allyn and Bacon, 1976.

Halff, H. M.; Ortony, A.; and Anderson, R. C. "A Context Sensitive Representation of Word Meanings." *Memory and Cognition* 4 (November 1976):378–383.

Johnson, D. D. "Word Lists that Make Sense and Those That Don't." *Learning Magazine* 4 (November 1974):60–61.

Johnson, D. D., and Pearson, P. D. *Teaching Reading Vocabulary*. New York: Holt, Rinehart and Winston, 1978.

Klausmeier, H. J., and Sipple, T. S. *Learning and Teaching Concepts*. New York: Academic Press, 1980.

Labov, W. "The Boundaries of Words and Their Meanings." In C. J. Bailey and R. Shuy (eds.). *New Ways of Analyzing Variations in English*. Washington, D.C.: Georgetown University Press, 1973.

Marzano, R. *Vocabulary and Concept Development*. Denver, Educational Press of America, 1983.

Thorndike, E. L., ed. *Thorndike Dictionary*. Chicago: Scott, Foresman, 1935, 1942.

ORGANIZING THE ELEMENTARY CLASSROOM

CHAPTER 13

Children's Literature

WHAT KIND OF STORIES DO YOU LIKE BEST?
SECOND GRADERS
...happy stories
...stories about like if a fairy helps you
...stories about me

FIFTH GRADERS
...funny stories
...Judy Blume books

OVERVIEW

In this chapter we will discuss the use and value of children's literature in the elementary classroom. We will demonstrate how essential components of the language arts can be taught through children's literature and how you can evaluate quality in the vast numbers of trade books for children. We will also discuss the importance of developing positive attitudes toward reading and how this can be accomplished by bringing books and children together. Lastly we will focus on the classroom and discuss methods for making literature an integral part of the language arts curriculum.

INTRODUCTION

We begin our final section of the text with a discussion of children's literature in the elementary school. Thus far we have focused on particular language skills that warrant special attention and specific knowledge to teach. This final section of the text focuses on methods and procedures for teaching language arts. In particular we want to discuss the use of children's books as one of the most important tools for teaching the language arts and for integrating curriculum.

One of the most important tasks of an elementary language arts teacher is to bring children and books together. Fortunately, this task has become easier in recent years. Although excellent books always have been available for children, the quality and quantity has increased steadily. The availability of children's books, both hardback and paperback, has increased as well. Children's books now can be found in department stores, drug stores, and supermarkets as well as in book stores and libraries. In addition, children can now purchase their own books relatively inexpensively.

Because of these trends, teachers must be knowledgeable about children's books and stay abreast of new trends and issues in children's literature. Perhaps the single best way to turn children on to reading, to teach them to listen, to model writing, and to help foster a love of language, is to give them a book they love. To do this, however, teachers need to have a thorough knowledge not only of good literature for children but also of children's interests and reading levels. The purpose of this chapter is to help you acquire this knowledge.

USING CHILDREN'S LITERATURE FOR SCHEMA AND LANGUAGE DEVELOPMENT

What is children's literature? Huck (1979) defines literature as "the imaginative shaping of life and *thought* into the forms and structures of *language*" (p. 4) (authors' italics). We particularly like Huck's definition because it exemplifies the theory proposed by Goodman and our emphasis throughout this book, the interaction between thought and language. Huck continues her explanation, "The province of literature is the human condition; life with all its feelings, thoughts and insights" (p. 4). Notice the emphasis Huck places on experiences, the sum total of our schemata about the world. "The experience of literature is always two dimensional, for it involves both the book and the reader" (p. 4). Again, Huck emphasizes the importance of what the reader brings to the printed page as well as what the reader takes from the printed page.

Children's literature, then, enhances the human condition by bringing thoughts, emotions, and feelings to children through the printed page. Through literature children have an opportunity to explore their own feelings, to build on their existing knowledge and understanding of the world, to develop and refine concepts and schemata. Herein lies a clear benefit of children's literature and its value as the foundation of the language arts program: It enables children to learn about themselves, their language, and their world in an interesting way.

In particular we want to describe and present examples of how children's literature can assist the language arts program in meeting some important goals.

Schemata Development

Literature exposes children to the larger world of events, ideas, and feelings. They have an opportunity to explore worlds different from their own and can build on and expand existing schema in a way they could not do with basal readers alone. Here are some examples of books which can be used to build schema.

Picture Books.

The Story About Ping by M. Flack and K. Wiese (Penguin, 1977). This is a classic story about a duckling and his home on the Yangtze River. Children see a slice of life on a Chinese houseboat.

Alexander and the Terrible, Horrible, No Good, Very Bad Day by J. Viorst (Atheneum, 1972). Children enter a day in the life of Alexander and experience the problems he encounters. As children empathize with Alexander, they learn that everyday problems are universal and a part of life.

The Hating Book by Charlotte Zolotow (Harper and Row, 1969). This is a delightful story about a girl who "hates" her friend only to be reunited with her later on. Children expand their understanding of the term "friendship" through this tale.

The Tenth Good Thing about Barney by J. Viorst (Atheneum, 1971). This book deals sensitively and intelligently with the concept of death through a eulogy to a dead cat, Barney.

The Storm Book by C. Zolotow (Harper and Row, 1952). Children follow the progress of a storm from its calm beginnings to the rainbow at the end—here they expand on their understanding of a storm and its sequential components.

Island of the Blue Dolphins by S. O'Dell (Houghton Mifflin, 1960) *Julie of the Wolves* by J. George (Harper and Row, 1972). These two poignant Newbery award-winning books describe an Indian and an Eskimo girl's survival and adaptation to other environments. Children learn about the concepts of survival and basic needs through these stories.

. . . And Now Miguel by J. Krumgold (Apollo Eds., 1970). This is a story of a Hispanic child growing up on a sheep ranch in New Mexico. Children learn about other cultures and ways of life as well as daily experiences in a different environment.

These books are examples of children's literature that clearly develop concepts or schemata in children's world. The list could run hundreds of pages long. Our point is that children's books open doors to experiences, ideas, and events that children can use to enrich their knowledge of the world. The process becomes cyclical—the more children read, the wider their knowledge base, and the wider the knowledge base children have, the greater is their comprehension of what they read.

Language Development

As children expand their knowledge base or schemata through reading children's books, they also expand their knowledge of language as well. Reading literature helps children develop language in at least three important ways: (1) in learning new vocabulary and concepts; (2) in becoming exposed to new or unusual syntactic structures; (3) in learning "book talk" or formal written language. We will give examples of books that help children in each of these areas (for additional ideas and resources, see two excellent articles by Noyce and Wyatt, 1978, and Pilon, 1978).

Push, Pull, Empty, Full by T. Hoban (Macmillan, 1972) and *Over, Under, and Through* by T. Hoban (Macmillan, 1973). Both books develop the concepts and vocabulary of contrasting words. Each book provides young children with examples and illustrations of these troublesome words.

The Phantom Tollbooth by N. Juster (Random House, 1961). In this book children read of the adventures of Milo as he journeys through "The Lands Beyond." Milo's story provides delightful motivation to learn the meanings of the "Mountains of Ignorance," "The Lands of Null," and the "Doldrums."

Charlotte's Web by E. B. White (Harper and Row, 1975). This classic book tells the story of Wilbur, the pig, who is befriended by a wonderful spider named Charlotte. Children become eager to learn the meanings of

congratulations	sedentary	supreme
humble	gullible	aeronaut

and listen to envision

This morning each thin strand was decorated with dozens of tiny beads of water. The web glistened in the light and made a pattern of loveliness and mystery, like a delicate veil. (p. 77)

and

In the hard-packed dirt of midway, after the glaring lights are out and the people have gone home to bed, you will find a veritable treasure of popcorn fragments, frozen custard drippings, candied apples abandoned by tired children, sugar fluff crystals, salted almonds, popsicles, partially gnawed ice cream cones and the wooden sticks of lollypops. (p. 123)

The Little Moon Theatre by I. Haas (Atheneum, 1981). A wonderful lyrical story unfolds about a troupe of traveling players, Jo Jo, Jip, and Nicolette. Children quickly learn to listen for the refrains

"Oh Madam!" said Jo Jo. "The Little Moon Traveling Theatre made that wish come true, so you still have one wish left to do!" (p. 9)

and

In the morning she flew off once more and the troupe packed up to go, to another village and another show. (p. 9)

This type of pattern book has great appeal to children, as they learn to listen for and enjoy the structures and lyrical patterns of language.

Fox in Socks by Dr. Seuss (Beginner, 1965). This book is just one of a whole series of classic Dr. Seuss books that can be used to teach rhyming words at the simplest level and to foster a love of language at another level. Children love hearing the rhymes of

Knox in box
Fox in socks. (p. 4)

and the more complex . . .

I can't blab
such blibbler blubber!
My tongue isn't
made of rubber. (p. 44)

A Boy, A Dog and A Frog by Mercer Mayer (Dial, 1967) and *The Silver Pony* by Lynd Ward (Houghton Mifflin, 1973). Here are two "wordless" books, or books without any words. These are excellent examples of a whole genré of books that recreate a story visually. Children can then "tell" the story in their own words. These types of books are excellent sources for developing language fluency and creativity.

The Dragon Takes a Wife by Walter Dean Myers (Xerox, 1972). A delightful tale of Mable, the fairy and a dragon who needed help in slaying the knight. Mabel Mae's use of nonstandard dialect is juxtaposed to the standard language of the dragon

"What's bugging you, baby?" asked Mabel Mae Jones . . .

"Well," said Harry, "each week, in order to win a wife, I fight the knight in
shining armor. . . ."
Mabel Mae's enchanting "magic words" delight young children.
"Fire, be hotter
And hotter than that!
Turn Harry on
So he can burn that cat!" (p. 7)

The book provides an excellent vehicle with which to discuss formal and
informal language, dialect differences, and language registers.

Each of these books and hundreds more provide children with examples of
language that they may not hear in their everyday world. Helping children become
comfortable with book language is an important goal of a language arts program,
and one for which children's books can provide a pleasant vehicle.

We have tried to emphasize the valuable contributions of children's books to the
language arts curriculum. They can easily become the foundation of a language arts
program because they contain the essential components for teaching children about
the world through language. We will return to this idea shortly.

EVALUATING LITERATURE FOR CHILDREN

We hope to have convinced you by now of the importance of children's literature in
the classroom. Given that you realize how children's literature can strengthen the
language arts program, how do you evaluate books so you can choose the best ones
for your classroom?

Evaluating literature for children is not an easy task, particularly since we, with
adult perspectives, must evaluate what is valuable and worthy for a child who
almost always has a different perspective from us. We do have traditional criteria for
evaluation (Huck, 1976) and these criteria are a good place to begin in the evaluation
process.

Plot

When we look at plot we attempt to answer the question "Is it a good story?" Plot
refers to what happens in the story. In most ficticious Western culture books, stories
have a beginning, a middle, and an end. Stories for young children have simple plots
with lots of action. In Maurice Sendak's *Where the Wild Things Are* (Harper and Row,
1963), Max is sent to bed without dinner and thus begins his imaginary journey to
where the wild things are. His happy rumpus is interrupted, however, with loneli-
ness and smells of good things to eat. He returns safely home and with his supper
waiting for him.

Books for older children have more complicated plots, with flashbacks and subplots that older children are cognitively capable of understanding. In *Ash Road* (Greenwillow, 1978), Ivan Southall presents a complex plot shifting in focus from one family to another as they react to a bushfire in Australia. In Jean George's *Julie of the Wolves* (Harper and Row, 1972), the heroine flashes back to an earlier experience which resulted in her running away from home. In both books, the authors skillfully keep the young reader's interest and attention through complex and exciting plots.

Characterization

A second important criteria for evaluation of children's books relates to the particular characters in the story, who they are, how they act, how realistic and multidimensional they are. Even animals presented in picture books need to be portrayed as realistic characters. Stereotyped, one-dimensional characters can lose children's interest. More lifelike characters such as the rabbit in Margery Williams *The Velveteen Rabbit* (Avon, 1975), Charlotte in E. B. White's *Charlotte's Web* (Harper and Row, 1952) and Amos, the mouse in Robert Lawson's *Ben & Me* (Little Brown, 1951) capture the interest and attention of children readily. The velveteen rabbit thinks and acts as a caring young child, Charlotte befriends Wilbur the pig as all children would like to be befriended, and Amos relates his experiences with Ben Franklin in a humorous yet credible way. Children are captured by Judy Blume and Beverly Cleary characters because they are so authentic. The characters think and act like the readers, making the same kinds of mistakes, having the same strengths and weaknesses, and yet changing and growing through the story.

Setting

Where and when the story takes place can add strength to the plot, theme, and characterization of a story (Huck, 1976). Regardless of the time period, elements of the setting need to be authentic, and the writer needs to accurately portray the events, actions, and surroundings of a particular period. For example, historical fiction books can be excellent sources of information about particular time periods and can add significantly to children's schematic understanding of history only if the information presented is accurate. Laura Engle Wilder's *Little House* series (Harper and Row, 1973), William Armstrong's *Sounder* (Harper and Row, 1972), Alice Dalgliesh's *The Courage of Sarah Noble* (Scribner, 1954) are all examples of historical fiction books in which the setting plays an important part in the excellence of the plots and the books themselves. In these books the setting is described sufficiently and accurately and provides a vivid framework for the story to unfold.

Style

The author's writing style is a crucial component in the evaluation of a good book. How vividly and sensitively the characters are portrayed, how the events unfold, how language is used, how detailed the setting is described all affect the quality of the story. Consider the moving text in which Uri Shulevitz uses metaphors and personification to describe a scene at *Dawn* (Farrar, Straus, 1974) . . .

> *The moon lights a rock, a branch, an occasional leaf. The mountains stand guard, dark and silent. (p. 6—7)*

or the realistic internal monologue of Alexander in Judith Viorst's *Alexander Who Used to Be Rich Last Sunday.* . . (Atheneum, 1978)

> *They brought a dollar for me and a dollar for Anthony because—Mom says it isn't nice to say this—we like money. A lot. Especially me. (p. 7)*

Both texts are extremely effective in creating the mood and tone that the authors intend to capture in the minds of the readers. Each uses a unique and contrasting style; both are effective.

Theme

The theme refers to the overriding meaning of the story, the message the author intends to impart on the reader. Often the themes of children's books relate to an understanding and acceptance of self and others, or of growing up. Examples of these books are books such as E. L. Konigsburg's *Jennifer, Hecate, William McKinley and Me, Elizabeth* (Atheneum, 1967) and Maia Wojcieckowska's *Shadows of the Bull* (Atheneum, 1964). Not all books have themes; some are written as adventure or fun stories. Other books, however, are written about particular issues and problems in our times: divorce (*I Love My Mother*, by Paul Zindel, Harper and Row, 1975); individuals with handicaps (*The Summer of the Swans*, by Betsy Byars, Avon, 1974); death (*First Snow*, by Helen Coutant, Avon, 1974) and racial discrimination (*Crow Boy*, by Taro Yashima, Penguin, 1976). When a theme is presented in a book, it must be handled sensitively and not presented in an overbearing, and didactic manner.

While we have provided a general outline for the evaluation of children's books, a word of caution is in order. Each of the elements—plot, characterization, style, and theme—interact with each other to form the whole. Sometimes elements are omitted; some books have no theme, plot, or characters. Still these books manage to tell a good story and one that is of interest and value to children.

Remember that in the end children are the best judge of a good book. Arbuthnot and Sutherland (1972, p. 3) summarize by saying that "a book is a good book for children only when they like it, a book is a poor book for children, even when adults rate it a classic, if children are unable to read it or are bored by its content."

SOURCES OF GOOD BOOKS FOR CHILDREN

Fortunately, in addition to our own critical evaluation of books, we have available a number of excellent resources for finding good books for children. Below we list some basic sources.

- *The Children's Book Council.* A nonprofit trade association of children's book publishers which encourages and supports projects and programs to bring children and books together. It publishes a newsletter, periodical books about children's literature, posters, bookmarks, pamphlets, and other materials promoting children's books.

- *The Elementary School Library Collection*, 8th edition, (Mary V. Gauer, et al., eds.). Designed as a guide for the acquisition of books for a basic elementary school library, materials are reviewed and compared with those of earlier editions.

- *Children's Literature in the Elementary School*, (Charlotte Huck, 4th edition, 1976). A basic text in children's literature. The text can be used to learn more about basic issues in children's literature and also as a sourcebook for excellent children's books.

- *The Best in Children's Books: The University of Chicago Guide to Children's Literature*, 1966–1972, 1972–1976. (Zena Sutherland, ed.). These excellent reference books and guides to quality literature for children include titles, reading level, subject matter, and type of literature for hundreds of books.

- *The Horn Book Magazine.* Devoted entirely to children's literature, this journal includes reviews of current books and articles about authors and illustrations.

- *Children's Book Awards—The Newbery and Caldecott Medals.* The Newbery Medal was named in honor of John Newbery, a British publisher who was the first to publish books especially for children. The award is presented each year to "the author of the most distinguished contribution to American literature for children."

    The Caldecott Medal was named in honor of Randolph Caldecott, a nineteenth-century illustrator of children's books. The award is given annually to "the artist of the most distinguished picture book for children."

    Each year two books are awarded the Newbery and Caldecott medals, and several books which are the runners up are declared Honor Books.

These lists are excellent sources for high quality books, and should be consulted whenever you are selecting books for children. These sources are but a few of many that can be useful guides in the ardous task of gathering the best available children's books. You should be sure to work closely with your school librarian and media specialist.

DEVELOPING POSITIVE ATTITUDES TOWARD WRITTEN LANGUAGE THROUGH BOOKS

We have stressed throughout this book that one important goal of language arts instruction is to develop a love of learning about language. One important component of that goal is to help children develop a love of books. We mentioned in Chapter 1 that this goal probably transcends all others. Often this goal can get lost in the myriad of assignments for language instruction. Even as you wade through the enormous amount of material covered in this book, you might be likely to respond, "Oh yes, I forgot about that!" Teachers in elementary classrooms can also forget. In the daily shuffle of worksheets, basals, test skills, and activities, children and teachers can lose their perspectives about the importance of developing a love of books, an interest and enthusiasm for books, and hence a positive attitude toward written language.

How do we help children develop positive attitudes toward books? Roettger (1980) asked fourth, fifth, and sixth graders this question. Interestingly, their responses were consistent with the results of studies (See Bissett, 1969) and also with what experts have suggested (Koeller, 1981). Responses in order of frequency were: (1) to allow children time each day to read "their own" books even if they haven't finished all their work; (2) to talk to children about their hobbies so they can help children find interesting books; (3) to tell children about interesting books and help them build pictures in their mind about what is happening; and (4) to allow children to share their books with each other and with the teacher.

Student Interests: Providing Books In Which Children Are Interested

Based on what these children have suggested, it is clear that children need time to read and discuss books of interest to them. As teachers we need to provide children with the freedom and time to do this every day. We need to allow children the same freedom to pursue their interests as we normally do in our own personal reading.

Let's look for a moment at your own personal interests and tastes in books. You probably remember beginning a book and then putting it down because you found it boring. Or, you can remember not completing a book you read half-way through. Again, it didn't appeal to you or you were distracted by another book or activity. You probably also remember choosing a book because the subject was particularly appealing at some point in your life—a biography of your favorite actress or hero, a "how-to" book, a book about a country or state you planned to visit. In short, your particular mood, your attitudes, your varied interests and tastes determine what you read, how long you read, when you read, and so on.

Do we allow children the same freedom to explore books, to choose books of interest to them, to put books down when they are boring, to put books away without finishing them? Usually, the answer is no. In sum, we do not allow children the freedom to actively pursue their personal interests in books.

What we are saying here is critical. Just as you are allowed the freedom of pursuing your own book interests, children should also. Indeed, one of the best ways to help children become book lovers is to provide them with a variety of books and then give them options to choose books according to their own interests.

Children's interests have been studied extensively. Researchers typically categorize children's favorite books by content (for example, space travel or animal stories) or genre, (for example, mystery or folktale). Further, children's interests have been categorized by age and sex interacting with content or genre—primary children like animal stories, intermediate girls like romance fiction, intermediate boys like adventure stories (Huus, 1964). Abrahamson (1980) argues that children's interest can be classified according to story structure as well. For example, he found that most of children's favorites chosen nationally in 1979 for the Children's Book Council consisted of stories with episodic plots involving confrontation with a problem and characters with opposing viewpoints. Huus (1964, 1979) has summarized the results of early and more recent studies in children's interests in books and found that sex, age, literary quality, language, authors, and the reading program itself all can influence children's interests in books. Koeller (1981) in a review of the literature on children's literature found,

- Parents were more sensitive to the reading interests of their children than either teachers or librarians and could better predict children's choices of reading materials.
- When you satisfy reading interest, you foster reading efficiency.
- Students' reading increases when they have access to a variety of reading materials and an opportunity to discuss these materials.
- There is a positive relationship between the number of books a student reads and that student's comprehension *and* attitude.

DETERMINING STUDENTS' INTERESTS

Personal interviews can be conducted with each child at the beginning of the year. On a 5 × 8 card, you can record children's descriptions of their own interests. You can also obtain information about their general reading habits, their home environment and their attitudes toward reading. All of this information will assist you selecting books for that child.

Name _____
Date Interviewed _____
What do you read at home? _____
Do you like books? Why? _____
What do you like to do? _____

What reading materials do you have at home?

What things are you most interested in?

What do you like to read about?

The 5 × 8 card illustrated above gives the kinds of questions you might ask, depending, of course, on the age level of children.

Another procedure for determining student interests in books is through informal observation of children. Watching children and then recording observational notes on what children are interested in can provide a sound basis for helping children choose books.

By filling out a student interest scale older children can provide you with detailed information about their interests. Items on this scale can be read to children or they can complete the scale independently. You then can order books from the library for groups of children interested in the same topic, or work with individual children who have difficulty motivating themselves to read anything.

STUDENT INTEREST INVENTORY

1 How do you feel when you read?
2 What are your favorite books? Why?
3 What are your least favorite books? Why?
4 How often do you read at home?
5 What books do you have at home?
6 What magazines do you have at home?
7 When do you like to read?
8 Do you like to read out loud? Why or why not?
9 What do you like to read about?
10 What is your hobby?
11 How often do you watch TV?
12 What are your favorite TV programs?
13 What do you and your friends like to do best?
14 Do you have a favorite sport?
15 What do you like to study about the most?

READABILITY: PROVIDING BOOKS THAT CHILDREN CAN READ

In Chapter 11 we discussed the individualized reading approach in which children independently choose and read their favorite books. In using that approach or in simply allowing children a full reading period every day, you need to remember the earlier quote by Sutherland and Arbuthnot, "a book is a poor book for children . . . if they are unable to read it." For children to enjoy reading, they must be able to independently read the books they choose. This is not a firm rule; children can certainly enjoy and obtain value from a picture book they can just look at, and even read in part. However, if children are provided with a constant diet of difficult books, they will never develop positive attitudes toward reading. We discuss this success factor in more detail in the last chapter of this book.

In choosing books for children to read, it becomes very important to know the approximate reading levels of both the children and the children's books. The former task is straightforward, as most teachers soon learn the different reading levels of their students. The second task is less straightforward. How can one possibly know the reading levels of books?

Before discussing "reading levels" per se, let's consider the issue of readability. What makes a book readable? A multitude of factors interrelating with one another contribute to readability.

- Title and book cover or jacket.
- Size of the book—number of and total pages, the physical size of the pages.
- Size of the print.
- Format, layout of the illustrations and/or text.
- Author's writing style.
- Language structure within the text—sentence length, and complexity.
- Concept load or density—how often new words are introduced and how they are reinforced.
- In a narrative story, the setting, characters, plot, theme, and so on.
- Vocabulary complexity.
- Background of the reader, how much information about the subject is already known.
- Reader's interest in the subject.
- Reader's purpose or motivation for reading the book.

All these factors and perhaps more contribute to the readability of a book, that is, how readable it is. Clearly, some factors lie within the control of the writer and the publisher—writing style, book format, and quantity and quality of illustrations. Yet, other factors lie within the subjective evaluation of the reader..For example, the total number of pages in the book will sometimes be a contributing factor in choosing to read or not to read a book, for example, whether you want a long, rambling book to read on a two-week vacation, or a short novel to read on a plane.

This discussion of readability is extremely important as a basis for understanding "reading levels" of books. The term *reading level* refers to a relatively standard procedure currently used to determine readability or reading level according to vocabulary and sentence length. A number of readability formulas use primarily these two factors to establish reading levels of books, usually categorized by grades, from grade 1 through adult (Dale-Chall Readability Formula, 1948; Fry Readability Formula, 1977; Spache Readability Formula, 1966).

The Fry readability formula is perhaps the one recognized and used most often because it is simple and can be administered rather quickly. The graph and directions for using the Fry to determine the reading level of a book is shown in Figure 13-1.

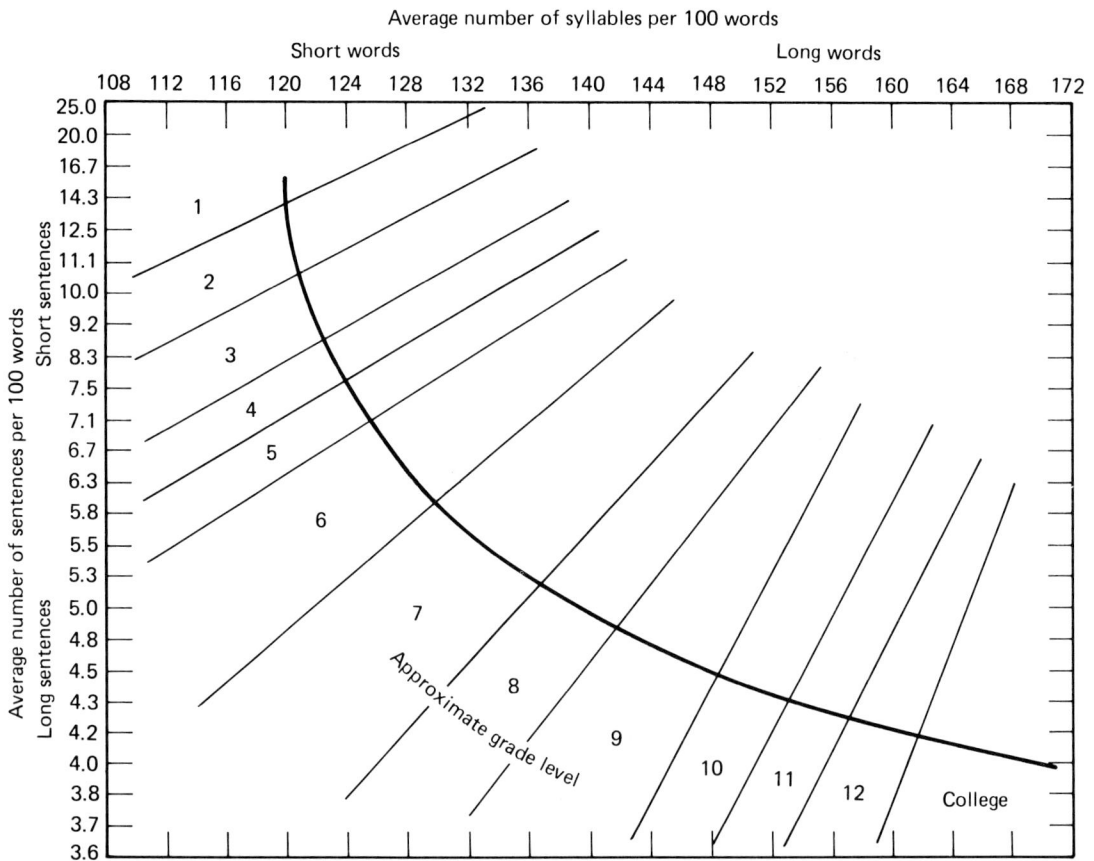

FIGURE 13.1 *Graph for Estimating Readability by Edward Fry, Rutgers University Reading Center, New Brunswick, New Jersey.*

The Fry readability formula represents one important method for determining the reading levels of children's books, but it must be interpreted cautiously. First, the criteria identified on the graph represent only two of many of which determine how readable a book is. Criteria within the subjective evaluation of the reader are particularly excluded. A book could have a high "reading level," but for a child with sufficient interest and background, the book may be quite appropriate. Second, the Fry graph is not as valid or reliable for determining the reading levels of primary grade books. It cannot differentiate lower-grade reading books as accurately as it can upper-grade materials. Thus, this graph provides the teacher with, at best, a rough guess of the reading level of a book.

Another procedure a teacher can use to match a student to a book is called the Cloze test. Developed by John Bormuth (1968) this test requires children to fill in every fifth word deleted from a passage. Bormuth developed tables from which the results can be converted to independent, instructional, and frustrational levels of difficulty. Using this procedure teachers can predict the ease or difficulty a child will have with a given book.

In the end perhaps the best technique for determining how readable a book is is that of observation. Remembering our task to make children successful at reading, we need to provide a variety of books at different levels for children. Beyond that we need to observe which books children choose, then listen to them read to see how appropriate the book is for that child.

USING CHILDREN'S LITERATURE IN THE LANGUAGE ARTS PROGRAM

In an appropriate classroom environment, children's literature can be used for language arts instruction. Children's books can form the base of the reading program, as we mentioned already when we discussed the individualized reading approach in Chapter 11. Alternatively, children's books can be woven into the reading and writing program to help develop an understanding of others and of language, and to model good writing. In this section we will discuss different ways to use children's books to accomplish some of the goals of language arts instruction.

Directions: Randomly select three 100-word passages from a book or an article. Plot the average number of syllables and the average number of sentences per 100 words on the graph to determine the grade level of the material. Choose more passages per book if great variability is observed, and conclude that the book has uneven readability. Few books will fall in the gray area, but when they do, grade level scores are invalid.

Example	*Syllables*	*Sentences*
First Hundred Words	124	6.6
Second Hundred Words	141	5.5
Third Hundred Words	158	6.8
Average	141	6.3

Readability: Seventh grade (see dot plotted on graph)*

For further information and validity data, see the *Journal of Reading* (April 1968) and the *Reading Teacher* (March 1969).

Reading Aloud to Children

The importance of reading aloud to children has been emphasized in the literature for many years (Koeller, 1981). Research has shown that reading aloud to children has a significant affect on children's reading and language growth (Chomsky, 1972; Durkin, 1966). Glazer (1981) lists several specific ways in which reading aloud affects language learning.

1 Instills a desire to learn to read.

2 Enhances facility with language.

3 Builds vocabulary and comprehension skills.

4 Increases schemata or world knowledge.

5 Provides for aesthetic education.

6 Allows the teacher to plan a balanced literature program.

7 Fosters an interest in literature.

8 Encourages group cohesiveness.

If you will recall from Chapter 1 the goals of language arts instruction, you will see that two of the three goals are served by reading aloud. For these reasons it is important to read aloud to children everyday. Fifteen or 20 minutes can be set aside before or after lunch or recess. It is important to view this time as valuable *instructional time*, not supplementary activity time. The attitudes and values established during this time are as important as any particular skill taught in the language arts curriculum.

How can reading aloud improve language arts skills? First, reading aloud children's books can encourage and build listening skills in children. Children thoroughly enjoy the listening experience when they want to hear a favorite book. We have rarely found a classroom where children did *not* enjoy listening to a story. Informally, you can encourage good listening skills by praising good listeners, by asking good questions, and by setting a purpose to the listening experience. Children are learning about the world, about language, and about the listening process at the same time.

Second, reading aloud to children can also enhance growth in writing. Through good literature children can hear how writers develop tone, mood, setting, plot, and character, and how they begin and end a story. Good literature provides children with good models of writing, and reading aloud and discussing these models is one excellent way of encouraging young children as authors. We will return to this idea shortly.

Before we move on to other methods of using children's literature in the language arts program, a word is in order about specific techniques of reading aloud to children. A teacher's technique definitely affects the literature experience. It is therefore important to read with expression and enthusiasm, to enunciate clearly, to maintain at least some eye contact with the children and to make the experience a positive one. Questions can be asked at the beginning to entice children to listen to the story. Questions and discussions can also occur during and at the end of the story as children will want to share their enthusiasm, interest, and ideas about the story.

Young children need to see the illustrations in picture books, and therefore it is very important to have them seated comfortably around you before you begin reading to them. If you know the text very well, you can hold it directly below you, thus allowing children to see the book at all times. Otherwise, you will need to hold the book to the right or left of your shoulder, while you read the text aloud.

Older children also enjoy being read to and can glean as much from this type of literature experience as young children can. They should have a voice in what is read to them; the books can then be used as a starting point for discussions about common experiences and problems in life. This experience also allows slower readers to enter the world of literature which they may not otherwise enter, and to participate in discussions about experiences common to them as well. A chapter can be read each day. Children enjoy the suspense and anticipation of predicting what happens and then evaluating their predictions in light of the next day's reading. In addition, older children can generate many writing ideas through these experiences.

Book Talks for Listening, Speaking, Reading, and Writing

A second technique for using a literature program for language arts instruction is through the use of book talks in the classroom. Book talks are informal presentations about books that have been read and enjoyed. Anyone can give a book talk, a teacher, librarian, or student. The purpose of a book talk is to motivate children to read and write. It is an excellent vehicle to share good books and good authors, and to create a classroom atmosphere in which books are treasured.

Book talks can be given to children of any age level. Teachers of first-grade children can read one or two sentences from a series of books and encourage children to check out the books for personal reading. Teachers could also read several books from the same author to help encourage writing. A book talk at this grade level would certainly differ in substance and length from one presented to older children with more reading proficiency; nevertheless, it is an educational and enjoyable activity for all age groups.

Witucke (1979) has several specific suggestions for book talks.

1 Include from four to eight titles revolving around a central theme—science fiction, biography, humor, new books, and so on.
2 Within this central theme select titles of general appeal to the recipients of the book talk.
3 Once the titles are chosen, decide how to tell about each book. Illustrations of the book can be shown. A brief segment of the book can be read, or paraphrased.

4 Include in the content of a presentation of a fiction book:
Introduction to the characters.
Exposition of the situation.
Inviting episode of the book.
Introduction to the setting.

5 Include in the content of a presentation of a nonfiction book:
Examples of anecdotes.
Illustrations.
Demonstration of a technique.

6 Decide on the order of the presentation—a stimulating and motivating beginning, the order of the books discussed, audience participation, an up-beat ending.

7 Rehearse the presentation before presenting it to the final audience.

8 Be sure to provide for a discussion after the presentation—allow children to borrow the books in which they are interested.

9 Bibliographies can be presented to children to stimulate reading in related areas.

10 Book talks can be audiotaped or videotaped for later use.

While Witucke's suggestions are aimed at teachers, they can be useful guides for children. Once children understand the concept of book talks, they can then create their own book talks.

Book talks are excellent vehicles for reinforcing and practicing all the language arts skills. Consider the four basic skills that are used.

1 Children must *read* the books.

2 Children must decide on an organizational framework and summarize or paraphrase the books through *writing*.

3 Children must give an *oral presentation* of the books.

4 Other children must *listen* to evaluate the books.

We recommend the use of book talks in place of the dreaded written book reports that so many intermediate grade children are forced to write. More language skills are used. More thought and organization must go into book talks. Once children understand the concept, they can use their creativity in trying to "sell" the books. In addition, book talks about particular authors help children become more aware of different authors and of their different styles. This is particularly appropriate for gifted children who could benefit from more detailed and lengthy study of authors and their works.

In addition, older remedial readers can improve their self-confidence and their attitudes toward reading and writing through book talks. These students can read young beginning reader books, books at their independent reading level, with the idea of then presenting book talks to primary grade children. More capable students can help the remedial students with planning the book talk. We know of one teacher who required her remedial sixth-grade students to plan and present a complete unit on children's literature to first- and second-grade classes. The presentation included researching and deciding which books to include and then reading them aloud to the classes and presenting book talks to encourage reading. The unit was thoroughly successful, and the teacher felt that her students' attitudes toward themselves and their reading improved through this activity.

WITCHES BIBLIOGRAPHY FOR A BOOK TALK

The Lion, the Witch and the Wardrobe, by C. S. Lewis (MacMillan, 1950).

The Little Broomstick, by Mary Stewart (William Morrow and Co., 1972).

Witch Water, by Phyllis Naylor (Atheneum, 1977).

The Witch's Daughter, by Nina Bawden (J. B. Lippincott Co., 1966).

The Book of Witches, by Ruth Manning Sanders (E. D. Dutton and Co., 1966).

The Witch of Blackbird Pond, by Elizabeth George Speare (Dell Publ., 1958).

HELPING CHILDREN BECOME AUTHORS AND ILLUSTRATORS

In our earlier chapter on writing we emphasized the importance of using literature to help students develop a sense of authorship. Graves and Hansen (1983) stress the importance of this concept of authorship for encouraging children to write. Children's literature is an excellent tool for encouraging writing and for building awareness of what an author is and what an author does.

For most children the concept of authorship is a remote one. Few children have ever met an author and few even understand the process of prewriting to writing to revision to publication. We ended our writing chapter with the concept of writing for the public. Now we want to show you how to develop a schema for authors through children's literature and writing.

Graves and Hansen (1983) have demonstrated that children as young as six or seven can develop a sense of authorship by writing daily about topics of interest to them and by "publishing" some of their works. They recommend illustrating and binding every fourth or fifth piece of work that children write. Before the books are bound, however, they are revised and edited via peer conferencing (recall the conferencing procedure from Chapter 6 on Writing). The books are then put on display and shared, read, and reread by peers.

Children's literature can be a valuable adjunct to this process. Through reading and listening to quality books, children can learn about authors and begin to know them as people. One way to do this is to choose an author of the week or month and then read a group of books by the same author. For example, one week can be declared a Dr. Seuss week in which the teacher reads a different book by Dr. Seuss every day. Children can then learn more about this author: his real name, his likes and dislikes, his background, and so on. They can then write *to* Dr. Seuss, write *about* Dr. Seuss, or write *like* Dr. Seuss. This particular activity can be used at the primary grade level and also with intermediate grade students who can be encouraged to write young children's picture books.

At the intermediate grade level children can be encouraged to read series books—for example, *The Narnia Series* by C. S. Lewis (MacMillan Publs.)—to develop an understanding of different authors, identifying their specific writing styles. Older children can also read a series of first-person narrative books, characteristic of contemporary fiction (Stewig, 1983). A cluster of books like *Are You There God, It's Me, Margaret,* by Judy Blume (Bradbury Press, 1970) can be read and evaluated as to the impact first-person narration has on the reader.

A wonderful book that raises issues of authorship responsibility is *Harriet the Spy,* by Louise Fitzhugh (Harper and Row, 1964). Harriet wants to be a journalist, and she practices by keeping a spy notebook on everyone she knows. Intermediate grade students immediately identify with Harriet and often decide to keep spy notebooks themselves. Harriet eventually gets herself into trouble with her notebook when her too candid notes are found by her friends. This incident can lead to excellent problem-solving discussions, debates, and role-playing situations where issues of honesty and condor must be measured against those of tactfulness. Children can discuss the different roles authors have in recording events and experiences and in expressing personal feelings. These activities also help children develop a sense of authorship.

Children love to draw and most children want to illustrate their own works. Studying illustrators as well as authors is an excellent motivator for children. Check at the school and local libraries to find books by a single illustrator. Maurice Sendak, a well-known children's illustrator, is the subject of a book about his art. Selma G. Lanes in *The Art of Maurice Sendak* (Harry N. Abrams, Inc., 1980) chronologizes the life of Sendak and his work as a children's illustrator. Gifted intermediate grade children can read part of this book. Young children of all ability levels can observe the wonderful array of art as represented by Sendak. They then can do additional projects based on Sendak's art. They also can write to Sendak himself. Some popular books written and illustrated by Maurice Sendak (published by Harper and Row) are listed below.

Outside Over There (1981)

Seven Little Monsters (1977)

In the Night Kitchen (1970)

Higglety, Pigglety, Pop! Or There Must Be More to Life (1967)

Hector Protector and as I Went Over the Water (1965)

Where the Wild Things Are (1963)

The Nutshell Library (1962)

Another wonderful illustrator of children's books is the Japanese artist, Mitumasa Anno. Anno has illustrated many wordless picture books. His style, like Sendak's, is unique and easily identifiable. Among our particular favorites are those books Anno has created depicting Europe: *Anno's Britain* (Philomel, 1982), *Anno's Italy* (Philomel, 1980), *Anno's Journey* (Philomel, 1978), and *Anno's Medieval World* (Philomel, 1980). His works demonstrate great attention to detail. Children can work in pairs and in small groups discussing the scenes and characters in Anno's books, trying to note the detail and characterization on each page.

Anno, like Sendak, is an excellent model for children in their attempts to illustrate their own "books." An understanding of illustrators is the goal of this activity. We want children to realize that as they write and draw they become authors and illustrators. This understanding is crucial to building self-concept and a positive attitude toward written language.

Last, we recommend that you bind children's works into books to help them become authors and illustrators. Binding their books ensures that they will value, indeed treasure, their written pieces. We have mentioned book-binding in previous chapters. Here we will show one way to bind a book. Teachers should include in their bound books a final page entitled, "About the Author and Illustrator." Here authors (that is, students) write something about themselves and their lives. This idea is an excellent one for helping children see that they too can become authors and illustrators.

Making Books

The basic materials necessary to make a book include scissors, rubber cement, wallpaper, cloth, wrapping paper, cardboard, plain white paper or construction paper, masking tape, and scotch tape. The procedure is given below.

A How to Make the Cover.

1 Cut two pieces of cardboard to desired shape.

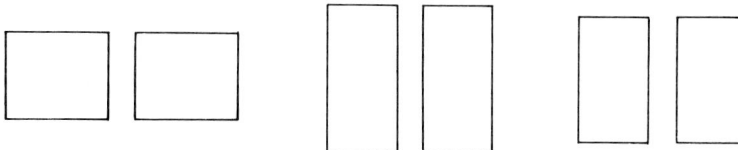

2 Tape cardboard with masking tape three-quarters to one-half inch apart.

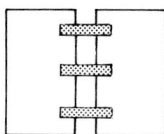

3 Cut cloth or paper one inch beyond the total cardboard area.

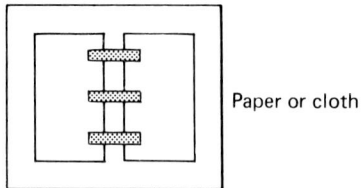

Paper or cloth

4 Fold cloth or paper over cardboard and scotch tape.

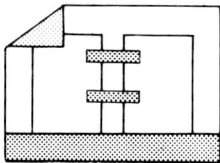

5 Cut plain or construction paper to fit one-half inch within all sides of covered paper.

6 Glue this paper onto folder paper and cardboard.

This is completed cover

Added extra page

Cardboard covered with cloth or paper

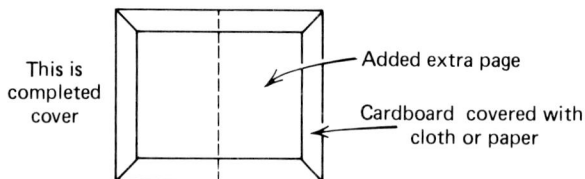

B How to Make the Pages of the Book.

1 Now fold plain or striped paper (this is your text) and add one extra page onto the bottom of your book. This last paper will be used to glue to the cover of the book.

2 Staple all the pages in the middle (or you can sew the pages together).

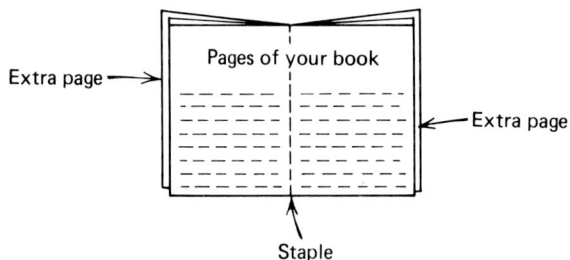

Extra page

Pages of your book

Extra page

Staple

C How to Glue the Cover to Pages.

1 Glue cover to bottom pages of book, front and back.

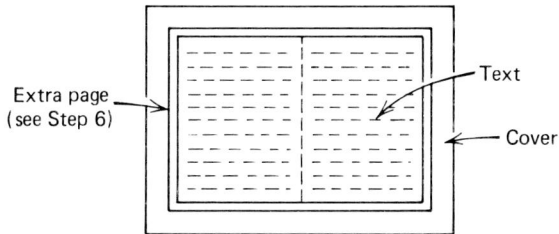

2 There is your completed book!

There are several other excellent activities that can be used to develop a sense of authorship in children. Graves and Hansen (1983) provide additional information and activities. We refer you to this article for further reading.

READING TO WRITE

While we can use children's authors and illustrators as motivators for entering the writing process, we can also use children's literature to stimulate writing. We want children to write all year, and they need ideas. One sixth grader we interviewed said the thing she did *not* like about writing was, "Sometimes you don't have very much to write, and they make us write, much more than what's in our brain, and then they yell at us because we're not writing, but there's nothing there." This is an interesting comment, and one you should analyze in detail. For now we want to suggest that we need to help children when "there's nothing there," and one way to do that is through children's literature.

Children's literature is an excellent medium to use to integrate reading and writing. In Chapter 11 on reading we mentioned the individualized reading approach where children read their favorite books. Several excellent writing activities can be generated after children read. Consider the following activities.

- Write about a favorite character.
- Write a different ending to the story.
- Write using the same language pattern as the author.
- Write a story about the same character.
- Write a sequel to the story.
- Write a script for a play based on the story (recall Reader's Theatre from Chapter 5)
- Write a different story based on an idea generated from another story.

At the primary grade level, there are dozens of wonderful books that can be used as patterns for children's writing. For example, in *Animal Should Definitely Not Wear Clothing* (Atheneum, 1970) Judi Barrett reiterates the title on each page with "because . . ." and then adds a picture and words to complete the thought ". . . it could be very messy for a pig." Children can then copy the familiar refrain from the chalkboard (good practice in handwriting) and add their own ideas, words, and pictures. Here is another excellent integrating activity; children use handwriting, writing, invented spellings, and reading skills.

We have already mentioned wordless picture books as stimuli to oral language development, and we mentioned that they can be used as a stimulus to writing as well. Mercer Mayer illustrates two wonderful books in *A Boy, a Dog and a Frog* and *A Boy, a Dog and a Friend* (Dial, 1967). Each is a miniature-sized book which sequences a series of events for the main character. Children can write captions for each character in a comic strip fashion. They also can write a play based on the books, or they can write the story in "book talk."

Older children can also benefit from wordless picture books. The *Silver Pony* by Lynd Ward (Houghton Mifflin, 1973) is an example of a more sophisticated picture book which intermediate grade children can enjoy. Students can do the same kinds of activities after "reading" the book—make captions, write a script, or write a story.

The number of ideas and activities we can generate about how to use children's literature is extensive and beyond our purposes here. Stewig (1983) has an excellent book, *Read to Write* which details more specific techniques for using literature as a springboard to writing. We refer you to his text for additional ideas.

A Final Word

All these strategies can be used to create an environment that encourages children to use language and to value books. Such an environment would certainly be a supportive one, one in which each child is treated as an individual and with understanding of his or her special needs. Bright children would be challenged cognitively and affectively by novels and stories several years beyond grade level readability. Poor readers would be equally successful reading books below grade level in terms of readability but of interest to them. The key is to provide enough variety in terms of difficulty and subject matter so that all students are *motivated* and *successful*.

Below we have included several additional ideas that can be used as a daily part of the language arts instructional program to foster literature growth and interest in children.

1 Have a book fair. Plan a schoolwide book fair to arouse children's interests in books. Children and parents can examine and purchase from a selection of hundreds of books they can actually see, feel, and touch. Get librarians, teachers, parents, and the principal involved. See an excellent article by Auten (1981) for references which include detailed directions for planning and implementing.

2 Have children make displays of books they have read. Children can make book jackets, dioramas, collages, art murals, bulletin board displays and models to illustrate their favorite books. Think of these activities as alternatives to making book reports.

3 Have children keep a daily log of their reading. This can be in the form of a diary or a journal or a file where they can write (a) their daily feelings about what they've read; (b) a synopsis of what they've read; (c) their reactions; and (d) number of pages read.

Allow them options in what they will record. They are more likely to maintain the log if it is intrinsically meaningful to them.

4 Create book clubs in which children can share and discuss books they have read. The clubs can be an excellent forum for book talks, and for discussing certain aspects of books—plot, setting, and so on. The club can also provide a vehicle for the study of different authors or genres.

5 Have children read books around a central theme or topic. See Moss (1978) for a detailed description of a ''Focus Unit'' in which children study a given topic from a variety of points of view and narrative structure.

This chapter lays the foundation for using children's literature in the elementary classroom. We will continue this discussion and present more ideas in the next chapter as we weave children's literature into an integrated language arts curriculum.

SUGGESTED ACTIVITIES

1 Read several children's books related to one central theme and write a ''book talk'' about those books.

2 Construct your own reading interest survey for either primary or intermediate grade children. Ask several children to complete the survey. Recommend three books to each child based on their interests.

3 Following the directions in this chapter, bind your own book. Then have a small group of children bind books using your model.

4 Read several Newbery and Caldecott books. Choose one picture book and practice reading aloud to a small group of children. Evaluate your oral reading techniques as discussed in this chapter.

REFERENCES

Abrahamson, Richard F. ''An analysis of Children's Favorite Picture Storybooks.'' *The Reading Teacher*, 34 (November 1980):167–170.

Arbuthnot, M. H., and Sutherland, Z. *Children and Books*. Glenview, Ill.: Scott, Foresman and Co., 1972.

Auten, A. "Bringing Children and Books Together." *Language Arts* 58, 4 (April 1981): 487–491.

Bissett, D. J. "The Amount and Effect of Recreational Reading in Selected Fifth Grade Classes." Doctoral dissertation, Syracuse University, Syracuse, New York, 1969.

Bormuth, J. R. "Cloze Test Readability: Criterion Referenced Scores." *Journal of Educational Measurement* 5, 3 (Fall 1968):189–196.

Chomsky, C. "Stages in Language Development and Reading Exposure." *Harvard Educational Review* 42, 1 (February 1972):1–33.

Dale, E., and Chall, J. "A Formula for Predicting Readability." *Educational Research Bulletin* 27, 1 (January 21, 1948):11–20.

————. "A Formula for Predicting Readability: Instructions." *Educational Research Bulletin*, 27, 2 (February 17, 1948):37–54.

Durkin, D. *Children Who Read Early*. New York: Teachers College Press, 1966.

Fry, E. "Fry's Readability Graph: Clarifications Validity and Extension to Level 17." *Journal of Reading* 21, 3 (December 1977):249.

Glazer, J. "Reading Aloud with Young Children." In Linda Lemme, (ed.). *Learning to Love Literature*. Urbana, Ill.: National Council of Teachers of English, 1981.

Graves, D., and Hansen, J. The Author's Chair. *Language Arts* 60, 2 (February 1983): 176–183.

Huck, C. S. *Children's Literature in the Elementary School*. New York: Holt, Rinehart & Winston, 1976.

Huus, H. "A New Look at Children's Interests." In Joan E. Chaprio (ed.). *Using Literature and Poetry Affectively*. Newark, Del.: International Reading Association, 1979.

————. "Interpreting Research in Children's Literature." *Children, Books and Reading*, Perspectives in Reading, 3 Newark, Del.: International Reading Association, 1964.

Koeller, S. "25 Years Advocating Children's Literature in the Reading Program." *The Reading Teacher* 34, 5 (February 1981):552–556.

Moss, J. F. "Using the 'Focus Unit' to Enhance Children's Response to Literature." *Language Arts* 55, 4 (April 1978):482–488.

Noyce, R., and Wyatt, F. R. "Children's Books for Language Exploration." *Language Arts* 55, 3 (March 1978):297–301.

Pilon, A. B. "Reading to Learn about the Nature of Language." In John W. Stewig and Sam L. Sebesta's (eds.). *Using Literature in the Elementary Classroom*. Urbana, Ill.: National Council of Teachers of English, 1978.

Roettger, D. "Elementary Students Attitudes Toward Reading." *The Reading Teacher* 33, 4 (January 1980):451–453.

Spache, G. D. *Good Reading for Poor Readers*, 6th edition. Champaign, Ill.: Garrand Press, 1966.

Witucke, V. "The Book Talk: A Technique for Bringing Together Children and Books." *Language Arts* 56, 4 (April 1979):413–421.

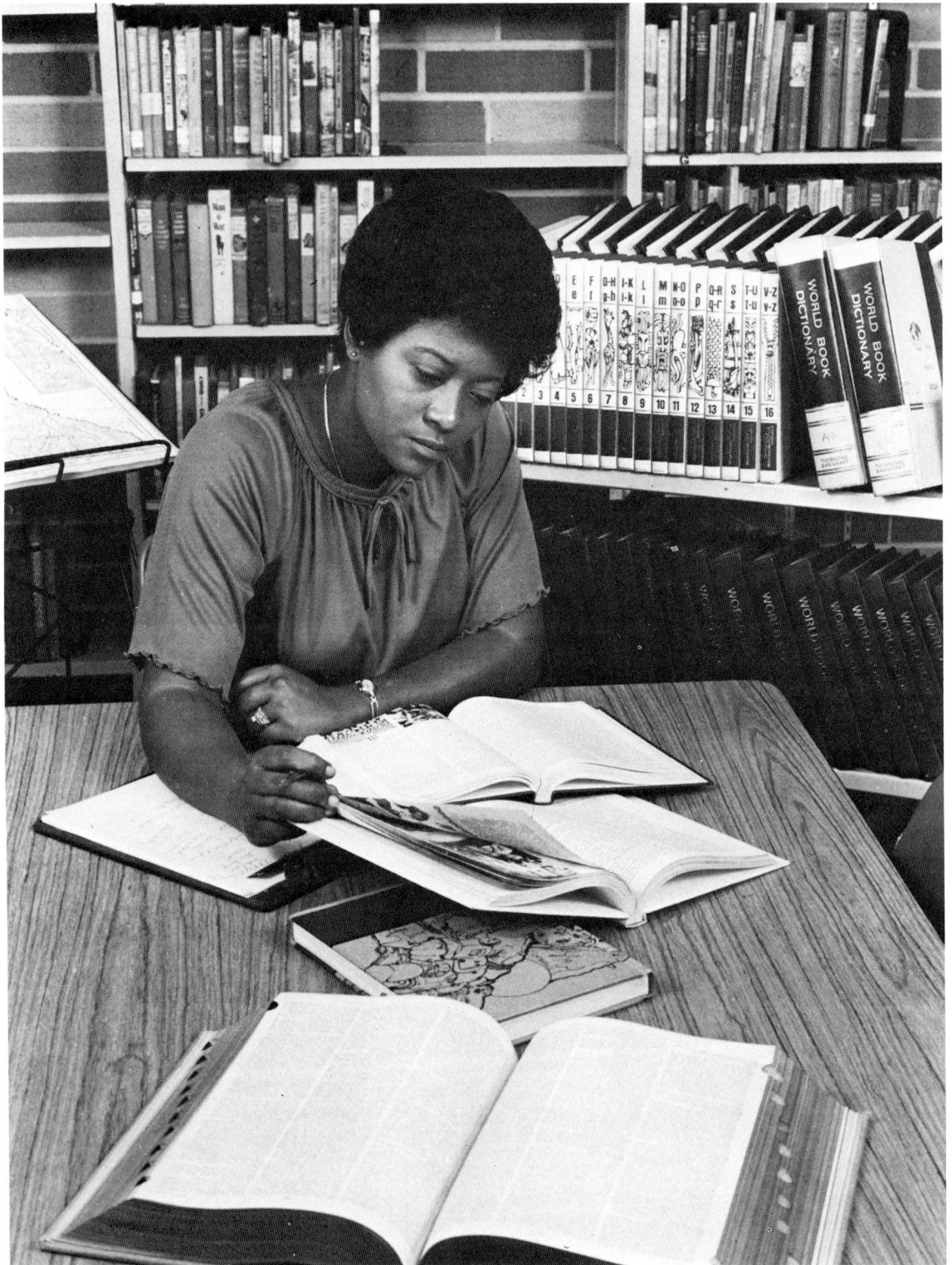

CHAPTER 14

Planning an Integrated Language Arts Curriculum

WHAT MAKES A GOOD TEACHER?
SECOND GRADERS
> . . . she helps more better than "Oh, you have to figure this out yourself."
> . . . If you do a paper and the teacher puts it up on the board.
> . . . If they are really nice, good to you.

OVERVIEW

At this time, we want to pull together the separate language arts skills and show you how to integrate these skills and organize a comprehensive language arts program. In the last chapter we focused on children's literature in the language arts program. This chapter will emphasis an integrated curriculum. We will present specific unit plans integrating reading, writing, listening, and speaking. Next we will show you how to expand the language arts into other subject areas, and create integrated units. Finally, we will present a sample of a specific project that integrates language into the curriculum.

RATIONALE FOR AN INTEGRATED CURRICULUM

In Parts 2 and 3 of this book, we presented each of the specific components of the language arts as a separate entity. Throughout the text, however, we emphasized the fact that the components are interrelated. We have presented specific "content" of reading and writing, for example, and also demonstrated how one closely relates to the other. We have also said that while you may be focusing on one language arts skill, you also can teach or practice several others.

Most educators would argue that there is a need to teach specific content in the language arts. As we said earlier, however, language arts instruction must be extended beyond the specific teaching to include experiences in and practice in using language holistically and in incorporating language into the curriculum.

We want to argue that incorporating language into the curriculum throughout the school day is a natural extension and practical application of the theoretical framework we have presented in this book. Integrating the language arts in this way can help children understand the relationship between thinking and language and between each of the language arts skills.

Presently, most instructional programs separate the teaching of specific skills and subskills in the language arts. We have encountered teachers who say they "don't have time" for "frill" activities such as integrating the language arts and using language across the curriculum. We have encountered primary grade teachers who don't teach social studies or science either because they say they "don't have time." We will show that you can teach subject area content and teach language arts at the same time. As you do this you are in fact developing schemata and language simultaneously.

At this point, it might be helpful to reread the scenarios described in the first chapter. Recall Mrs. Wright's students who were actively engaged in a variety of activities centered around the book *Stuart Little*. Recall Ms. Pilloud's sixth graders who were working on projects related to the theme of survival. These children were engaged in activities that presented language holistically and purposefully. They were using and practicing all the language arts we discussed in this text. Several of the theoretical issues mentioned at the beginning of the text are also relevant here.

- *Concepts and vocabulary development* are obtained slowly and through direct and multisensory experiences. Integrating the language arts allows children to read about, write about, talk about, hear, and experience words and concepts.

- *Schemata*, like concepts, are developed slowly and through varied experiences, activities, and exposures to different situations, concepts, ideas, and so forth. Again, the more varied the experiences, the better the success in developing schemata.

- Children need to understand and make sense of *larger units of discourse,* beyond the word, paragraph, or short story. The integrative approach helps children look at the whole and understand how the parts relate to the whole. It also helps children see how *separate language skills function together*—how reading and writing are connected, how creative drama and reading are connected and so on.

- Learning theorists argue that *material* needs to be *made meaningful* to be retained in long-term memory. Integrative units such as the ones described in the first chapter tie separate skills together around meaningful topics, thereby increasing the chances of retention in long-term memory.

- Linguists argue that *language* is best learned in natural situations and in meaningful context. Again, integrating the language arts helps children learn language in meaningful context.

Thus, while we want to teach children the separate skills of the language arts, we must not stop there. We also need to integrate the skills to provide interesting and meaningful experiences for children and to provide multiple opportunities for them to learn.

CURRICULUM PLANNING

Curriculum planning for integrating the language arts is not an easy task. Teachers' manuals and other "how-to" books may help you to teach specific skills, but rarely guide you to creating interesting, meaningful activities beyond these skills. As a language arts teacher, you must do the creating yourself. In this section we hope to assist you in this endeavor by presenting an organizing framework for language arts curriculum planning.

Huck's Web: An Organizational Procedure for Integrating the Language Arts

In Chapter 11, we presented semantic webbing as an instructional strategy to improve reading comprehension. Several reading educators have advocated the use of this type of webbing process as a powerful teaching strategy to use with both children and teachers. Constructing a web helps you visualize relationships among concepts, ideas, or events. Through this process, you can visualize units of study holistically, and at the same time you can see how the elements of those units fit together and relate to one another. The webbing process can be used directly with children, as in Johnson and Pearson's (1978) semantic mapping for concept development or in Freedman and Reynold's (1980) semantic webbing for story development already presented in Chapter 11. Alternatively, the webbing process can be used with teachers to develop curriculum guides. Norton (1977, 1982) adapted a Huck's web (Huck, 1976) for developing literature units to present to children, and Dole (in press) adapted the webbing process for integrating language arts with content area subjects. In this section, we want to show you how to use the webbing process as a curriculum guide to construct an integrated literature web around children's literature. We will then present some examples of completed webs.

The webbing process can help you to develop meaningful curriculum units (a series of lessons on a particular topic). Through the web, you can see how language arts skills become functional rather than separate skills to be studied in isolation during a preset time of the day. The webbing process has additional advantages as well.

1 It saves time in the initial brainstorming and planning of a unit.

2 It encourages you to think through a unit holistically, making sure that you bring in many language areas rather than one or two.

3 It improves the overall organization of your curriculum planning.

Steps in Constructing a Huck's Web. Charlotte Huck (1976) developed what is known as a Huck's web for integrating the language arts around a particular children's book. The steps for constructing a Huck's web are given below.

1 Choose a book that is of particular interest to children. You might want to begin with Caldecott or Newbery award-winning books, such as

Trumpet of the Swans, by E. B. White (Harper and Row, 1975)

Charlotte's Web, by E. B. White (Harper and Row, 1975)

The Girl Who Loved Wild Horses, by Paul Goble (Bradbury Press, 1978)

Bridge to Terebithia, by Katherine Paterson (Avon, 1979)

Strawberry Girl, by Lois Lenski (Dell, 1967)

A Wrinkle in Time, by Madeleine L'Engle (Farrar, Straus, Giroux, Inc., 1962)

A Gathering of Days, by Joan Blos (Atheneum, 1982)

The title of the book will be placed in the center of the web. The first part of the web would look like this.

```
                    Island of the
                    Blue Dolphins
```

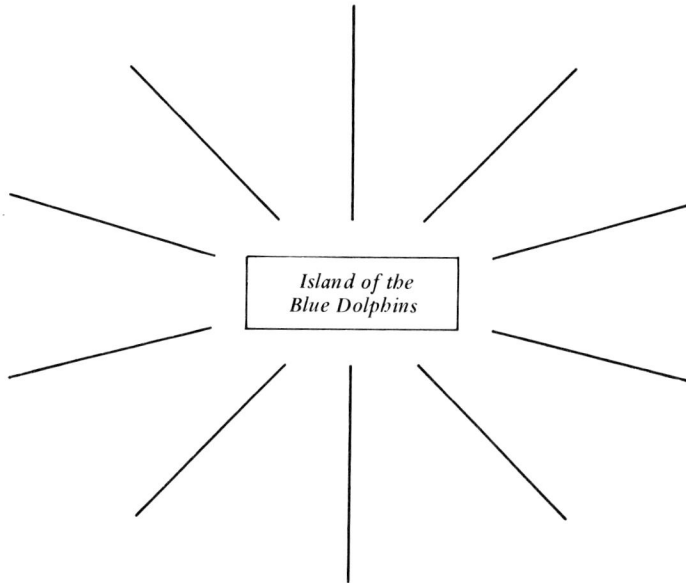

2 Next, choose several language arts areas to cover. These areas become the strands of the web and will determine the organizing activities for the curriculum unit.

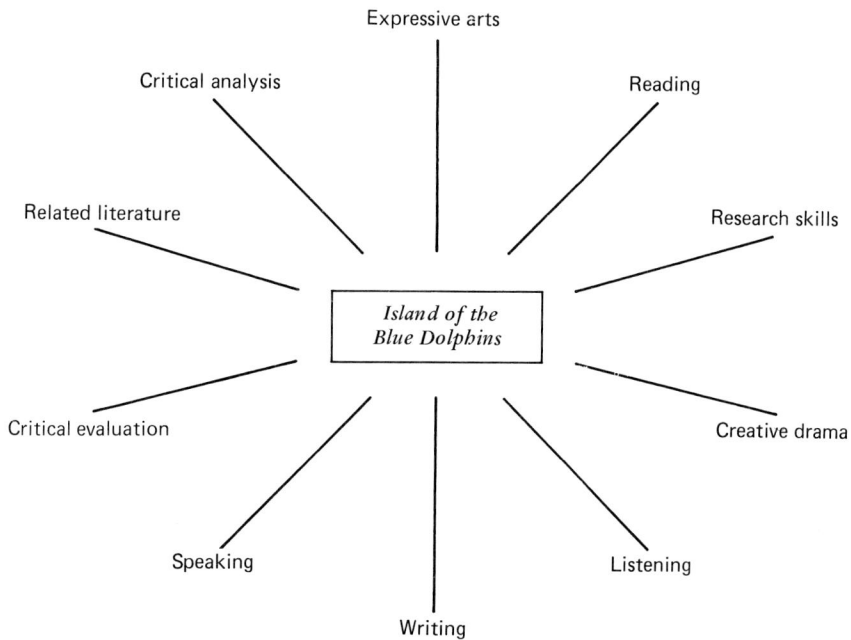

```
                         Expressive arts
        Critical analysis                    Reading

Related literature                                Research skills

                         Island of the
                         Blue Dolphins

Critical evaluation                               Creative drama

        Speaking                              Listening

                            Writing
```

3 Once the language arts areas have been chosen, fill in each of the area strands with activities. For example, under the writing and research strands could be included activities such as

---

ISLAND OF THE BLUE DOLPHINS

Research Skills

1 Find out more factual information about the Lost Woman of San Nicolas from old newspapers by writing to appropriate resources, or reading additional books.

2 Research the climate of the island. Construct a map that depicts the climate and what clothes and shelter would be needed for different times in the year.

Writing

1 Write a continuation of this story. What happens to Karana when she enters civilization?

2 Pretend you are Karana. Record a typical day on the island in diary form.

3 Write letters to California's Chamber of Commerce to find out more about the island.

An alternative approach to listing the activities is to list the skills to be covered in that language area. Many administrators are particularly concerned about meeting district objectives. The web can be written to ensure administrators that language arts objectives are being met through this curriculum unit.

ISLAND OF THE BLUE DOLPHINS

Writing

1 Children will write a formal letter with proper capitalization and punctuation.

Oral Language

1 Children will listen to state the main idea in the book.

2 Children will listen to recall in correct sequence the events in the book.

3 Children will listen to determine three things Karana did to ease her life on the island.

Research Skills

1 Find out more factual information about the Lost Woman of San Nicolas from: old newspapers, writing to appropriate resources, and additional books.

2 Research the climate of the island. Construct a map that depicts the climate and what clothes and shelter would be needed for different times in the year.

3 Research and list the possible foods to eat on the island.

4 Learn more about wild dogs.

ISLAND OF THE BLUE DOLPHINS by Scott O'Dell

Expressive Arts

1 Construct baskets that might be similar to the ones Karana made.

2 Draw a map of what the island would probably look like.

3 Make a large relief map of the island based on the drawing.

4 Compare this map with real maps of the island.

5 Create a large mural depicting the major events in the story in petroglyph form.

Oral Language

1 Read aloud the first chapter of the book. Have children listen for what happens on the island. On a large chart, write down what children predict the story will be about.

2 Have children role play various parts of the story.

3 Discuss the role of language as a form of communication. What other forms of communication do we use? How did Karana communicate with the Russian girl? Role play types of nonverbal communication.

Writing

1 Write a continuation of this story. What happens to Karana when she enters civilization?

2 Pretend you are Karana. Record a typical day on the island in diary form.

3 Write letters to California's Chamber of Commerce to find out more about the island.

Critical Analysis

1 Evaluate the character of Karana. What were her strengths? What were her weaknesses? Is she an admirable character? Why?

2 Discuss the importance of superstition in the novel. How did it affect Karana's life?

3 Compare and contrast Karana's life with and without her animal friends. What purpose did they serve?

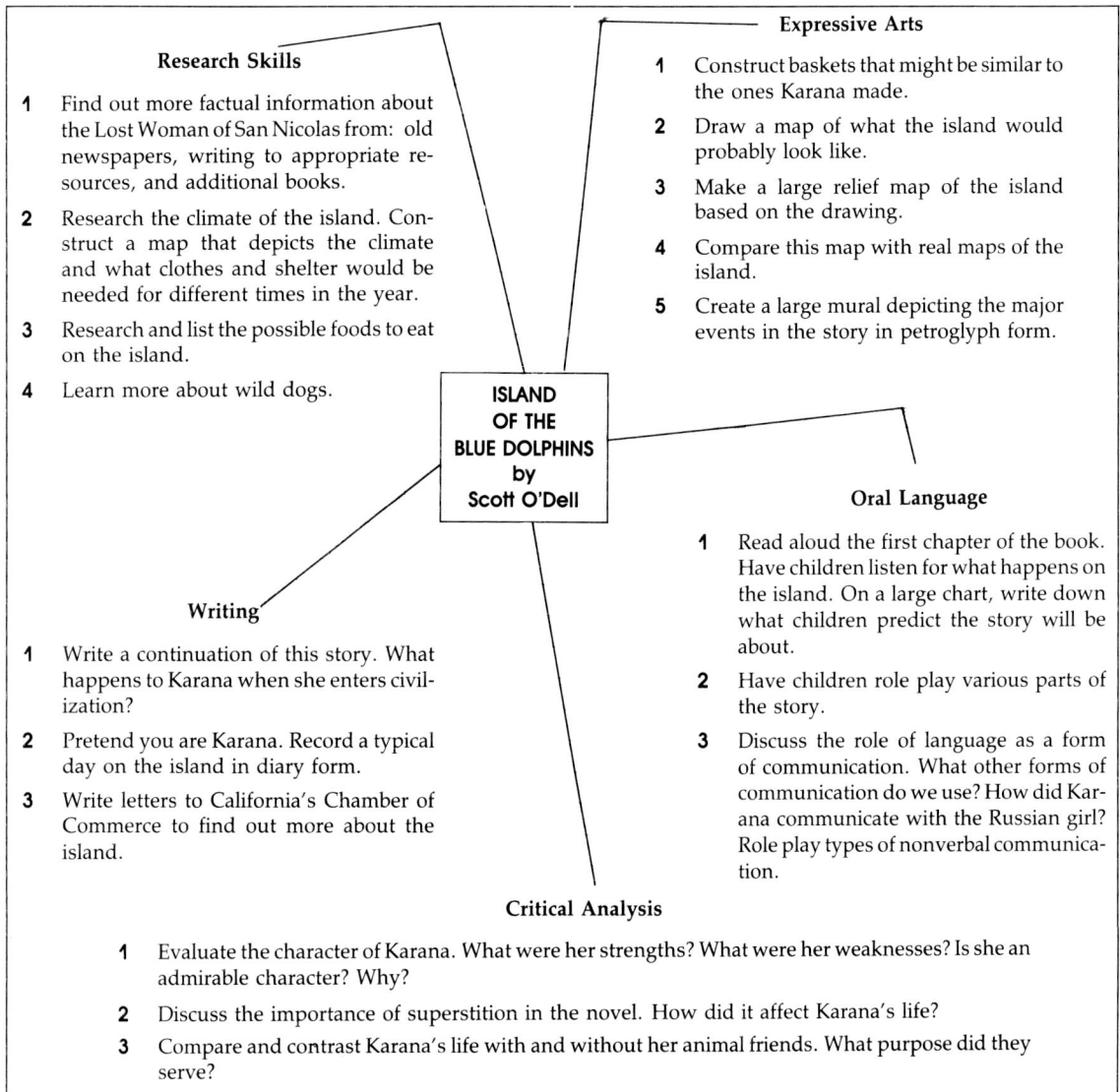

FIGURE 14-1 *Completed Huck's web for* Island of the Blue Dolphins.

Uses of the Web. Once all of the activities or objectives for the strands are created, the integrated web is complete. (We have included two examples of Huck's Webs (see Figures 14-1 and 14-2); notice that one is the base for Mrs. Wright's classroom (Figure 14-2), activities described in Chapter 1. The webs serve as concise, easy-to-read outlines or summaries of units you can teach in a week or in a month. They can be used in a variety of ways.

Science

1 Make a bird chart. Find a way to classify different types of birds.

Environment
Shapes of beaks
Size of bird
Nesting habits
Kinds of food
Migrating and Non-migrating

2 Observe and record bird behavior. Make a file of bird facts and vocabulary words.

Social Studies

1 In the classroom scene, Stuart talks about the reason for having laws. Discuss this with the class. Ask students to draw up a constitution for the class—write it on large butcher paper and post it where everyone can see it.

2 Draw a simple map showing the places Stuart traveled to or places the students have been or would like to go.

3 Make a scale model of a scene from the book. Include Stuart in the model.

STUART LITTLE*
BY
E. B. WHITE

Listening

1 Ask students to listen and to remember the sequence of events in a particular chapter.

2 Have students listen to find out how Stuart felt when he was alone on the river.

Writing

1 Keep a daily journal (writing occurs immediately after reading) pretending they are Stuart Little. They are to record what happens to them each day as a mouse—they may not use the exact occurrences from the book.

2 Make a language experience story and draw a picture of and describe the part children liked best in the book.

Expressive Arts

1 Ask students to draw a painting on each side of the paper. One depicts something Stuart does in the book, the other depicts something Stuart typically could do.

2 Have students pretend they are a family who just had a mouse. They role-play what they are going to do.

3 Students write a poem that Margalo could sing. Then set the poem to music with guitar or piano.

4 Students draw a large mural scene from *Stuart Little*.

* Unit written by Libby Hogan.

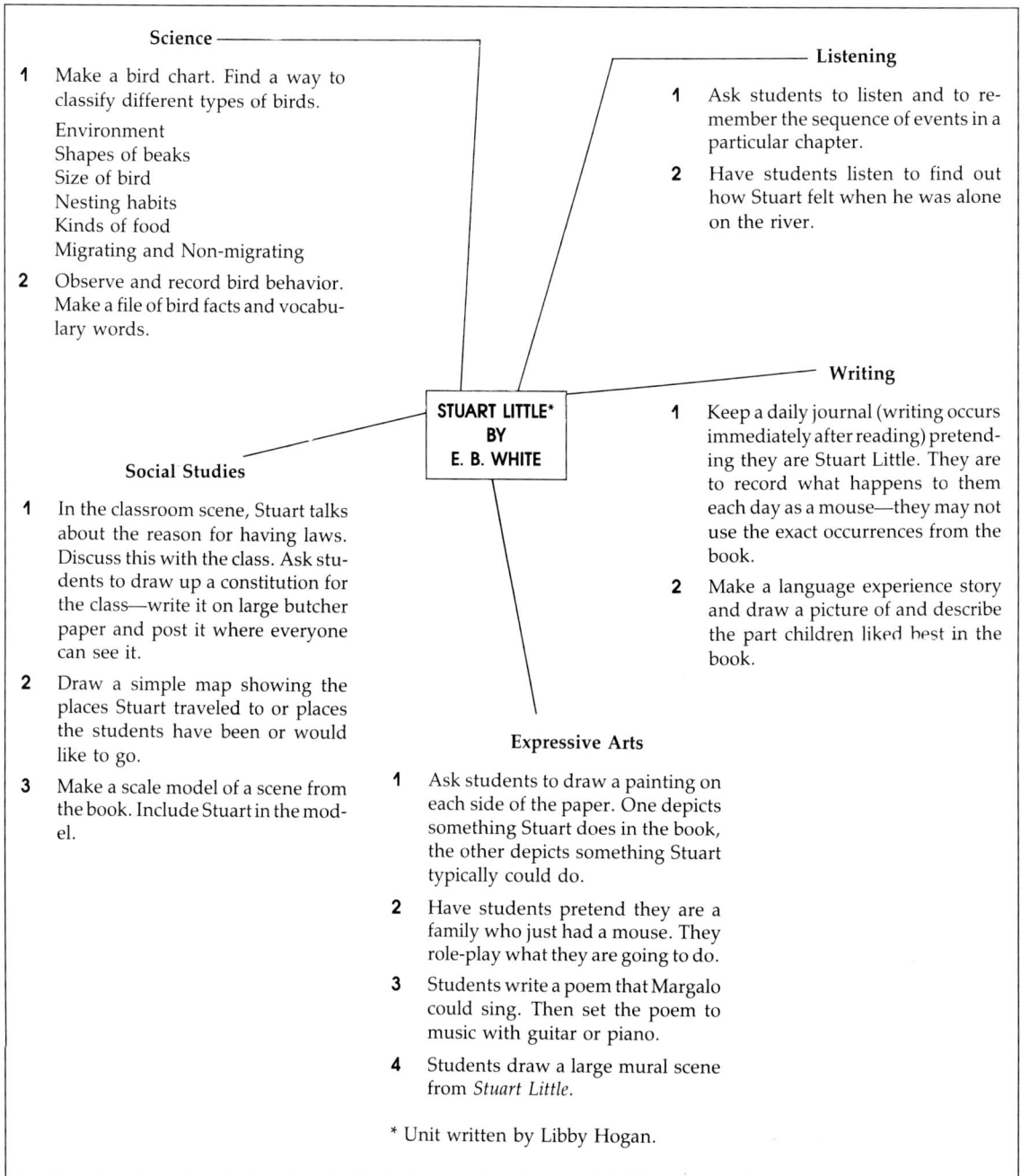

FIGURE 14-2 *Completed Huck's web for* Stuart Little.

1 You can construct longer, more detailed units expanding each of the activities in the language arts strands. Then you can teach the complete unit to the whole class.

2 Assign groups of children to different strand activities on the basis of interest or strength or weakness in the language area. Each group can create a product and, as a culminating activity, groups can share their products with other members of the class.

3 A whole unit can be assigned to a particular group of children to be completed independently and presented to the rest of the class. For example, a unit on *A Wrinkle in Time* might be particularly appropriate for a small group of gifted children interested in science-fiction novels. The web is an excellent vehicle for individualizing and differentiating instruction.

4 Activity cards can be constructed for each of the strand activities. Children could then choose to work independently on activities in which they are interested. This type of activity provides successful experiences for children when they are encouraged to work on activities in which they are interested and capable of completing independently.

Sample activity cards for two books are given here. The cards for *My Brother Sam Is Dead*, *by James Collier and Christopher Collier (Four Winds Press, 1974) are given below. Activities for Chapters 1, 2, 3 might include

---

1 In the first three chapters, religion often enters the story. Go to the library to *find out more about religion* in colonial America. Pick one type of religion to *report* on or write a general *summary* of religion during colonial times. At the end of your report, add three or four *paragraphs comparing* (finding similarities and differences between two things) the religious beliefs of the colonial people to religion as it is practiced today. How have religious beliefs changed? Why do you think those changes occurred?

---

2 Choose a battle from the early Revolutionary War (Lexington/Concord, Fort Ticonderoga or Bunker Hill) and *report* on it in a *newspaper article* for the *Connecticut Journal*. You are the reporter, writing information from the scene of the battle. Will there be bias in your article or will it be straight reporting of facts? Remember to include who, what, where, when, why, and how details about your battle.

---

* All Activity Cards were developed by Ellin Oliver Keene, Douglas County Schools, Colorado.

Activities for Chapters 4, 5, 6 could be

---

3 *Read* about the music and art in Europe and the colonies in the period between 1600 and 1800. Who were the composers and artists? *Write* a *description* of the music and art and bring some examples of the music and art to share with the class.

---

4 You are George III, King of England, making a *speech* to the British Parliament in the year 1772. They have asked you to address the problem of the colonial disturbance in America. *Read* about George III and British history of the time and make a speech as he might have, telling how the British felt about the colonial uprising.

---

5 In the book, prejudice toward Indians is described. If it were your task to eliminate prejudice toward handicapped people, what kind of a system would you design to accomplish the task? Don't forget to include education, other people and the media to help. Make your *presentation* to the president in the form of a speech, using *audio visual* material to supplement your speech.

Activity cards for *The Twenty-One Balloons*, by William Pène du Bois (Viking, 1947) follow.

CHAPTER 1

Who was the President of the United States in 1893 when Professor Sherman made his journey? Find out and write a letter from the President (you!) to Professor Sherman describing your term in office (you're very vain) and asking that he recount the details of his journey to you. Make your letter convincing.

CHAPTER 2

If you could start any kind of fad, what would it be? Try to start a fad in your classroom. Don't tell anyone what you're up to, and see if it takes hold! Do things that will encourage others to become part of the fad. After the fad has had a chance, decide how well you did. Conduct a discussion with your class. Tell them what you were up to and let them suggest things that you could have done to make the fad catch on more completely. Make a list of these suggestions and discuss them with your teacher.

CHAPTER 3

I'm sure that you, like Professor Sherman, have wanted to "get away from it all" sometime in your life. Now's your chance! Design some sort of contraption to take you away from your town. Make some rough sketches and write a description of your invention and a detailed account of where your contraption will take you and what you'll do there. Then make a precise (look it up!) drawing, using lots of color on a big piece of posterboard and hang it somewhere around school, along with your edited and revised written description. Perhaps you could really build your get-away machine!

We believe that the webbing process provides you, as a language arts teacher, with a flexible tool for organizing and individualizing the curriculum. In addition, through the webbing process, you are forced to integrate the curriculum, so that language arts skills are taken out of the content area textbooks and made a functional part of the world in which we live.

ACTIVITIES THAT CAN ENHANCE
LANGUAGE LEARNING THROUGH INTEGRATED WEBS

Making and binding books	Keeping logs, journals
Collages, montages	Writing poems
Storytelling	Puppet shows
Making relief maps	Constructing models
Making pamphlets, brochures	Dioramas
Field trips	Murals
Audiotaping	Advertising
Videotaping	Exhibits, displays
Creative dramatics	Making posters, bulletin boards
Role playing	Drawing, painting
Writing plays	Musical activities
Making filmstrips	Rhythmic activities
Making puppets	Constructing games
Making TV shows, newscasts	

LANGUAGE ACROSS THE CURRICULUM

We have already suggested that careful planning needs to be done to ensure that the language arts are not treated as isolated subjects. Many teachers and administrators seem to be unaware that language is the tool for every subject area taught. Teachers need to realize that they can enhance thinking and language learning throughout the day. For example, as we teach a science unit on ecosystems, we must be aware that we are using expressive and receptive language skills to develop an understanding of this science concept. We ask students to *record observations* in a notebook, *research* one aspect of ecosystems, *listen* to a scientist discuss tundra ecosystems, *ask* relevant *questions*, *discuss* advantages and disadvantages of different ecosystems. These activities revolve around the language arts skills. The skills become functional ones used to learn about specific subjects.

All the activities suggested in this book for the learning of different language arts skills can and should be applied to content area subjects. In this way, children have opportunities to learn and practice these skills repeatedly in different situations. Although we have already presented these ideas separately in previous chapters, we would like to present them together, hoping that they will now have more meaning for you.

EXPRESSIVE COMMUNICATION SKILLS

As units of study are presented to children, they have multiple opportunities for speaking and writing.

- Children interview a geologist who discusses different types of rocks.

  Interviewing guest speakers. Requires children to present their ideas understandably, ask relevant questions, respond intelligently.

- Children role play pioneers approaching Pike's Peak.

  Drama techniques. Requires children to role-play, read lines with expression and clarity.

- Children tell the story of how their grandparents lived during the Great Depression.

  Storytelling, oral history. Requires children to use appropriate expression and enthusiasm, hold the listener's attention.

- Children research and report on their favorite country.

  Report writing. Requires children to use research and study skills, prewriting, writing, and revision cycles.

- Children record daily changes in growth of small plants.

  Observation writing. Requires children to make careful notes, keep records, make lists, and charts.

- Children pretend they are an animal and report their experiences.

  Narrative writing. Requires children to create, extend, or expand on an idea.

RECEPTIVE COMMUNICATION SKILLS

Children also have multiple opportunities for the functional use of listening and reading skills through integrated units of study:

- Children follow instructions on how to make a telescope.

  Listening and following directions. Requires children to listen carefully and be able to hold and retain information in short-term memory, also to follow a sequence.

- Children listen to TV commercials and evaluate the usefulness of the marketed product.

  Listening to evaluate critically. Requires children to use prior schemata to listen and evaluate what they hear.

- Children listen to a guest speaker who tells of her volunteer experiences for Peace Corps in Senegal.

  Directed listening-thinking activity (DLTA). Requires children to use prior schemata to make predictions about what will be heard, to develop hypotheses, and listen for specific purposes and to prove/disprove based on concrete evidence.

- Children read *Julie of the Wolves* to predict Julie's methods of survival in the Arctic.

  Directed reading-thinking activity (DRTA). Similar to DLTA, only is used in reading and requires children to use prior schemata to predict, make hypotheses, and prove or disprove in a reading situation.

- Children read *Charlotte's Web* and make a map of the life cycle of Charlotte and her babies.

  Semantic webbing. Allows children to focus on any aspect of a story, to see interrelationships within a story.

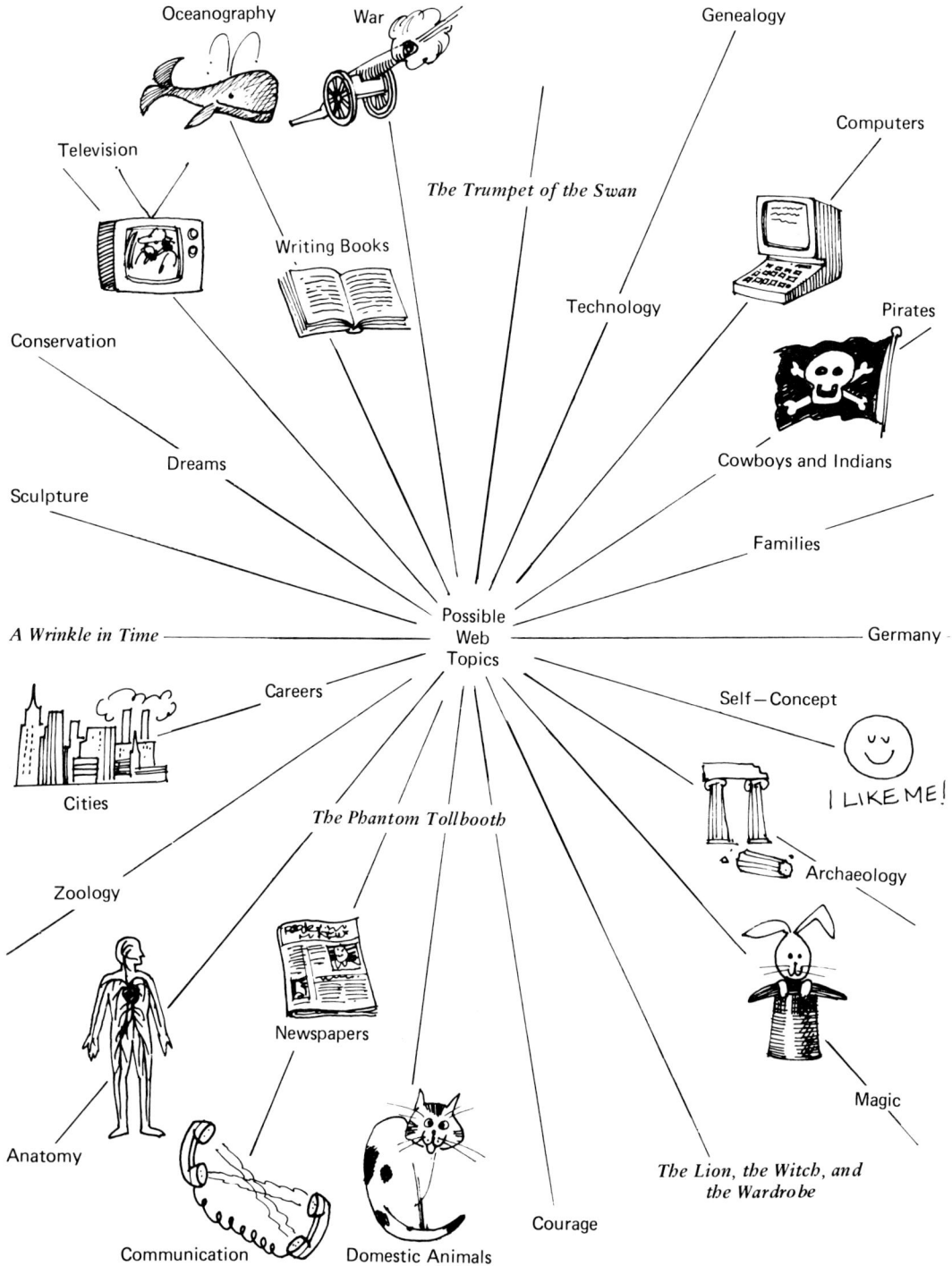

Oceanography

War

Genealogy

Television

The Trumpet of the Swan

Computers

Writing Books

Conservation

Technology

Pirates

Dreams

Cowboys and Indians

Sculpture

Families

A Wrinkle in Time

Possible Web Topics

Germany

Careers

Self—Concept

Cities

I LIKE ME!

Zoology

Archaeology

The Phantom Tollbooth

Anatomy

Newspapers

Magic

Communication

Domestic Animals

Courage

The Lion, the Witch, and the Wardrobe

FIGURE 14-3 *Possible topics for the webbing process.*

Expanding the Web: Integrating Language Arts with Subject Areas

As we have already shown, the webbing process is an excellent strategy to use for planning literature units, but its usefulness can be extended beyond that (see Figure 14-3). The webbing process can also be used to integrate the language arts with the subject areas of science, math, social studies, music, art, and so on (Dole, in press). Such an integrated curriculum provides children with multiple opportunities to reinforce, extend, and apply their skill learnings to real world experiences.

Expanding the web into other subject areas is a simple task. In the center of the web, we can use any topic, concept, or area of interest to children. Whereas the integrated literature web centered around children's literature, this new web can center around science, social studies or math curriculum. For example, an integrated web at the primary level could center around the social studies curriculum of "family," "all about myself," or "transportation." At the intermediate level, webs can center around science concepts like "ecosystems," "motion," or "anatomy."

This new integrated web is then constructed similar to the literature web, only other subject areas are included. We have included an integrated web to give you an idea of the range of possibilities open to you as you plan an integrated curriculum (see Figure 14-4). Notice that the web we have included is the base for the activities we described in Ms. Pilloud's class in Chapter 1.

Science

1 *Charting.* Ask students to identify the types of food available to Miyax, Sam, and Phillip. Have them prepare charts naming each food, how it is obtained, and prepared.

2 *Cooking/tasting.* From the food charts made, try to bring some of these foods in to the class to cook and/or taste.

3 *Climate.* Have students consider the effect of climate on the type of shelter required in a certain area. If they were living in their town but had no home, what shelter would they make?—Where and from what? Give reasons for these decisions.

Expressive Arts and Drama

1 *Model building.* Have students build three-dimensional models of different scenes and characters from each story.

2 *Plays.* Have students write a skit or play based on one part of the book they have read. Classmates will be cast in the roles. These can be presented to their own class or younger classes.

3 *Commercial making.* Have children make a television commercial based on their book as if it was a movie to be aired on TV.

4 *Collages.* Have students cut out magazine pictures and make a collage illustrating the concept of survival.

SURVIVAL
Related Literature
The Cay by Theodore Taylor
My Side of the Mountain by Jean George
Julie of the Wolves by Jean George

Research Skills

1 Each group of three students randomly picks one of ten places in the world decided by the teacher. The groups have to research to find out what they need to survive in that area. They have to decide if they could survive based on what's available to them. Factors to consider are food, shelter, clothing, climate. Students should be encouraged to use many different resources. Each group will report findings to class.

Language Arts

1 *Cookbooks.* Have students compile and bind together cookbooks of the various foods, recipes, and methods used in each of the three books.

2 *Debate.* Group students according to each book. Have them debate (supporting their book) about the pros and cons of survival (arctic vs. country vs. island). Have another class sit in to judge and decide which is best.

3 *Creative writing.* Have students write their own survival stories. These can be bound together as a class book.

Social Studies

1 *Map making.* Have students draw a map showing different places in the stories. En courage them to use scale and symbols.

2 *Sequencing.* Have students create a time-line, marking the events of each story in correct sequence. Also have them construct a time line of the characters' emotional responses to their ordeal.

* Written by Donna Pilloud.

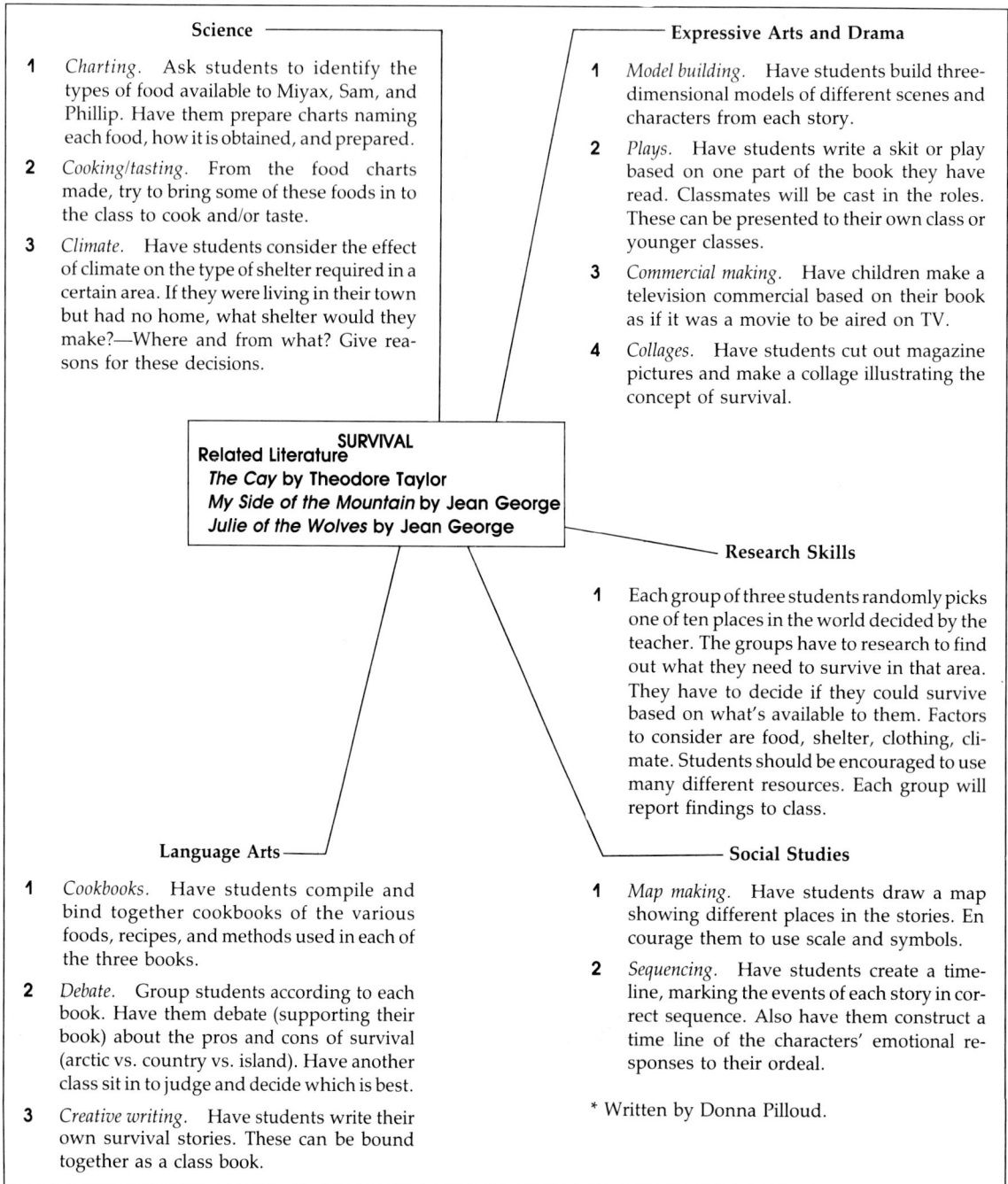

FIGURE 14-4 *Completed web on survival.*

An Example of an Integrated Curriculum

We will close this chapter by presenting an example of an integrated language curriculum and describing the activities and experiences so necessary for its success. We will focus on an intermediate classroom in which children are studying the Revolutionary War.

* Brainstorming

* Vocabulary and concept development

* Reading skills

* Teacher models and expands on what students say

* Reading

Introducing the Unit. Mrs. Pour teaches American History as part of the fifth-grade curriculum. At this time students are studying the events leading to the Revolutionary War. Mrs. Pour uses a social studies textbook, *The Making of Our America* (Allyn and Bacon, Inc.). Students already have an understanding of the colonization of America and have studied life in the early colonies.

Mrs. Pour begins this next unit with a brainstorming session using a semantic map (already described in Chapter 12 on Vocabulary). She places the word "Independence" on the chalkboard and circles it. She asks, "Can anyone tell me what 'independence' is, or what it means?" It is clear that children are not familiar with this term. "Okay, what is the root word?" Children respond correctly, "Independent." Mrs. Pour then uses the word in context. "What does it mean to be independent of someone or something?" One child responds, "You can do something by yourself." Mrs. Pour replies, "Yes, good. If you are independent, you can do something without help. You can do it by yourself." Another child offers, "You're free." Mrs. Pour nods and says, "Yes, we need to start writing some of these ideas on the board." The web begins.

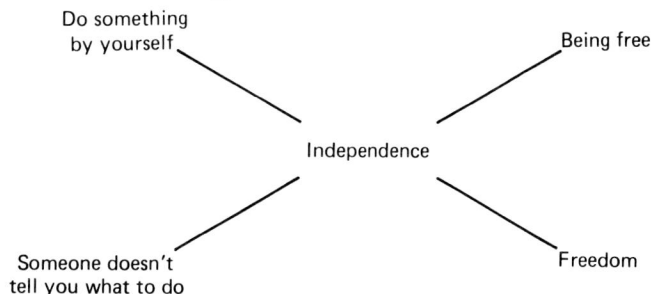

• Building schemata by relating the new to the known	Mrs. Pour then begins a discussion on what it means to fifth graders to be "independent." They respond by relating the idea of freedom to their personal lives. "My brother doesn't always tag along with me." "My mother doesn't tell me what to do." "I can do what I feel like doing." "Me and John hang around with nobody telling us what to do."
• Group discussion	Mrs. Pour then asks children how as youngsters they are *not* independent.
• Listening • Speaking • Taking turns	They discuss how their parents make rules, how the school makes rules, and how they do not have choices in some things. They also discuss their financial dependence on their parents. "Like, if my parents didn't give me a place to live, then I couldn't afford an apartment because nobody would give me enough money."
• Connecting the new to the known	Mrs. Pour then moves from the known to the new. "Now, remembering what it means to be independent, who can tell me what it would mean for the early colonies to be independent of Britain?" Children see the connection immediately and begin to generate ideas about the Colonies and their relationship to Britain. "The Colonists could do what they wanted and Britain wouldn't tell them what to do."
	In this way Mrs. Pour introduces the concept of independence. Notice that she begins the unit through discussion, brainstorming and semantic mapping.
• Building schemata • Developing language	Next, Mrs. Pour organizes the class for the three-week unit. The unit will involve children in listening, speaking, reading, and writing activities designed to build schemata and language abilities in this one particular area. She organizes by asking

• Directed-
reading-
listening-
thinking-
activity

TEACHER: What questions do you want to raise about the Colonists and Britain? What do you want to learn more about?

CHILD 1: What did the children do in those days?

CHILD 2: What was it like to live when the British told you what to do?

CHILD 3: Who was right?

CHILD 4: Why did the British tell them what to do?

CHILD 5: What happened?

• Writing
• Reading

Mrs. Pour hands out five pieces of large chart paper and has each child write his or her question at the top of the chart paper. She explains that children can choose one question that they are particularly interested in and be a part of a group that will answer that question for the whole class. The unit will culminate in an oral presentation to the other fifth-grade class about the Revolutionary War and the meaning of independence. Each group will be responsible for researching, reading about, and writing to answer the question and then developing some tangible product (for example, a slide-tape show, a chart, or graphs) for their oral presentation.

• Working
cooperatively
in groups

• Sharing

Working in Groups. Next, children break up into small groups to discuss further their topics. Children are instructed to brainstorm more specifically: (1) what they want to know, and (2) what procedures they need to go through to gather the information they need. A variety of resources and references are encouraged

Interviews

Guest Speakers

• Oral language

Children's fiction books

Nonfiction books

Social studies textbooks

Encyclopedias

• Listening	Museums Chambers of Commerce (for Eastern states) Historical landmarks (for Eastern states) Films, filmstrips Records, tapes Plays
	As each group discusses and brainstorms ideas for their research, Mrs. Pour invites two parent volunteers to assist her. These volunteers are available to help children focus more specifically on how they should gather their data. One group who wants to know what children did in those days decides they want to read some books about children who lived in that era. Assisted by the librarian, they find
• Reading	*Johnny Tremain*, by Esther Forbes (Dell, 1969) *John Treegate's Musket*, by Leonard Wibberley (Farrar, Straus and Giroux, 1959) *This Time, Tempe Wick?*, by Patricia Gauch (Coward, 1974) *My Brother Sam Is Dead*, by Christopher and James Collier (Four Winds Press, 1974)
• Oral Sharing	Each child decides to read one of the books and to tell the rest of the group what it is about. The parent aide suggests that they then could categorize certain things about living
• Classification and Categorization	Food Clothing Shelter Leisure activities Parents and children
• Chunking information	One child suggests that they could then write their own historical fiction story.

• Researching to gather information	A second group then decides to focus on living under British rule. They decide they need to find out specifically what the British told the colonies to do. They decide to gather their information through
• Reading • Listening • Speaking • Writing (notetaking)	Guest speakers (from local universities, museums) Social studies textbooks Additional trade books in the library They then think about how they can present the information they gather in an interesting way. They decide on a drama depicting British dominance over the colonies.
• Researching to gather information • Reading at the sentence and schema levels • Notetaking	A third group decides to focus on who was right— the British or the Tories. They decide to present a debate arguing each position. The group chooses sides so they can begin to gather data to defend their position. They brainstorm several sources to use. They decide they need facts, dates, a good knowledge of how each side felt, and critical thinking skills to determine which position was more believable.
• Critical listening • Speaking • Debating • Defending • Critical thinking • Sequencing of events • Brainstorming • Writing	The last group decides to develop a time line of the events leading to the Revolutionary War. Mrs. Pour suggests that they work together with the third group because both groups need a chronology of events leading to the war. They agree, and brainstorm together the different sources they can use to gather the information. The next day Mrs. Pour has each group prepare a list of things they need to do. Each group is assisted by the teacher or parent aides to ensure that they are headed in the right direction. The first group makes a chart listing their work.

Group 1

Read the book.

Talk about the book to the group.

Write charts.

Brainstorm ideas for book.

Write historical fiction story.

Bind the book.

Read to the class.

TEACHER'S PLANNING SCHEDULE

	Monday	Tuesday	Wednesday	Thursday	Friday
A.M.	Regular scheduling of subjects (math, reading, writing, spelling, music, physical education, art, and so on)				
1:00 to 1:30	Introduction of unit	Work in small groups	Small group work	Guest speaker	
1:30 to 2:00	Introduction	Small group work	Researching	Large group discussion	
	Recess				
2:15 to 2:45	Small group brainstorming	Small group work	Researching	Researching	

Each group works independently and also with Mrs. Pour, the parent aides, and the librarian. Guest speakers and field trips are attended by the whole class and discussed in context of the Revolutionary War and the concept of independence. One

- Speaking
- Listening
- Reading
- Writing

guest speaker develops the concept of "war" for students by helping them see the relationship between warring countries and students' own fighting with friends. One student who read *My Brother Sam Is Dead* presents to the whole class her argument that war is bad for everybody. Every four days, Mrs. Pour has a large group discussion in which a spokesperson for each group presents a progress report. Children discuss the difficulty they encounter gathering their data and also talk about what they are learning. (A secretary of each group also reports daily progress to Mrs. Pour.)

Sharing the Results.   The most exciting aspect of the project for students is to share what they learned. Each group has spent considerable time researching, reading, and writing to learn more to answer their questions. Thus they are anxious to share their learnings with others.

Mrs. Pour provides her class with a different audience to motivate them to do their best. She has encouraged them to use different media and different styles of presentation.

The presentations take a few days to complete. Children organize their presentations around the five questions they asked at the beginning. One child holds up a large cardboard with a question on it, and then that group proceeds to answer the question as best they can. The first group presents a large 3 foot × 5 foot chart that describes how children lived during the Revolutionary War. They have representative samples of some of the food of that era (corn, potatoes, and so on), the shelter (pictures of cabins, and of Boston). They present a short skit on how children would obey parental requests during that era.

Another group depicts British dominance over the colonies. They use Heathcote's model of drama presentation (see Chapter 5). They have to write a skit depicting the Tories in heated discussion over the latest of British rules—taxation of tea. They then listen to a dramatic presentation of the issues: "The Colonists Talk of Independence" and "America's Fight for Freedom," recordings in *Our Nation's Heritage Series* by the Chevron School Broadcast Company, 1970.

The Chevron School Broadcast,
Our Nation's Heritage Series
(Chevron Research Company, 1970)

1 Prologue to America.
2 The New World.
3 Exploring the New World.
4 Europe in the New World.
5 The English in America.
6 The Colonial Frontier.
7 The Revolutionary War.
8 Cornerstone of a New Nation.
9 The New Nation is Launched.
10 The New Nation is Tested.
11 The Nation Expands.
12 The Nation Divided.
13 Settling the West.
14 Industrial Revolution in America.
15 America Becomes a World Power.
16 Twentieth Century Begins.
17 The Nation in Prosperity and Poverty
18 America in World War II.
19 America in Midcentury.

A third group presents a scholary approach to the topic. They attempt to explain the sequence of events that led to the Revolutionary War. They have developed a large mural time-line depicting dates, events, and pictures of those events. They present the time-line to their audience. Each member of the group reads a date and an event, and then one to three members of the group present a short drama of the event.

The final presentation involves a debate over the concept of independence of the colonies. Students argue the position of each side and time is allowed for interchange of ideas and questions from the audience.

The closing of the unit is done with a large group discussion lead skillfully by Mrs. Pour. She writes independence again on the board, and asks students to now think about everything that comes into their mind. She writes and writes, because now the children have an expanded schemata and language base about this concept. They can relate it to the colonial times and to the needs of children and adults of that era. They can understand how sides were chosen and why issues were complex. They can state an argument for someone who wants independence and for someone who does not want to relinquish their hold.

Is this teaching the language arts? We want to argue that these experiences and activities practice and build all the skills needed to learn about language. Additionally, or perhaps at the heart of this is the thought processes. We are teaching students how to think and how to use language to learn about their world, to expand their schema and to develop language in all subjects.

Clearly, content area subjects can be learned through the expressive and receptive communication skills. Integrating the language arts with subject areas in meaningful units of study is one very effective way of creating interesting curriculum that provides children with important learning experiences.

TWENTY—ONE INTERESTING FICTION BOOKS IN SOCIAL STUDIES

Alcott, Louisa May. *Little Women*. Crowell, 1955.

Armstrong, William H. *Sounder*. Harper, 1969.

Blos, Joan. *A Gathering of Days*. Scribner, 1979.

Collier, James Lincoln and Christopher. *My Brother Sam Is Dead*. Four Winds, 1974.

Dalgliesh, Alice. *The Courage of Sarah Noble*. Scribner, 1954.

Farley, Walter. *Black Stallion*. Random, 1944.

Forbes, Esther. *Johnny Tremain*. Houghton, 1943.

George, Jean. *My Side of the Mountain*. Dutton, 1959.

George, Jean. *Julie of the Wolves*. Harper, 1973.

Gipson, Frederick. *Old Yeller*. Harper, 1956.

Houston, James. *Akaravak, an Eskimo Journey*. Harcourt, 1968.

McDermott, Gerald. *Arrow to the Sun: A Pueblo Indian Tale*. Viking, 1974.

Mowat, Farley. *The Dog Who Wouldn't Be*. Little, 1957.

O'Dell, Scott. *Island of the Blue Dolphins*. Houghton, 1960.

O'Dell, Scott. *Sing Down the Moon*. Houghton, 1970.

Paterson, Katherine. *Bridge to Terabithia*. Crowell, 1977.

Rawls, Wilson. *Where the Red Fern Grows*. Doubleday, 1961.

Speare, Elizabeth. *The Witch of Blackbird Pond*. Houghton, 1958.

Viorst, Judith. *The Tenth Good Thing About Barney*. Atheneum, 1971.

White, E. B. *Charlotte's Web*. Harper, 1975.

Wilder, Laura Ingalls. *The Little House Series*. Harper, 1953.

TWENTY-ONE INTERESTING BOOKS IN ART AND MUSIC

Adkins, Jan. *How a House Happens*. Walker, 1972.

Collier, James. *Jug Bands and Handmade Music: A Creative Approach to Music Theory and Its Instruments*. Grosset, 1973.

Cone, Molly. *Leonard Bernstein*. Crowell, 1970.

Harris, Leon. *The Russian Ballet School*. Atheneum, 1970.

Hosier, John. *The Sorcerer's Apprentice and Other Stories*. Walck, 1961.

Jones, Helen. *Robert Lawson, Illustrator*. Little, 1972.

Jones, Hetti. *Big Star Fallin' Mama: Five Women in Black Music*. Viking, 1974.

Landeck, Beatrice. *Echoes of Africa in Folk Songs of the Americas*. McKay, 1969.

Larrick, Nancy. *The Wheels of the Bus Go Round and Round; School Bus Songs and Chants*. Golden Gate, 1972.

Macaulay, David. *Cathedral, The Story of Its Construction*. Houghton-Mifflin, 1973.

Macaulay, David. *City. A Story of Roman Planning and Construction*. Houghton-Mifflin, 1974.

Macaulay, David. *Pyramid*. Houghton-Mifflin, 1975.

Mathis, Sharon Bell. *Ray Charles*. Crowell, 1973.

Noble, Iris. *Leonardo da Vinci; The Universal Genius*. Norton, 1965.

Posell, Elsa. *This Is an Orchestra*. Houghton-Mifflin, 1973.

Price, Christine. *Made in West Africa*. Dutton, 1975.

Rockwell, Harlow. *Printmaking*. Doubleday, 1974.

Skinner, Michael. *How to Make Rubbings*. Van Nostrand, 1972.

Sloane, Eric. *The Sound of Bells*. Doubleday, 1966.

Spier, Peter. *The Star Spangled Banner*. Doubleday, 1973.

Trevino, Elizabeth. *I, Juan de Pareja*. Farrar, 1965.

TWENTY-ONE INTERESTING FICTION AND NONFICTION BOOKS IN SCIENCE

Allison, Linda. *The Reasons for Seasons*. Little, Brown and Company, 1975.

Asimov, Isaac. *What Makes the Sun Shine?* Little, Brown and Company, 1971.

Babbitt, Natalie. *Tuck Everlasting*. Farrar, 1975.

Cob, Vicki. *Science Experiments You Can Eat*. Lippincott, 1972.

Cooper, Elizabeth K. *Science in Your Own Backyard*. Harcourt, 1958.

Cooper, Elizabeth K. and Padraic. *A Tree Is Something Wonderful*. Golden Gate, 1972.

Davis, Joseph A. *And Then There Were None: America's Vanishing Wildlife.* Holt, 1973.

du Bois, William Rene. *The Twenty-One Balloons.* Viking, 1974.

Eberle, Irmengarde. *Koalas Live Here.* Doubleday, 1967.

George, Jean Craighead. *All Upon a Sidewalk.* Dutton, 1974.

Henry, Marguerite. *Misty of Chincoteague.* Rand McNally, 1947.

Juster, Norton. *The Phantom Tollbooth.* Random, 1961.

Kalina, Sigmund. *Three Drops of Water.* Lothrop, 1974.

L'Engle, Madeleine. *A Wrinkle in Time.* Farrar, 1962.

L'Engle, Madeleine. *A Wind in the Door.* Farrar, 1973.

Lewis, C. S. *The Narnia Series.* MacMillan, 1951–55.

Macaulay, David. *Cathedral, the Story of Its Construction.* Houghton-Mifflin, 1973.

Milgrom, Harry. *Egg-ventures: First Science Experiments.* Dutton, 1974.

O'Brien, Robert C. *Mrs. Frisby and the Rats of NIMH.* Atheneum, 1971.

Rawlings, Marjorie K. *The Yearling.* Scribner, 1938.

Wrightson, Patricia. *Down to Earth.* Harcourt, 1965.

SUGGESTED ACTIVITIES

1 Construct a Huck's web around a special children's book. You might look in the appendix to find a Newbery book, or choose one with which you are already familiar. See Huck (1976) and two excellent articles by Norton (1977, 1982) for additional examples of Huck's webs.

2 Construct a content area web. Design the web around a particular social studies, math or science concept. Several examples have already been given. Be sure to locate and include several children's books related to the concept.

3 Talk to several teachers about how they view the language arts and content area instruction. See if any of them teach units such as the one we described in Mrs. Pour's class.

REFERENCES

Dole, J. A. "Reading and Language Arts Curriculum Planning Through the Integrated Web." *The California Reader* (in press).

Freedman, G., and Reynolds, E. G. "Enriching Basal Reader Lessons with Semantic Webbing." *The Reading Teacher* 33, 6 (March 1980):677–684.

Huck, C. S. *Children's Literature in the Elementary School.* New York: Holt, Rinehart and Winston, 1976.

Johnson, D. D., and Pearson, P. D. *Teaching Vocabulary Development.* New York: Holt, Rinehart and Winston, 1978.

Norton, D. E. "A Web of Interest." *Language Arts* 54, 8 (November/December 1977): 928–932.

———. "Using a Webbing Process to Develop Children's Literature Units." *Language Arts* 59, 4 (April 1982):348–356.

CHAPTER 15

Classroom Management

WHAT MAKES A GOOD TEACHER?

SIXTH GRADERS

... not too strict and not too light.

... they need to pay attention to the kids.

... she knows how you are really feeling.

... she makes the work fun to do.

... a lot of *patience*; teachers need a lot of patience.

... to know everything and to speak good you have to know a lot about your subject.

OVERVIEW

In this chapter we will discuss the organization and management of the language arts classroom. We do so by reviewing the current research and theory on classroom management and applying that information to language arts instruction. Specifically we cover the following topics: (1) classroom arrangement, (2) rules and procedures, (3) use of time, (4) engagement and success, (5) independent seatwork, (6) discipline, (7) peer teaching, (8) use of aids and paraprofessionals, and (9) use of computers. We complete the chapter with some concluding thoughts about the role of the teacher in the language arts program.

INTRODUCTION

At the beginning of this text we presented two different language arts classrooms and described some classroom activities. We described students working cooperatively on projects which used all the language arts skills. Students listened, talked, read, and wrote about subject area concepts and topics.

In the previous chapter we discussed how to create such a classroom by describing some ways to organize your language arts curriculum. We recommended integrating the language arts skills themselves and also infusing them into subject area curriculum. In this way listening, speaking, reading, and writing are used to teach concepts necessary for understanding science, social studies, math, and so forth.

In this chapter we want to conclude our discussion of how to create a successful language arts classroom. Such a classroom depends on the teacher's overall organizational skills and management ability. A good teacher runs an efficient classroom which minimizes disruption and maximizes learning and success. We want to present some information to help accomplish these important goals. While we do present ideas and strategies for you to use in class, we want to stress that the focus of this chapter is on you, the language arts teacher, and your ability to organize and manage the classroom.

Despite the agreement as to its importance there was little research in classroom management until the last 10 to 15 years. Prior to that time most teachers thought of classroom management as an art and relied on their "bag of tricks" to organize and run a classroom. In the last 15 years research on effective classroom management has to a large extent taken the mystery out of management and aided in moving it to an applied science. That is to say, we now know specific effective management techniques.

ARRANGING THE LANGUAGE ARTS CLASSROOM

One of the first considerations for the language arts teacher is how to arrange the classroom and allocate space. About planning the use of space Evertson et al. (1981) state

The basis for all decisions about the use of space in the classroom is the consideration of what activities will be taking place in that classroom. Of course, no decision need be final: better arrangements may present themselves and the needs of the students may change in time. There's a lot to be said for changing the room around just for the sake of variety—it gives the feeling of a fresh start. But to start out one must decide on a plan (p. 12).

In light of this Evertson (pp. 13–14) offers the following suggestions.

1 You'll probably want to cover large bulletin board areas with colored paper. You can probably obtain these in your school office or supply room—they'll be in large rolls. A neat border will help. Again, the supply room may have materials, or you can spend a few dollars for materials at a school supply center or store. For a few more dollars, you can buy a book of bulletin board ideas or some posters.

2 Be sure to leave some space for displaying a list of rules.

3 Keep high traffic areas clear. Don't put desks, tables, chairs in front of doors, water fountains, sink, and so on.

4 Count the desks and chairs. Make certain you have enough. Replace damaged furniture.

5 You may have a room in which students sit at tables rather than desks. If this is the case, you will need to plan for student storage carefully. Individual tote trays, boxes, or square plastic tubs are often used in these situations. Storing these must be considered when arranging your room. They should be easily accessible to the students.

6 Even if other arrangements are to be used later in the year, it might be wise to begin the year with desks in rows facing the major instructional area. This minimizes distractions for the children and allows the teacher to monitor behavior more readily and to become familiar with individual students' work habits.

7 Arrange the area(s) so that you can monitor the rest of the class when you are in the area working with a small group. Position your chair so that you face the room.

8 Arrange work areas so that you can monitor them when you are working with the class.

One important element to consider when arranging the language arts classroom is learning centers. *Learning centers* consist of materials and equipment arranged in a particular space or center so that children can work independently on a number of related assignments. One complete center can be located in a corner of the room, or two or three centers can be located in that same area depending on the extent and detail of the assignments (see Figure 15-1). Each center has enough materials, equipment, and assignments to ensure that children can work independently for an extended period of time.

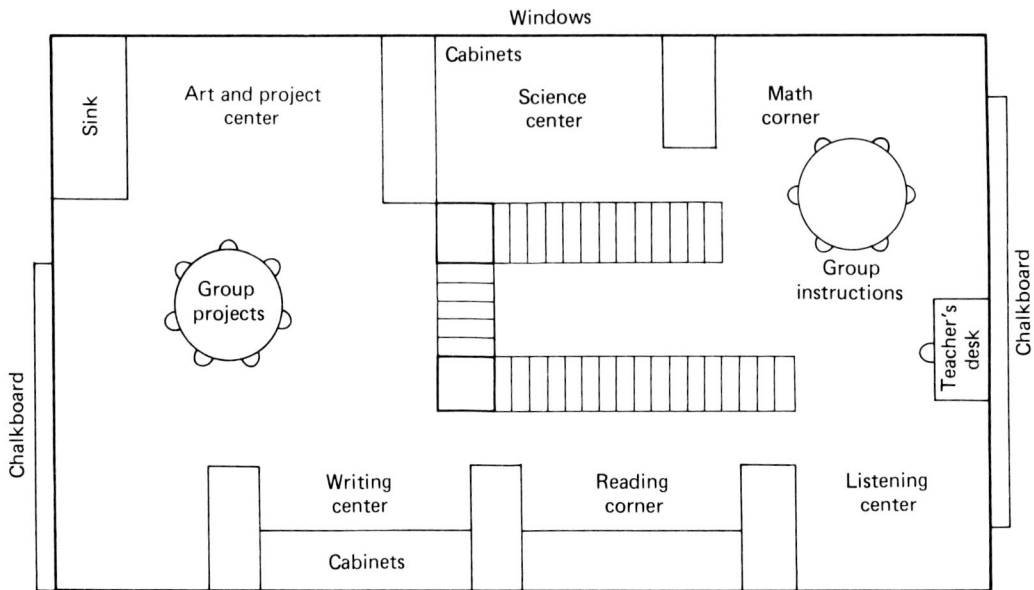

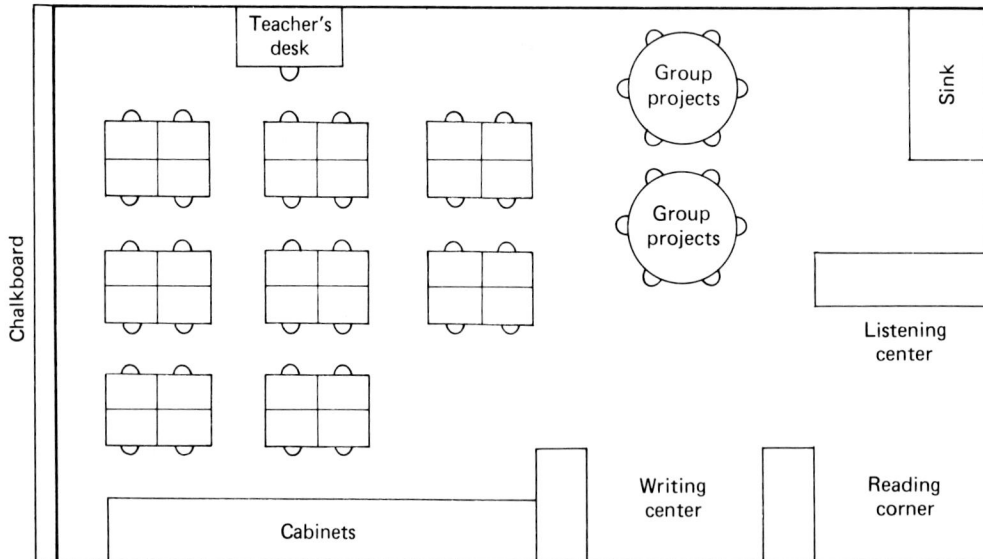

FIGURE 15-1 *Classroom arrangements.*

Although learning centers take time for teachers to plan and develop, centers can provide important learning experiences for children, and can give children the necessary practice and reinforcement of language arts skill learnings. For example, a letter writing center can be set up so that children can write letters to friends, relatives, pen pals or local newspapers and TV stations. Directions can be given on large charts for writing formal and informal letters and for addressing the envelopes. Activity cards can be included in a pocket in the learning center to provide children with ideas about people to write to or things to write for (see Figure 15-2).

Names of pen pals can be posted. Issues discussed in social studies or science can be posted, so that children can write to a local congressional representative or the newspaper to share their views.

In addition, integrated learning centers can be set up around the topic or concept themes similar to the ones discussed in the last chapter of this text. A center can also be set up around Huck's webs. Such activities can be written separately onto activity cards, and children can proceed through all or part of the web independently. Science or social studies learning centers can be set up for independent work on topics of particular interest to children. In this way, children can learn about some areas of interest that are not part of the regular curriculum for that particular grade. Language arts activities will always be central ones for any of these centers.

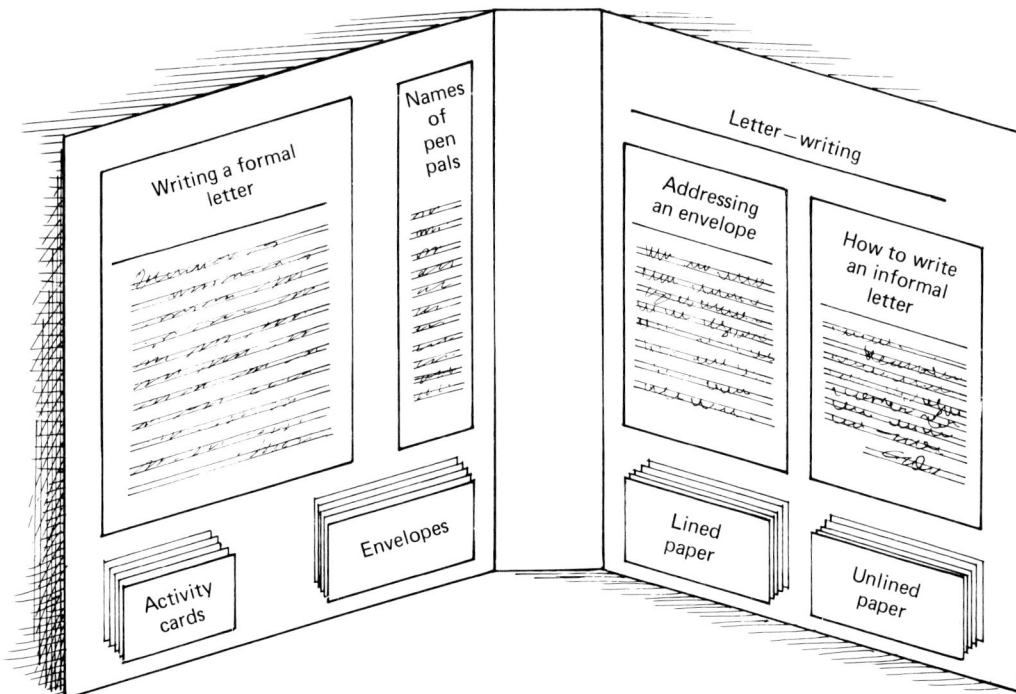

FIGURE 15-2 *Letter writing learning center.*

Below is a list of suggested materials for the construction of learning centers.

1 Reading Corner
- Book display racks.
- Shelves.
- Bean-bag chairs.
- Cushions.
- Books, all kinds of tradebooks and paperbooks.
- Magazines.
- Newspapers.

2 Writing Center
- Paper—Different shapes, sizes, colors, lined, unlined.
- Pencils, colored pencils, markers.
- Dictionaries, thesauruses.
- Blank books to write in, shape books.
- Comic strip without words.
- Activity cards, story starters.
- Pictures.

3 Listening Center
- Tape-cassette player, tapes.
- Earphone equipment.
- Accompanying storybooks.

Children can be assigned to centers, or alternately, centers can be used for supplementary activities. When centers are used as part of assigned seatwork, groups can be rotated through the centers.

TODAY'S ACTIVITIES

	Group A	*Group B*	*Group C*
9:00−9:30	With teacher	Listening center	Writing center
9:30−10:00	Listening center	Writing center	With teacher
10:00−10:30	Writing center	With teacher	Listening center

When centers are used for supplementary work, children can record their own progress through each center. A record follows as an example.

Name:	Kim Burn					
Date	Science Center	Art Center	Writing Letters Center	Literature Center	Indians Center	Reading Center
	10−1 Act. 1−5		10−1 Act. 1,2			
		10−2 Act. 1	10−2 Act. 3,4			
	10−3 Act. 6−10					
				10−4 Act. 1,2		

Below we have listed a number of useful books that describe in detail how to construct and use classroom learning centers. Careful planning in the use of learning centers can enhance classroom learning and provide additional stimulation for children.

Forgan, Harry W. *The Reading Corner.* Santa Monica, Cal.: Goodyear Publishing Co., 1977.

Forte, Imogene, et al. *Center Stuff for Nooks, Crannies and Corners.* Nashville, Tenn.: Incentive Publications, 1973.

Johnson, Hiram, et al. *The Learning Center Ideabook*, Boston: Allyn and Bacon, 1978.

Kaplan, Sandra, et al. *Change for Children.* Pacific Palisades, Cal.: Goodyear Publishing Co., 1976.

Kaplan, Sandra, et al. *The Teacher's Choice.* Santa Monica, Cal.: Goodyear Publishing Co., 1978.

Morlan, John E. *Classroom Learning Centers.* Belmont, Cal.: Fearon, Pitman Publishers, Inc., 1974.

Schaff, Joane. *The Language Arts Idea Book.* Pacific Palisades, Cal.: Goodyear Publishing Co., 1976.

Establishing Rules and Procedures

New teachers are commonly frustrated when they teach their first group of children. One of their first surprises is that they have to learn to control students before they can even think about the content of their lesson. The best advice we can give you is to learn how to establish rules and procedures with and for students. Once these are established, then you can concentrate on your language arts lesson.

Most elementary classrooms contain from 25 to 30 children each one expecting you, the teacher, to provide direction and guidance about procedures and rules. About rules and procedures Evertson (1981) states:

> *Although some teachers want their students to share in the responsibility of deciding on class rules, it is, ultimately the teacher's task to make certain that the set of rules and procedures is adequate and appropriate. If rules and procedures are constantly being revised, or if they are not followed properly, then you and your students will experience considerable frustration from interrupted tasks, lost time, and the interference of continually updating to modified rules and procedures. If, on the other hand, you establish a workable system, the year's progress will be much smoother (p. 28).*

Evertson strongly recommends that rules and procedures be established for the following areas, and activities.

1 Beginning class
   a Roll call, absentees, students who will be leaving early.
   b Tardy students.
   c Behavior during PA announcements.
   d Warmups or routines.
   e Distributing supplies and materials.

2 Instructional activities
   a Teacher-student contacts.
   b Student movement within the room.
   c Student movement in and out of the room.
   d Signal for student attention.
   e Headings for papers.
   f Student talk during seat work.
   g What students do when work is done.
   h Laboratory procedures: distribution of materials and supplies; safety routines; cleaning up.

3 Ending the class

   a Putting away supplies and equipment.

   b Organizing different classes' materials.

   c Dismissing the class.

4 Room areas

   a Student desks/tables and student storage area.

   b Learning centers/stations.

   c Shared materials, bookshelves, drawers, and so on.

   d Teacher's desk/storage areas.

   e Drinking fountain, sink, bathroom, pencil sharpener.
     School areas

5

   a Bathrooms, drinking fountains, office, library, and so on.

   b Lining up procedures.

   c Playground.

   d Lunchroom.

6 Whole class activities/seatwork

   a Student participation.

   b Cues or signals for getting student attention.

   c Talk among students.

   d Making assignments.

   e Passing out books, supplies.

   f Students turning in work.

   g Handing back assignments.

   h Makeup work.

   i Out-of-seat policies.

   j What to do when seatwork is finished.

7 Small group activities

   a Student movement into and out of the group.

   b Bringing materials to group.

   c Expected behavior of students in group.

   d Expected behavior of students *not* in group.

8 Other procedures

    a Beginning of school day.

    b End of school day.

    c Student conduct during interruptions, delays, and so on.

    d Fire drills, and so on.

    e Housekeeping and student helpers.

It is not enough to simply establish rules and procedures; they must be systematically explained, modeled, and reinforced, just as you would introduce any language arts skill. Further this should be done on the first day of school. As a matter of fact, at the primary level the first week to three weeks should be devoted to establishing rules and procedures.

TEACHER USE OF TIME

In recent years the use of time in school has been the focus of a large number of research projects. A generalization that can be made from much of that research is that far less time is spent in instruction than is commonly thought. To illustrate consider Figure 15-3.

Figure 15-3 indicates that about 25 percent of the school day is taken up by scheduled, nonacademic activities such as: recess, lunch, breaks between classes, and assemblies.

This means that about 75 percent of the school day is actually devoted to or allocated to classtime. Of that allocated classtime, 18 percent is taken up by nonacademic activities which include

Beginning managerial activities.

Transition time between assignments.

Giving assignments.

Working with one or two students while the others wait.

Ending managerial activities.

Social activities.

Interruptions.

Of these the major portion of time is spent in transition time between assignments and in giving assignments. If we factor out from the school day the nonacademic in-class activity and the scheduled nonacademic activity we are left with only 57 percent of the school day for instruction. But what does this mean for the language arts teacher? It does not mean that you should give students less time for lunch or recess or that they should exclude social activities, managerial activities,

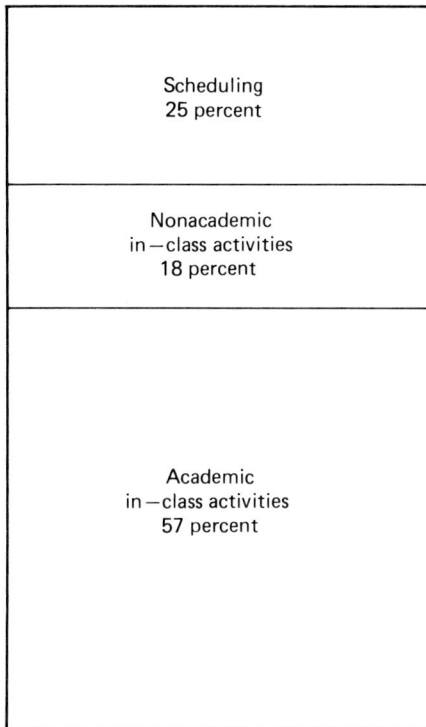

```
┌─────────────────────────────────┐
│                                 │
│          Scheduling             │
│          25 percent             │
│                                 │
├─────────────────────────────────┤
│          Nonacademic            │
│        in—class activities      │
│          18 percent             │
├─────────────────────────────────┤
│                                 │
│                                 │
│                                 │
│           Academic              │
│        in—class activities      │
│           57 percent            │
│                                 │
│                                 │
│                                 │
└─────────────────────────────────┘
```

FIGURE 15-3 *Use of time in school day.*

and so on from the classroom. It does mean that you should be *aware* of your use of time in classroom and should waste as little of it as possible.

ENGAGEMENT AND SUCCESS

Some major research findings concerning classroom management involve student engagement and student success. Many studies (Berliner, 1979; Bloom, 1974; Madaus, 1980; Ramey, Hillman and Matthews, 1982) have verified the finding that student academic success is a direct function of the extent to which students are successfully engaged in academic tasks. Commonly the term "time-on-task" is used when discussing engagement. There are three aspects: (1) engagement, (2) academic tasks, and (3) success.

Engagement refers to the extent to which students are actually doing what they are supposed to be doing in class. If the student is playing tic-tack-toe during a social studies class, the student is not engaged. *Academic tasks* are those that relate directly to the curriculum—even more specifically directly to what the students will be tested on (we will come back to this issue momentarily). *Success* refers to how successful students are in answering questions about the material being presented and performing the tasks (such as, homework and seat assignments) associated with a lesson.

One way of looking at the manner in which engagement, academic tasks and success interact to affect classroom activity is to add them to Figure 15-3 which depicted scheduled nonacademic time, in-class nonacademic time, and academic time. We have done this in Figure 15-4.

Figure 15-4 reports actual percentages calculated from a number of elementary schools in urban and rural settings. Five percent of the time academic instruction was occurring students were not engaged—not paying attention to the assigned task. Another 15 percent of the time that students were engaged, the teacher was working on content that was not considered relative to the curriculum. Another 5 percent of the time was lost to students' lack of success in the tasks they were supposed to perform. What is left when we take out all threats or distractions to learning is what is called "academic learning time." As Figure 15-4 indicates, this was 32 percent in the schools observed.

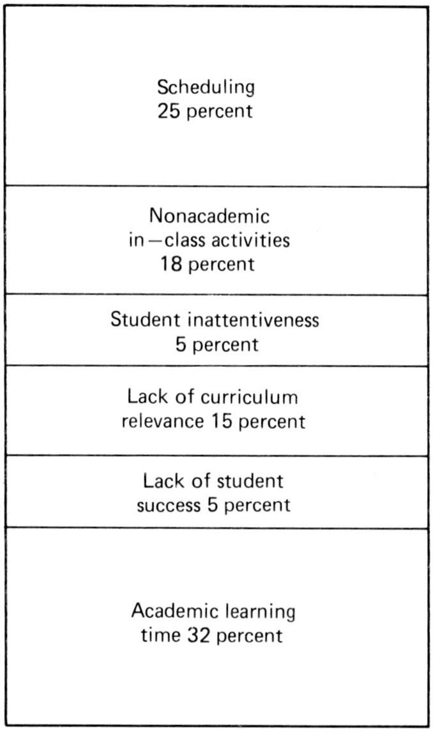

```
┌─────────────────────────────────┐
│                                 │
│         Scheduling              │
│         25 percent              │
│                                 │
├─────────────────────────────────┤
│         Nonacademic             │
│       in—class activities       │
│         18 percent              │
├─────────────────────────────────┤
│     Student inattentiveness     │
│         5 percent               │
├─────────────────────────────────┤
│      Lack of curriculum         │
│      relevance 15 percent       │
├─────────────────────────────────┤
│       Lack of student           │
│      success 5 percent          │
├─────────────────────────────────┤
│                                 │
│      Academic learning          │
│      time 32 percent            │
│                                 │
└─────────────────────────────────┘
```

FIGURE 15-4 *Academic learning time in school day.*

These figures are usually shocking to teachers. Commonly this information generates such questions as: "Does all instruction have to be geared toward the curriculum?" and "Should all the tasks students perform be easy so as to ensure success?" The answer is a definite *no* to both questions.

An effective language arts teacher is one who can teach all components of the language arts curriculum. Recall from Chapter 1 we discussed three goals of language arts instruction, to help students gain a love of learning language, to help them communicate effectively and to help them learn the skills of language. The school district curricula and tests often focus on the last goal only since it is the easiest one to measure on objective tests. Certainly an important component of effective teaching of the language arts is to help students develop listening, speaking, reading, and writing skills. We want to stress, however, that those skills are not the total language arts curriculum, and that you need to take students beyond those easily measurable tasks to teach them the full language arts curriculum.

Second, the effective language arts teacher is also one who varies the difficulty of tasks. With learning tasks where the teacher is present to provide immediate feedback to students, success rates of from 70 percent to 80 percent are sufficient; consequently, the tasks assigned can be relatively difficult for students. However, when students are working independently they become discouraged and frustrated if they are not highly successful. Consequently, relatively easy homework and well structured independent seatwork should be assigned (Brophy, 1982).

INDEPENDENT SEATWORK

First graders spend from 40 percent to 60 percent of an average reading lesson doing seatwork, but many of them don't seem to learn much from it. That's what Michigan State University researcher Linda Anderson (1982) concluded after watching students do reading seatwork in four schools.

Independent seatwork is potentially one of the most powerful and potentially one of the most unproductive instructional tools at a teacher's disposal. Some teachers consider independent seatwork "busy" work. They give students as many as 10 to 12 worksheets daily. These worksheets are given without regard to student ability or instructional level. Sometimes the worksheets can be too easy, as would be the case where third graders are asked to color simple pictures. Sometimes, particularly when the same worksheets are given to all children in the class, several children will not even be able to read the directions. Thus, for these children, the worksheets are frustrating and impossible tasks.

To be effective, worksheets must be carefully planned and administered. Below are some suggestions which can maximize the effectiveness of worksheets.

DO'S FOR WORKSHEET ASSIGNMENTS

- Do assign worksheets that children can successfully complete without direct assistance.
- Do assign legible and clear worksheets.
- Do assign instructionally appropriate worksheets.
- Do *vary* the types of assignments given on a daily or weekly basis.
- Do assign worksheets to "practice" a new skill, not to "introduce" it.
- Do give children practice in meaningful writing rather than by filling in the blanks.
- Do assign worksheets that children can read independently.
- Do encourage children to help one another if they encounter difficulty.
- Do encourage children to "practice" reading by reading books, not just skill worksheets.
- Do vary the worksheet assignments for differing abilities.
- Do assign more creative seatwork in addition to worksheets.

An important component in successful independent seatwork is variety. Worksheets are not the only type of activities that should be used. Below is a list of suggested alternative language arts activities.

1 Fold an 8 × 11 piece of paper in fourths. Have children write a sentence and illustrate what happened first, second, third, and last in the story they just read.

First	Second
Third	Last

Through this activity, children practice the skill of *sequencing*. They also write *complete sentences* and are asked to *paraphrase* parts of the story.

2 Have children draw a picture and describe in a few sentences the part of the story they liked best.

Through this activity children practice *paraphrasing*, *writing skills*, and *reading skills*.

3 Ask children to make a book jacket about a story they listened to or read. They should write the title, author and illustrator on the cover and then illustrate the cover. On the front insert of the jacket they should write a paraphrase of the story. On the back insert they can write about the author.

4 Children also can make book jackets for books they themselves wrote or other children in the class wrote. Through this activity children practice *writing* and *paraphrasing skills*.

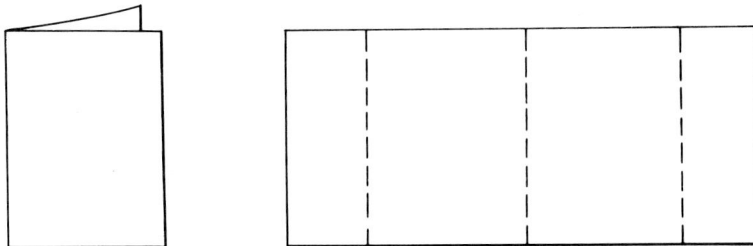

(dotted lines represent folds)

5 Have children draw a mural to depict the *sequence of events* in a story, the *main idea* in a story or the *climax* of a story.

6 Children can also *rewrite* a story into a play, or choose one component of the story to *dramatize* through role playing, puppetry, creative dance and movement, a monologue or dialogue.

7 Children can *rewrite* the ending to a story or continue the story through a sequel. They can *rewrite* the story through the eyes of another character in the story.

8 Children can try to "sell" a book or a story to other members of the class, through *writing* and *oral presentation*.

9 Older children can integrate the stories and books they *read* with other subject areas they are studying, for example, discuss *The Cay*, by Theodore Taylor, as an island in the Caribbean; *compare* and *contrast* survival in the semitropics, *The Cay* versus survival in the Arctic, *Julie of the Wolves*, by Jean George.

10 Have children answer guided questions about a book or story they are reading. Children respond in complete sentences rather than fill in the blanks.

DISCIPLINE

Probably the most talked about issue regarding classroom management in general is classroom discipline. What works and what doesn't work? Actually most of the factors we have already mentioned are related to discipline. To reduce the chance of discipline problems a teacher should

1 Identify and teach rules and procedures.

2 Use time efficiently.

3 Attend to student engagement and success.

4 Use well-planned and well-developed independent activities.

However, given that these tactics fail in a particular situation, how does a teacher handle discipline problems? There are many suggested techniques for handling disruptive students in the classroom. The techniques developed more recently are based on a cooperative or contractual arrangement between student and teacher rather than a model of teacher as authoritarian. For some teachers, a cooperative model represents a dramatic shift from their standard pattern of interaction. In this section we will review a current, major technique for handling classroom discipline—one proposed by Glasser (1977).

Glasser believes that the elementary school teacher is a major influence in a child's life, particularly in the development of a child's self-image. Glasser identifies eight underlying principles that he feels should govern all classroom interaction.

1 Get involved with students—be personal, warm, and friendly.

2 Deal only in the present, with what the child is doing now.

3 Work with students to help them make value judgments about their behavior.

4 If a student's behavior is detrimental to success, help the student to make a plan to change the behavior.

5 Get students to make commitments to their plans with a verbal statement, a handshake, or in writing.

6 Accept no excuses if students turn from their plan or break their commitment.

7 Inflict no punishment but do not interfere with natural consequences of misbehavior. Just keep working until change comes about.

8 Never give up. What this really means is hang in there longer than the child expects you to.

These eight principles have been translated by Medick (1980) into a 10-step procedure for handling discipline problems. A discipline problem is defined as a child who makes it difficult or impossible for others to learn or for the teacher to teach.

Step 1. Think about yourself and the child. Ask, "What am I routinely doing with this child?"

Step 2. Then ask, "Are these things working?" If the answer is "no," make a commitment to stop what you have been doing.

Step 3. Make a plan to do something every day with this student that is personal, friendly, and conveys the message, "I care about you." Be persistent even though a long time passes before your student responds favorably. Stay calm and courteous no matter how your student behaves.

Step 4. When a disruption occurs, issue a simple corrective or directive, such as, "Please stop it" or "Please be here on time"—nothing more. Continue Step 3.

Step 5. If Step 4 doesn't work, ask the child to evaluate his or her behavior: "What are you doing?" and "Is what you are doing against the rules?" If he or she denies doing anything, tell him or her what you see being done and state the rule being broken. Put the responsibility where it belongs—on the child. Don't say anything more—just wait. If you have been using Steps 1, 2, and 3, the questions in Step 5 are very effective in stopping misbehavior.

Step 6. If the child doesn't stop misbehaving then tell the child firmly and courteously, "We've got to get together and work it out." Take time to encourage the child to come up with the plan: help if necessary. The plan should be short-term, specific, possible, and involve some form of positive action more than "I'll stop it." Get a commitment from the child to follow the plan—shake hands on it, verbalize it, or put it in writing and sign it. It is important in Step 6 to impress on the child that the problem is going to be worked out. If the plan is not working and the child disrupts again, accept no excuses. Ask that child, "When are you going to do what you agreed to do in your plan?" Find out what went wrong. If necessary, renegotiate the plan and get a commitment from the child to follow it.

Step 7. If disruption continues, go through Step 6 once or twice. If this doesn't solve the problem, then isolate the child at a time-out location in the room or, if necessary, in the office. Say to the child, "I want you to sit here until you have a plan that will help you follow the rules or when you are ready to work out a plan with me."

Step 8. Step 8 is in-school suspension. If the child acts up during time-out, then he or she is referred immediately to the principal: "We want you to be in class, but we expect you to follow the rules. As soon as you have a plan that will help you follow the rules, you may return to class. If you need help with your plan, I'll help you."

If help with the plan is requested, the principal asks the child, "What did you do?" Then the principal asks, "What plan can you make that will help you do better?" Be prepared for lots of excuses.

Step 9. If a student continues to misbehave, he or she is declared out of control, and his or her parents are notified and asked to take the child home. However, the principal tells the parents and the child, "Tomorrow is a new day. We would like your child to be with us tomorrow so long as he or she maintains reasonable behavior. If behavior does not remain reasonable we will call you to take him or her home again."

When the child returns to school the following day, you go right back to Step 8—in-school suspension—until the child makes a plan to follow the rules.

Step 10. If consistent use of Steps 1 through 9 does not work, then the child must stay home permanently or receive special help provided either by the school district or community agencies.

The Glasser techniques for handling discipline problems are controversial but generally quite effective. Medick has both his and her perspectives in an excellent discussion entitled *Classroom Misbehavior* (1980).

PEER TEACHING

In our scenario of two language arts classrooms presented at the beginning of this text, we described children working together on language arts projects. Children can and do learn from each other and are therefore an important resource for teachers. Children have much to offer each other in terms of persistence, patience, an encouragement, and also in helping promote social growth and maturity.

There are a variety of ways in which children can be used to instruct each other in the language arts class. Assignments can be given in pairs rather than individually, and children can be asked to work together to complete reading worksheets, independent content area projects, or learning center activities. The pair assignments can be given to children who are at the same ability level, or the teacher can pair more capable students with ones who are in need of more assistance.

Group assignments can also be made where several children are responsible for each other's learning. In Chapter 6, we discussed peer conferencing in the writing process. Peers can work together on many language arts projects, researching and reporting on topic assignments or areas of interest.

Older children can also be solicited in helping younger children with a variety of tasks. For example, a first-grade class can be teamed with a sixth-grade class for writing assignments—writing a letter to Grandmother or a distant relative. Similarly, third graders could use the help of experienced sixth graders for their first report writing. Older remedial readers often enjoy reading books to young primary children and feel a sense of accomplishment in their own reading as well.

Many opportunities are available for some type of peer teaching in every language arts program. As you plan the instructional program, you need to build in time for children to learn from each other as well as from the "teacher."

AIDES AND PARAPROFESSIONALS

Managing an effective language arts classroom takes enormous energy and time. Instructing small groups of children and individualizing instruction for as many as six to eight different ability levels often requires more than one adult in the classroom. For these reasons, the use of aides and paraprofessionals is almost essential in today's classroom.

Aides, whether they are parents, students, or other volunteers, and paraprofessionals who have had some experience with children, can provide invaluable assistance to the language arts teacher. They can help in making some of the time-consuming learning centers that we mentioned earlier. Games, worksheets, bookbinding and other teacher-produced materials can be made by aides and para-professionals. They can also help teachers gather materials and resources for class units—films to order and obtain from the local library, filmstrips, books and other materials ordered and obtained from other schools or even the media center.

Because aides and volunteers often have had no background training working with children, many teachers have given these people "busy" work, such as grading papers. We suggest that teachers minimize their use of aides for these purposes. Research indicates that aides and paraprofessionals most directly affect school achievement when they are used in direct instruction.

COMPUTERS IN THE CLASSROOM

In October 1982 Market Data Retrieval, a research organization that maintains a data base covering all U.S. schools, colleges, and public libraries, conducted a survey of U.S. school districts. Related to microcomputer use they reported the following results:

- Of 15,314 school districts 8,947 (58 percent) used instructional computers, up 39 percent from the previous year.

- Of 82,422 school buildings 24,642 (30 percent) used instructional computers, up 50 percent from the previous year.

- The fastest growth in use of computers occurred in elementary schools, up 80 percent from the previous year.

- At that time a total of 10,499 of the nations 52,000 elementary schools (20 percent) were using microcomputers.

Since these results were reported the use of microcomputers has risen geometrically. It has been estimated (Hutchins, 1982) that by 1990 there will be three computers for every four desks in the elementary school classroom.

Given the current trend it is a fairly safe assumption that computers are here to stay in education. The majority of the software produced for microcomputers is for language arts and mathematics instruction. In Chapter 7 we mentioned how micro-computers can be used for sentence-combining practice. Because of the rapid change in hardware and software development a major problem facing the language arts teacher is keeping abreast of the field. There are a number of organizations available to teachers that provide information about educational hardware and software.

- Conduit. Conduit is a source for computer-based instructional materials that are reviewed, well-documented, programmed for ease of transfer and current. All materials are peer reviewed for conceptual validity, instructional usefulness, and overall quality (Iowa City, Iowa 52244).

- The International Council for Computers in Education (ICCE). This organization provides a way for educators to further instructional computing. ICCE is dedicated to effective and proper uses of computers in education and publishes a catalog of instructional materials specifically for computer education (Department 4A, Department of Computer and Information Science, University of Oregon, Eugene, Oregon 97403).

- Minnesota Educational Computing Consortium, (MECC). MECC is an organization created by four public education systems in Minnesota to coordinate and provide computer services to students, teachers, and educational administrators (2580 Broadway Drive, St. Paul, Minnesota 55113).

- Northwest Regional Educational Laboratory (NWREL). NWREL provides two major networks of computer information: Micro SIFT, a network clearinghouse for microcomputer software information for teachers, and Resources in Computer Education (RICE), a comprehensive data base that provides information on approximately 2000 microcomputer course-ware items and over 150 producers or developers of course-ware (300 S.W. Sixth Avenue, Portland, Oregon 97204).

- Technical Education Research Centers (TERC). TERC provides a service called the Computer Resource Center (CRC) for teachers. The center concentrates on microcomputer hardware, software, curricula, technical information to teachers, and has a library of journals, texts, manufacturer's literature, and manuals on topics related to electronics and computers in teaching (8 Elliott Street, Cambridge, Massachusetts 02138).

It is our strong recommendation that language arts teachers familiarize themselves with the current and future uses of microcomputers in the classroom.

THE TEACHER AS PRIMARY INSTRUCTIONAL AIDE

Even though we are now approaching a technology of instruction as is evidenced by much of the information in this chapter, there will never come a time when the responsibility shifts from the teacher to some instructional technique or piece of equipment as the primary tool in education. That is, the teacher is and will always be the primary instructional aid in the classroom. The informed, enthusiastic teacher will always generate enthusiasm and a desire for knowledge on the part of students. What are some ways to maintain enthusiasm in the language arts classroom? We have a few simple but useful suggestions.

1   Maintain and foster a love of language and the language arts. Effective language arts teachers are generally avid readers with a wide variety of interests which may range from the classics to children's literature. If you are enthusiastic about language and literature, your students will pick up this enthusiasm.

2 Be involved in your professional organizations. Many language arts teachers belong to the International Reading Association (IRA) or the National Council of Teachers of English (NCTE) or both. These organizations sponsor monthly journals such as *The Reading Teacher* and *Language Arts*, which contain current research based suggestions about effective language arts instruction. Membership in these organizations generally are worth their weight in classroom suggestions.

3 Enjoy yourself in the classroom. People usually do best what they like to do. Most, if not all teachers enter education because they like interaction with students. We recommend a playful and light atmosphere with your students and more importantly with yourself.

Enjoy teaching and your students will very likely enjoy learning.

SUGGESTED ACTIVITIES

1 Identify the rules and procedures you would require in the following areas: (a) passing out books, (b) cleaning up, (c) use of drinking fountain, bathroom, pencil sharpener. Compare your rules and procedures with those of another teacher.

2 Visit another teacher's classroom and observe his or her room arrangement. Is it conducive to efficient flow of traffic; efficient use of learning centers? What could be changed?

3 Using the information in Chapter 7 develop a learning center for the teaching of one aspect of grammar (for example, sentence patterns or sentence combining).

4 Interview two teachers in a building about their professional growth plans. How do they keep abreast of their field? What magazines and journals do they regularly read?

5 Interview two experienced teachers. Find out about their early experiences in teaching. Was it difficult to learn how to discipline children? Did they make the frequent mistake of trying to be friends with their students? How did they overcome this? What are the most important things to remember when teaching a class? Compare notes from these teachers. Do they agree? Do they have the same or different philosophies about managing the class?

REFERENCES

Anderson, L. M. *Student Responses to Seatwork: Implications for the Study of Cognitive Processing* Research Series No. 102. E. Lansing, Mich.: Institute for Research on Teaching, 1982.

Berliner, D. C. "Tempus Educare." In P. Pearson and H. Walberg (eds.). *Research in Teaching*. Berkeley: McCutchan, 1979.

Bloom, B. S. "Time and Learning." *American Psychologist* 29 (November 1974):682–688.

Brophy, J. E. "Teacher Praise: A Functional Analysis." *Review of Educational Research* 73 (Spring 1981):5–32.

———. *Classroom Organization and Management*. National Institute of Education, 1982.

Evertson, C.; Emmer, E.; Clement, B.; Sanford, J.; Worsham, M.; and Williams, E. *Organizing and Managing the Elementary School Classroom*. Austin, Tex.: Research and Development Center for Teacher Education, 1981.

Glasser, W. *Schools Without Failure*. New York: Harper and Row, 1969.

———. "Ten Steps to Good Discipline," *Today's Education* 66, 4 (November–December 1977):61–63.

Gordon, T. *T.E.T. Teacher Effectiveness Training*. New York: David McKay, 1974.

Green, J. L., and Smith, D. C. *Teacher and Learning: A Linguistic Perspective*. National Institute of Education, 1982.

Hutchins, C. L. "The Role of the Micro-computer in an Effective School." *Noteworthy*, Winter, 1982, pp. 8–12.

Madaus, G. *School Effectiveness: A Reassessment of the Evidence*. New York: McGraw-Hill, 1980.

Medick, J. M. *Classroom Misbehavior*. East Lansing, Mich.: Fanning Press, 1980.

Mid-continent Regional Educational Laboratory. "Helpful Tips for Teachers," *Noteworthy* (Winter 1982):77–80.

Ramey, M.; Hillman, L.; and Matthews, T. *School Characterstics Associated with Instructional Effectiveness*. Paper presented at Annual Meeting of the American Educational Research Association, 1982.

APPENDIX A

MARZANO LIST OF BASIC CONCEPT CLUSTERS*

1: Occupations
No. of concepts = 364
No. of clusters = 30

(a) Names of Occupations
RC: career, task, job
GLR: 2-job; 6-profession
NC: 20

(b) Supervisors
RC: manager, leader, sponsor, owner
GLR: 3-owner; 6-employer
NC: 22

(c) Royalty/Statesmen
RC: mayor, governor, queen, baron
GLR: 2-king; 6-squire
NC: 45

(d) Names for People in Sports
RC: player, boxer, coach, acrobat
GLR: 3-batter; 6-contestant
NC: 27

(e) Reporters/Writers
RC: author, poet, writer, reporter
GLR: 3-reporter; 6-historian
NC: 13

(f) Outdoor Professions
RC: hunter, cowboy, rancher, farmer, logger
GLR: 2-cowhand; 5-forester
NC: 31

(g) Artists
RC: painter, conductor, artist, musician
GLR: 4-musician; 6-sculptor
NC: 13

(h) Entertainers
RC: dancer, actor, clown
GLR: 2-actor; 6-actor
NC: 11

(i) Teachers/Advisors
RC: professor, student, counselor, teacher
GLR: 2-teacher; 6-tutor
NC: 11

* *Source:* Marzano List of Basic Concepts. Reprinted by permission of the author.

* *Note:* The following abbreviations are used throughout this appendix: RC = representative concepts; GLR = grade level range; NC = number of concepts; MA = math; SC = science; EN = English; and SS = social studies.

(j) Public Servants
RC: policeman, sheriff, officer, trooper
GLR: 1-fireman; 6-trooper
NC: 9

(k) Scientists/Discoverers
RC: scientist, biologist, discoverer, inventor
GLR: 3-inventor; 6-chemist
SC: botanist
NC: 20

(l) Areas of Work
RC: business, science, biology, education, medicine
GLR: 3-medicine; 6-politics
NC: 21

(m) Buying/Selling Related Occupations
RC: salesman, customer, merchant, vendor
GLR: 3-peddler; 6-vendor
NC: 11

(n) Small Businessmen
RC: butcher, grocer, blacksmith
GLR: 4-butcher; 6-milkman
NC: 14

(o) People Who Work in Offices
RC: businessman, secretary
GLR: 4-businessman; 6-typist
NC: 5

(p) Builders
RC: builder, manufacturer
GLR: 5-builder
NC: 3

(q) Printers/Publishers
RC: printer; publisher
GLR: 3-printer; 6-scribe
NC: 4

(r) People Who Clean-up
RC: garbageman, janitor
GLR: 4-garbageman; 5-janitor
NC: 3

(s) Occupations Related to Money
RC: banker, cashier
GLR: 4-banker; 6-teller
NC: 4

(t) Occupations Related to Prisons
RC: captive, guard, prisoner
GLR: 3-guard; 6-warden
NC: 8

(u) Occupations Related to Medicine
RC: nurse, patient, doctor
GLR: 2-doctor; 6-surgeon
NC: 7

(v) Occupations Related to Transportation
RC: pilot, porter, flier
GLR: 3-pilot; 5-seamen
NC: 8

(w) Clergy/Religious
RC: priest, bishop, cardinal
GLR: 3-cardinal; 6-missionary
NC: 11

(x) Repairmen
RC: plumber, carpenter, mechanic
GLR: 3-repairman; 6-mechanic
NC: 6

(y) Legal Occupations/Participants
RC: defendant, witness, judge
GLR: 3-judge; 6-lawyer
NC: 9

(z) Servants
RC: maid, servant
GLR: 3-maid; 5-usher
NC: 4

(a1) Occupations Related to Restaurants
RC: dishwasher, waitress, chef
GLR: 2-dishwasher; 5-chef
NC: 5

(b1) Messengers
RC: messenger, postmaster
GLR: 4-messenger; 6-postmaster
NC: 5

(c1) Occupations Usually Held by Youth
RC: babysitter, paperboy
GLR: 3-babysitter
NC: 2

(d1) Work Related Actions
RC: work, overwork, toil, employ
GLR: k-work; 6-retire
NC: 12

2: Types of Motion
No. of concepts = 321
No. of clusters = 24

(a) Motion (General)
RC: action, motion, mobile
GLR: 4-motion; 5-activity
NC: 9

(b) Lack of Motion
RC: stillness, dangle, pause, still
GLR: 2-rest; 6-suspend
NC: 22

(c) Beginning Motion
RC: beginning, start
GLR: 2-begin; 6-initiation
NC: 8

(d) Happening
RC: do, occur, react
GLR: k-do; 6-commit
NC: 11

(e) Completion
RC: end, finish
GLR: 2-finish; 6-complete
NC: 5

(f) Lack of Completion
RC: stop, ban, clog, delay
GLR: 1-stop; 6-stifle
NC: 17

(g) General Actions Involving Coming/Going
RC: journey, arrival, depart, roam, come
GLR: k-go; 6-depart
NC: 36

(h) Pursuit
RC: chase, pursue
GLR: 2-chase; 5-pursue
NC: 6

(i) Taking/Bringing
RC: take, mail, remove, place, deliver
GLR: k-put; 6-distribute
NC: 28

(j) Tossing Actions
RC: toss, throw
GLR: 1-toss; 4-thrust
NC: 11

(k) Pushing
RC: pull, push
GLR: 2-pull; 5-yank
NC: 9

(l) Vibration
RC: tremble, shake, jumble
GLR: 2-shake; 6-vibrate
NC: 17

(m) Shifting Motion
RC: shift, skid
GLR: 2-slide; 4-slip
NC: 5

(n) Jerking Motion
RC: bounce, lurch
GLR: 2-bounce; 5-budge
NC: 6

(o) Ascending Motion
RC: lift, hoist, rise
GLR: 1-blastoff; 6-ascend
NC: 6

(p) Descending Motion
RC: plunge, lower, drop
GLR: 1-fall; 6-slump
NC: 18

(q) Descending Motion
Done by Humans
RC: sit, crouch
GLR: k-sit; 5-stoop
NC: 6

(r) Reduction
RC: contraction, shrink, cramp
GLR: 4-shorten; 6-shrivel
NC: 8

(s) Expansion
RC: expansion, enlarge, sprawl, burst
GLR: 4-swell; 6-expand
NC: 22

(t) Force
RC: force, propulsion
GLR: 3-force; 5-pressure
NC: 3

(u) Closing/Opening Actions
RC: close, open
GLR: 2-open; 4-slam
NC: 4

(v) Joining Activities
RC: connection, join, merge, combine
GLR: 3-join; 6-mingle
NC: 32

(w) Separating Action
RC: separate, split, unfasten
GLR: 3-unfasten; 6-unwind
NC: 7

(x) Circular Motion
RC: spin, orbit, turn, encircle
GLR: k-around, 6-revolve
NC: 25

3: Size Quantity
No. of concepts = 310
No. of clusters = 11

(a) Size (Small/Large)
RC: tiny, large, small, vast
GLR: k-little; 6-monstrous
NC: 20

(b) Measurement Actions
RC: measure, rank
GLR: 3-weigh; 6-monitor
NC: 8

(c) Measurement Devices
RC: ruler, scale
GLR: 4-ruler; 6-gauge
NC: 12

(d) Things Commonly Measured
RC: address, diameter, countdown

GLR: 3-longitude; 6-angle
MA: radius
NC: 11

(e) Specific Units of Measurement
RC: inch, volt, pound, degree, gallon
GLR: 2-mile; 6-ounce
MA: centimeter
NC: 28

(f) Partitives
RC: bit, section, factor, segment,
       category
GLR: 1-dot; 6-portion
MA: subset
NC: 32

(g) Amount (General)
RC: amount, lot, entire, abundant, extra, another, plenty, most, lack only
GLR: 1-many; 6-unlimited
NC: 58

(h) Cardinal/Ordinal Numbers
RC: number, first, initial, two, three
GLR: k-two; 6-digit
NC: 66

(i) Specifiers
RC: each, this
GLR: k-the; 3-either
NC: 11

(j) Diminishers
RC: roughly, merely, mainly, rather, somewhat, hardly, nearly
GLR: 1-just; 6-precisely
NC: 32

(k) Intensifiers
RC: totally, sure, almost, quite, thoroughly
GLR: k-too; 6-thoroughly
NC: 32

4: Animals
No. of concepts = 289
No. of clusters = 15

(a) Animals (General)
RC: pet, creature, animal
GLR: 1-animal; 4-beast
NC: 11

(b) Cats/Dogs
RC: cat, tiger, dog, wolf
GLR: k-dog; 6-jackal
NC: 25

(c) Reptiles/Mythical Animals
RC: snake, reptile, monster, dragon
GLR: 2-dragon; 5-anaconda
NC: 13

(d) Baby Animals
RC: kitten, colt, chick, puppy
GLR: 2-puppy; 6-duckling
NC: 13

(e) Land Animals (General)
RC: deer, horse, elk, pig, goat, bear, zebra
GLR: 1-bear; 6-bull
NC: 44

(f) Rodents
RC: mouse, squirrel, rabbit
GLR: 2-squirrel; 6-weasel
NC: 18

(g) Primates
RC: monkey, gorilla
GLR: 2-monkey; 6-ape
NC: 6

(h) Sea Animals
RC: whale, fish, tuna, goldfish
GLR: k-fish; 6-catfish
NC: 24

(i) Shellfish and Others
RC: shrimp, eel, crab, oyster, octopus
GLR: 4-oyster, 6-sponge
NC: 21

(j) Birds
RC: robin, canary, gull, turkey, eagle, owl
GLR: 1-bird; 6-nightingale
NC: 30

(k) Insects
RC: butterfly, spider, mosquito, ant, moth
GLR: 1-bee; 6-mite
NC: 30

(l) Parts of Animals
RC: hide, pelt, antler, fur, tail, beak
GLR: 2-tail; 6-plume
NC: 14

(m) Animal Dwellings
RC: zoo, kennel, nest
GLR: 1-zoo; 6-stockyard
NC: 14

(n) Animal Equipment
RC: rein, horseshoe, collar, saddle
GLR: 3-saddle; 6-muzzle
NC: 10

(o) Animal Actions
RC: fly, buck, gallop
GLR: 1-fly; 6-shod
NC: 16

5: Feelings/Emotions
No. of concepts = 282
No. of clusters = 18

(a) Names for Feelings (General)
RC: feeling, emotion, mood
GLR: 4-mood; 6-sensation
NC: 6

(b) Fear
RC: fright, terror, startle, terrify, afraid
GLR: 2-afraid; 6-agony
NC: 23

(c) Actions Associated with Fear
RC: cover, wince
GLR: 6-flinch
NC: 3

(d) Worry/Shame
RC: shame, concern, worry, anxious
GLR: 3-worry; 6-anxiety
NC: 15

(e) Anger
RC: anger, revenge, fury, outrage, hostile, irate
GLR: 2-angry; 6-disdain
NC: 29

(f) Meanness/Cruelty
RC: cruel, vicious, mean
GLR: 2-mean; 6-destructive
NC: 13

(g) Irritability
RC: scornful, unfriendly, grumpy
GLR: 2-grumpy; 5-disagreeable
NC: 8

(h) Sadness
RC: sad, distress, sorry, grieve
GLR: 2-sad; 6-forlorn
NC: 18

(i) General Upset
RC: bother, disturb, sullen, upset
GLR: k-upset; 6-somber
NC: 16

(j) Excitement
RC: amazement, ecstasy, amaze, excite
GLR: 1-surprise; 6-passion
NC: 22

(k) Fun/Joy
   RC: happiness, pleasure, happy, gay,
          fun
   GLR: k-fun; 6-gleeful
   NC: 29

(l) Comfort/Contentment
   RC: comfort, calm, soothe, console
   GLR: 3-calm; 6-console
   NC: 23

(m) Jealous/Envy
   RC: envy, jealousy
   GLR: 4-jealous; 6-protective
   NC: 8

(n) Hope/Doubt
   RC: trust, doubt, suspicion
   GLR: 2-hope; 6-suspicion
   NC: 9

(o) Liking/Caring
   RC: care, love, like, revere, support
   GLR: k-like; 6-entrust
   NC: 28

(p) Neglect
   RC: neglect, overlook, omit
   GLR: 5-neglect; 6-overlook
   NC: 5

(q) Desire
   RC: wish, want, desire
   GLR: k-want; 6-yearn
   NC: 12

(r) Traits not Related to Emotions
   RC: ability, aspect, quality, trait
   GLR: 4-skill; 6-trait
   NC: 15

6: Food Types/Meals
No. of concepts = 260
No. of clusters = 14

(a) Types of Meals
   RC: supper, meal, feast, dessert
   GLR: 2-dinner; 5-refreshment
   NC: 14

(b) Food Types (General)
   RC: fruit, meat, seafood,
          nourishment, vegetables
   GLR: 1-food; 6-supplies
   NC: 16

(c) Sweets
   RC: honey, cookie, pudding,
          chocolate
   GLR: k-cake; 6-custard
   NC: 23

(d) Prepared Foods
   RC: noodles, muffins, bread, cereal,
          sandwich
   GLR: 3-bread; 6-cereal
   NC: 22

(e) Meats
   RC: ham, bacon
   GLR: 4-sausage; 6-steak
   NC: 8

(f) Dairy Products
   RC: butter, cheese
   GLR: 2-egg; 5-margarine
   NC: 6

(g) Ingredients Used to Prepare Foods
   RC: flour, dough, salt, pepper
   GLR: 3-sugar; 6-spice
   NC: 22

(h) Things to Drink
   RC: pop, tea, wine, soup
   GLR: 2-milk; 6-broth
   NC: 26

(i) Fruits
   RC: pear, plum, cherry, orange,
          banana

GLR: 2-apple; 6-melon
NC: 25

(j) Vegetables
RC: tomato, pumpkin, rice, acorn
GLR: 1-nut; 6-maize
NC: 40

(k) Actions Done to/with Food
RC: bake, boil, blend, ripen
GLR: 2-cook; 6-simmer
NC: 19

(l) Food Tastes
RC: bitter, rotten, juicy
GLR: 2-sweet; 6-rotten
NC: 15

(m) Eating/Drinking Actions
RC: taste, chew, drink
GLR: k-eat; 6-consume
NC: 16

(n) Hunger/Thirst
RC: hunger, appetite, thirst
GLR: 4-starve; 6-appetite
NC: 8

7: Time
No. of concepts = 251
No. of clusters = 11

(a) Time (General)
RC: lifetime, daytime, bedtime
GLR: 1-time; 5-mealtime
NC: 11

(b) Devices Used to Measure Time
RC: clock, watch
GLR: 2-watch; 5-calendar
NC: 5

(c) Parts of a Day
RC: noon, evening, night, minute
GLR: 1-day; 6-overnight
NC: 23

(d) Periods of Time Longer Than a Day
RC: season, winter, age, century
GLR: 2-summer; 6-centennial
NC: 22

(e) Months/Days
RC: January, February, Tuesday, Monday
GLR: —
NC: 19

(f) Relative Time
RC: today, future, past, ancient
GLR: 1-tomorrow; 6-ancestry
NC: 27

(g) Prior Actions (Relationship Markers)
RC: earlier, beforehand, prior, former, recent
GLR: 1-after; 6-previous
NC: 27

(h) Subsequent Action
(Relationship Markers)
RC: later, eventually, next, afterward
GLR: k-then; 6-latter
NC: 20

(i) Concurrent Actions
(Relationship Markers)
RC: as, while, now, meanwhile
GLR: k-now; 5-meanwhile
NC: 18

(j) Speed
   RC: hurry, frenzy, rush, fast, quick, swift
   GLR: 1-race; 6-hasten
   NC: 34

(k) Duration
   RC: frequent, permanent, rare, eternal, again, occasional, often
   GLR: 1-again; 6-daily
   NC: 45

8: Machines/Engines/Tools
No. of concepts = 244
No. of clusters = 14

(a) Machines
   RC: equipment, hardware
   GLR: 3-machine; 6-mechanism
   NC: 10

(b) Engines and Parts of Engines
   RC: engine, throttle, jet
   GLR: 3-motion; 6-diesel
   NC: 13

(c) Fuels
   RC: fuel, gas
   GLR: 2-oil; 5-petroleum
   NC: 8

(d) Appliances
   RC: oven, heater, refrigerator, television
   GLR: 1-TV; 5-griddle
   NC: 18

(e) Tools
   RC: wench, crowbar, hammer, saw, hoe, chisel
   GLR: 3-tool; 6-rasp
   NC: 38

(f) Tools Used for Cutting
   RC: axe, sword, blade
   GLR: 3-knife; 6-razor
   NC: 13

(g) Cutting Actions
   RC: chop, mince, grind, cut
   GLR: 1-cut; 6-mince
   NC: 23

(h) Fasteners
   RC: hook, clamp, strap
   GLR: 2-string; 6-rivet
   NC: 24

(i) Handles and Things Related
   RC: latch, key
   GLR: 2-handle; 6-knob
   NC: 9

(j) Miscellaneous Devices
   RC: lever, pedal, pulley, wand
   GLR: 2-roller; 6-gantry
   NC: 16

(k) Equipment Related to Vision
   RC: telescope, camera
   GLR: 3-camera; 6-periscope
   NC: 9

(l) Electronic Equipment
   RC: transmitter, teletype
   GLR: 4-robot; 6-computer
   NC: 7

(m) Utensils Used for Eating/Cooking
   RC: spoon, pot, sieve, glass, dish
   GLR: 1-pan; 6-ladle
   NC: 28

(n) Weapons
   RC: weapon, missile, gun, explosive, arrow
   GLR: 2-gun; 6-ammunition
   NC: 28

9: Types of People
No. of concepts = 237
No. of clusters = 15

(a) People (General)
RC: human, people, mankind
GLR: 2-people; 5-self
NC: 10

(b) Names for Women
RC: woman, widow, lass, female, girl
GLR: 1-girl; 6-housewife
NC: 17

(c) Names for men
RC: boy, male, sir, guy, gentleman
GLR: k-guy; 6-host
NC: 12

(d) Names Indicating Youth/Age
RC: infant, youth, child, elder, baby
GLR: 1-baby; 6-infant
NC: 20

(e) Names Indicating Friendship
RC: neighbor, ally, pal, lover, friend
GLR: 1-friend; 6-comrade
NC: 17

(f) Names for Spiritual/Mythical People
RC: fairy, spirit, saint, goblin, wizard
GLR: 2-fairy; 6-poltergeist
NC: 17

(g) Names Indicating Negative Characteristics of People
RC: liar, gossip, enemy, grouch, outlaw, thief
GLR: 3-thief; 6-pest
NC: 28

(h) Names Indicating Lack of Permanence for People
RC: guest, rover, runaway, visitor
GLR: 3-visitor; 6-wanderer
NC: 15

(i) Names Indicating Permanence for People
RC: settler, dweller, resident
GLR: 4-settler; 6-immigrant
NC: 17

(j) Names Indicating Size of People
RC: giant, midgit, pygmy
GLR: 2-giant; 6-pigmy
NC: 5

(k) Names Indicating Fame
RC: celebrity, hero, idol
GLR: 2-star; 6-idol
NC: 7

(l) Names Indicating Knowledge of a Topic
RC: expert, genius, novice
GLR: 4-expert; 6-amateur
NC: 7

(m) Names Indicating Financial Status of People
RC: millionaire, miser
GLR: 6-pauper
NC: 4

(n) Family Relations
RC: dad, mother, parent, sister, brother
GLR: k-daddy; 6-niece
NC: 45

(o) Names of People Indicating Political Disposition
RC: democrat, patriot, socialist
GLR: 5-confederate; 6-patriot
SS: republican
NC: 16

10: Communication
No. of concepts = 227
No. of clusters = 15

(a) Communications Involving Confrontation or Negative Information
RC: argument, complain, condemn, insult, threat, disobey
GLR: 3-complain; 6-curse
NC: 54

(b) Communications Involving General Presentation of Information
RC: tell, explain, show, claim, declare
GLR: k-show; 6-convey
NC: 26

(c) Communications Involving Positive Information
RC: truce, greeting, assure, support
GLR: 2-greeting; 6-congratulations
NC: 24

(d) Persuasion
RC: convince, influence, urge, suggest
GLR: 4-suggest; 6-coax
NC: 18

(e) Questions
RC: question, reply, quiz, ask
GLR: k-ask; 6-inquire
NC: 20

(f) Communications Involving Supervision/Commands
RC: command, require, obey, control, let
GLR: k-let; 6-dominate
NC: 38

(g) Giving Out Information Previously Withheld
RC: admit, confide, confess
GLR: 4-confess; 6-confide
NC: 4

(h) Promises
RC: vow, oath, promise
GLR: 3-promise; 6-pledge
NC: 5

(i) Recording or Translating Information
RC: quote, translation, record
GLR: 5-quote; 6-interpretation
NC: 8

(j) Exclamation (General)
RC: oh, alas, ha, hey, yes, hi
GLR: k-no; 6-bravo
NC: 30

11: Transportation
No. of concepts = 224
No. of clusters = 8

(a) Types of Transportation
RC: car, jeep, bus, bicycle, locomotive, buggy
GLR: 1-wagon; 6-chariot
NC: 53

(b) Work Related Vehicles
RC: tractor, bulldozer, wheelbarrow
GLR: 2-tractor; 6-narrow

SS: reaper
NC: 16

(c) Vehicles Used in Snow
RC: sled, toboggan
GLR: 2-sled; 6-snowplow
NC: 4

(d) Vehicles Used for Air Transportation
RC: plane, blimp, rocket

GLR: 1-airplane; 6-aircraft
NC: 16

(e) Vehicles Used for Sea Transportation
RC: ship, tanker, raft, battleship, barge, steamboat, sailboat
GLR: k-boat; 6-gondola
NC: 37

(f) Parts of Vehicles
RC: wheel, headlight, hull, oar, wing
GLR: k-boat; 6-gondola
NC: 37

(g) Actions Specific to Vehicles
RC: fly, sail, ride
GLR: k-ride; 6-cruise
NC: 18

(h) Things Traveled on
RC: street, intersection, route, alley, tunnel, railroad, path, seaway, airfield
GLR: 1-road; 6-passageway
NC: 43

12: Mental Actions/Thinking
No. of concepts = 195
No. of clusters = 12

(a) Thought/Memory (General)
RC: memory, thought, wonder, consider, think
GLR: 1-think; 6-ponder
NC: 20

(b) Subjects/Topics
RC: topic, scheme, plan, objective
GLR: 2-plan; 6-theme
NC: 10

(c) Mental Exploration
RC: search, experiment, examine, explore
GLR: 3-explore; 6-examination
NC: 15

(d) Mental Actions Involving Conclusions
RC: solve, compose, prove, discover, invent
GLR: 3-invent; 6-conclude
NC: 35

(e) Consciousness
RC: awake, dream, sleep, asleep
GLR: 1-sleep; 6-unconscious
NC: 26

(f) Interest
RC: attention, intrigue
GLR: 3-interest; 6-intrigue
NC: 5

(g) Teaching/Learning Actions
RC: coach, teach, learn, know
GLR: k-know; 5-instruction
NC: 25

(h) Processes and Procedures
RC: method, procedure, process
GLR: 5-process; 6-maneuver
NC: 5

(i) Definition
RC: definition, meaning
GLR: 5-definition
NC: 2

(j) Choice
RC: choose, decide, pick
GLR: 2-pick; 6-appoint
NC: 16

(k) Intelligence
RC: wisdom, smart, stupid, alert, aware, wise
GLR: 2-wise; 6-cunning
NC: 28

(l) Beliefs
RC: belief, superstition, custom
GLR: 4-custom; 6-philosophy
NC: 8

13: Nonemotional Human Traits
No. of concepts = 175
No. of clusters = 16

(a) Kindness/Goodness
RC: charity, courtesy, kind, polite, nice
GLR: 1-kind; 6-affectionate
NC: 31

(b) Eagerness/Reliability
RC: busy, poise, eager, confidence, diligence, trustworthy
GLR: 2-busy; 6-ambitious
NC: 37

(c) Lack of Initiative
RC: lazy, aimless, idle
GLR: 2-lazy; 6-idle
NC: 7

(d) Freedom/Independence
RC: freedom, independence, dependent
GLR: 4-freedom; 6-dependent
NC: 4

(e) Confidence/Pride
RC: sure, confident
GLR: 2-proud; 6-dominant
NC: 6

(f) Patience
RC: patient, impatient
GLR: 3-patient; 6-expectant
NC: 3

(g) Luck/Prosperity
RC: fortunate, successful, lucky
GLR: 2-lucky; 5-prosperous
NC: 7

(h) Strictness
RC: strict, stubborn, staunch
GLR: 3-strict; 6-staunch
NC: 5

(i) Humor
RC: witty, humorous, funny
GLR: k-funny; 6-humorous
NC: 4

(j) Spirituality
RC: spiritual, religious, sacred
GLR: 5-religious; 6-sacred
NC: 7

(k) Prudence
RC: prudence, modesty
GLR: 4-prudence; 5-modesty
NC: 2

(l) Shyness
RC: meek, timid, shy
GLR: 3-shy; 6-reluctant
NC: 7

(m) Dishonesty
RC: dishonest, phony, tricky
GLR: 5-tricky; 6-mischievous
NC: 8

(n) Loyalty/Courage
RC: loyalty, treason, courage, heroic, honor
GLR: 3-honor; 6-courageous
NC: 29

(o) Instability
RC: crazy, reckless, wild
GLR: 3-wild; 6-unstable
NC: 12

(p) Caution
RC: watchful, cautious, caution
GLR: 2-careful; 6-caution
NC: 6

14: Location/Direction
No. of concepts = 172
No. of clusters = 12

(a) Locations (General)
RC: direction, location, position
GLR: 3-distance; 6-location
NC: 9

(b) Boundaries
RC: corner, edge, margin, side
GLR: 2-side; 6-brink
NC: 15

(c) Planes
RC: diagonal, vertical, horizontal
GLR: 6-vertical
MA: diagonal
NC: 6

(d) Nonspecific or Context
Specific Locations
RC: there, somewhere, here
GLR: k-here; 4-elsewhere
NC: 9

(e) Compass Directions
RC: north, south, right, southern
GLR: 1-right; 6-midwest
NC: 26

(f) Back/Front/Middle
RC: back, end, front, middle
GLR: 1-back; 6-central
NC: 19

(g) Directions To/From
RC: at, to
GLR: k-from
NC: 3

(h) Inward/Outward Direction
RC: inside, internal, outside
GLR: k-in; 6-interim
NC: 17

(i) Up/On
RC: on, atop, up, upward
GLR: k-up; 5-atop
NC: 23

(j) Down/Under
RC: under, below, down
GLR: k-down; 6-downward
NC: 13

(k) Distance
RC: distant, beyond, close, local,
      away
GLR: k-away; 6-abreast
NC: 26

(l) Presence/Absence
RC: present, absent, presence
GLR: 3-present; 6-absence
NC: 6

15: Literature/Writing
No. of concepts = 171
No. of clusters = 9

(a) Names/Titles
RC: title, label, name, heading

GLR: 1-name; 6-inscription
NC: 15

(b) Types of Literature
RC: composition, story, fiction, fable
GLR: 1-story; 6-mythology
NC: 11

(c) Types of Books
RC: textbook, novel, manual, magazine, encyclopedia
GLR: k-book; 6-manual
NC: 34

(d) Poems/Songs
RC: poem, music, hymn, tune
GLR: 2-sing; 6-hymn
NC: 21

(e) Drawings/Illustrations
RC: illustration, drawing, diagram
GLR: 4-drawing; 6-graph
NC: 6

(f) Messages
RC: postcard, telegram, letter, bulletin
GLR: 1-letter; 6-slogan
NC: 19

(g) Things to Write with/on
RC: pen, crayon, notebook, paper
GLR: 2-paper; 6-manuscript
NC: 18

(h) Rules/Laws
RC: law, proposal, policy, rule
GLR: 3-rule; 6-contract
NC: 14

(i) Reading/Writing/Drawing Actions
RC: scribble, sign, copy, draw, write
GLR: 2-write; 6-illustrate
NC: 33

16: Water/Liquids
No. of concepts = 164
No. of clusters = 9

(a) Water (Different Forms)
RC: liquid, rain, hail, snow, ice
GLR: 1-water; 6-snowflake
NC: 22

(b) Actions Related to Water
RC: drip, seep, spray, pour, swim, dive, flow, boil, sprinkle
GLR: 4-sprinkle; 6-surge
NC: 51

(c) Equipment Used with Liquids
RC: fountain, pump, hose
GLR: 3-hose; 6-funnel
NC: 10

(d) Moisture
RC: dew, mist, haze
GLR: 4-mist; 6-moisture
NC: 10

(e) Slime
RC: slime, sediment, scum
GLR: 3-scum; 6-froth

SC: silt
NC: 6

(f) Bodies of Water
RC: river, pond, lagoon, reef, ocean, stream
GLR: 2-stream; 6-tributary
NC: 32

(g) Places near Water
RC: island, shore, seashore
GLR: 3-shore; 6-isle
NC: 12

(h) Directions Related to Water
RC: ashore, downstream, overboard, offshore
GLR: 4-underwater; 6-offshore
NC: 11

(i) Artifically Created Places near Water
RC: seaport, dock, dam, harbor
GLR: 3-harbor; 6-pier
NC: 10

17: Clothing
No. of concepts = 161
No. of clusters = 12

(a) Clothing (General)
RC: costume, suit, garment
GLR: 2-suit; 6-garment
NC: 10

(b) Parts of Clothing
RC: button, lining, pocket
GLR: 1-pocket, 5-seam
NC: 10

(c) Shirts/Pants/Skirts
RC: shirt, blouse, trousers, skirt
GLR: 1-dress; 6-gown
NC: 15

(d) Things Worn on the Head
RC: cap, bonnet, hood, hat
GLR: 1-hat; 6-visor
NC: 12

(e) Things Worn on the Hands/Feet
RC: boot, sock, sandal, gloves, shoe
GLR: 1-shoe; 6-stockings
NC: 13

(f) Coats
RC: shawl, cloak, coat, jacket
GLR: 1-coat, 6-shroud
NC: 9

(g) Clothing Accessories
RC: tie, belt, umbrella, comb, tassel
GLR: 2-ring; 6-tassel
NC: 25

(h) Armor
RC: armor, shield
GLR: 5-armor; 6-shield
NC: 3

(i) Actions Done to/with Clothing
RC: wear, fold, design, sew
GLR: 2-wear; 6-embroider
NC: 23

(j) Characteristics of Clothes and
Wearing Clothes
RC: threadlike, sheer, naked
GLR: 5-threadlike; 6-sheer
NC: 10

(k) Fabrics
RC: material, thread, silk, wool, cloth
GLR: 2-cloth; 6-satin
NC: 23

(l) Smell/Scent
RC: scent, fragrance, smell
GLR: 2-smell; 6-odor
NC: 8

18: Places Where People Live/Dwell
No. of concepts = 154
No. of clusters = 4

(a) Places Where People Live
RC: neighborhood, city, slum,
      country, town
GLR: 1-town; 6-empire
NC: 21

(b) Continents/Countries
RC: continent, country, United States,
      North America
GLR: 4-country
NC: 24

(c) States
RC: Washington, Oregon, Colorado
GLR: —
NC: 55

(d) Cities
RC: Denver, Seattle, New York
GLR: —
NC: 54

19: Noises/Sound
No. of concepts = 143
No. of clusters = 5

(a) Noises (General)
RC: noise, clatter, listen, hear, quiet
GLR: 1-sound; 6-lull
NC: 24

(b) Devices That Produce Sound
RC: horn, bell, telephone
GLR: 2-horn; 6-earphone
NC: 12

(c) Noises Made by People
RC: cheer, snore, shout, laugh, cry, mumble, chant
GLR: 1-laugh; 6-applaud
NC: 49

(d) Animal Noises
RC: peep, croak, moo
GLR: 2-quack; 6-yap
NC: 31

(e) Noises Made by Objects
RC: thud, creak, zoom, thump, jingle
GLR: 2-ring; 6-tinkle
NC: 27

20: Land/Terrain
No. of concepts = 142
No. of clusters = 8

(a) Areas of Land
RC: acre, area, spot, territory
GLR: 2-place; 6-premises
NC: 22

(b) Characteristics of Places
RC: tropical, rural, metropolitan
GLR: 4-tropical; 6-metropolitan
NC: 17

(c) Valleys/Craters
RC: cave, canyon, crater, ditch
GLR: 2-hole; 6-chasm
NC: 27

(d) Mountains/Hills
RC: mountain, slope, peak, hill
GLR: 1-hill; 6-embankment
NC: 21

(e) Forests
RC: jungle, meadow, glen
GLR: 2-forest; 5-woodland
NC: 12

(f) Fields
RC: orchard, vineyard, field
GLR: 2-field; 6-paddy
NC: 9

(g) Parks/Yards
RC: park, playground, patio, yard
GLR: 2-yard; 6-playground
NC: 11

(h) Bodies in Space
RC: earth, universe, planet
GLR: 2-world; 5-universe
SC: galaxy
NC: 23

21: Dwellings/Shelters
No. of concepts = 141
No. of clusters = 13

(a) Structures
RC: building, structure
GLR: 2-tower; 6-construction
NC: 8

(b) Places to Live in/Stay in
RC: apartment, mansion, motel,
        dwelling
GLR: k-house; 6-habitat
NC: 21

(c) Places of Protection/Incarceration
RC: fort, cell, prison
GLR: 1-cage; 6-dungeon
NC: 14

(d) Places Where Goods Are Bought/Sold
RC: store, market, drugstore
GLR: 1-store; 6-tavern
NC: 12

(e) Mills/Factories
RC: mill, workshop, factory
GLR: 2-shop, 6-studio
SS: refinery
NC: 12

(f) Places for Learning/Experimentation
RC: school, college, library, laboratory
GLR: 1-school; 6-university
NC: 17

(g) Places for Sports
RC: court, stadium
GLR: 4-gym; 6-arena
NC: 17

(h) Medical Facilities
RC: hospital, ward, clinic
GLR: 3-hospital; 6-clinic
NC: 7

(i) Places for Prayer/Worship
RC: chapel, shrine, church, cathedral
GLR: 3-church; 6-cathedral
NC: 10

(j) Places for Transportation
RC: airport, terminal, station, depot
GLR: 2-station, 6-depot
NC: 4

(k) Places Used for Storage
RC: hut, shed, warehouse, barn,
        storeroom
GLR: 1-barn; 5-storeroom
NC: 10

(l) Places for Farming/Ranching
RC: ranch, plantation, farm
GLR: 1-farm, 5-plantation
NC: 5

(m) Monuments
RC: monuments, landmark,
        memorial, totem
GLR: 5-totem; 6-memorial
NC: 4

22: Materials
No. of concepts = 140
No. of clusters = 7

(a) Containers
RC: carton, crate, package, barrel,
        sack, tub
GLR: 1-box; 6-bin
NC: 46

(b) Materials/Objects Used to Cover Things
RC: plug, canvas, cellophane
GLR: 2-cover; 6-tarpaulin
NC: 11

(c) Building Materials (Wood)
RC: board, plank, lumber
GLR: 2-wood; 6-shingle
NC: 12

(d) Building Materials (Nonwood)
RC: cement, pipe, pole
GLR: 2-bar; 6-pavement
NC: 25

(e) General Names for Objects
RC: object, thing
GLR: 1-thing; 6-substance
NC: 3

(f) Building Action
RC: build, install, repair, restore

GLR: k-make; 6-modify
NC: 31

(g) Wraping/Packing Actions
RC: wrap, bind, pack
GLR: 3-wrap; 6-unravel
NC: 12

23: The Human Body
No. of concepts = 128
No. of clusters = 11

(a) The Body (General)
RC: body, hips, limbs
GLR: 3-body; 6-carcass
NC: 11

(b) Body Coverings
RC: flesh, scar, hair, skin
GLR: 1-hair; 6-blubber
NC: 14

(c) The Head
RC: mind, cheek, cerebellum
GLR: 1-head; 5-skull
SC: medula
NC: 12

(d) Mouth/Throat
RC: teeth, lip, tongue, throat
GLR: 2-mouth; 6-fang
NC: 11

(e) Eyes/Ears/Nose
RC: ear, eye, nose
GLR: 2-eye; 6-eyelash
NC: 11

(f) Limbs
RC: arm, leg, hand
GLR: 1-hand; 6-knuckle
NC: 12

(g) Legs/Feet
RC: foot, leg, knee
GLR: 1-leg; 6-haunch
NC: 11

(h) Internal Organs
RC: liver, lung
GLR: 3-stomach; 5-lung
NC: 7

(i) Internal Bodily Fluids
RC: blood, vein, bleed
GLR: 4-vein; 6-perspiration
MC: mucus
NC: 15

(j) Bones/Muscles/Nerves
RC: rib, muscle, nerve
GLR: 2-bone; 6-nerve
SC: ligament
NC: 15

(k) Bodily Systems
RC: reproductive, respiratory
GLR: 5-reproductive
SC: circulation
NC: 9

24: Vegetation
No. of concepts = 116
No. of clusters =   5

(a)   Vegetation (General)
RC: shrub, bush, tree, vegetation
GLR: k-tree; 6-underbrush
NC: 18

(b)   Types of Trees
RC: pine, locust, elm, spruce, oak
GLR: 2-oak; 6-cedar
NC: 22

(c)   Parts of Trees
RC: branch, stump, leaf
GLR: 2-branch; 6-bough
NC: 15

(d)   Flowers
RC: blossom, seed, rose, daisy
GLR: 2-flower; 6-hemp
SC: pistil
NC: 38

(e)   Other Vegetation
RC: algae, grass, hay, root, grass
GLR: 1-grass; 6-thatch
SC: kelp
NC: 23

25: Groups of Things
No. of concepts = 116
No. of clusters =   5

(a)   Groups of Things (General)
RC: group, combination, network, bundle, assemble
GLR: 2-pile; 6-network
NC: 36

(b)   Small Groups of People/Animals
RC: gang, chorus, flock, club, crew
GLR: 2-class; 6-throng
NC: 22

(c)   Political/Social Groups
RC: republic, country, legislature, culture, tribe
GLR: 2-country; 6-civilization
SS: federation
NC: 27

(d)   Military Groups
RC: army, squad, patrol
GLR: 3-police; 6-squadron
NC: 15

(e)   Small Business/Social Groups
RC: committee, conference, audience
GLR: 4-council, 6-commission
NC: 16

26: Value/Correctness
No. of concepts = 108
No. of clusters =   4

(a)   Right/Wrong
RC: truth, mistake, correct, incorrect
GLR: 1-right; 6-fairness
NC: 29

(b)   Success
RC: succeed, fail, failure
GLR: 4-success; 6-failure
NC: 4

(c) Importance/Value
RC: important, main, good, worthwhile, terrific, magnificent, precious
GLR: k-good; 6-spectacular
NC: 49

(d) Lack of Value
RC: useless, awful, unfit, insignificant, faulty, bad
GLR: 2-bad; 6-negative
NC: 26

27: Similarity/Dissimilarity
No. of concepts = 108
No. of clusters =   4

(a) Likeness
RC: like, copy, equal, similar
GLR: 2-like; 6-equivalent
NC: 32

(c) Difference
RC: difference, separate, comparison, different
GLR: 2-different; 6-unequal
NC: 19

(b) Addtion (Relationship Markers)
RC: and, too, move over, indeed
GLR: k-too; 6-furthermore
NC: 18

(d) Contrast (Relationship Marker)
RC: but, whereas, although
GLR: k-or; 6-despite
NC: 39

28: Money/Finance
No. of concepts = 102
No. of clusters =   7

(a) Money/Goods You Receive
RC: fortune, prize, salary, treasure, reward
GLR: 1-prize; 6-wage
NC: 29

(d) Money Related Actions
RC: earn, spend, buy
GLR: 2-earn; 5-purchase
NC: 14

(b) Money/Goods You Pay Out
RC: tax, fee, price, cost
GLR: 3-cost; 6-debt
NC: 15

(e) Money Related Characteristics
RC: costly, free, cheap, poor
GLR: 3-free; 6-inexpensive
NC: 8

(c) Types of Money
RC: money, cash, penny, dime
GLR: 1-penny; 6-finance
NC: 24

(f) Places Where Money Is Kept
RC: safe, purse, bank
GLR: 2-bank; 6-mint
NC: 12

29: Soil/Metal/Rocks
No. of concepts = 102
No. of clusters = 6

(a) Metals
RC: iron, lead, graphite, uranium
GLR: 2-gold; 6-cobalt
SC: coke
NC: 45

(b) Rocks/Jewels
RC: stone, slate, jewel, ruby, rock
GLR: 2-rock; 6-gravel
NC: 22

(c) Characteristics of Rocks
RC: crude, sedimentary, bituminous
GLR: – –
SC: bituminous
NC: 4

(d) Actions of Metals
RC: rust, tarnish
GLR: 4-rust
NC: 3

(e) Soil Types
RC: dirt, clay, sand, dust
GLR: 2-sand; 6-ore
NC: 14

(f) Actions Done to Soil/Crops
RC: plow, cultivate, harvest
GLR: 3-till; 6-cultivate
NC: 14

30: Rooms/Furnishings/Parts of Dwelling
No. of concepts = 97
No. of clusters = 6

(a) Rooms
RC: kitchen, bathroom, den, hall, room, parlor
GLR: 2-room; 6-parlor
NC: 20

(b) Parts of Houses
RC: chimney, wall, roof, window, stairs, hearth
GLR: 2-wall; 6-hearth
NC: 22

(c) Fences
RC: fence, hedge, gate, curb
GLR: 2-gate; 6-curb
NC: 10

(d) Furniture
RC: table, chair, rocker, cabinet
GLR: 1-table, 6-rocker
NC: 16

(e) Decorations
RC: curtain, carpet, vase, rug
GLR: 3-rug; 6-canopy
NC: 16

(f) Linens
RC: pillow, blanket, sheet
GLR: 2-cover; 6-cushion
NC: 13

31: Attitudinals
No. of concepts = 92
No. of clusters = 7

(a) Truth of a Statement
RC: frankly, really, truthfully
GLR: 2-surely; 6-evidently
NC: 29

(b) Doubt about Truth
RC: perhaps, possibly, allegedly
GLR: 1-maybe, 6-technically
NC: 15

(c) Expectedness
RC: curiously, amazingly, ironically
GLR: 2-strangely, 6-remarkably
NC: 16

(d) Fortune
RC: happily, sadly, fortunately
GLR: 1-happily; 6-unfortunately
NC: 9

(e) Satisfaction/Dissatisfaction
RC: delightfully, disturbingly
GLR: 5-delightfully
NC: 6

(f) Correctness
RC: wrongly, rightly
GLR: 1-rightly, 4-incorrectly
NC: 6

(g) Wisdom
RC: wisely, foolishly, artfully
GLR: 2-cleverly; 6-prudently
NC: 11

32: Shapes/Dimensions
No. of concepts = 90
No. of clusters = 8

(a) Shapes (General Names)
RC: shape, form, frame, figure
GLR: 2-shape; 6-outline
NC: 10

(b) Circular or Curved Shapes
RC: circle, curve, sphere, round
GLR: 2-round; 6-oval
SC: circuit
NC: 20

(c) Rectangular or Square Shapes
RC: square, rectangular, cube
GLR: 2-block; 6-cubic
NC: 10

(d) Straightness/Crookedness
RC: stripe, strip, crooked
GLR: 2-line; 6-criss-cross
MA: linear
NC: 10

(e) Sharpness/Bluntness
RC: sharp, dull, taper
GLR: 3-sharp; 6-blunt
NC: 6

(f) Dimension
RC: long, length, height, thin, depth, wide
GLR: 1-long; 6-width
NC: 22

(g) Fullness/Emptiness
RC: hollow, empty, full
GLR: 2-full; 5-swollen
NC: 6

(h) Inclination
RC: level, steep
GLR: 2-flat; 6-erect
NC: 6

33: Destructive/Helpful Actions
No. of concepts = 87
No. of clusters = 4

(a) Destructive Actions to Nonhumans
RC: accident, wreck, dent, ruin, smash
GLR: 2-break; 6-collide
NC: 20

(b) Destructive Actions to Humans
RC: hurt, murder, cripple, torment
GLR: 2-hurt; 6-afflict
NC: 24

(c) Fighting
RC: scuffle, fight, war
GLR: 1-fight; 6-combat
NC: 17

(d) Actions Helpful to Humans
RC: help, nourish, cure, protect
GLR: k-help; 6-revive
NC: 26

34: Sports/Recreation
No. of concepts = 80
No. of clusters = 6

(a) Sports/Recreation (General)
RC: sport, match, contest
GLR: 1-game; 6-competition
NC: 11

(b) Specific Sports
RC: football, soccer, boxing, golf
GLR: 1-racing; 6-croquet
NC: 27

(c) Equipment Used in Sports
RC: racket, bat, hurdle, goal
GLR: k-ball; 6-javelin
NC: 22

(d) Exercising
RC: exercise, play, jog
GLR: k-play, 6-sprint
NC: 12

(e) Magic
RC: magic, trick
GLR: 2-magic; 6-magical
NC: 5

(f) Board Games
RC: cards, checkers
GLR: 2-cards; 6-checkers
NC: 3

35: Language
No. of concepts = 69
No. of clusters = 3

(a) Language and Language Conventions
RC: grammar, accent, dialect, diction
GLR: 3-language; 6-diction
NC: 19

(b) Words/Sentences
RC: sentence, phase, prefix, syllable
GLR: k-word; 6-phase

EN: pronoun
NC: 25

(c) Letters/Alphabet
RC: alphabet, symbol, notation, letter
GLR: 1-letter; 6-notation
NC: 25

36: Ownership/Possession
No. of concepts = 68
No. of clusters = 6

(a) Losing/Giving-up
RC: lose, dispose, exchange
GLR: 3-trade; 6-discard
NC: 14

(b) Possession/Ownership
RC: have, own
GLR: k-have; 6-possess
NC: 7

(c) Taking/Receiving Actions
RC: obtain, achieve, seize
GLR: k-get; 6-inherit
NC: 15

(d) Finding/Keeping
RC: find, locate, keep
GLR: 1-find; 6-retain
NC: 7

(e) Winning/Losing
RC: win, overtake, triumph
GLR: 2-win; 6-conquest
NC: 18

(f) Freeing Actions
RC: escape, flee, surrender
GLR: 3-free; 6-sacrifice
NC: 7

37: Disease/Health
No. of concepts = 68
No. of clusters = 6

(a) Diseases (General)
RC: disease, illness, sick, well
GLR: 2-well; 6-plague
NC: 16

(b) Specific Diseases/Ailments
RC: cancer, polio, cold, blind
GLR: 2-burn; 6-influence
SC: virus
NC: 18

(c) Symptoms of Diseases
RC: pain, weariness, sore
GLR: 4-ache; 6-fatigue
NC: 11

(d) Specific Types of Germs
RC: germ, bacteria
GLR: 3-germ; 6-organism
SC: enzyme
NC: 7

(e) Actions Related to Injury/Disease
RC: burn, wound
GLR: 2-burn; 6-paralyze
NC: 6

(f) Medicine
RC: medicine, drug, bandage,
      transfusion
GLR: 2-medicine; 6-surgery
SC: vaccine
NC: 10

38: Light
No. of concepts = 68
No. of clusters = 5

(a) Light/Lightness
RC: sunshine, lightness, gleam, bright
GLR: 1-light, 6-candelight
NC: 20

(b) Actions of Light
RC: sparkle, shimmer, brighten
GLR: 3-shine; 6-illuminate
NC: 14

(c) Darkness
RC: shade, dark, blot, blacken
GLR: 1-dark; 6-blacken
NC: 10

(d) Producers of Light
RC: flare, candle, lamp, beam
GLR: 1-light; 5-ray
NC: 13

(e) Clarity
RC: clarity, dull, vague
GLR: 1-dim; 6-transparent
NC: 11

39: Causality
No. of concepts = 59
No. of clusters = 2

(a) Causality
RC: result, cause, stimulate, reason
GLR: 3-reason; 6-motive
NC: 23

(b) Causality (relationship markers)
RC: by, because, hence, therefore
GLR: k-then; 6-hence
NC: 36

40: Weather
No. of concepts = 55
No. of clusters = 5

(a) Weather/Nature (General)
RC: climate, nature, environment
GLR: 3-weather; 6-environment
NC: 6

(b) Storms
RC: storm, downpour, hurricane, tornado, torrent
GLR: 2-wind; 6-torrent
NC: 22

(c) Clouds
RC: cloud, cirrus, cummulus
GLR: 3-cloud
SC: cummulus
NC: 6

(d) Natural Catastrophies
RC: flood, disaster, earthquake, avalanche
GLR: 3-drought; 6-avalanche
NC: 14

(e) Characteristics of Weather
RC: icy, sunny, foggy
GLR: 3-foggy; 6-wintry
NC: 7

41: Cleanliness/Uncleanliness
No. of concepts = 53
No. of clusters = 3

(a) Uncleanliness/Filth
RC: garbage, trash, junk, dirty, filthy
GLR: 4-trash, 6-sanitation
NC: 27

(b) Cleanliness
RC: wash, clean, purify
GLR: 2-wash; 6-sanitation
NC: 15

(c) Tools for Cleaning
RC: broom, soap, toothbrush
GLR: 3-brush; 6-toothpick
NC: 11

42: Popularity/Knowness
No. of concepts = 52
No. of clusters = 3

(a) Popularity/Familiarity
RC: familiar, popular, obvious, common
GLR: 3-common; 6-standard
NC: 24

(b) Lack of Popularity/Familiarity
RC: unknown, private, secrecy
GLR: 3-secret; 6-privacy
NC: 10

(c) Likelihood
RC: likely, certain, doubtful
GLR: 2-sure; 6-definite
NC: 18

43: Physical Traits of People
No. of concepts = 51
No. of clusters = 4

(a) Physical Traits
RC: strong, strength, weak, clumsy
GLR: 2-strong; 6-graceful
NC: 22

(b) Neatness
RC: neat, tidy
GLR: 3-neat; 5-tidy
NC: 4

(c) Attractiveness
RC: pretty, handsome, gorgeous
GLR: 2-lovely; 6-majestic
NC: 15

(d) Size as a Physical Trait
RC: slender, skinny, husky
GLR: 1-fat; 6-lanky
NC: 10

42: Touching/Grabbing Actions
No. of concepts = 50
No. of clusters = 3

(a) Feeling/Striking Actions
RC: feel, stroke, nudge, slap, pound
GLR: 2-pat; 6-prod
NC: 26

(b) Grabbing/Holding Actions
RC: grab, clasp, pluck, grip
GLR: 1-hold; 6-clench
NC: 19

(c) Specific Actions Done With the Hand
RC: point, wave

GLR: 2-point; 4-salute
NC: 5

45: Pronouns
No. of concepts = 49
No. of clusters = 5

(a) Personal
RC: you, he, she, it
GLR: k-you
NC: 6

GLR: k-who; 4-whom
NC: 4

(d) Interrogating
RC: what, when, why
GLR: k-which; 4-whichever
NC: 12

(b) Possessive
RC: my, your, mine
GLR: k-my; 2-mine
NC: 10

(e) Indefinite
RC: no one, everyone, each
GLR: k-some; 4-nobody
NC: 17

(c) Relative Pronouns
RC: who, whom, which

46: Contractions
No. of concepts = 49
No. of clusters = 1

(a) *Not*
RC: can't, won't, hasn't
GLR: 1-don't; 6-isn't
NC: 14

(d) *Is*
RC: It's, he's, who's
GLR: 1-it's; 4-here's
NC: 14

(b) *Have*
RC: I've, we've, you've
GLR: 2-I've; 4-they've
NC: 5

(e) *Would*
RC: I'd, we'd, she'd
GLR: 2-I'd; 4-we'd
NC: 6

(c) *Will*
RC: they're, he'll, you'll
GLR: 1-I'll; 4-he'll
NC: 6

(f) *Are*
RC: we're, they're, you're
GLR: 3-you're; 4-they're
NC: 4

47: Entertainment/The Arts
No. of concepts = 48
No. of clusters = 4

(a) Plays/Movies
RC: performance, movie, plot, scenery
GLR: k-show; 6-climax
NC: 14

(b) Music/Dance (General)
RC: music, concert, ballet
GLR: 2-dance; 6-conduct
NC: 11

(c) Instruments
RC: drum, violin
GLR: 3-piano; 5-fiddle
NC: 12

(d) Art
RC: art, picture, sculpture
GLR: 1-picture; 6-mosaic
NC: 11

48: Walking/Running Actions
No. of concepts = 46
No. of clusters = 5

(a) Running/Walking
RC: run, jog, walk, trudge, hobble
GLR: k-run; 6-tread
NC: 26

(b) Lurking/Creeping
RC: crawl, prowl, lurk
GLR: 2-crawl; 6-slither
NC: 6

(c) Kicking
RC: kick, stomp
GLR: 2-stamp; 6-trample
NC: 5

(d) Jumping
RC: hop, leap
GLR: k-jump; 5-leap
NC: 6

(e) Standing/Stationary Actions
RC: stand, straddle
GLR: 2-stand
NC: 3

49: Mathematics
No. of concepts = 46
No. of clusters = 4

(a) Branches of Mathematics
RC: math, geometry
GLR: 3-arithmetic; 5-algebra
NC: 5

(b) Mathematical Quantities
RC: minimum, maximum, percent
GLR: 4-total; 6-percentage
NC: 18

(c) Equations/Formulas
RC: formula, exponent
GLR: 5-equation
MA: divisor
NC: 9

(d) Mathematical Operations
RC: addition, subtract, divide
GLR: 2-add; 6-minus
NC: 14

50: Auxiliary/Helping Verbs
No. of concepts = 46
No. of clusters = 2

(a) To Be
RC: are, is been
GLR: K-are; 4-being
NC: 8

(b) Primary Auxiliaries
RC: do, does, have
GLR: k-do; 1-had
NC: 8

(c) Modals
RC: will, could should
GLR: k-can; 2-shall
NC: 11

(d) Semi-Auxiliaries
RC: is about to, is going to

GLR: 2-add; 6-minus
NC: 12

(e) Linking Verbs
RC: stay, remain, become
GLR: 1-stay; 4-remain
NC: 7

51: Events
No. of concepts = 44
No. of clusters = 3

(a) Dates/Events (General)
RC: occasion, event, circumstance
GLR: 4-event; 6-instance
NC: 16

(b) Festive/Recreational Events
RC: holiday, festival, parade, carnival

GLR: 1-party; 6-ceremony
NC: 23

(c) Political Events
RC: campaign, election
GLR: 5-election; 6-campaign
NC: 5

52: Temperature/Fire
No. of concepts = 40
No. of clusters = 5

(a) Temperature
RC: temperature, Fahrenheit, warm, heat
GLR: 1-cold; 5-temperature
NC: 20

(b) Insulation
RC: insulation, insulate
GLR: 6-insulate
SC: insulator
SS: fireproof
NC: 4

(c) Fire
RC: fire, blaze, flame, burn, flicker

GLR: 1-fire; 6-smolder
NC: 6

(d) Products of Fire
RC: ash, smoke
GLR: 2-smoke; 6-ember
NC: 6

(e) Fire Producers
RC: burner, firewood
GLR: 4-firewood
SC: burner
NC: 4

53: Images/Perceptions
No. of concepts = 39
No. of clusters = 2

(a) Visual Images/Perception
RC: reflection, vision, image, represent
GLR: 2-sight; 6-portray
NC: 10

(b) Looking/Perceiving Actions
RC: look, glance, notice, peer, observe
GLR: k-see; 6-glower
NC: 29

54: Life/Survival
No. of concepts = 38
No. of clusters = 2

(a) Life/Birth/Death
 RC: life, live, death, birth, hatch,
    spawn
 GLR: 1-live; 6-existence
 NC: 25

(b) Survival/Growth
 RC: survive, thrive, mature
 GLR: 2-grow; 6-evolve
 NC: 13

55: Conformity/Complexity
No. of concepts = 34
No. of clusters = 2

(a) Conformity to a Norm
 RC: original, unique, strange, distinct
 GLR: 2-strange; 6-distinct
 NC: 15

(b) Complexity/Order
 RC: complex, plain, elaborate
 GLR: 3-pure; 6-elaborate
 NC: 19

56: Difficulty/Danger
No. of concepts = 30
No. of clusters = 2

(a) Difficulty
 RC: difficulty, ease, impossible,
    simplify
 GLR: 2-easy; 5-simplify
 NC: 13

(b) Danger
 RC: safety, hazardous, unsafe, peril
 GLR: 2-safe; 6-peril
 NC: 17

57: Texture/Durability
No. of concepts = 30
No. of clusters = 2

(a) Texture
 RC: hard, soft, rough, coarse
 GLR: 1-hard; 6-coarse
 NC: 21

(b) Durability
 RC: filmsy, fragile, durable, strong
 GLR: 2-strong; 6-grail
 NC: 9

58: Color
No. of concepts = 29
No. of clusters = 2

(a) Colors
RC: red, blue, orange, yellow
GLR: k-green, 6-amber
NC: 25

(b) Paint
RC: paint, dye
GLR: k-paint; 6-enamel
NC: 4

59: Chemicals/Acids
No. of concepts = 28
No. of clusters = 2

(a) Chemicals
RC: oxygen, hydrogen, sodium
GLR: 2-helium; 5-nitrate
SC: boron
NC: 25

(b) Acids
RC: acid, sulfuric
GLR: 5-acid
SC: hydrochloric
NC: 3

60: Facial Expressions/Actions
No. of concepts = 21
No. of clusters = 4

(a) Facial Expressions
RC: smile, frown
GLR: 2-smile; 4-sneer
NC: 6

(c) Actions Associated with the Mouth
RC: lick, suck
GLR: 2-lick, 5-spit
NC: 5

(b) Actions Associated with the Nose
RC: smell, sneeze
GLR: 2-smell; 6-snore
NC: 4

(d) Breathing
RC: puff, exhale
GLR: 2-blow; 4-breathe
NC: 6

61: Electricity/Atoms
No. of concepts = 21
No. of clusters = 2

(a) Electricty
RC: electric, electronic, radiation
GLR: 3-electricity
NC: 8

(b) Molecules/Atoms
RC: molecule, atom, proton
GLR: 5-ion; 6-electron
SC: nucleus
NC: 13

APPENDIX B

Newbery Medal Books

1922   Van Loon, Hendrik. *The Story of Mankind.*

1923   Lofting, Hugh. *The Voyages of Doctor Dolittle.*

1924   Hawes, Charles. *The Dark Frigate.*

1925   Finger, Charles J. *Tales from Silver Lands.*

1926   Chrisman, Arthur. *Shen of the Sea.*

1927   James, Will. *Smoky, The Cowhorse.*

1928   Mukerji, Dhan Gopal. *Gay Neck, the Story of a Pigeon.*

1929   Kelly, Eric P. *The Trumpeter of Krakow.*

1930   Field, Rachel. *Hitty, Her First Hundred Years.*

1931   Coatsworth, Elizabeth. *The Cat Who Went to Heaven.*

1932   Armer, Laura Adams. *Waterless Mountain.*

1933   Lewis, Elizabeth Foreman. *Young Fu of the Upper Yangtze.*

1934   Meigs, Cornelia. *Invincible Louisa.*

1935   Shannon, Monica. *Dobry.*

1936   Brink, Carol Ryrie. *Caddie Woodlawn.*

1937   Sawyer, Ruth. *Roller Skates.*

1938   Seredy, Kate. *The White Stag.*

1939   Enright, Elizabeth. *Thimble Summer.*

1940   Daugherty, James. *Daniel Boone.*

1941   Sperry, Armstrong. *Call It Courage.*

1942   Edmons, Walter. *The Matchlock Gun.*

1943   Gray, Elizabeth Janet. *Adam of the Road.*

1944   Forbes, Esther. *Johnny Tremain.*

1945   Lawson, Robert. *Rabbit Hill.*

1946   Lenski, Lois. *Strawberry Girl.*

1947   Bailey, Carolyn Sherwin. *Miss Hickory.*

1948   DuBois, William Pène. *The Twenty-One Balloons.*

1949   Henry, Marguerite. *King of the Wind.*

1950   DeAngeli, Marguerite. *The Door in the Wall.*

1951   Yates, Elizabeth. *Amos Fortune, Free Man.*

1952   Estes, Eleanor. *Ginger Pye.*

1953   Clark, Ann Nolan. *Secret of the Andes.*

1954   Krumgold, Joseph. *. . . and now Miguel.*

1955   DeJong, Meindert. *The Wheel on the School.*

1956   Latham, Jean Lee. *Carry on, Mr. Bowditch.*

1957   Sorensen, Virginia. *Miracles on Maple Hill.*

1958   Keith, Harold. *Rifles for Watie.*

1959   Speare, Elizabeth George. *The Witch of Blackbird Pond.*

1960   Krumgold, Joseph. *Onion John.*

1961   O'Dell, Scott. *Island of the Blue Dolphins.*

1962   Speare, Elizabeth George. *The Bronze Bow.*

1963   L'Engle, Madeleine. *A Wrinkle in Time.*

1964   Neville, Emily. *It's Like This, Cat.*

1965   Wojciechowska, Mai. *Shadow of a Bull.*

1966   de Trevino, Elizabeth Borton. *I, Juan dePareja.*

1967   Hunt, Irene. *Up a Road Slowly.*

1968   Konigsburg, E. L.. *From the Mixed-Up Files of Mrs. Basil E. Frankweiler.*

1969   Alexander, Lloyd. *The High King.*

1970   Armstrong, William H. *Sounder.*

1971   Byars, Betsy. *The Summer of the Swans.*

1972   O'Brien, Robert C.. *Mrs. Frisby and the Rats of NIMH.*

1973   George, Jean Craighead. *Julie of the Wolves.*

1974   Fox, Paula. *The Slave Dancer.*

1975   Hamilton, Virginia. *M. C. Higgins, the Great.*

1976   Cooper, Susan. *The Grey King.*

1977   Taylor, Mildred D. *Roll of Thunder, Hear My Cry.*

1978   Paterson, Katherine. *Bridge to Terabithia.*

1979   Raskin, Ellen. *The Westing Game.*

1980   Blos, Joan W. *A Gathering of Days: A New England Girl's Journal.*

1981   Paterson, Katherine. *Jacob Have I Loved*.

1982   Willard, Nancy. *A Visit to William Blake's Inn: Poems for Innocent and Experienced Travelers*.

1983   Voigt, Cynthia. *Dicey's Song*.

APPENDIX C

Caldecott Medal Books

1938 Lathrop, Dorothy, illus. Helen Dean Fish (text selected by). *Animals of the Bible*.

1939 Handforth, Thomas. *Mei Li*.

1940 d'Aulaire, Ingri and Edgar Parin. *Abraham Lincoln*.

1941 Lawson, Robert. *They Were Strong and Good*.

1942 McCloskey, Robert. *Make Way for Ducklings*.

1943 Burton, Virginia Lee. *The Little House*.

1944 Slobodkin, Louis, illus. James Thurber. *Many Moons*.

1945 Jones, Elizabeth Orton, illus. Rachel Field. *Prayer for a Child*.

1946 Petersham, Maud and Miska. *The Rooster Crows*.

1947 Weisgard, Leonard, illus. Golden MacDonald. *The Little Island*.

1948 Duvoisin, Roger, illus. Alvin Tresselet. *White Snow, Bright Snow*.

1949 Hader, Berta and Elmer. *The Big Snow*.

1950 Politi, Leo. *Song of the Swallows*.

1951 Milhous, Katherine. *The Egg Tree*.

1952 Mordovinoff, Nicholas, illus. (Nicholas, pseud.). William Lipkind (Will, pseud.). *Finders Keepers*.

1953 Ward, Lynd. *The Biggest Bear*.

1954 Bemelmans, Ludwig. *Madeline's Rescue*.

1955 Brown, Marcia. *Cinderella* (translated from Charles Perrault).

1956 Rojankovsky, Feodor, illus. John Langstaff (retold by). *Frog Went A-Courtin'*.

1957 Simont, Marc, illus. Janice May Udry. *A Tree Is Nice*.

1958 McCloskey, Robert. *Time of Wonder*.

1959 Cooney, Barbara. *Chanticleer and the Fox* (adapted from The Canterbury Tales).

1960 Ets, Marie Hall, illus. Aurora Labastida (co-author). *Nine Days to Christmas.*

1961 Sidjakov, Nicholas, illus. Ruth Robbins (retold by). *Baboushka and the Three Kings* (Russian folktale).

1962 Brown, Marcia. *Once a Mouse* (retelling of a fable from the Hitropadesa).

1963 Keats, Ezra Jack. *The Snowy Day.*

1964 Sendak, Maurice. *Where the Wild Things Are.*

1965 Montresor, Beni, illus. Beatrice Schenk DeRegniers. *May I Bring a Friend?*.

1966 Hogrogian, Nonny, illus. Sorche Nic Leodhas. *Always Room for One More* (derived from a Scottish Nursery rhyme).

1967 Ness, Evaline. *Sam, Bangs, and Moonshine.*

1968 Emberley, Ed, illus. Barbara Emberley (adapted by). *Drummer Hoff* (based on a seventeenth-century folk verse—John Ball shot them).

1969 Shulevitz, Uri, illus. Arthur Ransome (retold by). *The Fool of the World and the Flying Ship* (Russian folktale).

1970 Steig, William. *Sylvester and the Magic Pebble.*

1971 Haley, Gail. *A Story—A Story* (retelling of an African tale).

1972 Hogrogian, Nonny. *One Fine Day* (inspired by an Armenian folktale).

1973 Lent, Blair, illus. Arlene Mosel (retold by). *The Funny Little Woman* (Japanese tale).

1974 Zemach, Margot, illus. Harve Zemach (retold by). *Duffy and the Devil* (Cornish tale).

1975 McDermott, Gerald. *Arrow to the Sun* (adaptation of a Peublo Indian tale).

1976 Dillon, Leo and Diane, illus. Verna Aardema (retold by). *Why Mosquitoes Buzz in People's Ears* (West African tale).

1977 Dillon, Leo and Diane, illus. Margaret Musgrove. *Ashanti to Zulu: African Traditions.*

1978 Spier, Peter, illus. *Noah's Ark* (includes Spier's translation of a seventeenth-century Dutch peom, the Flood, by Jacobus Revius).

1979 Goble, Paul. *The Girl Who Loved Wild Horses.*

1980 Cooney, Barbara, illus. Donald Hall. *Ox-Cart Man.*

1981 Lobel, Arnold. *Fables.*

1982 Van Allsburg, Chris. *Jumanji.*

1983 Brown, Marcia. *Shadow* (trans. of a French poem by Blaise Cendrars).

PHOTO CREDITS

In addition to the credits that appear in the text, we acknowledge here the permission of the authors and publishers indicated to reproduce the following material:

1 Figure 3.1, p. 26. from *Language Development: Form and Function*, by Lois Bloom Copyright 1970 by MIT Press. Reprinted by permission of MIT Press, Cambridge, Mass.

2 Figure 3.2, p. 27. from *Reading Instruction for Classroom and Clinic*, by Edward Fry Copyright 1972. Reprinted by permission of McGraw-Hill Book Company, New York.

3 Figure 3.4, p. 30. from *Language Development*, 2 Ed. by Philip S. Dale Copyright © 1976 by Holt, Rinehart and Winston. Reprinted by permission of Holt, Rinehart and Winston, CBS College Publishing.

4 Figure 6.2, p. 118. Reprinted with the permission of The National Council of Teachers of English.

5 Figure 8.1, p. 148. Reprinted with the permission of The National Council of Teachers of English.

6 Tables 1 & 2, pp. 287−288. from *Teaching Reading Vocabulary* by D. Johnson and P. David Pearson. Copyright © 1978 by Holt, Rinehart and Winston. Reprinted by permission of Holt, Rinehart and Winston, CBS College Publishing.

AUTHOR INDEX

A

Abbott, J., 248
Abelson, R.P., 19
Abrahamson, R., 303
Allen, R.V., 242
Ames, W., 151–152
Anderson, L.M., 363
Anderson, R., 272, 277
Applebee, A., 102
Arbuthnot, M.H., 300, 305
Armstrong, M., 95, 113
Ashton-Warner, S., 228, 242
Askov, E.N., 170
Aukerman, R., 226, 252–253, 256

B

Barbe, W.B., 167, 170, 172, 248
Barker, L.L., 198
Barnhardt, C., 226
Bereiter, C., 50
Berliner, D.C., 361
Biren, P.L., 170
Bissett, D.J., 302
Block, K., 153
Blodgett, E.G., 61
Bloom, B.S., 361
Bloom, L., 26
Bloomfield, L., 226
Blumberg, P., 153
Bormuth, J., 307
Bradley, V.N., 141
Bradsford, J.D., 18
Braine, M., 38
Bredin, D.M., 154

SUBJECT INDEX